Parks for Texas

This book inaugurates the

CLIFTON AND SHIRLEY CALDWELL TEXAS HERITAGE SERIES

Books about Texans and their architecture, built environment, and photography, as well as historic preservation and the flora and fauna of the state

In 1940 the Central Texas congressional candidate for reelection, Lyndon B. Johnson, capitalized on recent New Deal developments in his Tenth District by encouraging publication of *The Highland Lakes of Texas*. This planning guide from federal and state partner-agencies illustrated through charts and graphs, and pen-and-ink scenes, the sweeping opportunities offered by new lakes, new highways, and new parks along the Colorado River. That fall, Civilian Conservation Corps Co. 854 commenced work on Inks Lake State Park, and transformed this model American recreation landscape into reality. *National Park Service, Lower Colorado River Authority, and State Parks Board*

PARKS
FOR TEXAS

Enduring Landscapes of the New Deal

JAMES WRIGHT STEELY

University of Texas Press
Austin

Requests for permission to reproduce material from this work should be sent to Permissions, University of Texas Press, P.O. Box 7819, Austin, TX 78713-7819.

∞ The paper used in this publication meets the minimum requirements of American National Standard for Information Sciences—Permanence of Paper for Printed Library Materials, ANSI Z39.48-1984.

Library of Congress Cataloging-in-Publication Data

Steely, James Wright.
    Parks for Texas : enduring landscapes of the new deal / James Wright Steely. — 1st ed.
        p.   cm.
    Includes bibliographical references (p.   ) and index.
    ISBN 0-292-77734-5
    1. Parks—Texas—History.   I. Title.
SB482.T4S74   1999
333.78'3'09764—dc21   98-28537

After all, nature has to give some help in establishing a state park. It requires
more than a cow pasture and an excited chamber of commerce to make a park go.

—State Representative W. R. Chambers, *Dallas Morning News,* 28 August 1945

For cheerfully taking the family on summer vacations to state parks and for explaining the difference between CCC and WPA, this work is in memory of
Thomas Brazelton Steely Sr.

And to honor the hands and hearts of those who created the New Deal state parks this work is dedicated to
The Alumni of the Civilian Conservation Corps.

CONTENTS

PHOTO SECTIONS

TABLES

New Deal parks had aged some twenty years when the author first encountered their rustic cabins and outdoor cookers, such as this giant pit grill directed by summertime chefs about 1935 at Lake Corpus Christi State Park. If depression era Americans expressed dismay at relief workers creating recreation parks for the automobile class, their common experiences in the Second World War soon enough expanded the middle class to envelop even former CCC enrollees. By the 1950s, war veterans—now a class unto themselves—all brought their children of the baby boom to these state parks for summer vacations. Their campfire yarns might center on relatively recent war experiences, but their outdoor cooking intentionally rekindled traditions of pioneer days and brought yet another generation into contact with the great outdoors. *Harpers Ferry Center, National Park Service*

AUTHOR'S NOTE

On the terrain motives become clear . . . —Barbara Tuchman, "The Historian's Opportunity" (1966) from *Practicing History* (Knopf, 1981), p. 61.

INSPIRATION

This work began a long, long time ago with a small boy in a state park, climbing up rough stone walls of a mountain cabin, all the way to its roof. Who could build such a perfect house? Later a job took the young man to other state parks, offering similar cabins, with fireplaces inside, too. Why did these perfect houses appear hundreds and thousands of miles from each other? Answering these questions led years later to a master's thesis, and further discovery of a seemingly endless inventory of parks to visit throughout the country. The answers continue to emerge, deep in lonely files and archives, and in the worn faces and bright eyes of the aging fellows who indeed built these perfect houses.

As friend John Jameson prepared an expanded work on Big Bend National Park, he encouraged his editor at the University of Texas Press to read that state-park thesis to find out who built some of those perfect houses in the Chisos Basin. From that introduction came this book assignment. Here the questions expanded to: where did the idea for "state parks" come from? who planned these parks? how were they financed? when did the concept of a park system appear? what determined the location of each park? why do these places endure?

Oddly enough, most of these questions concerning Texas state parks have never been answered, at least not in print, nor all in one place. Delightful stories—and some downright myths—have served as official answers for many years. For example:

- from the *St. Louis Post-Dispatch* in 1925: "On a golden afternoon of the war year 1916, Mrs. Isabella Neff called her son, Pat, out to the old homestead near Waco and asked him to write the provisions of her last will and testament. . . . 'That 10-acre pecan grove along the banks of the Leon River, [she instructed Pat] . . . I wish to give my State for a permanent park.'"

- from an internal "history" of the Texas Parks & Wildlife Department in 1968: "Miriam A. Ferguson signed [a] bill creating Texas State Parks Board in 1925 (39th Leg.) and appointed 1st Board with Pat Neff as chairman."

The truth, as it is available in surviving documents, oral histories, and the parks themselves, is of course much more interesting than these expedient fabrications. This work originally encompassed a more complete accounting of Texas state parks and the State Parks Board, not always one and the same. But because the early history is mostly political, and not exactly one of concrete accomplishment, it now stands separately. Because the extraordinary development of facilities made possible during Franklin Roosevelt's New Deal offers a most complete explanation for the state parks still enjoyed today, this volume concentrates on that depression-era episode.

BACKGROUND

As this story unfolds, the reader should keep a few eccentricities of Texas politics in mind, and be aware of peculiarities in this narrative.

- Texas politicians in the early to mid-twentieth century hailed with few exceptions from the Democratic party, although the party itself acknowledged many diverse factions, and some outright renegades.
- Texas elections for state office occur in even-numbered years, with late spring primaries and sometimes a summer primary runoff or two. Until the last generation or so, Democratic candidates surviving the last runoff had effectively won the office; the November general election served as mere ceremony and attracted large turnouts only in presidential election years.
- Texas governors, like state representatives and congressmen, until 1975 stood for election every two years. With three exceptions—William Hobby, Miriam Ferguson, and Ross Sterling—every governor between Reconstruction and the Second World War won two consecutive terms; most served four full years.
- Elected state officials take office, and the Texas legislature begins its 120-day (after 1930) regular session, in January of odd-numbered years. Any number of thirty-day "called" or "special" sessions may be held during

the two following years, at the discretion of the governor and technically only to address topics identified by her or him.

- State government is funded through appropriations from the legislature for two fiscal years—each of duration between 1 September and 31 August—called bienniums. The federal government in this era observed a fiscal year between 1 July and 30 June, just to confuse matters.

- This historical narrative progresses chronologically, with no overt foreshadowing. A minimum of backward glances serve only to provide background on new characters, or briefly to restate important prior events. Terms unknown to the players are avoided in the text, for instance, "the World War" is used after 1914 and before emergence of a second global conflict; and "depression" before later analysts declared it the Great Depression.

- Use of the terms *preservation* and *conservation* have changed somewhat since the early twentieth century. Briefly, national park supporters described themselves as *preservationists,* disturbing nature as little as possible, and national forest promoters were labeled *conservationists,* protecting the productivity of the land while harvesting and renewing its resources.

- Other words and their usage in the historic era might now seem strange. *Reform* became a popular term for positive change—largely through government solutions—during the Progressive Era, which strongly affected national and state politics between the 1890s and the 1930s New Deal. *Relief* in this era spelled "survival in a crisis," first for European victims of the First World War and then for anyone suffering from the Great Depression. *Welfare* and *security* replaced *relief* just before the Second World War, although *security* soon took on additional meaning in the context of national defense. All these terms can easily mean something different today.

- The Civilian Conservation Corps, by design or happenstance, functioned in two six-month *periods* each year for recruitment, camp placement, camp reassignments, facility planning, and other purposes. Beginning in April 1933 periods were named by their consecutive number (first, second, third, etc.); those beginning on 1 April were often called *summer period,* and those beginning on 1 October were known as *winter period.*

- The dating system herein of day/month/year (e.g., 4 March 1933) is used throughout the narrative, except in direct quotes, not just because of the military connections to the CCC, but also for the happy disposal of commas.

- Direct quotes are honored for original spelling, punctuation, and grammar. Thus the device of "[*sic*]" is used sparingly, rather than frequently. The language of the era, particularly through the words of D. E. Colp and Pat Neff, enliven their thoughts and emotions. They speak to us now as they did to their peers, with some faults and quirks, but quite effectively.

• The bedrock story of state recreation parks is revealed through primary sources from many repositories. Political and social contexts of parks are covered through secondary sources as well as the thoughtful voices of experts in those fields, especially historians such as Seth McKay, Rupert Richardson, and Arthur Schlesinger, who lived through this period. Where a substantial body of work exists on particular parks, their principal historians reveal important details best, and for these works the reader is referred to the bibliography herein.

• The book is intended to be a running narrative for most readers, but likely will also be a reference source for others, particularly those who seek the origins of their favorite park. Frequent markers of subtitles and dates should help the reader "surf" through the text without getting lost, and regularly "dive in" where a particularly interesting vignette appears.

• Exhaustive effort has been made to find the *full names* of individuals mentioned, particularly for women who applied "Mrs." to their husband's names for the durations of their adult lives. If initials appear, the author could not find the full name, with the exceptions of Harry S. Truman (of course) and James Burr V. Allred, named for three uncles, one known by all as simply "V."

• Finally, the reader has been spared an overdose of acronyms, but common use in the 1930s and 1940s of virtual names such as CCC, WPA, and FDR is honored here with discretion (see List of Terms and Abbreviations).

ACKNOWLEDGMENTS

As implied in this work's dedication and introduction above, Tom Steely dispensed early inspiration and clarity on New Deal programs, resulting in his son's deep appreciation of the era. Though a college student in the late 1930s, Steely took full advantage of the nation's new highways to range from the Tennessee River to the Rio Grande in pursuit of recreation, jobs, and then in 1942 a commission in the U.S. Navy. Along the way he studied the pioneering adult-education programs of the CCC and WPA and made notes on the best places for family vacations. After the war and upon commencement of that family, mother Jane took over vacation planning and

THE ENDURING LEGACY

By 1941 the State Parks Board endorsed postcard views of its new statewide facilities to attract visitors.

Approach to Recreation Center, Abilene State Park, Abilene, Texas

The Massachusetts "Colourpicture" company produced this invitation to Abilene State Park, but the faraway artist who tinted it failed to capture the color of the distinctive red sandstone used in construction. *Author's Collection*

The original portals to Garner State Park featured handsome stone work and hammered metal lettering. Their removal was necessary to avoid a dangerous highway entrance. *Author's Collection*

BRIDLE PATH BRIDGE IN MINERAL WELLS STATE PARK, MINERAL WELLS, TEXAS

Mineral Wells State Park reverted to the city, but this graceful "bridle path" stone-arch bridge survives as one of the earliest CCC achievements in Texas. *Author's Collection*

Big Spring State Park features a mountaintop pavilion with spectacular views. *Texas Parks and Wildlife Department, Bill Reaves*

Lake Sweetwater Metropolitan Park's excellent CCC work is now sadly neglected. *Photo by the Author*

Balmorhea State Park's pool creates an oasis around San Solomon Springs. *Photo by the Author*

Grayson State Park reverted to Loy County Park near Denison, but retains its landmark CCC water tower bastion. *Photo by the Author*

Big Bend National Park's Lost Mine Trail still features an elaborate CCC drainage system and occasional CCC limestone paving. *Photo by the Author*

Indian Lodge in Davis Mountains State Park exhibits exemplary CCC work in its adobe walls, cottonwood beams, and cedar furniture from the mill at Bastrop State Park.
Texas Department of Transportation, J. Griffis Smith

Gonzales State Park, now a city facility, remains a memorial to the 1936 Centennial. Its museum complex includes this centenary monument to the Revolution.
Photo by the Author

Bastrop State Park hosts an active chapter of CCC alumni, who in 1991 dedicated an Official State Historical Marker recognizing their 1930s accomplishments.
Photo by the Author

forever linked the scent of pine-shaded mountain cabins with the taste of chocolate-chip cookies.

My own college training proved fortunate during pursuit of a New Deal research topic. At East Texas State University, Joe Fred Cox, Keith McFarland, Robin Rudoff, Otha Spencer, and Bob Ward saw no lines between history and current events, and writing about both. University of Texas at Austin professors Blake Alexander and Wayne Bell in the 1980s reluctantly allowed research on "recent" New Deal public works. Alexander perked up when he saw connections to Franklin Roosevelt's love of architecture, and Bell warmed to the topic when he discovered that CCC workers carved quotes from Thoreau into fireplace mantels at Bastrop State Park. Instructor Eugene George offered his library and advice on craftwork in CCC parks, and Professor Joe Frantz inspired this work's political vein so much that he should have written its foreword, but alas he departed too soon.

My career in public service provided essential background—in addition to support and friendships—from the inner workings of state and federal governments. At the Texas Highway Department, Frank Lively combined the joy of travel and fellow travelers with further lessons on correct grammar and short sentences. At Texas Parks and Wildlife, Zane Morgan and Sue Moss ably compared Frederick Jackson Turner with Walter Prescott Webb, and later provided access to early park records and CCC inventory projects. At the Texas Historical Commission, Curtis Tunnell (the boss), Cynthia Beeman, Ned Coleman, Lee Johnson, Dwayne Jones, and Frances Rickard connected people and history with places, and constantly confirmed that the twentieth century has history, too. Former staff historian Amy Dase deserves special credit for insisting that the passive voice is passé.

While affiliation with the Texas Historical Commission greatly aided research for this work (and vice versa!), *Parks for Texas* remained an independent project. Limited financial support came from the Texas Parks and Wildlife Department for its 1986 CCC booklet; *Texas Highways* Magazine for a 1989 article on the CCC; the Rice Design Alliance lecture series; and West Texas A&M University for its 1993 symposium on the New Deal.

At various agencies, archives, libraries, and museums, a number of staff members opened wide the doors of their collections. These include professionals at the Texas Department of Transportation, the Legislative Reference Library, the University of Texas at Austin's architecture and planning library and architectural drawings collection, Sul Ross State University, the Austin History Center, the Bell County Museum, the Panhandle-Plains Historical Museum, and the state historic preservation offices in Iowa, Kentucky, Minnesota, Missouri, Nebraska, and Oklahoma.

Special mention is deserved for Ethan Carr, Elaine Harmon, Laura Harrison, John Paige, Dorothy Waugh, and Conrad Wirth of the National Park Service; Jimmy Rush and Dave Pfeiffer at the National Archives; Donaly Brice and John Anderson at the Texas State Archives; Ralph Elder at the Center for American History's Barker Texas History Collections; Mike Graham, Cindy Martin, and David Murrah at Texas Tech's Southwest Collection; Penny Anderson, Doug Barnett, and Chris Long at the Texas State Historical Association; Ellen Brown and Kent Keeth at Baylor University's Texas Collection; H. G. Dulaney and Mac Reese at the Sam Rayburn Library; Jeff Goble at the Fort Croghan Museum; Lucy and Dave Jacobson of the Fort Davis Historical Society; Gene Allen, Sarah Hunter, and Peggy Riddle of the Dallas Historical Society; and Sally Abbe with the City of Lubbock. The families of Tom Beauchamp, Sr., George Nason, Sr., and Lawrence Westbrook happily provided insights and photographs of their New Dealer ancestors.

Texas Parks and Wildlife headquarters staff who dug deep in files and shared their knowledge include Susie Ayala, Jim Bigger, Art Black, Sarah Boykin, Mary Candee, Dennis Cordes, Nola Davis, Elena Ivy, Norma Nanyes, Earl Nottingham, Andrew Sansom, June Secrest, Debbie Tilbury, Jim Watt (grandson of James and Miriam Ferguson), John Williams, and Steve Whiston. Several superintendents and staff provided extensive assistance on their state parks for this work, especially Mark Abolafia-Rosenzweig, Ron Alton, Angela Ernhardt, Richard Grube, Michelle Ivie, Brent Leisure, Mike Moncus, Ned Ochs, Terry Rodgers, and Roger Rosenbaum.

A number of independent researchers and organizations graciously shared their findings on New Deal parks, including Jean Baker, Dee Barker, Charles Bauer, Eliza Bishop, Dorothy Blodgett, Donaly Brice, Jeffrey Crunk, Bill Dobbs, Lila Knight Ethridge, David Faflik, Martha Doty Freeman, Doris Freer, Bill Green, Hardy-Heck-Moore (Marlene Heck and Terri Myers), Ken Hendrickson, Nancy Hengst, John Jameson, George Kegley, Ann Lanier, Jane Manaster, Mildred Massingill, Peter Flagg Maxson, Mike Murray, Ralph Newlan, Nan Olson, Bob Parvin, Elizabeth Pink, Carlian Pittman, JoAnn Pospisil, Tom Scott, Sam Sterling, Sharon Toney, USDA Forest Service (John Ippolito), USDA Soil Conservation Service (Dave Fischgrabe), University of Texas at Austin's Borderlands Archeological Research Unit (Solveig Turpin and Dan Utley), Maria Watson-Pfeiffer, and Evangeline Whorton. Crucial to understanding particular parks and their larger roles in the state system were the efforts of Margaret Agnor, Gail Beil, Fred Dahmer, and Lady Bird Johnson (Caddo Lake); Ann Bode and Patsy Light (Goliad); Clay Davis, Lisa Hart Stross, Tory Laughlin Taylor, and Dan Utley (Mother Neff); Betty Howell, Peter L. Petersen, and Lueise

Tyson (Palisades and Palo Duro Canyon); Jean Price and Ruth Mitchell (Possum Kingdom); J. C. Martin and T. J. Zalar (San Jacinto); and Julie Strong (Garner, Goliad, and Zilker).

CCC veterans who opened their memories and hearts for this work include Leslie Crockett, Marvin Martin, Ray Mason, Ernest Rivera, Clay Smith, Red Smith, and the members of CCC Alumni Lost Pines Chapter 167 based at Bastrop State Park. Roscoe Bowers—who served at Lampasas, Big Bend, Davis Mountains and Garner—continually provided great details from his sharp wit and memory. Veteran J. B. Braziel's collection of CCC company lists, assignments, and other details thankfully filled many gaps not explained in official sources.

Finishing in the category of indispensable for advice and assistance are Linda McClelland and Tom DuRant at the National Park Service, Mary Jane Fehr (widow of Arthur Fehr) of Austin, and John Jameson at Kent State University. John follows a long line of New Deal researchers from East Texas State University starting with Nancy Ruth Lenoir (of Paris, Texas) and her 1965 honors thesis "The Genesis and Demise of a New Deal Agency: the CCC." University of Texas Press sponsoring editor Shannon Davies believed steadfastly in this project and waited with extreme patience for its conclusion, while copy editor Helen Simons expertly polished the final draft, and David Cavazos and Lois Rankin supervised production. The author's wife, Barbara Stocklin Steely, supported this work through research, travel, and stamina throughout its duration.

Any errors or misinterpretations are the author's own, and corrections or exposures of major and minor gaffes will be happily received!

LIST OF TERMS AND ABBREVIATIONS

Board of Control: state agency created in 1919 to oversee government functions not assigned to executive branch departments; duties included oversight of state historical parks and their local park commissions through 1949.

CCC: Civilian Conservation Corps; federal agency created in 1933 by executive order and act of Congress, generally enlisting one young male per indigent family, between the ages of seventeen and twenty-eight, for assignment to conservation work projects.

Centennial: 1936 celebration marking one hundred years of Texas independence from Mexico and creation of the Republic of Texas.

Centennial Commission: full-title, Commission of Control for Texas Centennial Celebrations; also federal United States Texas Centennial Commission.

CWA: Civil Works Administration; federal agency in winter 1933–1934—financed by PWA, and directed by Harry Hopkins—that sponsored small public works for temporary employment of 219,000 Texans.

DRT: Daughters of the Republic of Texas; organization founded in 1891 and closely involved with preserving San Jacinto, the Alamo, and other state historic sites.

ECW: Emergency Conservation Work; the official name of the program under which the CCC operated until 1937; the term "Civilian Conservation Corps" was always applied to the workers themselves, as opposed to the ECW bureaucracy; reauthorization of the CCC in 1937 dropped the ECW title.

FERA: Federal Emergency Relief Administration; federal agency 1933–1935—directed by Harry Hopkins—that provided relief funds to the states and sponsored small public works projects.

Forest Service: bureau of the U.S. Department of Agriculture (USDA); a.k.a. U.S. Forest Service, and—now preferred by the agency—USDA Forest Service; also Texas Forest Service, associated with Texas A&M College (now University); both agencies directed CCC companies in forestry work.

Inspector: traveling agent of the National Park Service who advised park project designers on appropriate plans and techniques; also traveling agent of the Civilian Conservation Corps who periodically audited camp conditions.

NCSP: National Conference on State Parks; founded in 1921 at a meeting in Iowa, served as connection between NPS and state park officials.

NPS: National Park Service, bureau of the U.S. Department of the Interior; directed CCC companies in local, state, and national park work.

NYA: National Youth Administration; federal agency 1935–1943—directed in Texas 1935–1937 by Lyndon B. Johnson—that employed high school and college students, during or between semesters, on small public works projects and job-skill training.

PWA: Public Works Administration (formally Federal Emergency Administration of Public Works); federal agency 1933–1941—headed by Interior secretary Harold Ickes—that provided grants and loans to large-scale public works projects.

RFC: Reconstruction Finance Corporation; an enterprise of the federal government after 1932, first acting as a bank of last resort for large private companies, then as source of federal relief funds to states, then as underwriter of New Deal programs such as the CCC.

SCS: Soil Conservation Service; bureau of the U.S. Department of Agriculture; directed CCC companies after 1935 on public and private lands in soil conservation work.

SH: State Highway; as SH 66.

SES: Soil Erosion Service; bureau of the U.S. Department of the Interior; directed CCC companies 1933–1935 on public and private lands in soil conservation work.

TPWD: Texas Parks and Wildlife Department; state agency created in 1963 by merger of the State Parks Board and the Game and Fish Commission, to direct most outdoor recreational activities in Texas, including state parks.

Veterans: in New Deal context, war veterans of any U.S. conflict from the Spanish American War through the First World War; in modern context, surviving alumni of the Civilian Conservation Corps.

WPA: Works Progress Administration (after 1939, Work Projects Adm.): federal agency 1935–1943, replacing FERA—and first administered by Harry Hopkins—that employed heads of households on local public works projects as well as on artistic and scholarly assignments.

Parks for Texas

Created in 1923 through legislation pushed by Governor Pat M. Neff, the Texas State Parks Board developed an immediate strategy of soliciting land with highway frontage, donated by tourism-conscious communities. Preparing for one of several automobile caravans to barnstorm such park-minded towns, board members in July 1924 gathered with close colleagues in San Antonio: (left to right) David E. Colp of San Antonio, chairman; Phebe K. Warner of Claude, "secretary and statistician"; Pat Neff of Waco, governor; Mrs. W. C. Martin of Dallas, vice chairman; Robert M. Hubbard of Texarkana, State Highway Commission chairman; Katie Welder of Victoria, "historian"; and Hobart Key of Marshall, "attorney and sergeant at arms." *Texas Parks and Wildlife Department*

Prologue

1883–1932

See Texas First

Texas should have led all other states in the Union in the ownership and maintenance of State parks, especially in view of the fact that of the forty-eight states
she is the only one that once owned title to all her lands. When she entered the
Union, she refused to surrender her public domain. Texas, however, has now
sold or given away practically all of her public lands, aggregating one hundred
and seventy-two million acres. She did not reserve one beauty spot, nor set
aside anywhere one acre of land to be used and enjoyed by the public in the
name of the State.—Governor Pat Morris Neff, *The Battles of Peace,* 1925[1]

IN THE NAME OF THE STATE

In midwinter of 1883 John Ireland stepped into the perennial challenge
of a freshman Texas governor pitted against a more seasoned bunch of
legislators. Fortunately Ireland brought to his new position a progressive vision of what this rapidly growing state could be, in both financial
security and magnificent image. With admirable political skills, Ireland fulfilled a campaign promise by halting the state's overextended land-grant
programs. He consequently saved some 27 million acres of public domain
in West Texas as an earnings base for the permanent school fund. To settle
another charged debate, the governor selected native red granite from Burnet County for the mammoth new State Capitol in Austin. Thus Ireland
spared his fellow Texans possible embarrassment over the building contractor's preference for Indiana limestone.

And with an eye to the forthcoming fiftieth anniversary of the Texas
Revolution, Ireland pushed the same legislature to preserve the two most
beloved historic sites in the state. The Alamo church, centerpiece of the
famous 1836 battle but by Ireland's day a forlorn relic in bustling downtown
San Antonio, became state property with a $20,000 payment to the Roman

Catholic diocese. At San Jacinto, where Sam Houston defeated Santa Anna's army and ensured Texas independence, the state acquired for $1,500 a ten-acre cemetery along Buffalo Bayou to memorialize that epic clash.

Governor Ireland and his fellow lawmakers might not have envisioned great public parks or dedicated pleasure grounds at these two sites. Nor did they imagine that the mythic desert of public domain in West Texas held any scenic wonders worthy of declaration as great natural parks. So, with exception of the Capitol grounds and state cemetery in Austin, enjoyed by local citizens since the 1850s as shady retreats from city life, the Alamo and San Jacinto represented the first efforts by the state to preserve special places for public gratification.

Texas leaders in the 1880s danced on the edge of growing national trends for government stewardship of public lands, as well as guardianship of the public's collective identity in scenery and battlefields. Only a few years before, in 1872, U.S. president Ulysses Simpson Grant declared the astonishing Yellowstone reservation in Wyoming the nation's, and the world's, first "national park." The State of New York stopped disposal of public lands in its Adirondack Mountains in 1883 and two years later designated Niagara Falls—already a major tourist attraction—as its first state park. The federal government also actively acquired landmarks of Civil War heroism, by the 1890s adding Shiloh and Vicksburg battlegrounds to a list of wartime cemeteries that already included Gettysburg and Antietam.

Other related trends embraced directly by Texans in the late nineteenth century influenced acquisition of Alamo and San Jacinto real estate as well. Transportation improvements, confined locally to better roads and bridges but extending across the state and nation through long-distance railroad connections, opened unprecedented opportunities for pleasure travel. Consequently, visitors on holiday or business in the burgeoning city of San Antonio—many qualified by their curiosity as tourists—added Alamo pilgrimages to travel itineraries. On an annual cycle, the Texas Veterans Association mustered on San Jacinto Day, sometimes in cities convenient to rail traffic, but often on April 21st with other pilgrims at the battlefield itself.

Summertime gatherings for retelling war stories also increased in popularity with Civil War veterans, who formed Texas affiliates of national organizations and hosted huge open-air reunions on dedicated campgrounds. Likewise black Texans, enjoying free movement in the post-war South, celebrated emancipation with grand outdoor picnics around June 19th. All these summer festivals strongly resembled the multiple-day rituals of "camp meetings," traditional revivals of rural church congregations. In fact, by the 1890s permanent religious campgrounds throughout Texas and the nation regularly hosted fair-weather secular programs, many on the Chautauqua and Lyceum educational circuits that crisscrossed the country by train. As more and more families railroaded to summer vacations, seeking educational as well as recreational holidays, the scenic grandeurs of the American West— Yellowstone and a growing list of national parks—became fashionable destinations with rustic hotels and fabulous meadows for camping. Finally at the turn of the century, competition for all these diversions with affordable European vacations rose to such intensity that rail-agent promoters of domestic travel implored summer pilgrims to "See America First."

THE FIRST STATE PARKS FOR TEXAS

In 1891 the Texas Veterans Association, an aging group supporting further state land acquisition at San Jacinto, received a burst of energetic assistance. The newly formed Daughters of the Republic of Texas (DRT) proclaimed from Houston that the nearby battlefield would be a major focus of their service. As the Daughters quickly grew into a statewide society, they exerted pressure on the legislature for San Jacinto appropriations. In addition, their Houston chapter took over the veterans association's plan and fund to erect a substantial monument at the site.

These Daughters of the 1890s proved the vanguard in Texas for a national movement of women's organizations that supported many broad and specific social concerns. These encompassed urban-reform issues of the time, such as child-labor abuses, health, recreation, and the need for public parks. Women's groups also promoted public education and the teaching of history, as illustrated by the Daughters' initial interest in battlegrounds and monuments. Unfortunately the Texas legislature did not respond in progressive fashion to the initial pleas of the DRT. An economic depression discouraged most innovations on the part of state government, although some legislators seemed interested at least in the novelty of honoring their heroes of the revolution. "We believe that the field of San Jacinto," maintained Representative E. W. Smith of Tyler in 1893, "should be the property of the state . . . but in our opinion, Texas is not now in the mood, nor in the proper financial condition, to undertake such work."[2]

Four years later, though, the state's economy had recovered and the Daughters found their own eloquent sponsor for land acquisition and improvements. Senator Waller Thomas Burns of Houston, a rare Republican in the legislature and a self-proclaimed progressive, orchestrated a legislative visit to the site. He declared such a tour was crucial, so that "the members of this honorable body may have the privilege of standing on that historic ground . . . immortally hallowed by the devotion and consecrated by the blood of the sons of Texas." With such oratory in 1897 Burns successfully extracted $10,000 from his colleagues and Governor Charles Allen Culberson "for the establishment of a public park." Although Culberson deleted additional funds for improvements, in the following four years a special state commission closed on 336 acres at San Jacinto.

While Daughters in Houston struggled to improve their state's expanded investment at San Jacinto, other chapters achieved measured success with the mercurial legislature. In 1905 newly enrolled Daughter Clara Driscoll convinced lawmakers to purchase the *convento,* or Long Barracks, property adjacent to the Alamo church for $65,000. And state officials agreed, upon further urging of Daughters in La Grange, to acquire the small cemetery at Monument Hill that entombed Texans killed during the republic's ill-fated Mier Expedition. Finally, in 1907 the Austin government directed $25,000 toward the first state-financed improvements at the battleground "hereafter [to] be known and styled 'San Jacinto State Park'," the first officially so named.[3]

With the seventy-fifth anniversary of the Texas Revolution approaching in 1911, legislators endorsed a number of commemorative activities, including major improvements to the Alamo. They also arranged for reinterment of Stephen Fuller Austin's remains from his Brazoria County burial to an elaborate new tomb at the capital city's state cemetery. And during this official enthusiasm the grave of Elizabeth Patton Crockett, Alamo martyr David Crockett's widow who accepted a Texas land bounty in Hood County seventeen years after her husband's death, received an imposing state monument at Acton near Granbury.

Other communities stepped forward during the next two years with offers of land, missing the jubilee but nonetheless inspired by state government's occasional patronage for Texas Revolution landmarks. Patriots in Goliad County proposed donation of the "Fannin battlefield," site of the ill-fated surrender on Coleto Creek about ten miles from the city of Goliad, plus sale of the ruined *presidio* La Bahia just south of town for $10,000. The 1913 legislature and Governor Oscar Branch Colquitt declined the old fort's purchase but accepted the 13-acre battleground donation for what became known as Fannin State Park. The city of Gonzales tendered a much larger offer of 150 acres from its city parklands in honor of the Battle of Gonzales, which took place not here but about four miles west of town. Embracing this donation with greater zeal, lawmakers appropriated $7,500 for improvements to their new Gonzales State Park.

The next governor, James Edward Ferguson, in 1915 openly supported this trend of land acquisition for state historical parks. Ferguson skillfully played a populist issue when he convinced the legislature to purchase 50 acres for $10,000 at Washington-on-the-Brazos, where Texans signed their 1836 declaration of independence. "I admonish you," Ferguson pressed lawmakers, "to preserve and beautify this hallowed ground . . . where citizen and alien may gather in the years to come, and from the white dust of travel find rest and recreation."[4] That same year the town of Refugio donated its entire public square to commemorate the nearby execution of Captain Amon Butler King and his men by Mexican troops. With addition of this King's State Park, the state now owned a scattered number of memorials, all commemorating the 1836 revolution and republic decade.

State officials entrusted management of the Alamo to the DRT, while memorials at Acton and La Grange became the responsibility of local volunteers. The five loosely designated "state parks"—Fannin, Gonzales, King's, San Jacinto, and Washington—were consigned to governor-appointed local commissions. They, in turn, reported separately after 1919 to the state's new Board of Control, which also managed the Capitol grounds and state cemetery among several diverse institutions. Texas had state parks, as did a number of states by 1920, but no state park system.

PAT NEFF'S CRUSADE FOR A SYSTEM

The "good roads" movement, expanding throughout the nation after 1900, promoted all-weather thoroughfares and a vast network of interconnecting routes. After 1910 good roads and bridges served as foundations for an astonishing proliferation of automobile sales to farmers, laborers, and middle-class city dwellers alike. Among many social changes wrought by this fantastic revolution, the independent nature of intercity auto travel induced overnight drivers to shun an entrenched urban and railroad-associated hotel routine in favor of any pastoral spot beside the open road. And as a national craze, free-wheeling jaunts in the rubber-tired machine ironically coupled with a "back to nature" movement, providing a quick escape to the breezy countryside for anyone who otherwise toiled day to day in stifling surroundings. But picnicking and camping motorists soon overwhelmed the most inviting roadside landscapes, and private landowners howled at the resulting damage. Many towns offered some relief by establishing camping sites at shaded outskirts, in an age-old tradition of accommodating pilgrims along their journey.

Pat Morris Neff proudly claimed to be the first Texas gubernatorial candidate to campaign for office by automobile, and he happily stretched his frugal travels through auto-camping. Before his party's primary election of August 1920, Neff declared he had driven some 6,000 miles in his Model T, speaking several times each day including stump—or bumper—deliveries in thirty-seven counties where no other governor had ever set foot. Despite his widespread popularity, though, the new chief executive met stubborn resistance in the 1921 legislature for his progressive ideas of water conservation and efficient government.

The governor's vision was then affected at a very personal level: his mother died a few months into his first term and bequeathed their family's small camp-meeting grove in Coryell County as a park "to the public." From his recent experiences in auto camping, the governor merged an idea of state-sponsored roadside campgrounds with his mother's gift of country-lane parkland and hit upon a major proposition for his second term. Also responding to pressure from a group in the Davis Mountains to create some sort of scenic reserve there, in 1922 Neff launched a veritable crusade to develop "State Parks for Texas," as he titled one of his mass-market articles. "Each year the host of those who take their vacation by automobile is multiplied," Neff observed, urging drivers to "see Texas first," on their weekends and holidays. "Texans can find no better channel to advertise her charms," he reasoned, "than by catering to the ever-increasing throng of vacationists who are certain to go where hard-surfaced highways and convenient camping sites abound."

Henceforth Neff roundly—if erroneously—criticized previous generations for not reserving "one beauty spot, nor set[ting] aside anywhere one acre of land to be used and enjoyed by the public." [5] When Neff referred—infrequently—to the five existing state parks, he called them "sacred shrines" or simply "memorials," and he introduced his park-system bill in 1923 with the very different concept of roadside parks. When the measure emerged from legislative committees, it called primarily for the donation of potential sites, with the exception that a large park somewhere in the Davis Mountains might be financed by a future legislature. Pleased even with this first noncommittal legislative step, Neff signed the bill and approved a $1,500 appropriation for site inspections.

Retaining an important Neff recommendation, the bill established the State Parks Board to carry out inspections, and the governor appointed its members: David Edward Colp, San Antonio good-roads promoter; Hobart Key, Sr., Marshall businessman; Mrs. W. C. Martin, Dallas newspaper correspondent; Phebe Kerrick Warner, Claude newspaper columnist; and Katie Owens Welder, Victoria rancher. These five positions represented geographical distribution across the state, Neff proudly noted, and the three females all strongly supported parks and recreation initiatives through the Texas Federation of Women's Clubs. Neff soon appointed his newfound friend Dave Colp chairman of the parks board, and the two agreed that women's groups would make ideal contacts for donations and ultimately for pressing legislators to fund a state park system.

Meanwhile Stephen Tyng Mather, director of the National Park Service (NPS) and its dozen western preserves, busily nourished a nationwide movement for *state park systems.* An ardent naturalist, Mather expressed dismay over an invasion of automobiles into his parks that wildly accelerated after the World War. "We have had, in the Yellowstone," he told a state parks group in 1922, "some sixty thousand people in a single season coming by automobile from every state in the union, from Texas, Maine, and California."[6] Targeting both motor tourists and meddling congressmen who clamored to create their own national parks, Mather reasoned that state parks could serve as pressure valves for federal treasures like Yellowstone and Yosemite. American scenery that did not meet his exceptional standards for any new national parks might be preserved, and more freely attract tourists, as state parks.

Texas parks board chairman Dave Colp maintained spirited correspondence with Mather's National Conference on State Parks throughout the 1920s. Yet the conference's slogan for a roughly 500-acre "state park every hundred miles" failed to move Colp and Neff away from their pursuit of fifty-acre "small parks" and "beauty spots" as "waysides" for intercity motorists. Neff and parks board members attracted much publicity and some fifty small-park donations during several barnstorming motorcades into south, west, north, and east Texas towns. But a growing number of "large park" boosters in Texas—promoting the Davis Mountains as well as the Big Bend, the Frio River, Palo Duro Canyon, and Caddo Lake—grew frustrated with the State Parks Board and its failure to facilitate destination parks for summer vacationers. Thus, poorly lobbied and disinclined legislators received no solid proposals to acquire land for the large parks, and they refused to accept even the small donations—citing long-term management costs—until 1927.

That spring, with Neff employed in Washington, D.C., Colp survived a grueling Austin senate hearing on his small-park donation list and surprisingly emerged with twenty-three new "state parks" from Beeville to Van Horn (see Appendix B). He promised legislators and Governor Daniel James Moody that each park could survive through operation profits, and in fact a handful including Alto Frio and Hillsboro apparently thrived under local management. Of far greater significance, however, and with no participation of the State Parks Board, the same legislature passed a bill, introduced by Senator Thomas Bell Love of Dallas, instructing the highway department to develop the Davis Mountains State Park Highway. This project presented an intriguing compromise for the debate between small- and large-park enthusiasts, projecting an eighty-mile scenic loop into the mountains west of Fort Davis upon donated right-of-way.

Thereafter, Colp and his board repeatedly lost momentum to other state-park interest groups, as well as an inevitable rise of commercial auto camps and popular new "motels." Preparations in Houston for the 1928 Democratic National Convention, pushed by local leaders, brought impressive state-assisted improvements to San Jacinto State Park. And the approaching centennial of Texas independence inspired still larger budgets for all state historical parks under the Board of Control, plus the Alamo. Dur-ing the 1931 legislature Colp, with incalculable help from Senator Margie Elizabeth Neal of Carthage, managed to secure important legislation for more concession deals on donated state parklands. He could take no credit that year, though, for creation of Goliad State Park, encompassing the old mission Espíritu Santo ruins; nor for reservation of state lands at popular fishing waters in Aransas County, to be called Goose Island State Park; nor for dedication of state property at Caddo Lake in deep East Texas as a "pub-lic park"; nor for a two-year contract signed by Palo Duro Canyon land-owners with the local chamber of commerce to allow public access to the Panhandle's premier scenery for the first time.

In sum, these initiatives proved that in the decade following Pat Neff's proposal for a state park system, widespread community interest in parks emerged even at the remote frontiers of Texas. Unfortunately in 1932 the darkening clouds of national economic depression placed tremendous strains on government at all levels, and incidentally caused a dramatic de-crease in leisure travel. Responding to the growing crisis, President Herbert Clark Hoover encouraged all governors to meet ballooning unemployment with "energetic yet prudent pursuit of public works."[7] Texas Governor Ross Shaw Sterling dutifully signed a bill addressing the growing problem of transient workers drifting into Texas cities. He encouraged hand labor as a substitute for machinery on the state's own public works projects, limited mostly to highway construction and university buildings.

In late summer Congress declared an emergency and approved distri-bution of funds from the federal Reconstruction Finance Corporation to states and counties for direct relief. At the same time, the momentum of discontent brought Hoover's presidential opponent, Franklin Delano Roo-sevelt, to the forefront of public attention. Promising sweeping and pro-gressive changes in government and conservation practices to end this dev-astating depression, candidate Roosevelt broadcast over nationwide radio: "I pledge you, I pledge myself, to a new deal for the American people."

That election summer Dave Colp struck a sweetheart deal with the donation of land in Burnet County and a concession contract for develop-ment. This popular retreat known as Sherrard's Cave, complete with wooden dance floor underneath rolling limestone hills southwest of Burnet, compared favorably with Carlsbad Caverns National Park in New Mexico, Colp bragged. On Thanksgiving Day—just after Roosevelt's election as president, to take office in March 1933—Pat Neff, now chief executive of Baylor University, delivered a dedication speech at the entrance of newly renamed Longhorn Cavern State Park.

Flushed with this single success, Colp next threw his energies to a fa-vorite site, Palo Duro Canyon, and feverishly sought a federal loan from the

Reconstruction Finance Corporation for visitor improvements there. Despite the depression, conditions must have seemed like a dream come true for Colp: good roads, cheap gasoline, federal funds, and a weary public desperately needing recreation! Fifty years after state acquisition of the San Jacinto cemetery, and ten years after the crusade for a state park system began, in midwinter at the approach of 1933, Colp should have been ready for the park development opportunities of a lifetime.

for State's Business Too

Into
Dance
ural Ball

e to Gulf,
r to See
Office

s Held

s Escorted
Motor
en

erguson turn-
oms of half a
e adopted an
ce for the
the inaugural
in Gregory

as Mrs. Fer-
receiving line
ung into the
e, played and
the Old Gray

her husband
ield home to
embers of her
led by a
scort.

'If You Love Me Like I Love You - - -'

—Photo by Jordan-Ellison

A few minutes after this picture was taken while Mrs. Miriam A. Ferguson was being sworn in as governor, she was telling the audience "If you love me like I love you, nothing can cut our love in two." And you might say the official family of Texas was in that frame of mind during the oath taking, if you look at the pleasant expression on their faces.

At the left you see Justice C. M. Cureton, ready to administer the oath of office. Immediately behind him is James E. Ferguson, husband and advisor of the governor. The central figure in the picture is Mrs. Ferguson, and unfortunately Lieut. Gov. Edgar E. Witt got behind the microphone. But that is he. And Speaker Coke Stevenson, at the right, seemed to be enjoying the party.

Housewif
Becomes
Lone S

Ma Pledges C
Giving Reli
In Inaugu

Celebratio

Reduction of
Come Quicl
Govern

By R. W
Associated
Mrs. Miriam A
back to the offic
Texas Tuesday,
cannon boomed
and a throng tha
house of repr
blocked capitol 1
partmental offic
acclaim.
For the secon
years, Mrs. Ferg
left hand on a Bi
age through its lo
pacity, and swore
impartially discha
all the duties incu
Sterling

Through one of the twists of fate that make history so compelling, Miriam A. Ferguson in January 1933 returned triumphant to the Texas governor's mansion after an absence of six years. Under *Austin American* front-page headlines following her inauguration, "the official family of Texas" included (second from left to right) Jim Ferguson of Temple, also former governor and loyal husband; Governor Ferguson; Edgar E. Witt of Waco, lieutenant governor; and Coke Stevenson of Junction, Speaker of the House. This entire cadre of leadership already had demonstrated little interest in state parks, but their clamoring acceptance of federal assistance in months to come facilitated the multimillion dollar effort to create a vast park system for Texas. *Austin American, 18 January 1933*

Chapter 1

1933, FIRST HALF

The Worst of Times, the Best of Times

Actually Texans were not particularly concerned with events at the state capital, busy as they were discussing the actions and efforts of Franklin D. Roosevelt and the New Deal in Washington, D.C. The new president was trying many experiments to end the Great Depression and restore prosperity.

More and more Texans, along with the residents of other states, were made to feel that all really important governmental action occurred at the federal level.—Seth McKay, in *Texas after Spindletop* [1]

CUSSING AND DISCUSSING THE DEPRESSION

The nation's economic slump, threatening since 1929 to dash realistic hopes for a Texas state park system, showed promise at the beginning of 1933 as possible salvation for the ten-year-old movement started by Pat Morris Neff. Only a few months earlier State Parks Board Chairman David Edward Colp hardly viewed his paper list of undeveloped parks as relevant to the issue of unemployment relief. Now, as the Washington government extended an extraordinary helping hand with cash for destitute Texans, officials quickly identified public parks as ideal sites for short-term labor-intensive work projects that benefited entire communities. A number of state recreation sites, including a few like Beeville and Hillsboro that were on Colp's list but really maintained by home governments, would be ready to greet spring visitors after winter relief work in the form of brush cleanups, tree pruning, erosion prevention, and road grooming. Of greatest import to Colp, a federal relief-funds loan for parkland purchase and improvements at Palo Duro Canyon seemed a strong possibility, justifying his bumbling but persistent optimism throughout the past decade.

Across the nation a similar pattern developed in response to the three-year-old crisis, worsening with each winter as the traditional season of lowest employment. The National Conference on State Parks, based in Washington, D.C., observed the increasing use of beautification work for unemployment relief and asked various park experts to discuss the trend. In the organization's January 1933 issue of *State Recreation,* Robert Moses, New York State Council of Parks chairman, expounded that "parks and parkways afford almost the best opportunities for the employment of large numbers of relief workers."

Horace Albright, National Park Service director, followed Moses's remarks with confidence that "in a year or two most of us will have forgotten recent depressed conditions." Albright's perspective of continual expansion in his agency under President Herbert Clark Hoover, despite the depression, led him to encourage immediate development and expansion of state parks nationwide "for filling the recreation needs of a constantly growing number of outdoor enthusiasts." Seasoned landscape architect James L. Greenleaf pointed out more grimly that states with active park programs should not otherwise respond to the depression with funding reductions. "The fundamental purpose of our state parks," Greenleaf pleaded, "is to preserve for all time the re-creative values of our best in air, mountain, river, lake and forest for the upbuilding and saving of the people. Are the people worth it? Of course there can only be one answer unless we are contemptible evaders." [2]

Relishing this theme of a remedy in nature, President-elect Franklin Delano Roosevelt promised vast extension, upon his inauguration in March, of highly successful relief programs developed while he was governor of New York. His depression employment formula of conservation for both land and people, assigning droves of unskilled laborers to huge reclamation projects and mass tree plantings, implied still more improvement of parks as public works programs. And if Texas leaders agreed that only federal intervention could relieve their own exhausted efforts to weather the crisis, the state would receive a lion's share of attention. Roosevelt pledged cooperation with Southern governors, even displaying hints of populism that amplified the Austin homecoming of Governor-elect Miriam Amanda Wallace Ferguson. Most importantly, Texans in Washington lately maneuvered into positions of tremendous power, starting with John Nance Garner of Uvalde as vice president-elect and Jesse Holman Jones of Houston as a board member of the Reconstruction Finance Corporation (RFC), the government's very source of relief dollars.

Jones's RFC enjoyed much favorable publicity in the winter of 1932–1933, including praise from Panhandle columnist and State Parks Board charter member Phebe Kerrick Warner. "Tragic as the depression has been," she explained in an early 1933 news column, "State Park projects have thrived under it as the parks furnished an opportunity for public work . . ."

Warner cited three hopeful undertakings funded through the RFC, starting with an Armstrong County road extending across Palo Duro Canyon and opening parts of its wonders to automobile traffic. Another scenic road project, the Davis Mountains State Park Highway, Warner continued, likewise was "being built by home people and almost entirely out of the materials on the ground." At the same time, she noted, work on "Long Horn Cave State Park near Burnet," following its formal dedication the previous Thanksgiving, "has been going forward . . . all winter and by tourist time it will be in excellent condition for visitors." Praising many related projects in parks and playgrounds, she added that the federal money had been "spent for labor which has provided [relief] for many homes in the most respectable way." Warner spoke for each of these communities as she reasoned, "[w]e may just as well be at work building this road across our county as sitting around idle and cussing the depression."[3]

Despite the optimism of park enthusiasts in Texas and beyond, realities of the depression for all Americans grew difficult to evade in the winter of 1932–1933. Emergency assistance for Texans through RFC relief loans between November 1932 and January 1933, as estimated by the West Texas Chamber of Commerce, addressed "an average monthly relief load of approximately 112 000 families per month and approximately 59 000 nonfamily persons per month. This would be equivalent to a relief load in the state of Texas of approximately 10% of the population."

Other statistics for the winter, as new governors took office in January but President-elect Franklin Roosevelt prepared for a March inauguration, were "startling," according to depression historian Robert McElvaine. "From the top of prosperity in 1929 to the bottom of depression in 1933, [gross national product] dropped a total of 29 percent, consumption expenditures by 18 percent, construction by 78 percent, and investment by an incredible 98 percent. Unemployment rose from 3.2 percent to 24.9 percent." McElvaine estimates that, "[b]y almost any standard the United States was in its worst crisis since the Civil War."[4]

Governor Ferguson, the 1933 Legislature, and Relief

Miriam Ferguson took the oath of office on 17 January 1933 inside the Capitol's House of Representatives, and six years after her first term (1925–1927) again became governor of Texas. To her right during the swearing-in ceremony stood her "former governor-husband" James Edward Ferguson, according to the *Austin American*. And to her left Lieutenant Governor Edgar E. Witt swore to uphold his office for a second consecutive term. Defying long-time custom for various reasons, no other former governors welcomed the fifty-seven-year-old grandmother into her second administration. During her inauguration speech to a nonetheless packed House chamber and radio microphones, Governor Ferguson told her audience that "the people . . . have sent us here to bring relief."

> On every hand there is want, and need, and hunger that has already led to despair and desperation. Hope is nearly gone. The burdens of government are falling heavily on the masses. Reduction of taxes must come and come quickly, or the government will fall and fall quickly. . . . [Y]ou and I take up the most serious and desperate task that ever confronted the people of our state.[5]

But the governor and the legislature, true to long-time custom, "apparently did not trust one another fully," remarks historian Seth McKay, "and there was little effort to work together on the financial problems of the state." Legislators did review a new 40,000-page study, their parting gift from former governor Ross Sterling, recommending broad restructuring of state government from 129 bureaus and commissions into 20 encompassing departments. The Griffenhagen Report, as it was called, endorsed a single conservation agency to manage state recreation parks in addition to game, fish, and forestry programs. But the worsening depression and political disagreements rendered the report obsolete on arrival.[6] Fortunately for indecisive Texas lawmakers, federal money continued to flow into Texas to cover the staggering costs of relief and to engage the unemployed in public works such as roads and parks—for the time being.

Less than three weeks after her inauguration, Governor Ferguson received an alarming letter from A. W. McMillen, field representative of the Reconstruction Finance Corporation. "You are aware that considerable sums of money," wrote McMillen on 4 February 1933, "have been made available in the State of Texas by the [RFC] for the relief of destitution. For example, the amount made available, for the months of January and February, was approximately $2,500,000." These funds, he continued, "are not in lieu of, but are merely supplementary to, State and local efforts." In other words, the RFC wanted to know, what has the Texas government contributed to match these federal funds?

Governor Ferguson presented the RFC letter to the legislature with her own message of 15 February attached. "I beg to say that if this relief work is to continue for any length of time," she wrote, "I feel sure that the Federal Government is going to require the State to co-operate in some material way to carry on the work." Adding that McMillen also criticized the method of fund distribution in Texas, through regional chambers of commerce, she called for a joint committee of the House and Senate "to confer with my Department with a view to making recommendation to the Legislature as to what might or can be done in the premises."[7]

Within two weeks of her appeal to the legislature on behalf of federal funds, on 1 March 1933 Governor Ferguson created by executive order the Texas Relief Commission. On recommendation of Reconstruction Finance Corporation officials, she then placed responsibility for distributing federal relief funds in the hands of this new five-member state board, thus removing the private commerce offices from the program.[8]

A few days later the Texas Relief Commission appointed an executive director, Lawrence Whittington Westbrook. The Belton native had served between 1928 and 1932 as a state legislator from Waco, which enhanced his relations with new lieutenant governor Edgar Witt of Waco. And as a Bell County alumnus Westbrook passed the Fergusons' test of loyalty as well. He ranked as lieutenant colonel in the Texas National Guard and had recently proved his skills as successful organizer of the Texas Cotton Cooperative Association.[9] Now placed in command of all federal relief funds transmitted to Texas, Colonel Westbrook began organizing his new outfit, while the Forty-third Legislature considered making the Texas Relief Commission a full-fledged state agency.

In the meantime some lawmakers debated the reorganization outlined in the Griffenhagen Report, while others set to work preparing a relief-bonds proposal to be presented later for statewide vote. And all these Texans watched closely to see what the coming "new deal" in Washington would mean to the state, the nation, and citizens everywhere hit hard by the depression.

FDR AND HIS NEW DEAL

"Nothing to Fear But Fear Itself"

The country's banking system teetered on collapse in early spring 1933, prompting national anxiety and compelling governors, including Miriam Ferguson, to declare statewide bank holidays. Beneath this gloom of depression and cold overcast skies on 4 March 1933 — a Saturday — fifty-one-year-old Franklin Delano Roosevelt took the oath of office outside the Capitol in Washington, D.C. He broke from the traditional response of "I do" by reciting the entire presidential pledge for his nationwide radio audience, then turned vigorously to the shivering crowd of 100,000 to deliver his rousing inauguration speech. Responding directly to the national banking crisis, he assured the nation it had nothing to fear from such material panic. Progressive government would save the day.

"This nation asks for action, and action now," President Roosevelt declared, outlining his battle plan for advancing against the economic crisis. "We must act, and act quickly," he emphasized, underlining Governor Ferguson's own recent inaugural assertion that relief "must come and come quickly." Roosevelt lectured on the basics of financial reform, then confronted the paramount problems wrought by more than three years of depression, compounded—he believed—by the nation's poor conservation practices of many generations.

> Our greatest primary task is to put people to work. This is no un-solvable problem if we face it wisely and courageously. It can be accomplished in part by direct recruiting by the Government it-self, treating the task as we would treat the emergency of war, but at the same time, through this employment, accomplishing greatly needed projects to stimulate and reorganize the use of our natural resources.[10]

The vice-presidential oath for Texan John Nance Garner completed the transition of government later that day. Garner "marched to the north side of the Capitol" to the House chamber, according to his biographer Lionel Patenaude, "with the entire House of Representatives accompanying him, to be sworn in as vice-president of the United States."[11] The next day—Sunday—Roosevelt called for a special session of Congress, and on Monday he directed that all banks in the nation would close during that week. Assembling legislative proposals with his "brains trust" of advisors early in the week, Roosevelt sent a banking reform bill to the Thursday opening of Congress, where Garner called the Senate to order at noon. While waiting for the bill to work its way through Congress in a few hours, the president and a close group of advisors discussed the next bold steps of their New Deal.

The Civilian Conservation Corps

Roosevelt had proposed the previous fall a relief idea to establish "work camps for youths," remembered his advisor Rexford Guy Tugwell, who then gathered information for such a program. Now, five days after inauguration, several new cabinet officers joined the president as he "sketched out a plan to put 500,000 men to work on a variety of conservation tasks," writes historian John A. Salmond. Harold LeClaire Ickes, the crusty progressive Republican from Chicago and now Secretary of the Interior, Henry Agard Wallace as Secretary of Agriculture, and George Henry Dern as Secretary of War participated in this afternoon speculation. Aides prepared a draft bill by 9 P.M., and thereafter a lively White House deliberation advanced the proposal to detail. The Departments of Agriculture, Interior, and War would jointly administer this effort to recruit and direct a civilian legion for "useful work in forest improvement," according to Tugwell.[12]

That night Congress approved the bank reorganization bill, which limited gold circulation and instructed the Reconstruction Finance Corporation to purchase stock in the strongest banks. The RFC, with long-time Roosevelt friend and Texan Jesse Holman Jones now de facto chairman, thus entered the Roosevelt administration as its first New Deal agency.[13] The president's second week moved rapidly through multiple tasks of preparing critical relief legislation, plus legalization of beer and reopening the banks. "As soon as the banking crisis was under control," Schlesinger outlines, Roosevelt "turned to the idea of emergency conservation work. . . . 'I think I'll go ahead with this,' he said, '—the way I did on beer'." He issued a memorandum to the Departments of Agriculture, Interior, and War and brought in Secretary of Labor Frances Perkins—a trusted New York colleague and now the first woman ever appointed to a presidential cabinet—with her sprawling U.S. Employment Service for recruitment. "I am asking you to constitute yourselves an informal committee of the Cabinet," the President wrote on 14 March, "to co-ordinate the plans for the proposed Civilian Conservation Corps."[14]

Ickes, Wallace, Dern, and Perkins met the next day to discuss organization of this "CCC," and where it should fit into Roosevelt's broad plans for public works and unemployment relief. Their combined vision for employing youths on conservation projects looked to recent statistics that placed one in four Americans between the ages of fifteen and twenty-four among the nation's transient population and among those "totally unemployed," recounts Salmond.

> A further 29 per cent worked part-time only. This was an American crisis. These young people, endlessly tramping city streets or stagnating in country towns, were in a situation not of their own making. Bewildered, sometimes angry, but more often hopeless and apathetic, they were a generation already deeply scarred. The government could no longer afford to ignore their plight.[15]

The "informal committee" quickly affirmed the need for a youthful conservation army, but cautioned the president to keep this program "confined to forestry and soil erosion projects." They felt that labor leaders and Congress would support his proposal so long as it did not interfere with private employment and even other public works programs. Later on Wednesday Roosevelt conducted his third press conference and presented several details about the conservation plan, including proposed pay for the "usefully employed" at $1 per day.

On Tuesday, 21 March 1933, Roosevelt issued to Congress his message on "relief of unemployment," including specific request for authority to create a civilian conservation corps. Urging passage within two weeks, the president now estimated that 250,000 men could be enrolled in time for summer employment, half the strength of his recent thinking but still a staggering figure compared to the U.S. Army's regular enlistment of 174,000. Congressional hearings on emergency conservation work stretched through the next ten days, centering on wages, appearances of militarism and comparisons with Germany, and funds for the program. After much colorful oratory and maneuvering, a modified Senate bill highly favorable to the president prevailed. A significant amendment survived from the House debates, attached by Republican Oscar Stanton De Priest of Illinois, the single African American member of Congress. In recruiting this corps of American youth, De Priest inserted, "no discrimination shall be made on account of race, color, or creed." [16]

Conservation work would be funded, Congress assured, by unexpended balances of $300 million from the Reconstruction Finance Corporation's 1932 public works authorizations. In addition, Chief Forester Robert Y. Stuart had argued in committee hearings that the program should not be confined to federal lands. He convinced Congress to avoid "a mass movement of men from states east of the Mississippi River," Salmond summarizes, "where about 70 per cent of the [nation's] unemployment was located, to states west of the Rocky Mountain region, where 95 per cent of the [federal] public domain lay." Stuart thus set the landmark stage for "cooperative agreements made with the states to allow work in state forests and parks."

Congress returned the bill, popularly known as the Emergency Conservation Act, to Roosevelt on 31 March. Its wording gave him broad powers to organize—and name—the program as he wished and to pay its workers at whatever pay scale he deemed appropriate. Less than four weeks after he took office, the president signed this first unemployment relief measure into law. Throughout the cooperating cabinet agencies, preparations kicked off to mobilize the provisions of the act. On 5 April the President issued an executive order officially creating the New Deal experiment he had already named: the Civilian Conservation Corps. [17]

TEXAS MOBILIZES FOR THE NEW DEAL

The Texas Rehabilitation and Relief Commission

In Austin, Texas Relief Commission director Lawrence Westbrook labored throughout March 1933 to beat the Reconstruction Finance Corporation's deadline for central disbursement of federal relief funds. RFC funds came to Austin and, based on needs identified in county applications, then passed to local volunteer committees "to help the destitute unemployed pending their reabsorption into remunerative occupations," Westbrook declared with flourish. He determined that state oversight of federal funds would meet the RFC's scrutiny, and insisted on accountability at all levels. "Work permitted to be paid for by these funds must be," he specified, "constructive work of a public and, if possible, permanent nature . . . in exchange for the [relief] payments made, whether in cash or in kind."

Housed in the governor's suite at the Capitol and working with the RFC's March grant of almost $1.5 million, the relief commission busily distributed funds to 242 applicant counties. Westbrook's list of "eligible work projects" resembled earlier suggestions that spawned local public works through the winter of 1932–1933, such as roads, cemeteries, vegetable gardens, and parks. Perhaps based on the most successful of the initial RFC-funded relief work, now "Planning and building of municipal and county parks" rose to the top of the eligible list.[18]

As a parallel effort to combine public works with beautification, in early April 1933 State Highway Engineer Gibb Gilchrist hired his department's first "landscape engineer." The highway commission—with particular enthusiasm from its tree- and park-enthusiast chairman, Walter Raleigh Ely—authorized Gilchrist to pay $225 per month from existing budgets to landscape architect Jac L. Gubbels. The Dutch-trained designer came with impressive credits including 1928 work at San Jacinto State Park, 1932 assistance at Longhorn Cavern State Park, and recent beautification at the State Cemetery in Austin. Gubbels' assignment included training Highway Department engineers "to get the spirit of beautification along the highways," as Gilchrist put it, "and preserve the natural beauty spots."[19]

On 20 April Governor Ferguson announced that state lawmakers should enact emergency legislation to make the Texas Relief Commission "a proper technically correct" agency for two years. That day Westbrook and RFC official Aubrey Williams addressed the Texas House of Representatives. Williams noted that despite the success of distributing RFC relief funds, "very little use" had been made in Texas and other states of other public-works programs available from Congress since 1932. Texans could build permanent water and sewer plants and even more highways under existing programs, if only reluctant state officials would apply for available federal funds. (Notably, the nonconformist State Parks Board chief D. E. Colp already had acted exactly as Williams suggested by applying for RFC funds to develop state parks at Palo Duro Canyon and the Davis Mountains.)

After reminding legislators that Texas had already received almost $7 million from the RFC in the previous eight months, Williams held out the final carrot. "The sum of one hundred thousand dollars annually has been put down for administrative purposes," from Washington to run the state relief commission, he told House members. A group of representatives soon introduced a bill to make Westbrook's office a bona fide agency and to rename it the Texas Rehabilitation and Relief Commission. Supported by federal funds, the director received a $4,000 annual salary, and the agency received a two-year mandate to "administer all funds made available by the Federal Government," including those from the recently passed Emergency Conservation Act.[20]

Just as Westbrook's responsibilities rapidly enlarged, he received notification from Washington that his office would be enlisting Texas applicants in the new Civilian Conservation Corps. He "immediately left for Washington" for consultation with the Department of Labor on recruitment, according to *The Texas Weekly,* as "the first call has been issued for 900 men." The Texas Relief Commission director also sought "to investigate the possibilities of securing for Texas some of the projects to be carried out."[21]

Mobilizing for Emergency Conservation Work

Since becoming a working agency of the federal government in early April 1933, the Civilian Conservation Corps had moved rapidly toward its goal of placing 275,000 men in work camps by 1 July. States, in addition to being given recruitment quotas for their own citizens, received camp allotments for actual work projects. In mid-April the newly appointed director of Emergency Conservation Work (ECW: the official name of Roosevelt's experiment), Robert Fechner, telegraphed all governors asking them to identify work projects and camp sites that fit the requirements for CCC company assignments.

Governor Ferguson replied to Fechner on 15 April, expressing satisfaction that Texas had been allotted "one hundred and twenty camps of two hundred men each for a period of six months." Having no federal public land within its boundaries, Texas stood to benefit hugely from the ECW provision that camps could be assigned to state and local public lands, as well as to private tracts. Westbrook's initial visit to Washington, amplified by an influential delegation in Congress, had ensured for Texas a healthy portion of the new conservation-work program. Texas could now expect to participate in the CCC through both recruitment (12,000 young men) and project assignments (potentially 120 camps, which would be occupied by 24,000 men). Ferguson assured Fechner that "the State Forest Service, the State Reclamation Engineer, the Board of Water Engineers and the Director of the Texas [agricultural] Experiment Stations are preparing proposals" for CCC camps.

> It is understood, of course, that the selection of work projects and camp sites under the provisions of the Act is left to your discretion in order that you may most effectively carry out the program of the President. It was with this thought fully in view and with the feeling that the healthful and wholesome environment prevailing in this State, especially in its unsettled sections, would appeal to you, that I have taken the action above referred to.[22]

Westbrook's staff spent the next two weeks exploring and confirming the Texas conservation camp assignments. Backed by widespread public support for both the president and the governor, as well as a fortune in favorable publicity for the newly established CCC, Westbrook accomplished wonders in acquiring land donations. Two particular successes included 468 acres on Caddo Lake and 560 acres in the Davis Mountains, specific parklands that had eluded the State Parks Board for more than ten years!

On 29 April Ferguson forwarded detailed proposals by air express to Fechner, hoping to distribute her 120-camp quota among twenty-six projects across the state. The governor summarized the proposed projects "under three general heads as follows: A. Forestry, B. Flood Control and Land Reclamation, [and] C. Prevention of Soil Erosion." However, her attached list and map actually divided them as eleven "State Park," eleven "Flood Control," and four "combination park and flood control" projects. A note at the top of the list stated, "This summary is inclusive of 12 Forestry Projects."

Despite the governor's identification of up to fifteen park projects, the State Parks Board received no opportunity to propose camp sites. Perhaps Ferguson and Westbrook excluded Colp—still undisputed chairman of the parks board—because Washington's conservation-work officials initially emphasized forestry. Or perhaps this governor still, as eight years before, had no truck with Colp and his ad hoc agency. Nevertheless the Texas state-park proposals acknowledged Colp's old wish list for "large parks," with specifications for Caddo Lake (road, swimming pool, twenty-five cottages), Davis Mountains (roadwork, dams, twenty-five cottages), and Guadalupe Mountains (roads). Noted characteristics of these sites did not describe current state land ownership, or lack thereof.

The list also proposed new work at Longhorn Cavern (where concession development had begun in 1932 under State Parks Board contract), to include trails, roads and twenty overnight cottages. Other "state parks" on the list and map included heretofore unsolicited sites at Jacksonville, Jasper, and Sweetwater. New parks to be combined with flood-control projects appeared at Abilene, Blanco, Normangee, and the Nueces River in Live Oak County. The remaining park proposals on the 29 April list, coupled with Longhorn Cavern and Blanco, would form an intriguing north-to-south line of parks along new State Highway 66 at Mineral Wells, Stephenville, Hamilton, and Lampasas, honoring the old slogan of "a state park every hundred miles" but cutting the distance between parks to about forty miles.[23]

The Dignity and Prestige of Pat Neff

While Westbrook compiled the initial conservation-work proposals, Governor Ferguson cycled through her appointment lists and came upon two openings at the State Parks Board. Phebe Kerrick Warner's second term expired in 1933, and either because of poor connections with Ferguson or declining health, she was not reappointed. However, to fill Warner's energetic shoes, in a flash of brilliance Ferguson appealed to former governor and founder-extraordinaire of the State Parks Board, Pat Morris Neff of Waco. Neff had recently accepted the presidency of Baylor University, but he continued to oversee Mother Neff Park each summer. And he had maintained occasional contact with Colp and the surviving potential of their state park movement. Ferguson telegraphed Neff, mindful of the state park projects being proposed to Washington, with her offer.

> KNOWING YOUR GREAT INTEREST IN AND LOVE OF STATE PARKS I THINK THE PUBLIC SERVICE WOULD BE GREATLY BENEFITTED IF YOU WOULD ACCEPT APPOINTMENT ON THE STATE PARK BOARD STOP THE FEDERAL GOVERNMENT IN ALL PROBABILITY WILL ENDEAVOR TO EXTEND STATE PARK PROJECTS MATERIALLY STOP IN ASKING YOU TO SERVE I HAVE IN MIND ADDING DIGNITY AND PRESTIGE TO THE MOVEMENT.[24]

Neff responded the next day, 29 April—just as the Texas park project proposals went to Washington—that "it would give me great pleasure to serve on park board." With one more State Parks Board appointment to fill, the position held since 1923 by Hobart Key of Marshall, the governor then asked Neff for a recommendation. At first Neff coolly replied, "I am not able to think of anyone I would be willing to recommend for appointment on park board." But on 11 May, Ferguson chose Gus Frederick Urbantke, an Austin educator and insurance agent who knew the Fergusons through previous state appointments, and who probably knew Neff as well. By consulting with neither Colp nor Neff on the ECW park proposals, Ferguson displayed her old habit of crude timing and failure to coordinate simultaneous events, particularly concerning state parks. Also, with the appointments of Neff and Urbantke, Ferguson ended Neff's original regional-representation structure of the board.[25]

Refining the ECW Program

Governor Ferguson's (and Westbrook's) confusion over camp assignments —mixing forestry projects with state park sites—reflected similar discord at the federal level. The conservation-work advisory council struggled to divide CCC start-up responsibilities between the sponsoring agencies, opening old wounds between Interior and Agriculture and their respective National Park Service and U.S. Forest Service bureaus. The latter attempted at first to set up all the nation's CCC camps and administer their day-to-day operations. Even state-park proposals went initially to the Forest Service instead of NPS for approval, which caused immediate problems for the Texas applications. A forestry official in Washington reviewed Ferguson's 29 April proposals and submitted a naively critical report to Fechner.

Texas "State Park projects seem principally to consist of construction of dams to create lakes and ponds and of building construction," the reviewing forester groused on 3 May. "These parks are for the most part not forested. Possibly some work might be projected as to these parks that would come within the scope of the Act, but it seems evident that project plans, as submitted, cannot be approved." [26]

Fechner wrote Ferguson on 8 May acknowledging the negative review, but added, "the study is being continued and possibly a more favorable attitude may be justified later on." In the same letter, confirming that the president had proceeded with his indulging and slow process of ratifying each camp site personally, Fechner revealed the first handful of Roosevelt's CCC assignments for Texas. "You may be interested to know that the President has approved the erection of one work camp in Texas on state forest land, [and] three work camps on private [forest] land to perform work which would be in the public interest. . . . While of course this is a very modest start," Fechner told the governor, the first four CCC camps in Texas received assignments in (1) Jasper, (2) Angelina and Nacogdoches, (3) Trinity, Walker, and Houston, and (4) Polk counties. [27]

This initial selection of only four Texas sites reflected glaring flaws within the conservation-work organization, as both CCC recruitment and camp assignments nationwide moved at an alarming crawl. The U.S. Forest Service could not handle the transport and care of 250,000 recruits, and the president could not postpone the enormous demands of his office to approve camp sites one at a time. So Fechner asked the Army to intervene, and on 12 May its staff presented a new approach to mobilization, asking the president to grant wartime powers for commanding and transporting recruits, and for securing campsites and supplies from host communities without the bother of open-market procedures. Roosevelt approved this plan that day, even agreeing to forego his personal site approvals and speed up project selection.

Two days later, officers of the Army's Eighth Corps Area headquartered at Fort Sam Houston in San Antonio visited College Station to consult with Texas Forest Service officials. From there they traveled to Lufkin "to reconnoiter camps for four companies of the Civilian Conservation Corps," according to the *San Antonio Light,* which trumpeted these "first camps for tree army workers in Texas." [28]

On 15 May the National Park Service, also breaking from dependence on the U.S. Forest Service in conservation-work management, established four district offices across the nation. "Their main purpose," described then assistant director of the park service Conrad Wirth, "was to process applications and give careful review and general supervision to planning and carrying out work . . . for the state, county, and metropolitan parks CCC program." Texas fell into District III, in the Rocky Mountain region combining the Utah Basin and the Southwest, according to Wirth and his boss Horace Albright, who then named the supervising district officers. "Herb Maier, an excellent architect who had done some work for the National Park Service," Wirth recalled, "agreed to take the Rocky Mountain district, with headquarters in Denver."

Indeed, Herbert Maier had designed between 1924 and 1929 some of the best examples of park buildings in the national park system, according to his critics. Maier's four museum commissions at Yellowstone National Park epitomized more than a decade of attempts to produce service facilities that harmonized with the landscape, particularly through small buildings of local stone and wood, completed with hand tools and natural finishes. Maier had studied architecture at the University of California at Berkeley and engineering in San Francisco. About 1920 he began designing museum dioramas and then complete buildings for a variety of clients, including the National Park Service. He worked regularly with NPS chief naturalist Ansel Hall at the University of California at Berkeley through the spring of 1933, when his park service friends nominated him for a new district officer position to help direct NPS State Park Emergency Conservation Work.[29]

Also on 15 May Governor Ferguson wrote to Fechner, Congressman Sam Rayburn, and others that she had just signed legislation creating the Texas Rehabilitation and Relief Commission. She immediately instructed Westbrook "to proceed to Washington for the purpose of conferring with the heads of Federal Departments . . . and with members of the Texas delegation in the National Congress. . . . Accompanying Col. Westbrook will be a committee of engineers and technicians whose duty it will be to explain the details of projects already submitted and to discuss others in prospect."[30]

Westbrook proceeded not a moment too soon, because the bulk of Texas conservation-project applications had not recovered from the negative U.S. Forest Service review of early May. Ferguson telegraphed Fechner on 16 May that she had just learned that the Army "issued instructions to forward all Texas quota except eight hundred sixty men to camps [in] other states."

I FEEL THAT HEARING SHOULD BE GIVEN RELATIVE THESE APPLICATIONS BEFORE ORDERING TEXAS QUOTA OTHER STATES AND EARNESTLY REQUEST SAME BE EXTENDED STOP HAVE FULLEST DESIRE COOPERATE WITH NATIONAL PROGRAM IN EVERY WAY BUT HOPE THIS WILLINGNESS WILL NOT PREJUDICE INTERESTS THIS STATE UNNECESSARILY[31]

At last on 27 May Fechner sent a memo to National Park Service director Albright listing ten Texas state park projects approved for CCC camps, some to receive more than one two-hundred-man camp each. Westbrook's visits with Washington officials, especially members of the powerful Texas congressional delegation, linked perfectly with the National Park Service's break from rival U.S. Forest Service control of project locations. Now on Fechner's approved list, Caddo Lake would definitely receive a CCC camp, and two camps would be assigned to the Davis Mountains for park development under NPS supervision. In addition, the curious chain of new parks along SH 66 would be fulfilled through one CCC camp each for Mineral Wells, Stephenville, Hamilton, Lampasas, and Blanco. Fechner's list dropped several sites from Governor Ferguson's initial submittal, notably Guadalupe Mountains and Longhorn Cavern. But a new project at "Tres Palacios" promised a state park near the popular coastal resort community of Palacios in Matagorda County. And a new site approved in Randall and Armstrong counties acknowledged intense regional lobbying for major state park development at Palo Duro Canyon.[32]

New Deal Politics and D. E. Colp

Assignment of Emergency Conservation Work projects in Texas, with associated CCC camps, depended as much on politics as on appropriate geography. As the new program intended, the initial four CCC reforestation camps in Texas landed squarely in the sprawling eastern Big Thicket, long exploited for its prime timber and now urgently in need of conservation work. And certainly, building state parks at the alluring landscapes of Caddo Lake, the Davis Mountains, and Palo Duro Canyon had been proposed by nonpartisan park supporters for years.[33]

But most of the newly approved ECW park areas in May 1933 fell within important political turf as well as suitable landscapes. Caddo Lake's submittal, for instance, benefited from the powerful influence of U.S. Senator John Morris Sheppard, serving in Washington since 1902, and Palo Duro Canyon from that of Congressman Marvin Jones, representing the Panhandle since 1916. SH 66 passed through the congressional districts of powerful Washington old-timers Thomas Lindsay Blanton and James Paul Buchanan, who both strongly supported employment through New Deal public works for their constituents.

The proposed chain of parks along SH 66 must have received encouragement from state officials, too, including State Highway Commission chairman and park enthusiast Walter Ely. In addition, the SH 66 towns of Stephenville, Hamilton, and Lampasas all lay within fifty recreation-driving miles of Waco, home to Lieutenant Governor Edgar Witt, Texas Relief Commission director Westbrook, and State Parks Board appointee Neff.

Finally, the newly approved CCC camp sites at both Mineral Wells and Palacios actually served, in part or whole, National Guard training facilities at, respectively, Camp Wolters and Camp Hulen. Lieutenant Colonel Lawrence Westbrook of the Texas National Guard could be the only explanation for these two odd "state park" CCC camps.

State Parks Board chairman Colp, absent from the astonishing series of recent developments that virtually guaranteed a state park system for Texas, could be found only behind the intense push for Palo Duro Canyon. Colp seemingly had traded his kingdom for a single horse in the spring of 1933, since Westbrook quickly built a powerhouse commission that now controlled public park works throughout the state. Thus Colp failed miserably to secure development prospects for most of the park communities he had courted for a decade, as these now missed assignments of CCC camps. As one pitiful result, early park donor A. B. Mayhew—whose 26.5 acre "Alto Frio" River site in Uvalde County had been presented to Pat Neff in 1924, then achieved great success as a concession operation by 1926—successfully petitioned the legislature in April to return the land.[34] Yet Colp, to his credit, now doggedly pursued the $141,000 RFC loan for acquisition and development of parkland at Palo Duro Canyon, still in private hands.

Colp and Fred Emery, owner of a large part of upper Palo Duro Canyon, had earlier consulted with RFC and National Park Service officials in Washington, D.C., about their park idea. Emery and his wife had recently acquired their partners' interests in the original Arnold Ranch/Byers Brothers holdings in Palo Duro Canyon. Their two-year agreement with the Canyon Chamber of Commerce for public park use of Section 101—Emery's most desirable and accessible scenery—expired on 30 April 1933, and Emery remained eager throughout the spring to strike a more permanent deal with Colp and the State Parks Board.

To Emery's delight, Washington park planners Conrad Wirth and Herb Evison displayed a keen interest in Palo Duro development. Fortunately and economically, they modified Colp's and Emery's vision of a Palo Duro park from that of an elaborate resort atmosphere to one more sensitive to the natural environment. Development estimates fell accordingly, and Colp lowered his federal loan request to $120,000. Officials then asked Colp to shift responsibility for his proposed "Goodnight Trail" canyon access road to the Texas Highway Department. And, reiterating their initial response of late 1932 to Colp, these officials insisted he secure legislative authority for his parks board to accept and service a potential loan.[35]

Panhandle park supporter James Guleke and others, with some input from long-time Palo Duro proponent Phebe Warner, took on the legislative challenge. In mid-April they prodded Amarillo state senator Clint C. Small to introduce a bill meeting the federal loan requirements. Small guided the legislation quickly through the Capitol by noting "many of the State parks in this State are badly in need of improvement, and . . . improvement thereof will create employment which is so sorely needed at this time." In early May, Colp, Guleke, and the State Board of Water Engineers conducted a survey in Palo Duro Canyon for the Goodnight Trail right-of-way, starting its west end at the Panhandle-Plains Museum in Canyon. At its east end, the parkway would extend to the "first automobile crossing over the canyon proper," reported the *Amarillo Sunday News-Globe,* referring to the recently completed Claude-to-Wayside road. Warner, "pioneer booster for Palo Duro Canyon as a state park," the paper added, joined the survey party at one stop and "pledged the support of Panhandle women." Promoting the parkway in May through publicity and several speeches to regional organizations, Colp repeatedly noted that "the only remaining problem is obtaining of the right of way to be deeded to the state." [36]

Other state-park and related bills moved successfully through the legislature's regular session in the spring of 1933, albeit with little or no collaboration from Colp. Freshman senator John Sayers Redditt of Lufkin sponsored a resolution establishing procedures for the federal government to acquire natural-resource lands in Texas. The state forester would approve any land purchased for national forests, this new law required, and the State Parks Board "must first approve the purchase of any land for National Parks in the State."

One more park bill, equal in potential to Senator Small's funding initiative for Palo Duro Canyon, "provided for the creation of the Texas Canyons State Park." Cosponsored by representatives B. Frank Haag of Midland, Everett Ewing Townsend of Alpine, and Robert McAlpine Wagstaff of Abilene, this bill and attached resolution acknowledged the qualities of the little-known Big Bend region. Moreover, although 150-acre Goose Island State Park had been created in 1931 from unassigned state land, this Big Bend measure breached traditional resistance by creating a state park directly from the state's public school lands. [37]

As the regular session neared an end, the legislature agreed to two voter referendums for an August vote. To satisfy Washington's insistence on Texas contributions to match federal relief payments, a statewide bond measure would offer $20 million for unemployment relief. And to match President Roosevelt's quick action on federal tolerance of beer, Texans would decide on its legal sale in their state. Lawmakers also agreed—for the first time since 1917—upon twenty-one new congressional district boundaries, effective in August, based on the 1930 census that allowed Texas three new seats. Before the session ended on 19 June, the State Parks Board claimed one minor victory in addition to Small's loan measure. Under the Board of Control's budget, the parks board could spend $375—its first funding in eight years—plus "any park rents, concession, privilege, or other park receipts," in each of the two coming fiscal years.[38]

THE CCC BEGINS STATE PARK WORK IN TEXAS

Filling Positions of Responsibility

Beginning on 30 May 1933 the newly appointed district officer for NPS Region III, Herb Maier, traveled through his vast new district, from North Dakota to Texas, according to his reports. Maier fixed his itinerary on "contacting the state authorities, breaking in the procurement officers, appointing inspectors and surveying the proposed work projects."

> It must be borne in mind that the state parks in the third district are in a large measure either primitive areas that have recently been deeded to the state or are located in states where park development has not reached the degree of perfection [as] in some of the eastern states. This places a responsibility for creative work and the establishing of policy on the National Park Service in this district. Although this adds to the burden of work it affords a real opportunity for service.[39]

In Austin, Maier reviewed applications for traveling inspector positions to be his eyes, ears, and design hands at each park site under development. He found Victor Brock and Frederick Amerman Dale, both with the backgrounds in engineering and conservation that Maier needed as quick studies for what he called "park-minded" landscape design. Dale, a New York City native with degrees from New York University and Massachusetts Institute of Technology (1914), possessed considerable experience in public works management. He had moved to Austin in 1930 to direct construction of a privately financed hydroelectric dam on the Colorado River between Llano and Burnet but had lost his job when the depression dried up capital for the project.[40] Quickly hired by Maier and initially headquartered at Westbrook's relief commission offices, Dale became in effect the first Texas state park engineer.

Maier's federal payroll allowed for the appointment of several other professional and skilled positions at each new park site. These jobs ranged from project superintendent to—as appropriate for the terrain and master-plan development—engineer, landscape architect, and architect. Positions for "Local Experienced Men" hired to join the CCC camps offered additional work to carpenters, stone masons, blacksmiths, and other master craftsmen idled in their communities by changing technologies and the depression. In addition to paying these "technical men," the National Park Service estimated that each CCC camp would expend a total of $18,000 over the course of its six-month assignment.

The question of command over this substantial job bank and considerable depression payroll signaled the inevitable clash between Colp's State Parks Board and Westbrook's agency. When Maier during his whirlwind district tour sought to find Colp, the national parks official discovered that the state board had no office, no employees, and a $375 annual budget beginning only in the coming fiscal year! Alarmed that the parks board could not disburse federal salaries throughout the state, and that the board certainly could not offer engineering services or an architectural design office, Maier's superiors—Wirth and Albright—turned to Governor Ferguson for an immediate remedy. She responded to Albright on 7 June that indeed the "State Park Board has no paid administrative nor fiscal set-up."

> Due to this fact and to necessity for definite and responsible relationship with your department it is requested that you designate Texas Rehabilitation and Relief Commission . . . to act in behalf of this state in connection with administration of park projects carried on under Emergency Conservation program. . . . Chairman Colp of State Park Board joins me in this request.[41]

Now Colp definitely found himself elbowed out of an impending park development boom far greater than he or Phebe Warner or Pat Neff ever imagined. Along with the funds to pay for all professional and craft positions at the state park projects, the National Park Service also arranged especially for Texas to receive a $500-per-month overhead allowance for a central state parks office; all these funds would now go to the relief commission. Almost as important as funding, the ability to place trusted colleagues and long-time friends in well-paying jobs fell to Westbrook instead of Colp. Now the most generous role Colp could fill would be with further land negotiations at Palo Duro Canyon, and perhaps at other potential park sites if the CCC program continued beyond its initial six months.

Caddo Lake State Park

On 5 June one of the first project superintendents hired, Captain Waller K. Boggs, arrived at Caddo Lake to prepare for the first CCC camp officially assigned to state park work in Texas. Boggs joined members of the Marshall Chamber of Commerce and its Marshall Park Board—chaired by former State Parks Board member Hobart Key—representing the local effort to establish a park on Caddo Lake. As they conducted an inspection tour of several donated sites totaling some 468 acres, Boggs informed his local contacts that he represented the "State Park Board and the Emergency Relief Commission"; acknowledging service for the moment to two masters in Austin. "Nature has provided a park in the rough," he described to an area newspaper, "and it requires only the hand of man to make it one of the outstanding beauty spots in the Southwest."

These dense piney woods actually fronted on Big Cypress Bayou west of the main body of Caddo Lake and just north of Karnack, and included the abandoned nineteenth-century settlement Port Caddo. Karnack resident Thomas Jefferson Taylor II—owner of a reputed 15,000 acres in the area—had donated the initial ten acres at Port Caddo. The Port Caddo Motor Club added its small resort at the old landing. Other land donors included the Harrison County Colored Country Club and the Dallas Caddo Club, among several institutions and individual owners who had acquired small tracts of land at this popular retreat over many years.[42]

CCC Co. 889 arrived on 17 June at Karnack by train from Fort Sill, Oklahoma, to begin work on project "SP-1-T": the first authorized, National Park Service–supervised state park in Texas. Other CCC companies preceded 889 to their job assignments—notably on 10 June at Palacios (Co. 1805), and on 16 June at Davis Mountains (879 and 881) and Blanco (854)—but all took up their shovels as Emergency Conservation Work began moving brush and earth across the United States. Commanded by U.S. Army Reserve lieutenant T. V. Webb, the 220 CCC enrollees at Caddo Lake set to work establishing their tent-camp garrison and clearing the underbrush that choked about a hundred acres in the planned development area of the new park. NPS inspector Victor Brock visited the camp in early July and reported the men busy on their first assignment, "building a one-half mile road from the county road to the campsite." Identifying the necessary cooperation for access roads common to most conservation-work sites, Brock added that Caddo Lake's "approach road—19 miles long from Marshall—is a poor one. The Chamber of Commerce is asking the State [Highway Department] to put it into shape."[43]

Davis Mountains State Park

Fort Davis correspondent Barry Scobee in early June reported under top-ranked headlines of the *Alpine Avalanche* that "Real State Park In The Davis Mountains May Be A Reality." While the Texas Highway Department slowly progressed through federal relief funding on its Davis Mountains State Park Highway, the region's dream of offering more than a linear parkway finally sprang to life with the donation of some 560 acres in Keesey Canyon just west of Fort Davis. The J. W. Merrill family (contributing 200 acres), Joe W. Espy (200 acres) and the Union Trading Company with other

Fort Davis citizens (160 acres) assembled title to this compact valley of Keesey Creek. The site boasted a perfect entrance along the new park highway, building westward up Limpia Creek from town toward Mount Locke and the University of Texas McDonald Observatory under construction there. This rolling landscape—where grassy hills rise steeply above each side of creek beds, then break into dark stone pinnacles along the ridge tops— became the home of CCC companies 879 and 881 when they arrived on 16 June from Fort Bliss.

"Cars and trucks of Fort Davis and Marfa brought 400 from the railway at Marfa last Friday morning," Scobee wrote on 23 June. "[A]nd since then they have been busy in getting a complete camp organized and built, with running water, bath houses, frame kitchens, attractive streets, floored sleeping tents, a medical dispensary, and sanitation." The correspondent provided a wealth of detail about the new camp, including its mixed education and ethnic makeup, the crucial hand tools for their work, and how the operation of the camp immediately boosted the local economy. "Boys from college campus and cotton rows, from city streets and open plains, are in the Davis Mountains State Park C.C.C. camp and having the time of their young lives. Four hundred are present, including a score or so of Mexicans and twice that number of colored men."

Initial park development, Scobee revealed over several weeks, would include roads in the canyon and up to the mountaintops, a dam and lake on Keesey Creek, and several cottages of adobe or stone. "A great vision is behind all this," Scobee reflected, "and the 'visioners' have been those who have seen the possibilities of the Davis mountains for the last twelve years— former Governor Neff, Tom Love, Governor Sterling, and later the members of the state highway commission, and numerous others of which [D. E.] Colp is an important and leading one." [44]

Palo Duro Canyon State Park(s)

Colp suffered from more bad timing—he thought—when Herb Evison of the National Park Service in early June 1933 asked federal offices to detain Colp's favorable Palo Duro Canyon loan application. Colp and Fred Emery were very close to a deal with the RFC, based on Senator Clint Small's recent enabling bill, for the State Parks Board to acquire more than 14,000 acres—eight miles long and three miles wide—of Emery's holdings. However, passage of the Emergency Conservation Act and subsequent assignment of CCC camps, coupled with a major realignment of federal relief-fund offices, quickly left Colp's loan idea behind in the rapidly changing policies of Washington, D.C.

Colp reluctantly gave his blessing for the shift of Palo Duro development hopes to the conservation-work program. With James Guleke's persistent urging and the help of Congressman Marvin Jones and Senator Tom Connally in Washington—plus full support of the National Park Service—on 1 June President Roosevelt approved the incredible assignment of four CCC camps to Palo Duro. Several Amarillo citizens, unimpressed with this positive news because they had no guarantee the Emery land deal would succeed, combined resources and purchased yet another tract in Palo Duro, part of the old H. C. Harding place. Now billed as the Palisades, this 320-acre tract directly south of Amarillo forthwith received one of the four Palo Duro CCC camp allotments when its donors promised immediately to present their land title to the State Parks Board.[45]

The complicated purchase of Emery's land negotiated by Colp required the state to pay Fred and his wife Millie a mere $10, but to pledge installments from park income for several years to come. Colp missed completely the prudent step of calling the State Parks Board to a meeting (and they had not met since perhaps 1930) for their own validation of the deal. Yet he certainly acted on precedent, having pulled off the Longhorn Cavern contract a year earlier in much the same way.

With Colp's agreement, the Emerys placed their deed in escrow with an Austin bank pending confirmation that an Emergency Conservation Work project would indeed be assigned to Palo Duro Canyon. Since the Emerys still owed money on their Palo Duro land, the contract called for state payments first to address their original liens recently extended to 1942. Then the parks board would continue paying on the Emerys' vendor's lien for another six years, retiring all debts (for a total of $361,000) in 1948. All these figures depended upon half the income from planned entry fee charges of 20 cents per adult, 10 cents for children, and 35 cents for each auto, plus 20 percent of all provision sales.[46]

Since Governor Ferguson had recently assigned responsibility for state park decisions to the Texas Rehabilitation and Relief Commission, Westbrook now scrutinized Colp's handiwork. Upon Westbrook's insistence, Colp in mid-June turned the Emery documents over to Attorney General James Burr V. Allred for ratification. Sure enough, Westbrook and his commissioners did not like Allred's response, particularly since it clarified the point that the state held no deed to Emery's land. Instead they all found only Colp's promise of federal improvements and an obligation to pay off two huge liens "for some five or six times the value of the land," according to one examiner. Simultaneously the National Park Service balked at the arrangement, because the president all but forbade the federal government from erecting public buildings on private land.[47]

Meanwhile, U.S. Army surveyors could not locate a source of water, essential for the hundreds of CCC enrollees expected to encamp very soon, within Emery's chunk of Palo Duro. Already suspicious of Colp's land deal and now convinced that drinking water could not be found in Palo Duro Canyon, Washington park planners shifted this large CCC allotment to the next available Texas site: the recently authorized "Texas Canyons State Park."

The Brewster County site then ran immediately into the same water problem. "Colonel King, a medical officer from Fort [S]ill," wrote park service inspector Fred Dale of events in late June, "positively turned down all sites in the Big Bend country. The camps are now headed [on paper] toward the Palo Duro again, water at the [Palisades] site having been discovered in the meantime." CCC Co. 856 arrived on 21 June 1933 at "Palisades State Park," attracting little attention but launching at least the backup plan for park development somewhere in Palo Duro Canyon.[48]

Although Dale initially surmised that the CCC-camp shell game caused the "Amarillo people [to] have received the situation philosophically," considerable Panhandle fury rained upon the relief commission. Westbrook and his commissioners gave in on 29 June, and Army technicians approved a piped-in water supply for Emery's Section 101 site, thus satisfying National Park Service requirements to confirm the CCC camp location.

All these delays caused the Army to dispatch for Palo Duro more recently formed CCC units made up of middle-aged military veterans, including many who had been Bonus Marchers just weeks before in Washington, D.C. Late on 11 July approximately two hundred men of CCC Co. 1829 arrived at the Amarillo train depot from their conditioning camp at Fort Sill, and the next morning local citizens formed a car and truck caravan to transport enrollees to their Section 101 camp site. On the same day, CCC companies 1824 and 1828, also composed of war veterans, arrived from Fort Sam Houston, Texas, and joined the ragtag motor caravan shuttling to and from the canyon. "Undaunted" by a sudden thunderstorm that swept through the growing encampment, writes historian Peter L. Petersen, "the men continued to set camps and by nightfall, a 'tent city' of more than 600 men had been established."[49]

A Burgeoning State Park System

The *Hamilton Herald* dutifully reported every initial step of establishing the CCC camp for Hamilton State Park, to be built a few miles south of the city on SH 66. "A thrill of excitement and curiosity swept over Hamilton on Tuesday [20 June] at noon [with] the expected arrival of the quota of reforestation army boys," the article related. Their camp at the city fairgrounds came "equipped with city water, electric lights, and many other modern conveniences such as are required by the government for the use of the reforestation army." [50]

Despite community enthusiasm over the planned SH 66 parks for Hamilton, Blanco, Clifton, and Mineral Wells, inspector Dale judged these grounds "not really of national park character." But recently employed inspector P. H. Elwood offered that park improvements at Mineral Wells, like the other small highway parks, "will in reality be a roadside retreat of a higher order if well planned and executed and supervised." The Mineral Wells CCC camp, although initially assigned like the Palacios camp to the Army's adjacent summer training grounds, "is divided between improvement of national guard quarters at Camp Wolters, where the CCC camp is garrisoned," Dale acknowledged, "and work on a 60 acre park a half mile north of Mineral Wells." In contrast, the larger SH 66 park sites selected for Lampasas and Stephenville, plus nearby Meridian, offered "interesting topographical relief and impressive scenery," Dale reported in anticipation of extensive improvements at each. [51]

By the first of July, President Roosevelt and Robert Fechner's conservation-work organization met their ambitious goal by placing 274,375 men nationwide in CCC camps. "The Army had successfully undertaken," summarizes CCC historian John Salmond, "the largest peacetime mobilization of men the United States had ever seen, had built more than 1,300 camps, and had installed recruits in all of them. The CCC was off to a fine start." The Texas state parks system found itself up and running as well. From the state's quota of forty-one CCC camps—with assignments ranging from reforestation and soil erosion to park projects—fifteen companies of CCC enrollees set to work by midsummer developing the long-contemplated miracle of a state park system of twelve new recreation parks.

Inspectors Dale, Brock, and Elwood busily motored the highways and backroads of Texas, visiting each of the camps, offering advice and reporting on their progress. When these federal officials paused long enough in Austin to type their meticulous weekly reports to boss Herb Maier in Denver, they helped establish a central design office with a staff funded by the National Park Service. "Mr. [B. L.] Austin, the architect . . . is working the drafting board here," Dale reported on 1 July to Maier. Roy Ferguson soon joined the office as a "landscape engineer" to help draw the first boundary maps and plot the first CCC construction duties for an eventual master plan at each park. "Design for rock entrance which will be used for many parks has been prepared and also working drawings for this entrance," Dale typed for Maier.

"You will appreciate, however," he explained in words echoing now-familiar speeches of their president, "that our first consideration must be keeping the men usefully employed." [52]

TABLE 1

The First Texas State Parks of the New Deal

First Period, Emergency Conservation Work, June–Fall 1933[1]

NPS Number	Official Name	CCC Company
SP-1	Caddo Lake State Park	Co. 889
SP-2	Lampasas State Park	Co. 896
SP-3	Stephenville State Park	Co. 817
SP-4	Davis Mountains State Park	Co. 879
SP-5	” ” ” ”	Co. 881
SP-6	Hamilton State Park	Co. 882
SP-7	Blanco State Park	Co. 854
SP-8	Mineral Wells State Park	Co. 1811
SP-9	Tres Palacios State Park	Co. 1805
SP-10	Palisades State Park	Co. 856
SP-11	Clifton State Park	Co. 878
SP-12	Meridian State Park	Co. 1827(V)[2]
SP-13	Palo Duro Canyon State Park	Co. 1829(V)
SP-14	” ” ” ” ”	Co. 1828(V)
SP-15	” ” ” ” ”	Co. 1824(V)

[1] Texas CCC assignments in 1933 spanned the months from June through September; this duration later was designated the ECW "first period." Subsequent six-month periods began in October and April, primarily to facilitate movement of CCC companies and their settlement at new camp assignments during the fair weather of fall and spring. Early NPS project-number assignments to Texas state parks varied, but within a few months the list stabilized to those recorded here. John A. Salmond, *The Civilian Conservation Corps, 1933–1942: A New Deal Case Study* (Durham, N.C.: Duke University Press, 1967), p. 45; various CCC camp rosters; "Thirty-nine CCC Camps in Texas," *Farm and Ranch,* circa November 1933, clipping in "New Deal" vertical file, Barker Texas History Collections.

[2] "(V)" signified a CCC company of war veterans.

INTERLUDE

The CCC: a Well-Grounded, Well-Rounded Plan

"What is the CCC?" enrollee Harold Buckles inquired in late 1934 from his Caddo Lake State Park assignment. "What do they do? How is the organization run?" The young "forest soldier" placed himself in the shoes of local citizens who encountered his associates of CCC Co. 857, and to address typical curiosity he contributed an informative essay to the *Marshall News Messenger.* "Those are questions that are asked every member of the CCC," he began. "They are not questions that can be answered briefly, for it's a big organization, doing big things."[53]

The Civilian Conservation Corps clearly sprang in March 1933 from the progressive dreams and innovations of Franklin Delano Roosevelt. Yet the new president relied heavily upon the ideas and wisdom of many advisors to breathe life into the CCC, as well as to shape its administration and its specific conservation tasks. Indeed one of the earliest visions for such a New Deal program emerged from conversations between advisor Rex Tugwell and the U.S. Forest Service. Their initial proposal for a "forest army" or "tree army" imposed lasting nicknames for the CCC, long after park development and soil conservation joined forestry on its list of basic assignments in 1933. Some CCC admirers did acknowledge the expanded missions, attaching the moniker "soil soldiers" to appropriate camps and, eventually, "army in overalls" to the vast program. Beyond the notions of conservation and specifically reforestation, the concept of the CCC—that of a seasonal, quasi-military[54] home for young men assigned to rustic work in the outdoors—lay grounded in numerous American traditions and institutions.

Boy Scout and concurrent girl-camper institutions that appeared about 1910, and enjoyed enormous American youth participation, provided perhaps the most superficial influence on the 1933 CCC. Certainly the popular ideal for families to send sons and daughters off to summer camps offered a comforting model for parents of younger CCC enrollees, even if they lacked the means for such higher-class rituals.

Coincidentally in 1910 Franklin Roosevelt, who could not ignore his cousin Theodore's support for conservation and particularly the Boy Scouts, encountered an influential speech on youth and conservation. Dubbed "The Moral Equivalent of War," this rousing delivery at Harvard University by William James proposed a universal draft as the progressive answer to "childishness" in "our gilded youths." James proposed, in remarkable anticipation of Roosevelt's later consideration of destitute youths, "If now . . . there were, instead of military conscription, a conscription of the whole youthful population to form for a certain number of years a part of the army enlisted against Nature, the injustice would tend to be evened out, and numerous other goods to the commonwealth would follow."[55]

The World War draft and enlistment experience of the late 1910s lingered into the 1930s as an American tolerance for entrusting the nation's youth to temporary military guardians. And the country's interest in maintaining defensive "readiness" after the 1914–1918 war—resulting in widespread support for reserve units, the National Guard, and a summer-soldier program called Citizens Military Training Camps—motivated a collective patriotic fervor for responding to the government's call to service.

As a more immediate but obviously non-Roosevelt premonition of the CCC, in January 1933 one Republican U.S. senator called for the War Department to establish year-round Citizens Military Training Camps for unemployed youth. James Couzens of Michigan "introduced a bill . . . authorizing the Army to house, feed, and clothe unemployed young men from the ages of seventeen to twenty-four at military posts," notes historian John Salmond. Chief of Staff Douglas MacArthur frowned on the idea, but his subalterns reviewed the Army's capacity for such a mission. When Congress took no immediate action in Hoover's last weeks as president, the measure "was soon quietly shelved." [56]

Ironically, no matter how hard the new president and Congress downplayed the ultimate military nature of the CCC, an undeniable martial atmosphere prevailed in CCC camps. The War Department soon served a highly visible role in the CCC's combination of uniformed reserve officers as camp commanders, Army field kitchens and mess halls for hearty camp food, surplus World War uniforms for initial CCC enrollee clothing, plus wartime tent and barrack designs for housing. Moreover, accommodation in the CCC for older, unemployed war veterans seemed considerably more than an afterthought in this rapidly mobilizing "forest army."

Creating a New Deal Program

The Emergency Conservation Act, rather than designate or create an entirely new bureau, authorized the President "to utilize such existing departments or agencies as he might," according to one account, "to carry out his 'pet project'." Although this experiment received the organization name "Emergency Conservation Work" (ECW), Roosevelt's original term "Civilian Conservation Corps" stuck, and it applied everlasting to the workers themselves, as opposed to the ECW bureaucracy directing them. (Reauthorization of the CCC in 1937 dropped the ECW title.) To carry out ECW, Roosevelt drew upon a number of previous initiatives that called for cooperation between cabinet agencies, all to accomplish temporary assignments from the chief executive or Congress.

Calvin Coolidge, for instance, in 1924 asked his Secretaries of Agriculture, Commerce, Interior, Labor, and War to help organize "[c]ountry recreation for as many of our people as possible" through the not-repeated "First National Conference on Outdoor Recreation." In 1930 just before the depression truly alarmed Congress, a couple of its members outlined a multi-million-dollar "Federal-Aid Park Commission, to be composed of the Secretaries of the Interior, Agriculture and Labor." In both cases planners hoped that the control of vast resources by each agency would play an even grander role when brought together for a wide-reaching national goal. [57]

Just ten days after taking office, on 14 March 1933, Roosevelt named his Secretaries of Agriculture, Interior, Labor, and War as an "informal committee of the Cabinet to co-ordinate the plans for the proposed Civilian Conservation Corps." In his second "fireside chat" the president drew his nation's collective ear to a discussion of Emergency Conservation Work, calling its legislation a "well-grounded, well-rounded plan." [58] The president

projected, and arranged funding for, an initial six-month experiment beginning officially on 5 April 1933. Authorization of a second six-month "period"
to begin in the fall of 1933 set the pattern for CCC terms of enlistment,
and—theoretically—the completion time for all "technical agency" (National Park Service, U.S. Forest Service, etc.) projects. The administration
of the program as it was initiated (and as it changed through time, with
such changes indicated briefly in the following discussion) relied heavily on
the Departments of Labor, War, Agriculture, and Interior.

The Labor Department administered most CCC enrollment through
state selection agencies (in Texas, the relief commission) and county welfare
boards across the nation. Roosevelt's campaign proposal of employing a million men in reforestation was adjusted after inauguration to a half million
and finally settled on 250,000 (this enrollment cap later expanded), plus
25,000 "Local Experienced Men" hired as trade and craft experts. Single
young men, one per family, between the ages of 18 and 25, could enlist for
six-month periods upon qualification of family relief needs. These young
men (the age limit was lowered to 17 in 1935) filled the largest category of
CCC "Juniors." Regional managers of the Veterans' Administration chose
physically fit ex-servicemen, married or not, who had acted in any U.S.
conflict from Morocco to Cuba to Europe in the World War, to fill CCC
"Veterans" companies totaling 10 per cent of all CCC enrollment. Junior
enrollees could be posted to any camp in the United States (African Americans after 1935 remained in their home states per enrollment quotas); Veterans remained in their home states per enrollment quotas; Native Americans generally remained on their reservations. A brief experiment early in
the New Deal with female camps failed but inspired later agencies.

The War Department—primarily through the U.S. Army—condi-
tioned, transported, fed, clothed, housed, and paid CCC enrollees the minimum $30 per month, of which at least $25 went directly to parents or guardians. The RFC funded all ECW expenses, including those required for
Army support. Through its nationwide "service corps area" regions (Texas
fell into the Eighth Corps Area headquartered at Fort Sam Houston), the
Army positioned each CCC encampment and contracted within local communities for construction of its barracks and other facilities. The standard
military "company" averaging 200 men became the ideal CCC camp complement (some Veterans companies accepted 250 men; all companies reduced enrollment in 1936 to 160, the next year returning to 200). However,
camp populations always fluctuated with enrollment gains and losses. Each
company received a permanent unit number, with its "hundred" digit—
third from the right—identifying its home corps area (in Texas, for example: 889, 1805, 2875).

The Army also observed, at first, its own established racial arrangements, generally assigning African American recruits to kitchen and other bivouac duties in each CCC camp. (After 1935, CCC officials ordered segregation of whole camps as either "White" or "Colored," and limited African American enrollment to quotas within each state.) Mexican Americans held no separate status, but received camp assignments in proximity to Hispanic communities. The Army (and from 1935 the Navy and Marines) summoned reserve officers to six-month rotations as CCC camp commanders and assistants. The Army also retained whole CCC companies, usually African American, for internal duties at military posts (such as Forts Bliss, Clark, and Sam Houston in Texas).

To provide leisure time activities at CCC camps, the Army promoted team sports—even chess!—and transported enrollees to other camps for competitive events. The results of these activities and other enrollee news appeared regularly in *Happy Days,* a privately produced but officially sanctioned weekly newspaper for the CCC. Beginning in December 1933 the Army also administered an extensive educational program, hosting teachers during off-work hours in most CCC camps to provide rudimentary and advanced classroom courses.

The Agriculture Department supervised CCC workday projects through its U.S. Forest Service on federal, state, and private woodlands. The chief forester directed conservation and recreation work in national forests, and cooperated with state conservation agencies on state and private tracts—for example, the Texas Forest Service extension of Texas A&M College. (The federal soil erosion program was transferred in 1935 to Agriculture, and thereafter its Soil Conservation Service supervised appropriate CCC camps.[59])

The Interior Department supervised CCC workday projects through its National Park Service in national parks, and cooperated with state park agencies and, later, with local governments in county and "metropolitan" parks. Interior's Soil Erosion Service (until 1935), Indian Office, and other bureaus also supervised CCC camps assigned specifically to conservation tasks on federal, state, and private lands. Erosion control work consisted of drainage correction, terracing, and vegetation planting, available to private landowners for conservation of their agricultural lands.

Roosevelt selected Robert Fechner—born in Tennessee and raised in Georgia, avowed labor unionist and vice president of the American Federation of Labor—to administer Emergency Conservation Work and head the CCC. Fechner accepted an enormous and unprecedented task, but drew considerable criticism during his service. "He was a stolid and unimaginative man," observes historian Kenneth Hendrickson, "who viewed the mission of his agency in the narrowest possible context. He also possessed an abrasive personality which caused frequent irritation among his close associates; but on the other hand he was totally dedicated to his task and served ably." [60]

State Park Emergency Conservation Work

The park service developed a numbering system, as did all cooperating bureaus, to indicate the budgeted project and on-site assignment of each CCC company. The categories for national park (NP-) and state park (SP-), and later county park (CP-) and "metropolitan area" (MA-), each prefixed consecutive project numbers within a state. The host state's initial letter sometimes followed this combination (for example, SP-1-T, Caddo Lake State Park in Texas). To further confuse the outsider, when officials assigned more than one CCC company to a single park, the park received additional numbers for each 200-man camp (the single Palo Duro Canyon State Park project once hosted four concurrent CCC camps and thus carried park numbers SP-13, CCC Co. 1829; SP-14, Co. 1828; SP-15, Co. 1824; and SP-16, Co. 1821!). Park numbers remained the same, unless an interruption in development occurred (single-camp Caddo Lake later carried designations SP-27 then SP-40). A CCC company's number also remained the same, traveling with its members no matter where—or under which technical bureau—it found itself (CCC Co. 889, first assigned to Caddo Lake State Park, SP-1-T, moved to Graham for its second six-month assignment as Soil Erosion Service camp PE-78-T—standing for Private land, Erosion service camp number 78, Texas).

To increase flexibility of the 200-man camps, Roosevelt approved in July 1933 the use of "side camps," sometimes called "spike camps," for temporary assignments. A technical agency could detach and supervise no more than 10 percent of a CCC company, free from Army control, for remote jobs away from the main camp. However, much larger side camps later proved the 10-percent rule itself to be highly flexible. [61]

Interior secretary Harold Ickes, extremely busy in early 1933 planning a range of New Deal relief and conservation experiments, assigned NPS director Horace Albright as his representative on the four-department advisory council. Albright turned to the assistant director, Conrad Wirth, to represent his direct interests at the council, and Wirth remained in this position after Albright left the park service later in 1933. Wirth in turn hired S. Herbert Evison from the National Conference on State Parks to coordinate nationwide "State Park Emergency Conservation Work" under NPS. Evison's organization, as a consequence—after its April 1933 issue of *State Recreation* and 25–27 May annual conference at Palisades Interstate Park,

New York—for the immediate future subordinated its activities to his federal assignment.[62]

Wirth fully acknowledged the direct relationship that the National Conference on State Parks and Evison had developed since 1921 with state park authorities. "Herb knew the state park people," Wirth explained, "he was a former newspaperman and a good writer, and to the Park Service he was a godsend."

> There was no sign of any sort in [the NCSP membership] that indicated a desire on the part of the federal park people to take over the states' responsibilities or even to tell them what to do. Both federal and state people realized there was a lot to be gained by the exchange of ideas . . . . While the army finance officer paid [each CCC camp's] bills, we asked the state authorities to act as our procurement agents. The CCC camps were turned over to them, and, although the camp superintendents and the technical men who supervised the work were paid out of federal funds, they reported directly to the state park authorities.[63]

Drawing a literary breath after explaining the complex framework of the CCC, historian Arthur Schlesinger in *The Coming of the New Deal* supplies this classic Rooseveltism:

> When someone complained that this complicated setup violated the principles of sound organization, Roosevelt replied, "Oh, that doesn't matter. The Army and the Forestry Service will really run the show. The Secretary of Labor will select the men and make the rules and Fechner will 'go along' and give everybody satisfaction and confidence."[64]

On 12 July 1933, a day after arriving at the Amarillo train depot, CCC companies 1824(V) and 1828(V) from Fort Sam Houston, and Company 1829(V) from Fort Sill, Oklahoma —all middle-age military veterans—established a 600-man tent city on the rim of Palo Duro Canyon. Though hampered by State Parks Board's land-title problems throughout their service here, CCC enrollees soon built the first road into this spectacular section of the canyon, opening its vistas and campgrounds to park visitors for the first time. The CCC camp, eventually housed in wooden barracks, hosted other companies through 1937 and is still marked by their stone recreation-hall chimney not far from the park entrance. *National Park Service, National Archives*

Chapter 2

1933, SECOND HALF

Assuming Full Responsibility

[I]t is the unanimous judgement of the State Parks Board of Texas that it
should have entire supervision under the direction of the National Park Service
of all the State park work and general activities pertaining to . . . our State park
system. Under your direction the parks board stands ready to assume full
responsibility and control of the present work now being carried on by the
Federal Government.— State Parks Board minutes, 17 October 1933 [1]

ORGANIZATION AND AUTHORIZATION

Convening and Recording Minutes!

By the first of July 1933, throughout Texas word had spread of CCC
camps, state park construction, and the resulting windfall for local
business. Official activity increased dramatically for D. E. Colp, State
Parks Board chairman, visiting communities with parks and others that
wanted parks and CCC camps. He performed "the job of a super-man,"
according to his friend and Palo Duro Canyon landowner Fred Emery.
"Heretofore, [Colp] had only one park to look after," Emery remembered,
"but now a gigantic amount of work had been thrust upon him. Being
limited by insufficient help and desiring to please, he worked night and day,
driving over the State . . . and did not find time to rest." [2]

Actually, by the time the ECW program and the Texas Rehabilitation
and Relief Commission had placed twelve state parks under construction,
Colp awkwardly stumbled for sound footing. Perhaps on the advice of
friends at NPS, or perhaps as the result of soul-searching, Colp at last called
a meeting of the State Parks Board on 7 July. At 9 A.M. in the Victoria home
of Katie Welder, Colp met with his host and Hobart Key of Marshall, who
also held Claude board member Phebe Warner's proxy for any decisions

made. Key accepted the title "secretary pro tempore," and produced the first minutes compiled by the board in its ten years of existence.

Such newfound professional behavior alone should have defined this meeting as historic, but its participants missed a few parliamentary details. Colp's lack of communication with Governor Ferguson—clearly a two-sided problem—resulted in a failure by all at Victoria to realize both Warner and Key had been replaced some two months before by the governor. Consequently, the board now met without new appointees Pat Neff and Gus Urbantke. And Tom Lamar Beauchamp, appointed to the board in 1929 but also missing from the Victoria gathering, had apparently never met with his colleagues.

With no clue of the board's spurious attendance, chairman Colp declared a quorum and launched into a paradox of both humdrum business and issues effecting the very life of the parks board. His first agenda item resulted in the approval of leasing "the State Park at Beeville," a 128-acre donated site accepted in 1927, to the Bee County American Legion Post.

Then Key introduced a resolution declaring the board's intention to "re-assume full supervision and control of all Park work." Colp had initially agreed in June, their statement recorded, "in order to facilitate and forward the garrisoning and improvement of the State Parks," to cooperate with the Texas Rehabilitation and Relief Commission in exchange for office space and assistance. Not only had the relief commission not furnished such facilities to the board, but "all plans for improvement and all work in connection with said Parks improvement and all employment for said work is now being done by the office of the [relief commission] Director," Lawrence Westbrook. As a result, a state recreation park system was being assembled "without reports to or recommendations of any character from the Parks Board and without consultation with or approval by the Board of any plans for improvement of such Parks." The Victoria gathering "duly passed" its manifesto, demanding from the relief commission a full accounting of current park plans and finances pending the board's assumption of full partnership with federal park development in Texas.

Satisfied with their momentary demonstration of resolve, members then discussed—as if through established routine—several potential parkland acquisitions. They declined a donation offer of the 20,280-acre E. H. Fowlkes Ranch, site of McDonald Observatory construction in the Davis Mountains, because of considerable "indebtedness" on the land. The group grudgingly noted that Clifton had received a CCC camp "which is working on the City Park, without authority, request or approval of this Board," and that their Longhorn Cavern property should "be properly policed or contract canceled at first opportunity to do so." Before adjournment, these would-be park planners placed in "escrow" donations of parklands "contingent on ability to improve by [CCC] camp or otherwise," at Abilene, Brownwood, and Sweetwater.[3]

A New Deal for Palo Duro Canyon

In early July Governor Ferguson dispatched first-gentleman Jim Ferguson to Washington, D.C., for meetings with federal officials on the state of relief programs in Texas. He joined Westbrook, "who has been here conferring with Harry L. Hopkins, administrator of Federal emergency relief," according to the 15 July *Dallas News*. Together they called on several Roosevelt cabinet heads, and congressmen including Sam Rayburn. While in Washington, Westbrook evidently sounded an alarm with NPS officials about the questionable land deal for Palo Duro Canyon State Park. By 22 July park service district officer Herb Maier had traveled from Denver to Austin for a conference with state park planners on this topic, and Maier's supervisor Herb Evison journeyed from Washington to Amarillo to organize an emergency conference with Colp.

On the morning of 23 July, Maier and his inspectors Fred Dale and P. H. Elwood, plus architectural draftsman B. L. Austin, flew from Austin to Amarillo to join the investigation. Immediately after touching down in Amarillo, Maier reported, the federal officials joined Colp and Amarillo Park Board members at Palo Duro:

> and spent afternoon and evening with them on horseback trip down into the gorge and along the canyon floor. . . . It was found to be a fortunate condition that, while the area which has been obtained as park land comprises only a small part of the canyon, the entire Palo Duro is in practically a primitive state so that lands adjoining the park land are and will, no doubt, remain in character with the park.[4]

Maier's testimony avoided discussion of Colp's dubious Palo Duro acquisition strategy, perhaps because this veteran NPS architect fell under the dramatic canyon's spell. Elwood added to the compliments, noting that Palo Duro "is in reality a small Grand Canyon, colorful and picturesque in astounding contrast to the flat surrounding country." The next morning Maier led an inspection of the canyon rim, pointing out ideal locations for campgrounds, picnic areas and "lodge development." By the end of the day discussions centered on "obtaining an additional section of land #101 adjoining the entrance," Maier wrote, "to protect the approach to the park entrance and provide a setting thereto as well as to afford a rim location for the lodge."[5]

Emery, who still held the majority of Section 101, met the afternoon of 24 July with Evison at Amarillo's Herring Hotel to discuss previous and present land questions. "Mr. Evison stated that if they (the National Park people) were to continue the work with the CCC camps at Palo Duro Park, that the 'park' area must include ALL of Section No. 101, instead of only 30 acres; otherwise, they would call the deal off. . . . The point was conceded by Emery."[6]

Maier and Evison, satisfied that the best features of Palo Duro Canyon had now been acquired in an acceptable agreement for the federal government, shuttled back to Austin. On the afternoon of the 25th they met with Westbrook, and the next day "held an all morning conference with Mr. Colp," Maier summarized simply. Colp set to work revising the Palo Duro transaction, producing a warranty deed that included all of renowned Section 101 for a total transaction of 15,103.85 acres. Park revenue through the following fifteen years—Colp projected—would pay off the first liens, due in 1942, then continue to pay Emery's vendor's lien. By 1948 Emery would receive $263,897.96, but with his existing first lien debts the total cost to Texas for Palo Duro Canyon State Park would be $377,586.25. As Attorney General Allred reviewed this new arrangement, Fred and Millie Emery signed the warranty deed on 28 July.[7]

The day before, Westbrook received a request from ECW's director Robert Fechner to name new CCC "Work Camps in this State" for a possible second six-month work period. Although the State Parks Board finally had begun to participate in federal assistance to Texas parks, Westbrook still controlled the assignment of all CCC camps. The state relief director responded to Fechner on 12 August with a list of eighteen proposed camps— the first five being for continued development at Clifton, Davis Mountains, Meridian, Palo Duro Canyon, and Stephenville state parks. He requested new CCC assignments for Abilene, Barreda (near Brownsville, one of the 1927 donated parks), Bonham, Grayson County, Indian Hot Springs, Sweetwater, and Zilker city park in Austin. "Special application also is made," Westbrook wrote, "for a State Park Camp at the site of old Fort Baker, between Groesbeck and Mexia," meaning the 1834 site of Fort Parker in Limestone County. Westbrook also asked for four CCC camps to begin development in Brewster County of "Santa Helena Park" and "Chisos Mountain Park," both on state lands within the legislature's authorized Texas Canyons State Park.[8]

FDR, Road Trips, and the CCC

From his first days as president, automobile-enthusiast Franklin Roosevelt commanded various motor outings about the capital, often venturing far into the countryside outside Washington. One Sunday motorcade in April carried the president and Mrs. Roosevelt, along with Secretary of the Interior Harold Ickes and park service director Horace Albright, to the Virginia mountains and the developing Shenandoah National Park. They visited former president Herbert Hoover's rustic camp on the Rapidan River, about ninety miles from the White House. The camp had been established as an executive retreat in 1929 by the park service and was still under NPS management. Roosevelt expressed little interest in utilizing the well-equipped facility.

This change-of-the-guard attitude from his new president strongly affected Albright, who had hinted for some time about a move to private employment. In spite of early demonstrated support from Roosevelt and Ickes, their parks director soon submitted his resignation effective 9 August. With the park service's cooperation in the CCC safely in Conrad Wirth's hands, and a successful transfer to his agency of many more federal sites and responsibilities, Albright left government service to become manager of the United States Potash Company in New Mexico. One of Stephen Mather's and Albright's trusted colleagues since 1920, Arno Bertholt Cammerer, rose from assistant director to head the service, which also became on 9 August officially—and awkwardly—the "Office of National Parks, Buildings and Reservations" to reflect its expanded role.[9]

In mid-August the president enthusiastically planned a return trip to the Virginia mountains, this time to visit pioneer CCC camps there. The elaborate 15 August visit brought FDR face to face with enrollees of the CCC, rapidly becoming the most popular and successful of his New Deal initiatives. Presidential advisor Rex Tugwell joined "most of those who had been through the organizing of the past months" at the Big Meadows banquet. The president was observed to be in high spirits as he expressed his ideas for conservation and recreation and portrayed his ideal public works projects to Tugwell:

> [Roosevelt] elaborated a scheme for a multitude of little forests—town and country woodlands. He agreed that we ought to plan a scattering of lakes—little lakes at the head of rivers and on small streams created by simple dams—where wildlife could find refuge and where recreation facilities could be provided for literally millions of people.[10]

Tugwell felt the CCC camp visits that day energized the motoring president, just as Roosevelt hoped the CCC would invigorate America's youth and the movement for conservation. Historian Salmond notes that Roosevelt's summer venture to the Virginia camps "confirmed for the President that the CCC was a success. It came as no surprise, therefore, when on August 18 he extended the Corps at full strength for another six months," to begin officially on 1 October.[11]

The day after Roosevelt announced continuation of the CCC, Westbrook again wrote Robert Fechner in response to a survey of the ECW's first six-month period. "The entire recruiting program in Texas was carried on without a hitch," Westbrook beamed. "We were able to have our full quota at the Conservation Camp on schedule." Obviously most interested in CCC recruitment and its effect on relief efforts, the Texas relief commission director said little of actual CCC work projects. "Our reports indicate," he acknowledged of life in the camps, "that it would be a fine thing if the government could arrange for better recreational facilities in many of the camp units." Westbrook predicted that a second six-month period would record even more success. "The outstanding fact in relation to the whole Emergency Conservation Work Program is that the young men are virtually 100 percent pleased with their jobs." [12]

Bread Bonds and New Parklands

Texans stepped up to their ballot tables on 26 August and voted in a two-to-one majority for the legalized sale of 3.2 percent beer. Then by a three-to-two margin they voted in favor of the U.S. Constitution's 21st Amendment, to repeal the 18th Amendment that, for fourteen years, had prohibited alcohol consumption. In the same election Texans approved two to one a state constitutional amendment allowing sale of $20 million in relief bonds. This money, Governor Ferguson and the legislature assured voters, would aid Texans impoverished by the unending depression. Moreover, these funds would satisfy Washington's demand for a state match to federal relief dollars, which already totaled about $7 million through April and now included more than $500,000 in State Park Emergency Conservation Work. Ferguson called the legislature to meet in September for a special session to sell the first "bread bonds" to meet the coming winter season of greatest unemployment. [13]

Just before the legislative session began and probably on recommendation of the attorney general, Colp called the State Parks Board to its second official session in two months. This time Colp utilized an up-to-date membership list, and on 11 September he convened with bona fide board appointees Tom Beauchamp, Pat Neff, Gus Urbantke, and Katie Welder. At some unrecorded point, the board affirmed Colp's leadership as chairman, then elected Neff as vice chairman and Urbantke as secretary.

Adding to Westbrook's recent proposals for new park sites, Colp had been busy since July convincing more Texas communities that state park development would come to those who donated land. Utilizing their 1931 authorization to accept new parklands without specific legislative action, board members approved a resolution to "acquire" several sites. These included three donations accepted at their erroneous July meeting—those from Abilene, Bastrop, and Sweetwater—and added Balmorhea, Bonham,

Brownwood, Chisos Mountains (Texas Canyons State Park), Ottine, Stamford, and Thorp Spring.

Buescher State Park near Smithville, a hundred-acre site accepted by the legislature in 1927, also found its way onto the "acquired" list, probably for additional donated acreage. In further acknowledgment of CCC park development previously arranged through the relief commission, the parks board agreed to another list "heretofore accepted conditionally," including parks at "Blanco, Caddo Lake, Fort Davis, Hamilton, Lampasas, Meridian, Mineral Wells, Palo Duro Canyon, Stephenville and Palisades." Only the present CCC park developments at Clifton—indignantly criticized at the July meeting as a city park—and "Tres Palacios" failed to make the retroactive acceptance list. Interestingly, the Hamilton CCC camp had closed more than a month before when Fort Sam Houston's hospital admitted forty members of Company 882 "because of . . . exposure to typhoid fever infection by contact with civilian typhoid carriers in the vicinity of the company's worksite," according to the *Hamilton Herald-Record*.[14]

At last, fortified with approval from Attorney General Allred, board members signed Fred Emery's vendor's lien to sell more than 15,000 acres of Palo Duro Canyon to the State of Texas. Emery, present at this board meeting, later described that when "Ex. Gov. Neff signed this Resolution . . . I remember him saying, 'Well, we will sign this now and probably in a couple of years we can go to the Legislature and get an appropriation to pay it off'." Through Neff's inexhaustible confidence in eventual legislative support for state parks, and through Colp's and Emery's determination to consummate a deal, Palo Duro Canyon State Park became a reality.[15]

1st Called Session, 1933 Legislature

Having cut the state budget by 21 percent in regular session, Texas lawmakers convened for special session in September for another round of depression-related measures. Authorized by the August election, the legislature approved immediate sale of $5.5 million in relief bonds to prepare for winter demands and to match additional federal assistance. Responding to the bond sale—as well as to loud but unsubstantiated criticism of Westbrook's performance in distributing federal relief funds throughout the state—the legislature reorganized his Texas Rehabilitation and Relief Commission. The agency would logically distribute new state relief funds, but official County Relief Boards would now join the checks and balances of depression bureaucracy. Also, the legislature restored Governor Ferguson's original name for Westbrook's bureau: Texas Relief Commission.[16]

In October Representative E. E. Townsend of Alpine, a cosponsor five months earlier of the Texas Canyons State Park law, introduced a new bill greatly expanding this park's potential. His new measure added Presidio County land within the possible boundaries that had previously concentrated on Brewster County, appropriated $1,500 to pay for any state land withdrawn from the Permanent School Fund for the park, and reserved the "mineral estate" for the school fund. As Townsend's bill became law on 27 October, the name of this grandiose dream also changed to "Big Bend State Park."[17]

Described territory for the Big Bend park represented an immense chunk of Texas, though the new law mentioned no ultimate acreage for the projected park. Townsend's $1,500 appropriation seemed microscopic by comparison, but embarrassingly cheap land in Brewster County had dropped to even lower values during the 1920s and the ensuing depression. "Big Bend's promoters," observes historian Peter L. Petersen, "though pleased with this action, were not totally satisfied and immediately began a campaign to gain national park status." What made the park so attractive, Petersen confirms, "in addition to its rugged scenic beauty, was the incredibly low cost of land acquisition. Literally tens of thousands of acres were available at a cost of no more than one cent per acre. Compared to widely quoted asking prices of $10 to $25 per acre for Palo Duro [Canyon] land, the advantages of Big Bend were especially obvious during a period of economic retrenchment."[18]

In the meantime, after conferring with NPS district officer Maier, Governor Ferguson called upon the State Parks Board to meet jointly with the Texas Relief Commission on 30 September. Maier addressed the feuding officials, pointing out that the federal government expected to spend $1.7 million on Texas parks through one year of ECW projects. He asserted that the parks board, therefore, needed to prove for the federal government that it could operate all new state parks once their design and development phases concluded and facilities opened for public use.

"The principal results of the joint meeting," Maier reported, "were the outlining of two bills to be presented next week to the legislature." In order to supplement Westbrook's overworked technical staff, the Texas Reclamation Department with its own staff of surveyors and engineers would be asked to cosponsor state park development with the ECW program. State Reclamation Engineer A. M. Vance already had shown himself friendly to the State Parks Board, directing in the previous two months topographical surveys of both Buescher State Park near Smithville and the nearby proposed Bastrop State Park. By the end of the joint September meeting, Colp and his colleagues agreed also to ask the legislature for $25,000 to fund "a two year period of park maintenance," according to Maier.[19]

State Representative John W. Laird of Lufkin introduced both measures for directing essential resources to the impoverished State Parks Board. One bill mistakenly authorized the State Board of Reclamation Engineers to help with park planning, and another called for a reduced appropriation of $15,000 for park maintenance and a Texas match to federal park dollars. Observing the doomed paths subsequently traveled by Laird's two bills, Maier wrote that "there is evidence that politics are playing a hand." The session ended on 13 October, "without at the last minute passing these bills."[20] This latest exercise in frustration at least helped members of the State Parks Board understand they desperately needed a technical staff and operating funds in order to assume control of current and future state park development in Texas.

The CCC Proves Its Worth

As the first period of the ECW program drew to a close in October and November, the Texas state park system advanced dramatically with federal New Deal assistance. No major structures or buildings had been completed on parklands during the almost-six-month period, but everywhere new roads, cleared underbrush, and the beginnings of several substantial dams verified the imminent development of first-class facilities. The conservation-work partnership between the NPS, the CCC, and the U.S. Army—founded as a hopeful experiment only months before—proved a hearty match for the diverse geography of Texas and even its convoluted politics. "Few states in the Union," wrote traveling inspector Elwood, "possess the contrasts, both scenic and climatic, that are found in Texas. In a single week it was my duty and good fortune to enjoy the langorous [*sic*] luxury of sub-tropical Caddo Lake and the green slopes and forest clad summits of the Davis Mountains."

Inspector Dale reported in October that the Meridian CCC war-veterans camp had begun the monumental task of a large earthen dam on Bee Creek. His colleague Elwood helped Meridian superintendent Louis J. Bryan select a "lodge site and principal road locations," and called this Bosque County scenery "the most promising of all the proposed Texas lake parks." At Blanco, Dale noted that "[w]ork at this park is progressing very satisfactorily" under superintendent Nottie H. Lee, with a "stone masonry arch" bridge and the "concession house" under construction, along with two dams and a "concrete slab highway bridge across the Blanco River." Inspector Harvey H. Cornell, dispatched to Texas by Herb Maier for special investigations, relayed that Palo Duro Canyon's rim-to-floor "down road" needed "an additional shovel," or earth mover, to push construction past "1/5 completed" and to "release men for other projects."[21]

To meet the demand of overseeing state park projects across the vast expanse of Texas, District Officer Maier announced on 8 October the arrival of another inspector, George Lister Nason. Like his able colleague Dale,

Nason had studied engineering, graduating in 1910 from the University of Minnesota. In addition, the new inspector shared master's degree landscape architecture training at Harvard University with National Park Service chief landscape engineer Daniel Hull (both graduated in 1914) and fellow District III inspector Harvey Cornell (1921). From 1924 to 1932 Nason directed the St. Paul, Minnesota, city park system while Theodore Wirth, father of NPS assistant director Conrad Wirth, superintended the adjacent Minneapolis park system. And Hull during the 1920s had approved the trend-setting rustic designs for several national park facilities by then-independent-architect Maier.[22]

Nason spent his first week on the job conferring with Maier in Austin and studying various park plans at the central design office. He then hit the road for visits with local officials at Bastrop, Sherman, and Bonham to discuss forthcoming work at their nearby parks. Back in Austin the next week, Nason met with Jac Gubbels, landscape engineer at the Texas Highway Department with prior Texas state park experience, for expert advice on native plantings. Before his second week ended Nason greeted Congressman Thomas Blanton at Abilene, then traveled to Amarillo to confer with Maier, Congressman Marvin Jones, and others on Palisades and Palo Duro Canyon state parks. Beginning his third week as inspector, Nason flew from Austin to Marshall to meet at Caddo Lake with CCC camp and local officials, including former State Parks Board member Hobart Key (who died a few months after this meeting). There Nason "suggested acquiring additional property from T. J. Taylor to the south which will give them a frontage on the highway to Jefferson." Nason spent the balance of the third week driving to park inspections at Mineral Wells, Stephenville, Meridian, and Clifton and back to Austin, where he reported to Lawrence Westbrook on park progress.[23]

STATE PARKS BOARD ASCENDING

Colp and Colleagues Assert Authority

While Nason acquainted himself with Texas state parks and their Austin administration—at the Texas Relief Commission under Westbrook—the State Parks Board intensified its contest for authority. Chairman Colp had persuaded friends at the highway department to provide an office in their new State Highway Building near the Capitol, and on 17 October the parks board met there to discuss its recent failure to receive funds from the legislature. After meekly accepting 140 acres of the National Guard's "state park" at Palacios—the perfect symbol of CCC camp assignments chosen by Westbrook without their consultation—parks board members reached the turning point.

Legislation dating from 1923 and reinforced in 1931 and 1933, they reasoned, clearly placed control of Texas recreation parks with the State Parks Board. Colp and his colleagues invoked their ten-year investment in this enterprise and issued a rambling but decisive declaration of independence, telegraphed the next day to NPS assistant director Wirth in Washington, D.C. "The statutory law of Texas," they asserted, "as interpreted by the legal authorities of the State[,] place on the State Parks Board the responsibility of all work pertaining to the park work of the State."

Wirth immediately telegraphed Governor Ferguson, asking "[w]hat is the effect of [Colp's] telegram and recent laws passed by legislature on our present arrangements[?]" He pointed out that the park service had kept faith with Texas by recommending fourteen CCC state park camps for the second period ECW, pending approval of operational funding. "Keenly disappointed in failure of legislature," Wirth added, "to enact law providing funds for permanent maintenance of parks." He promised to call Ferguson "over long distance phone in the morning" to discuss the matter. "Please advise by wire," he requested in the meantime, "whom we are to deal with in connection with State Park Emergency Conservation Work."[24]

Ferguson did not deposit in official records the contents of her ensuing correspondence, but evidently she suggested that Wirth seek a legal opinion on the matter. About three weeks later at a meeting in Fort Worth of all District III inspectors and procurement officers with Herb Maier and Herb Evison, the answer came, as recorded on 8 November by Inspector Nason. "Word was . . . received that the Attorney General of the State of Texas," he typed in his weekly report, "had ruled that the Texas State Parks Board was in charge of the administration and construction of Texas State Parks instead of the Texas Relief Commission."[25]

Chairman Colp quickly responded to the news from Attorney General Allred by calling a meeting of the parks board on 9 November. Members Colp, Tom Beauchamp, and Gus Urbantke met with Nason, representing the National Park Service, and Westbrook, still arguing for control of federal park development. Following the legislature's recent failure to fund the State Parks Board, Westbrook apparently had agreed to pass to the board "$500 – 600 per month overhead" already provided by the National Park Service to his relief commission. Westbrook thus felt he retained considerable leverage over the parks board. "Colonel Westbrook read a letter to the Park Board," Nason reported of their meeting, "in which he states that he was unwilling longer to continue in charge of the State Park work unless complete administrative authority was turned over to him by the Parks Board."

Recessing to private quarters and phoning absent board members Neff and Welder, Colp and his quorum emerged confident and defiant. They decided, matching the reverse psychology of Westbrook, that Allred's decision did not allow the parks board to delegate authority to the relief commission! The board would "assume full control and handle any and all matters pertaining to the improvement of the Texas State Parks." As Maier summarized, the "Texas State Parks Board has been awarded jurisdiction over State Park ECW work . . . with the result that the Relief Commission has retired from this activity."[26]

The Governor Disavows Palo Duro Canyon

Although Westbrook displayed little respect for the State Parks Board in general, he had added up the numbers of its Palo Duro Canyon land deal and honestly concluded that the state came up short. Yet his own relief commissioners, the governor, and the attorney general had approved the Palo Duro deal. Westbrook continued through the fall to warn Governor Ferguson, Wirth, and CCC director Fechner that expensive federal improvements were being made on land the state might not be able to retain.

After an energetic exchange of charges and countercharges between state and federal offices, in early December Ferguson simply washed her hands of the Palo Duro affair. Following the attorney general's assignment of state park authority to the parks board, Governor Ferguson dictated a curious letter to Fechner stating that "the management of the C.C.C. camps is under the State Parks Board of which D. E. Colp, Austin, Texas, is chairman. For this reason [the governor's] office is out of touch with such projects." Fechner shot back that "in my opinion, no one but the Governor of a State is responsible for the continuation of Emergency Conservation Work within the State."[27]

Despite this squabbling between faraway office suites, construction on the Palo Duro "rim-to-bottom road" reached completion in the fall. The Canyon Chamber of Commerce sponsored a gala commemoration in November to celebrate this first public access into the most spectacular part of the canyon, according to historian Petersen. "Nearly 6,000 people watched as Congressman Marvin Jones removed a symbolic barrier from the pathway," Petersen relates. "[T]he building of a road down the side of the canyon in less than six months was an achievement which would have been difficult if not impossible without the labor of the Civilian Conservation Corps."[28]

The Winter Period ECW

Westbrook and the Texas Relief Commission already had chosen CCC campsites for the second six months of ECW work to begin in the fall of 1933. While the State Parks Board dutifully accepted the donations of first- and second-period ECW parks, many of these sites—such as Clifton, Stephenville, and Lampasas—had never before been courted by Colp. Likewise, many previous state park donations promised development for years by Colp—like Beeville, Big Spring, and Frio River sites—had not yet received a chance to participate in this New Deal development boom. At least the logic and lobbying for the handful of "large parks" promoted in Texas for many years found Westbrook and Colp in agreement over substantial developments under way at Caddo Lake and the Davis Mountains.

No one on the State Parks Board expressed more interest in identifying new development projects than Neff. He understood that for park improvements the CCC topped any highway-worker or prison-trusty labor force he had previously imagined. His mother's 1921 bequest of parkland on the Leon River in Coryell County had received some improvements in the 1920s, but Neff realized that this six-acre bottomland would hardly rate a two-hundred-man CCC camp for an entire six-month development period. The day in November when inspector Nason learned of the legal decision in favor of the parks board, he coincidentally met with Neff "with regard to an addition he was proposing to Mother Neff State Park." [29]

But for now the second period of CCC camp assignments continued most park developments begun in early summer and added new sites only at Abilene, Bonham, Bastrop, and Grayson County. The City of Abilene assigned 507 acres of municipal property below Lake Abilene, southwest of Buffalo Gap, for their park that received robust support from both Congressman Blanton and a CCC company of war veterans brought in from northern Arizona. Bastrop had received enthusiastic federal consideration since late summer, and several donors offered about 750 acres for initial development. This area combined with added donations to the nearby 1927 Buescher State Park to create a large area in the "lost pines" to occupy the work of two CCC camps. Sam Rayburn encouraged Wirth to recommend a second-period state park camp near the congressman's home town of Bonham, and inspector Nason helped select a 532-acre donation southeast of the city. Grayson County commissioners, also in Rayburn's district, purchased 372 acres between Sherman and Denison for a new lake and park, which they proposed only to lease to the state for recreation use.[30]

By the first of December the National Park Service had approved twelve Texas sites for parks development during the coming months, supported by an initial complement of sixteen CCC companies. The new "winter period" technically started on 1 October but really had no uniform beginning date, as supervising agencies staggered assignments to allow many initial ECW projects a few more weeks for completion. "About 450 of the 1,400 camps" nationwide, news releases explained, "will be moved for the winter from the deep snow areas to places where work can be carried on throughout the season." Moderate-climate Texas immediately benefited from this policy, and with the shifting of camps several new companies arrived from out of

TABLE 2

State Parks of the Second-Period ECW

Fall 1933–March 1934

NPS Number	Official Name	CCC Company
SP-2	Lampasas State Park	Co. 896
SP-3	Stephenville State Park	Co. 817
SP-4	Davis Mountains State Park	Co. 879
SP-7	Blanco State Park	Co. 854
SP-8	Mineral Wells State Park	Co. 1811[1]
SP-11	Clifton State Park	Co. 878[2]
SP-12	Meridian State Park	Co. 1827(V)
SP-13	Palo Duro Canyon State Park	Co. 1829(V)
SP-14	” ” ” ” ”	Co. 1828(V)
SP-15	” ” ” ” ”	Co. 1824(V)
SP-16	” ” ” ” ”	Co. 1821(V)
SP-18	Bonham State Park	Co. 894
SP-21	Bastrop-Buescher State Park	Co. 1805
SP-22	” ” ” ”	Co. 1811[1]
SP-24	Grayson State Park	Co. 857
SP-26	Lake Abilene State Park	Co. 1823(V)

[1] CCC Co. 1811 transferred on 2 January 1934 from Camp Wolters at Mineral Wells to Bastrop.

[2] Co. 878 headquarters moved on 3 December 1933 to Belton as soil erosion project PE-76, leaving a 30-day side camp at Clifton; NPS officials declared Clifton State Park complete on 3 January 1934, when the side camp left for Belton.

state. Texas received a total of forty-two CCC camps of all types for the period, posted to various conservation jobs throughout the state.[31]

A conspicuous omission from the second-period list was SP-1, Caddo Lake, whose CCC Co. 889 shipped out on 30 November to a new Soil Erosion Service assignment at Graham, Texas. The National Park Service decided by the end of the first ECW period to halt work at Caddo Lake despite praise from all its personnel who encountered this "very pretty bayou," as inspector Nason called it in October. "A log concession building, the pavilion and a large part of the road-ways and two docks" stood complete, according to Nason, but the park needed expansion into specific and general tracts from 468 to "a few thousand acres" to justify another CCC period. A deeper problem with political support for this park might have stemmed from the state's new congressional districts effective in August: Harrison County and the state park side of Caddo Lake shifted from Martin Dies' District 2 to Wright Patman's District 1 just as the NPS solicited applications for the second development period.[32]

Davis Mountains State Park officially lost one of its CCC camps in late fall, as low re-enlistment for the new period left companies 879 and 881 with far fewer that two hundred enrollees each. So their members consolidated to retain one full-strength company for the winter in Keesey Canyon. Without Westbrook's patronage, the Palacios National Guard project closed, as did the Mineral Wells camp in January once its state-park component reached an acceptable halting stage. Both of these National Guard CCC camps—Co. 1805 from Palacios and Co. 1811 from Mineral Wells—then transferred to the large enterprise in Congressman James Buchanan's district for a combined Bastrop-Buescher State Park. And Palisades State Park, where "the State has exerted the least energy . . . in pursuing the ECW development," according to Maier, lost its CCC camp on 2 December. The day before, however, through the help of Congressman Jones a fourth company of war veterans arrived at the grander project elsewhere in Palo Duro Canyon. As four companies of some eight hundred men now tackled this state park development, the Palo Duro CCC effort became "the largest in the United States on any single project," according to NPS officials quoted in the *Amarillo Globe*.[33]

The Civil Works Administration

About the time Colp and the State Parks Board gained control of their destiny, and CCC camps shifted around the nation to winter quarters, the national unemployment problem rose toward its annual maximum. Despite the success of ECW projects and other New Deal relief and employment experiments, in the fall of 1933 President Roosevelt's relief administrator Harry Hopkins estimated that four million able-bodied Americans would not be able to find work until the next spring.

To address this mounting crisis Hopkins proposed the Civil Works Administration to undertake small public works projects in communities across the country, beginning in mid-December. As the Reconstruction Finance Corporation had proved during the previous winter, in three to four months otherwise-jobless men could complete a surprising variety of civic tasks such as roads, schools, airports, sewer systems, playgrounds, and parks. This new, temporary program would be funded with $400 million transferred from Harold Ickes's slow-starting Public Works Administration and would be directed by Hopkins's Federal Emergency Relief Administration staff through the state relief agencies. "Indeed," muses New Deal historian Arthur Schlesinger of Roosevelt's approval, "the whole effort might [have been] conceived as a means of tiding the unemployed over one more winter, by which time PWA could begin to take up the slack."[34]

In Texas, management of the new federal program fell to the Texas Relief Commission just as Westbrook relinquished the commission's command of state park development to the State Parks Board. In the shift of park responsibilities, Fred Dale—first inspector hired by the NPS to coordinate park projects across the state, and recently named head of its Austin central design office—chose a transfer to the relief commission as Westbrook's field engineer, effective 11 November. Back at the fledgling Washington office of the Civil Works Administration, "Hopkins had no planning staff, no shelf of light public works, no formulated program," Schlesinger explains, so "[p]roject ideas, generated in the atmosphere of pressure, came both down from Washington and up from the field." Once again, Westbrook found his agency directing a huge federal effort of broad latitude in placing and designing projects, with Dale's expertise crucial to its statewide implementation.[35]

Perhaps as a demonstration to outshine Colp and company, or through genuine interest in recreation, Westbrook steered a handful of substantial CWA projects toward undeveloped "state parks." By the end of the year as the new program's employment climbed to its national goal of four million, landscape development took place at the old Beeville and Jefferson Davis (Hillsboro) state parks accepted in 1927, as well as at two recent applicant parks, near Normangee and at "Love's Lookout" north of Jacksonville. The CWA also reconstructed a stone chapel at Goliad State Park, following drawings produced by San Antonio architect Atlee Bernard Ayres.

The program sponsored large park "clubhouses" at city lakes near Brownwood and Sweetwater, both on lands recently accepted by the State Parks Board for future improvements. New park buildings also appeared at Austin's Zilker Park, subject of an unsuccessful CCC-camp application submitted earlier by Westbrook, and at the city lake near Paris, recently examined by inspector Nason. And as a result of this program a similar "community house" rose on the south shore of Lake Mineral Wells upon city property, but some distance from recent CCC development at Mineral Wells State Park.[36]

All of these central park buildings exhibited striking and deliberate qualities of NPS design standards: low, horizontal lines with rustic-finish local stone and woodwork. Although individual commissions by local architects—for example, Thomas Broad in Paris and Charles Henry Page in Austin—these buildings nonetheless displayed the characteristics of park facilities as pioneered and recommended by park service district officer Maier. In the preceding seven months, Maier had carefully trained his regional inspectors in the art of park design, so that they in turn could inspire local architects hired to produce specific state park facilities for CCC construction. Although no longer working under Maier, Frederick Amerman Dale still implemented his NPS training while he supervised CWA park projects in the winter of 1933–1934. Ironically Dale's new assignment allowed him to oversee the immediate construction of large and excellent park buildings throughout Texas, while his former colleagues moved at much slower paces through the more ponderous ECW organization.

The Best of Times for Texas State Parks

Thus the worst year of the depression for many, and the first year of the New Deal for all, ended with a glimmer of hope for the nation and nothing short of a miracle for Texas state parks. The *Dallas News* on 10 December featured a long and supportive state parks article based upon press releases from Colp. "It was an ill wind that made the need of the Civilian Conservation Corps," reporter Alanzo Wasson wrote, "but one which has been laden with profit for the State Park Board."

Colp indicated in this article that the state now boasted thirty-two parks, "apart from the six hallowed by deeds of heroism [Fannin, Gonzales, Goliad, King's, San Jacinto, and Washington], . . . under care of the Board of Control." His list included twenty-eight "small parks" lumping sites acquired between 1927 and recent board resolutions, and four parks "that may be called large" at Bastrop, Big Bend, Davis Mountains, and Palo Duro Canyon. Colp claimed that all these sites, totaling "something more than 400,000 acres have been gathered together for park purposes" and donated to the state. Oddly, he left Longhorn Cavern and Mother Neff off the list, as well as any financial details of the Palo Duro Canyon deal. "The chairman of the board, Mr. Colp," the reporter continued, "under spur of no other reward than the gratification of a patriotic ambition, has worked indefatigably to convert the scenic beauties of the State from private possessions into a public heritage." [37]

Indeed, Colp rolled at long last into the real business of state park development with the flash and dash of his old Essex automobile—quite a change from Westbrook's low-key operation. Colp and the parks board hired Robert O. Whiteaker as park engineer at $3,000 annual salary in federal money to replace Fred Dale and represent the state as chief technical advisor. The board moved its offices from the Highway Building to the Senate chambers of the Capitol, to be near their new federal procurement officer, Senate secretary Bob Barker. Colp and Whiteaker met frequently with NPS officials, both in Austin and at the parks themselves, from Abilene to Bastrop and Palo Duro Canyon to the Davis Mountains. Colp worked long and hard to establish the trust of federal officials, and by mid-December Maier reported on this "new set-up that has by now had time to somewhat iron itself out. It was found that the Texas State Park Board is cooperating with the ECW in a much more satisfactory manner than obtained with the Relief Commission." [38]

Maier's inspectors, now including George Nason, Harry L. Dunham and Harvey H. Cornell, also crisscrossed the state guiding existing work and investigating potential new projects. A competent group of park superintendents controlled most of the current projects, moving projects faster and greatly pleasing their federal advisors. These included W. F. Ayres at Stephenville, Louis J. Bryan at Meridian, W. Rex Byram at Palisades, D. B. Cutler at Caddo Lake (during the first period), Nottie H. Lee at Blanco, Sam O. Miller at Palo Duro Canyon, and F. A. Riney at Abilene, who had engineered the adjacent city lake years before. Colp's newly gained command of park development brought the quiet privilege of patronage, and he wasted no time hiring old friend and Army Reserve major E. A. Kingsley. Upon Colp's encouragement, federal officials assigned the former San Antonio and Dallas city engineer to Mineral Wells State Park, where he successfully finished several projects before that camp's move in early January to Bastrop.[39]

While not yet designated a conservation-work project, the potential Big Bend State Park attracted continued attention from the NPS through the fall and winter. The recent departure of Horace Albright—who all but swore the nation would yield no new national parks—opened the investigations of several potential sites by a generation of younger, broader minded and wider traveled planners. Inspector Nason met with State Representative E. E. Townsend in November at Austin "with regard to the ecology of the Chisos Mountains," agreeing to continue the search for drinking water crucial to approval of any CCC camps for developing the park. "The Chisos Mountains," wrote Nason in late December when he first visited the Big Bend, "of which some 225,000 acres are under public control, present an opportunity in park design greater than anything I have yet seen. One wonders if in all the world there could be a greater excellence. The possibility of design is tremendous. It has not a single anti-climax, and each ascending climax is an astounding park within itself."[40]

The 10 December *Dallas News* article on state parks attempted to express similar sentiments for the recreation potential of the entire Texas system. The newspaper further noted that although CCC camps planned some time off for a Christmas vacation, most enrollees would return quickly to push development through the off-season winter months, so that state parks would be ready for the summer 1934 tourist season. "The work is mostly that of cleaning up, but some roads are being made inside the parks, some dams and camp houses built and later there will be some tree planting," the article summarized. "As yet but little use has been made of the State parks, one reason being that few people in the State and fewer out of it know how great the attraction some of them offer. It is the belief of Mr. Colp that next year there will be more pilgrims to them as a result of the work that is being done."[41]

Preoccupied with a federal loan for Palo Duro Canyon as the year began, Colp had entered 1933 with little awareness of what astounding events lay ahead. Apparently uninterested in Washington politics, and definitely put off by state politicians, he certainly did not anticipate the coalition between the popular Roosevelts and the populist Fergusons, nor could he have anticipated such grand results. A number of well-placed individuals, in addition to those in the White House and in the Austin Governor's Mansion, chose to address the depression with unprecedented public relief programs, many focusing directly on labor-intensive, conservation-minded, and spirit-lifting park development. These concepts, and the rallying of public resources to back up such progressive ideas, not only breathed new life into Texas state parks, they probably saved the state parks movement from oblivion.

Sadly, at these best of times for state parks, Phebe Kerrick Warner faded from the public scene with little credit for her long, hard work to establish a park at Palo Duro Canyon. She missed the July State Parks Board revival meeting in Victoria, and by the next meeting two months later, expiration of her term had been confirmed. Ten years before, on 19 October 1923, Phebe Warner had written to her new friend D. E. Colp expressing delight over their mutual appointments to the new State Parks Board, but forecasting a difficult road ahead.

> I feel like the rest and pleasure and State Pride of the present and all the future generations of Texas has dropped down on that board. Can we do it? Can we PUT IT OVER? One of the theories of my life is that "Anything that ought to be done can be done if attempted in time and at the right time." [42]

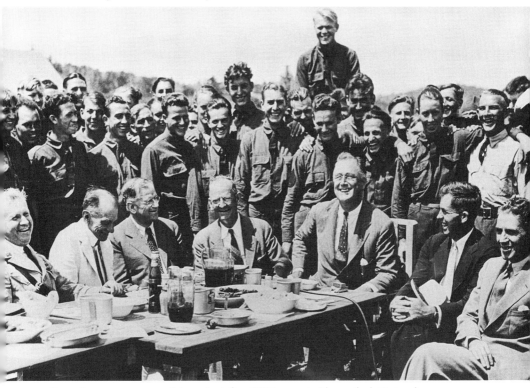

On 12 August 1933 at one of the nation's first CCC camps in Shenandoah National Park, Virginia, President Roosevelt joined (second from left) his personal secretary Louis Howe, Secretary of the Interior Harold Ickes, CCC director Robert Fechner, and (on FDR's left) Secretary of Agriculture Henry Wallace and his assistant Rexford Tugwell. *Harpers Ferry Center, National Park Service.*

Miriam Ferguson in June 1934 rescued the State Parks Board from loss of federal assistance with its first budget of $25,000. This act perhaps explains a rare meeting of board member Pat Neff (seated right) with the "Governors Ferguson," Miriam and Jim, in her Capitol office. *Collection of the Bell County Museum, Belton, Texas, The Miriam Ferguson Collection.*

Lawrence W. Westbrook, lieutenant colonel in the Texas National Guard, throughout 1933 directed the Texas Relief Commission and most federal programs in Texas, including assignment of its first CCC camps. *Lawrence Westbrook Family.*

George Lister Nason represented the ideal New Deal park designer: degrees in both engineering and landscape architecture, and by 1933 friendships among federal park architects, who made him their senior inspector for Texas. *George Nason Family.*

During summer 1938 congressional recess, on the steps of his Uvalde home Vice President John Garner (right) greeted Boy Scouts from Tyler, led by State Parks Board member Tom L. Beauchamp (in kerchief) on a tour of state parks. *Tom L. Beauchamp, Jr., Collection.*

The partnership aspect of New Deal state park construction is represented in fall 1933 at Palo Duro Canyon's road project by Army captain Charles D. Apple, state project superintendent J. O. Miller, and an enrollee of CCC Co. 1821(V). *R. E. Terry, National Archives.*

Federal partners despised cornerstones, but the 12 May 1934 commencement of Guy Carlander's lodge at Palo Duro Canyon was cause for ceremony by D. E. Colp (with trowel) and NPS inspector George Nason (to Colp's left). *National Park Service, National Archives.*

Key figures behind federal assistance to Texas parks, Herbert Evison (left), director of NPS state park cooperation, and Conrad Wirth, NPS assistant director, strongly urged development of Big Bend, which they explored in 1935. *Harpers Ferry Center, National Park Service.*

Paramount to federal design and support for Texas parks, particularly Big Bend, NPS director Arno Cammerer (in dark glasses) and NPS regional director Herb Maier (seated) in 1936 included Mexico in their review of the Rio Grande park. *Harpers Ferry Center, National Park Service.*

During a rare visit by a First Family member to a CCC park project in Texas, Eleanor Roosevelt in March 1938 inspected barracks of Co. 1823(CV) at Huntsville with Lieutenant K. K. Black (left) and Captain Van B. Houston. *The Texas Collection, Baylor University, Waco, Texas.*

On 1 August 1935 a distinguished inspection party visited Palmetto State Park (left to right): George Nason, Pat Neff, Dave Colp, Herb Maier, Albion Blinks, Gus Urbantke, Olin Boese, Herb Evison, and Conrad Wirth. *National Park Service, National Archives.*

By summer 1938 the State Parks Board had lost all female representation but matured to a businesslike organization: at Palmetto State Park, first executive secretary William Lawson stood fourth from left, and at his elbow were members Wendell Mayes, Raymond Dillard, and Tom Beauchamp; also present were J. V. Ash, Kennedy N. Clapp, Jake Sandefer, H. G. Webster, and, perhaps, the park manager. *The Texas Collection, Baylor University, Waco, Texas.*

War production was in full swing and projects like Garner State Park were providing military recreation when, in September 1943, Franklin D. Roosevelt stopped at Uvalde to share New Deal memories with his former vice president John N. Garner. *U.S. Navy, National Archives.*

Congressmen Contribute to Big Bend Park Fund

Perhaps the most important individuals in securing CCC camps for state park development, members of the seniority-rich Texas Congressional delegation usually wielded such influence only for the benefit of home districts. With a rare exhibit of statewide solidarity, in 1939 several Congressmen gathered on the steps of the nation's Capitol, offering contributions for a private campaign to purchase land for the proposed Big Bend National Park. At the left is U.S. Representative R. Ewing Thomason of El Paso, who introduced in 1935 the first national Big Bend legislation. Continuing to his left are Wright Patman of Texarkana, Milton West of Brownsville, Martin Dies of Orange, Lyndon Johnson of Austin, Clyde L. Garrett of Eastland, an unidentified individual, Fritz Lanham of Fort Worth, and William Robert Poage of Waco. *E. E. Townsend Collection, Archives of the Big Bend.*

Indian Lodge,
Davis Mts. State Park, Tex.

Dudley Studio,
Alpine, Texas.
108C

Inspired by adobe pueblos of New Mexico—or specifically by 1934 drawings of mesa-top Acoma Pueblo west of Albuquerque—"Indian Village" in Davis Mountains State Park remains a zenith in visitor accommodations for Texas state parks. Construction by CCC workers began in 1934 and lasted through installation of electrical service in 1937 by enrollees from "Big Bend State Park" far to the south. Now named Indian Lodge, this rambling hotel originally sported an earth-tone adobe finish but in 1938 received water-resistant whitewash applied by a "side camp" from the CCC company at nearby Balmorhea State Park. *Dudley Studio postcard, Alpine, Author's Collection*

Chapter 3

1934–1935

Colp and Neff Smite the Rock

After several years' existence without operating funds, the State Parks Board found itself suddenly flooded with opportunities by the National Park Service.
—State Auditor and Efficiency Expert, first audit of State Parks Board, December 1934[1]

A NEW DEAL STATE PARK SYSTEM EMERGES

New Relationships

The 1930s depression created a curious atmosphere, particularly after implementation of the New Deal, of great endeavors amid doldrums, of momentary prosperity amid poverty. For example, while unemployment statistics and dismal images of the depression presented a tragic and embarrassing picture of American culture, simultaneously the technology of travel and its consumers supplied a very different vision. In 1934 Chrysler introduced "airflow" streamlining in automobiles. General Motors developed revolutionary new diesel locomotives to pull equally advanced streamlined passenger trains. The world's great shipyards busily assembled the largest ocean liners ever to call at American ports, including the French *Normandie* and the British *Queen Mary*. In 1934 airmail service first threaded together the far-flung ports and nations of the Pacific Ocean.[2]

And Americans witnessed their president frequently range to his home in New York and his Warm Springs retreat in Georgia, as he gleefully explained the importance of travel and recreation for all. Thus no better illustration of the depression's ambiguities could be found in 1934 than the ambitious creation of state parks, for those who owned automobiles and had time for vacations, by laborers who owned little and had few prospects for private jobs. Yet this image thrilled Roosevelt, and millions of Americans, who perceived harmony in everyone doing something for someone else and, in theory, everyone doing something for oneself at the same time. Upon this fortunate blending of affluence with generosity Roosevelt built his New Deal, as Texans built new highways and a state park system.

As FDR's Emergency Conservation Work settled into its second period over the winter of 1933–1934, his Civilian Conservation Corps began to tackle ever more sophisticated projects. In Texas as in most of the nation, initial New Deal state park projects received CCC camps the previous June and July, halfway through the first ECW period. Even then, "[t]he last half of the first six-month period," admitted Conrad Wirth of the supervising National Park Service, "was a time for settling down and getting ready for the second CCC period" beginning in the fall. While much had been accomplished prior to January 1934—brush cleared, roads graded, dams begun, stone entry markers erected, and methods of inter-agency cooperation determined—now in the new year major building projects took shape throughout the growing Texas state park system (see Table 2).[3]

Serious investigation by the NPS of potential sites for designation as national parks or monuments also revealed in 1934 an increasing federal respect for Texas resources. Roger Wolcott Toll, superintendent of Yellowstone National Park and chief park service field investigator, on 3 January 1934 met state-park inspector George Nason for a briefing in Austin, then journeyed to several sites of interest to Washington officials. Toll first reviewed a strange panorama at Ottine in Gonzales County that featured "quaking bogs, mud geysers, sulphur water and soda water," according to Nason, who joined State Parks Board chairman D. E. Colp and engineer R. O. Whiteaker on the trip. A few days later at Palo Duro Canyon State Park, Toll and Nason met park builders and outspoken rancher-writer J. Evetts Haley. Haley accompanied Toll on the last leg of his Texas investigation, with a four-day adventure led by State Representative E. E. Townsend into the Big Bend country of the Rio Grande. "Toll's subsequent report," credits Big Bend historian John R. Jameson, "endorsed the Big Bend area for a national park and . . . remarked that it 'gives promise of becoming one of the noted scenic spectacles of the United States'."[4]

Designing State Parks

Assigned a painstaking task of assembling an effective design team for Texas, park service district officer Herb Maier became adjunct professor for several architects with little or no park planning backgrounds. Brought together by the depression and virtual shutdown of private construction, this seasoned park designer and his recently unemployed architects accepted a difficult commission: to render carefully considered designs for functional and permanent facilities, to supply their drawings fast enough to keep sixteen 200-

man CCC construction camps busy, but to restrain each exercise to a project that could be completed within the six-month ECW period.

The federally financed central design office at Austin first addressed "general control plans" for each state park development and designed the early primitive facilities built by the CCC. Drawings for simple but adequate projects such as latrines and picnic tables issued quickly from Wirth's Washington office. The second conservation-work period brought more elaborate designs from the Austin staff, now consisting of both architects and landscape architects, the latter from a relatively new profession but with a surprising number of recent graduates available for park work. By early 1934 the staff included Olin Boese, Mr. Hanson (or Hansen), Olin Smith, and Mr. Worchester, according to inspectors' reports. These apprentice park planners drafted plans for a swimming pool at Abilene, a substantial concession building at Bastrop, a polo field and concession center at Lampasas, a "housekeeping cabin unit" at Palo Duro, and a two-story concession pavilion at Stephenville.

Elsewhere state parks either neared completion with minimal facilities —at Blanco, Clifton, and Mineral Wells—or focused for the period on dam construction. Engineers from the Texas Board of Water Engineers designed and inspected the impoundment structures that occupied a majority of CCC workers through the winter at Bonham, Davis Mountains, Grayson, Meridian, and Stephenville. This work leaped to greater efficiency with the federal acquisition of steam shovels that allowed CCC crews to work on two and three shifts per day.[5]

Maturing as a district officer, Maier asked his field staff to study photographs of select NPS rustic facilities—many of his own design—from an album he called "The Library of Original Sources." Roaming in and out of Denver and his other district states Maier inspired his Texas design team—initially the four draftsmen in Austin and his three field inspectors—through "an amazing ability to clearly express the qualities of naturalistic architecture and landscape design," writes NPS historian Linda Flint McClelland.[6]

To supplement the state's central drafting office, Maier agreed during the second CCC period to employ design professionals on site at several important projects. For select parks, landscape experts would direct sensitive manipulation of the terrain and planting of appropriate vegetation. At Bonham State Park, for example, landscape architect F. K. McGinnis of Dallas joined the technical staff in revitalizing chalky hills that had lost much of their thin topsoil. McGinnis prescribed the transplanting of "[p]ecans, red oak, red cedar, hackberry and such shrubs as redbud, coralberry, sumac, yucca and many other plants which are . . . suitable for carrying out the naturalistic park planting," Bonham's newspaper reported. "Particular care will be exercised, not only in the moving and planting, but in placing these plants in their proper environment. An attempt will be made to get a start of bluebonnets as the bluebonnet is the State Flower."[7]

Maier and his inspectors especially recognized the benefits of constructing major building groups at Bastrop—because of its proximity to Austin and San Antonio—at Davis Mountains, and at Palo Duro Canyon. Thus by January 1934 at Palo Duro, seasoned Amarillo architect Guy Anton Carlander gladly deserted his idle city desk for a field office to design a canyon-rim lodge and other facilities for park visitors. At Davis Mountains State Park, architect J. B. Roberts and landscape architect Roy S. Ferguson supervised initial construction of roads and park buildings, and developed the idea of a hillside "Indian Village" for overnight guests. Inspector Nason judged their work near Fort Davis exemplary, particularly the scenic-drive overlook shelter derived from Maier's 1924 Glacier Point Lookout at Yosemite National Park. "I rather feel that this is due to the presence continually," Nason reported, "of a resourceful architect on the actual job. Such an architect should probably be placed in the other parks where buildings are going up."[8]

Although the Austin design office produced drawings for the Bastrop concession building in early December, ambitious plans for this park called for just such a "resourceful architect." On 15 January Colp called twenty-nine-year-old Austin architect Arthur Fehr to offer him the position of "architect-foreman" at Bastrop State Park. Fehr had graduated in 1925 from a University of Texas curriculum centered around the study of Greek and Roman classical buildings but sprinkled with some instruction on the Spanish Renaissance and early Texas pioneer shelters. He drafted for San Antonio architect Harvey Partridge Smith and master wood craftsman Peter Mansbendel on Spanish Colonial building restorations, studied one summer in France, then designed apartments in New York before the depression brought a halt to construction. After returning to Austin, Fehr worked infrequently and during 1933 collected only a few hundred dollars in fees. The federal job at Bastrop offered a $3,600 annual salary plus expenses.

Fehr immediately threw himself into the Bastrop project amid some four hundred CCC workers plus technical staff, including numerous Local Experienced Men (LEMs) hired to direct stone and wood crafts. He even rented a room in Bastrop from one of the project's LEMs, master carpenter "Uncle Joe" Pfeiffer, "an unusually qualified woodcrafts foreman," in the estimation of inspector Harry Dunham. During Fehr's first month on the job, he designed a crane for the quarry yielding park building stones, devised a mortar formula to match the deep red stone, directed stone masons on the concession building's masonry pattern, and studied old and abandoned homes in the area for window details and the possible purchase of their large hardwood framing timbers. He also helped set up a blacksmith's forge for repairing tools and manufacturing building hardware, and a lumber mill that quickly cut three walnut logs for future fireplace mantels and furniture.[9]

Fehr's previous architectural instruction and experience, and those of his newly hired counterparts, had predicted no scenario quite like this. The depression had thrown these able designers into a strange and wonderful adventure, not unlike that of Frederick Law Olmsted in the last century at New York City's Central Park: park designer and construction superintendent commanding great resources to create nothing less than a great public landscape.

Mr. Westbrook Goes to Washington

With abandonment of the CCC camps at the Palisades and Mineral Wells sites, park officials and local leaders appealed for additional development through Civil Works Administration labor. After inspecting Mineral Wells State Park in early January 1934, Nason observed that "[t]his camp ended . . . with an unsatisfactory completion": a small dam finished, but roads roughly graded and the concession building left without a roof. Colp had made arrangements with the mayor, Nason added, to finish the job through the city's civil-works allotment, but final consent lay with Lawrence Westbrook in Austin, as his Texas Relief Commission approved all such projects throughout the state.

"Colonel Westbrook agreed," Nason continued, "to make arrangements to get C.W.A. work started at the earliest possible moment" at Mineral Wells. Whatever deal Westbrook made to assign relief workers directly to the park, implementation became difficult when federal authorities announced termination of the program effective at the end of March. Then Westbrook announced his resignation at the end of January. The state relief administrator quickly left for Washington, D.C., to become assistant director of the Federal Emergency Relief Administration—sponsor of the nationwide CWA program—under presidential advisor Harry Hopkins.[10]

Putting on New Deal Dress

In mid-January, Colp reported on behalf of Governor Ferguson to Robert Fechner in Washington that the value of Texas parklands plus recent improvements equaled more than $5.5 million. "Our success in this park business," Colp flattered the ECW director, "is largely due to the co-operation of your Department." While Colp expressed genuine gratitude for the "improvements, men and money furnished by your department," this and other correspondence indicated that the State Parks Board chairman could not yet fully distinguish between the functions of Fechner's program, the NPS, and even the CWA.

Colp partially hit upon Fechner's contributions as he emphasized one unqualified benefit of state park development in the off-season, gushing that "towns near the ECW camps have 'had a harvest' during construction work. It is estimated that more than a hundred fifty thousand dollars new money is brought into all towns near the camps from what the enrollees, foremen and superintendent and their families spend, together with what the visitors spend while visiting friends and relatives in the camps." Colp added, "Not a vacant house to be found in the vicinity of these camps. Hotels and restaurants all doing good business." [11]

Under pressure from the NPS—not Fechner—to ensure operation of state parks following development, Colp in the same letter extended his old familiar optimism about forthcoming action. "[W]e feel very confident," he told Fechner, "at the next session of the Legislature they will make ample appropriation for whatever is necessary to carry on this work in a big way." Indeed, shortly after Governor Ferguson in late January called the legislature into its second special session, primarily to sell more "bread bonds," Representative W. M. Harmon of Waco sponsored a funding bill that included $25,000 immediately and a like amount in the next fiscal year for the State Parks Board. [12]

Meanwhile board members assembled on 22 February at the Capitol for their first meeting of 1934, to monitor progress of their funding request and to consider third-period CCC park projects. As the board for the first time independently considered camp applications, NPS inspectors visited the best development prospects, recommending Goose Island (a state park since 1931), Lockhart, and nearby Ottine. At this meeting board members voted to accept a ninety-nine-year lease for 14,000 acres in San Patricio County on the Nueces River and proposed Lake Corpus Christi. The board also agreed to accept "on condition of deed" both a large Harris County plantation on Cedar Bayou and Galveston Bay southeast of Baytown, and a part of "Old Independence" in Washington County, once the home of Sam Houston and a number of early academies.

Colp and his colleagues unanimously accepted one more donation, although Secretary Gus Urbantke's minutes recorded neither the motion nor the theatrical oratory in support. Vice Chairman Pat Neff—advised by federal officials since early November that the approximately six-acre Mother Neff park could be developed only with a sizable expansion *under public ownership*—thus pledged an "additional 250 acres" of family land along the Leon River in Coryell County to the state. [13] Even after this board meeting, Neff postponed legal transfer of his land to the state, perhaps because a commencement of CCC development in the spring of 1934 would necessitate closing the park in the coming summer months. So he gambled on a successful project application for the fall and proceeded with his own traditional summer program of public addresses and reunions at Mother Neff Park.

As the legislative special session neared its end, "prospects were bright for an appropriation being passed," NPS inspector Harry Dunham recorded of the parks board's funding proposal. In this fairly positive atmosphere, Senator Margie Elizabeth Neal managed to establish the Texas Centennial Commission for planning the statewide celebration two years hence, and endowed it with $100,000. But Colp's and Neff's optimism and the "harvest" of good business for communities hosting CCC camps still had not impressed this legislature. The parks funding "bill was finally killed in the last hours of the session," Dunham wrote reluctantly on 28 February, the day after final business.[14]

In response, Colp called the parks board into conference again on 1 March. The NPS insisted, Colp told the group, that the state of Texas should contribute at least $22,500 to furnish and equip nine state parks upon completion of their development. "Failure to appropriate the funds," a newspaper story explained, "would result in discontinuance of 10 CCC camps" currently at work in Texas state parks. With legislative assistance denied, the board agreed to request directly from Governor Ferguson a "deficiency appropriation," an emergency procedure for state agencies short of cash between legislative sessions. With only $375 budgeted for the year, Colp certainly could prove that his sprawling park system could not meet its obligations. The board's request of $25,000 would equip new parks with furnishings and equipment and cover staff salaries and office expenses for one year. The governor's office promptly sought Attorney General James Allred's opinion on the legality of such an action.

While awaiting Allred's decision, Colp helped generate handsome and timely publicity in the 18 March Sunday edition of the *San Antonio Express*. In this full-page, illustrated article headed "Texas Parks Putting on New Dress; Uncle Sam Foots the Bill," a thorough summary of the previous New Deal year of development concluded that "by the middle of next year, Texas will have one of the best State Parks Systems in the United States." Photographs created a montage of scenes featuring the "lost pines" of Bastrop State Park, the new low-water bridge at Blanco State Park, the new road to McDonald Observatory at Mount Locke in the Davis Mountains, and the dramatic geography of Palo Duro Canyon. Details from Colp conveyed his improved understanding of the ECW program as well as his growing affection for the CCC enrollees building his state parks.

"'Besides improving the park system, these CCC camps are making good American citizens out of the young men who are employed to work for them,' Chairman Colp said." [15]

Expanding the System

Applications from Texas for CCC state park camps in the third-period CCC assignments sought to continue most current projects but also to expand the maturing system with many new developments. In the parks board's collective judgment, Big Spring, Goose Island, and Longhorn Cavern deserved the high level of improvement afforded by CCC camps, since these bona fide state parks—created in 1927, 1931, and 1932 respectively—resulted from much more difficult origins than most others from the recent year of New Deal enthusiasm. The unusual San Marcos River landscape near Ottine enjoyed NPS support, as did San Solomon Springs near Balmorhea and Chisos Mountain prospects in the Big Bend. The Lake Corpus Christi park proposal likely originated from boosters in the Nueces River drainage, helped immeasurably by their congressman, Richard Mifflin Kleberg, who concurrently arranged federal assistance to complete the lake itself.

Nationally, in the first two CCC periods the Department of Agriculture took a lion's share of camps—in the first period: 1,268 compared to Interior's 243—with most assigned to national forests in the western states. "In the periods that followed," remembered Wirth, "adjustments between the two departments . . . were worked out to the satisfaction of both." [16] Now with approval from Washington to assign more CCC camps to the park service, Interior's State Park Emergency Conservation Work program stood to benefit from many more approved applications.

Only two days before the third-period assignments would begin, Texas Attorney General Allred announced that "Gov. Miriam A. Ferguson may legally authorize a deficiency appropriation for the state park board." Without this commitment of $25,000 to "equip buildings constructed at nine state parks by the Federal Government" and to cover administrative costs, the NPS might have given up on Texas and assigned its growing allotment to other states. Fortunately, the attorney general—for the second time in five months—and now the governor guaranteed life-saving support for the struggling State Parks Board. After 1 April 1934 more than nine Texas state parks continued their development and over the next two months ten more state parks received new CCC camps—for an eventual total of twenty-one companies busily preparing for the depression's recreation tourists. [17]

NPS officials deemed the park projects at Blanco and Lampasas finished, and their experienced CCC companies moved to new assignments at Longhorn Cavern and Big Bend. The Longhorn camp arrived on 19 May to

TABLE 3
State Parks of the Third-Period ECW
April–September 1934

NPS Number	Official Name	CCC Company
SP-3	Stephenville State Park	Co. 817[1]
SP-4	Davis Mountains State Park	Co. 879
SP-8	Mineral Wells State Park	Side Camp[1]
SP-10	Palisades State Park	Side Camp[2]
SP-12	Meridian State Park	Co. 1827(V)
SP-14	Palo Duro Canyon State Park	Co. 1828(V)
SP-16	” ” ” ” ”	Co. 1821(V)
SP-18	Bonham State Park	Co. 894
SP-21	Bastrop-Buescher State Park	Co. 1805
SP-22	” ” ” ”	Co. 1811
SP-24	Grayson State Park	Co. 857
SP-26	Lake Abilene State Park	Co. 1823(V)
SP-29	Palmetto State Park	Co. 873
SP-30	Zilker Metropolitan Park	Co. 1814
SP-31	Lake Worth Metropolitan Park	Co. 1816
SP-32	Lake Corpus Christi State Park	Co. 886
SP-33	Big Bend State Park	Co. 896
DSP-1	” ” ” ”	Co. 1855[3]
SP-35	Longhorn Cavern State Park	Co. 854
SP-37	Goose Island State Park	Co. 1801
DSP-2	Big Spring State Park	Co. 1857[3]
DSP-3	Hereford State Park	Co. 1862(V)[3]
DSP-4	Balmorhea State Park	Co. 1856[3]

[1] CCC Co. 817 dispatched a side camp of 108 enrollees about 1 April from Stephenville to complete work at the Mineral Wells State Park, with no further mention of this park's transfer back to the city during CWA labor applications. "History Company 817 McGregor, Tex. SP-38-T," *Official Manual 1936*, p. 49.

[2] Work resumed in July on the incomplete Palisades concession building with a side camp from companies at Palo Duro Canyon. Francis H. Gott, NPS Inspector Report, July 1934.

[3] Under the special drought relief program launched 1 July 1934, Co. 1855 arrived on 24 July as DSP-1, "Drought State Park," a second company for Big Bend. Ross Maxwell, *Big Bend Country* (1985), p. 57. Big Spring, Hereford and Balmorhea also received drought camps in July.

assume development of the Burnet County cave that had received little recent improvement under its concession operator. Big Bend Company 896 enrollees set up camp in the Chisos Mountains on 25 May following discovery of water on 16 April in the remote basin below Casa Grande mountain.[18] The late arrival date of these camps, well after the official 1 April beginning date of the new ECW period, reflected the program's nationwide tendency to spend a few more weeks on unfinished projects and to help the Army avoid transportation bottlenecks from moving and establishing too many camps at once.

As the Stephenville job wound down, more than half of Company 817 traveled north on State Highway 66 to Mineral Wells State Park. Specific municipal, or "metropolitan," camps began work at Zilker Park in Austin and Lake Worth near Fort Worth, although they received "SP"—state park—prefixes for accounting and design coordination purposes. Later in the period, Hereford received a newly assembled company of war veterans to begin work on city land not yet donated to the state. But Palo Duro Canyon lost two of its CCC Veterans companies at the beginning of the third period, probably due to difficulties of war-veteran reenlistment in those camps.

The parks board's application for a CCC camp at Independence, like the state's earlier attempt to secure a camp to reconstruct old Fort Parker, failed to win NPS approval. Another failed camp application, one probably aimed at development for the coming Centennial celebration in 1936, was that for "Sam Houston State Monument" in Harris County. The project received a number, SP-28, but appeared as "discontinued" on the third-period camp rosters. Yet, seemingly to further the Centennial promotion theme of catchy names for some parks, the new project at Ottine became "Palmetto State Park" in honor of the dwarf tropical plants that carpet this San Marcos River jungle.

On 12 May 1934, the day before Mother's Day, with great fanfare Pat Neff presented an "additional" 250 acres of Coryell County land for the expansion of Mother Neff State Park. The significance of the gift was heralded in a Baylor University press release:

> This tract of land joins Mother Neff Park bequeathed by the mother of Gov. Neff to the public for park purposes, and is the mother of the entire park system of the state in that it was this gift that suggested to Gov. Neff the idea of the State Parks. . . . About 100 acres is heavily timbered, rough, mountainous land, with a cave, bluffs, and springs on it, making it eminently desirable for park purposes."[19]

Now the title "Mother Neff State Park" truly described for the first time land actually owned by the state of Texas, since Neff evidently never transferred the original tract. His assertion that this park equaled its 6 initial acres plus the recent 250 acres still continued to shroud the park's statistics in confusion, since the entire tract from which Mother Neff Park had been carved after 1921 stood in the county tax rolls at exactly 250 acres.

Third-period CCC state park assignments in Texas with some exceptions reflected a maturing program of recreation destinations. Each, like Mother Neff, featured a minimum of 250 acres, accessibility to the state's rapidly expanding New Deal–assisted road system, and the preservation of unique natural features. The system's emphasis, however, remained west of a line drawn across Texas from Dallas through San Antonio, with the NPS particularly partial to far west development now beginning in the Big Bend.

The Pioneer Experience

While outdoor recreation stood above all other purposes in developing a New Deal state park system, by 1934 several related concepts joined the highly flexible definition of "state park." These public lands filled the vast margin between urban parks and the national parks, simultaneously blessed and cursed by that huge assignment. As the late NPS director Steve Mather had proposed as early as 1921, state parks across the nation now offered overnight camping sites for automobile tourists, either for a weekend drive from the city or en route to an extended vacation in a distant national park. In more specific definitions from early park promoters, state parks should preserve "characteristic scenery . . . peculiar to the state."

The National Conference on State Parks, under strong influence from the NPS, now focused that definition on service to urban populations. State parks, declared the NCSP, "provide large wild, natural, unspoiled areas within easy reach of large centers of population or thickly settled areas." Despite these certainties, park planning in 1934 remained a largely intuitive profession. Its experts had standardized the practice only through various pamphlets and such instructions as Maier's "Library of Original Sources" photo album of successful park facilities. Yet in Texas and elsewhere site selection and improvement resulted in a remarkable collection of resources matching the public's idea of "park."

Trees—usually pine forests—for shade and character linked the appearances of such distant Texas parks as Caddo Lake, Bastrop, and the Big Bend. Even in forested areas, and in locales from Bonham to Meridian and Abilene, the presence of stone outcrops and loose boulders attracted park designers, both for the story in their geology and the availability of building materials. A compact variety of terrain also allowed multiple development possibilities—such as at Big Spring, Palmetto, and Palo Duro—so that visitors could enjoy seclusion and experience changing landscapes along drives and hikes. With or without trees and boulders, the creation of a recreation water source completed the usual formula, hence the construction of dams in several parks—and the Abilene swimming pool venture as a cheaper alternative—plus the appeal of large municipal lakes near Corpus Christi and Fort Worth.

Former Interior secretary John Barton Payne also noted that state parks could preserve "historical sites . . . so that in a sense the life of the state as man has dealt with it is preserved for future generations." By implying that a "pioneer" encounter with the virgin land could be interpreted through state parks, Payne hit upon a secret of the visitor experience, and a model for constructing state park facilities even when scenery provided the primary attraction. Indeed, the frontier-settler notion of using local materials with primitive finishes helped early national park designers, including Maier, settle on their particular brand of "rustic" park buildings. In the national parks this meant that utility buildings—such as stores, offices, garages, water and sewer stations—should blend in with the dominant natural environment. But for state parks all these ideas extended to creating a more inclusive encounter for the visitor, especially the overnight automobile tourist not interested in camping on the ground.[20]

Thus the NPS responded to appeals from Colp and local communities by encouraging designs of small lodges and "housekeeping cabins" at select state parks. The first of these, architect Guy Carlander's "Coronado Lodge" near the park entrance of Palo Duro Canyon, began to take shape after its cornerstone dedication on 12 May 1934. Colp and State Parks Board secretary Gus Urbantke attended the canyon-rim ceremony, bringing with them from Austin an old newspaper friend, Raymond Brooks, who had visited Palo Duro in 1921 during an early legislative look at potential parks. As work progressed on Coronado Lodge, the project's ample CCC manpower also developed the canyon floor "Cow Camp" some distance from the entrance, featuring a grouping of stone cabins.[21]

For Big Bend, the park service now proposed that initial development include both a sprawling lodge and a nearby cottage group at the Green Gulch entrance to the Chisos Mountains Basin. "My preliminary theory of the lodge," George Nason wrote in early May, "is a Spanish Hacienda type, somewhat 'U' shaped in form, with the open end of the patio looking directly into the distant blue view to the north." After hiring El Paso architect William G. Wuehrman to develop this plan, Nason later assigned troubleshooting "architects Boese and Thompson" to assist with plans for the cottages. Interestingly, upon driving the battered trail south of Marathon and encountering the Chisos Mountains for the first time, newly hired inspector B. Ashburton Tripp remarked that "the park area and its approach are an invitation to those who will undergo anything for a peek at grandeur. The question is, will they do it a second time? Will they urge their friends to take a chance? Accessibility is one necessary element in this scheme."[22]

At Bastrop, architect Arthur Fehr worked on drawings for a prototype stone cottage while he supervised completion of the entry gateway and directed construction of the concession complex. By now he referred in his daybook to the concession building as a "refectory," the NPS term for a main park building that offered dining services along with meeting space and public toilets. On 9 May, Fehr submitted the cottage plans to Maier's district office—recently moved to the State Capitol in Oklahoma City—and waited for his proposal to pass from there to Washington and back with requisite architectural criticism.

Fehr's cottage floor plan outlined a compact bungalow with a large fireplace and living room opening onto two sleeping porches. Its small kitchen squared an outside corner created by one porch and the chimney, with clever side access to the fireplace hearth for cooking. "The squat, massive chimney," an appraisal read, "extreme batter of the walls, roofs of very low pitch, and the low walls which seem to knit the structure to [its] site are elements which add up to a total effect that is extraordinarily individual and attractive." No indoor plumbing appeared with the proposal, as Fehr intended a central latrine and shower building for the eventual cottage group, to be called "Pioneer Village." [23]

Less than a week after completing the Bastrop cottage drawings, Fehr received orders from the NPS for a one-month posting to the Davis Mountains housing project. That park's adobe "Indian Village" construction already underway "was a distinct shock to me," complained inspector Nason upon visiting Fort Davis in early May. The original design was by departed architect J. B. Roberts, with subsequent work by central office architect Olin Smith. "While it is being built more or less in accordance with the sketches prepared last fall," Nason explained, "it is distinctly lacking in character and atmosphere." Fehr's assignment here, along with his friend William Calhoun Caldwell, would "give it the character it should have," Nason reported.[24]

Fehr and Caldwell spent the next weeks "[c]ollecting data on 'West of the Pecos'," Fehr wrote, searching the Davis Mountains and Big Bend region for historic buildings and design inspiration. "W.C.C. and I cannot quite see an Indian village on the side of a mountain," Fehr reacted initially. "We are very much in mind to convert the whole scheme to Mexican—probably we should call it just -Texan-." Finally they notified Nason that their recommended "change is rather drastic," as they settled on an adobe pueblo complex for the north slope of Keesey Canyon.

Though they did not acknowledge specific precedents for their lodge refinements, Fehr and Caldwell probably encountered two significant sources during their Trans-Pecos travels. First, the existence of large nineteenth-century adobe haciendas in the Big Bend expanded their design possibilities for dried mud bricks beyond the local examples of aging U.S. Army construction at old Fort Davis. And second, recently produced drawings of Acoma Pueblo northwest of Albuquerque—showing ancient rough-lined, flat-roofed, mud-plastered apartments with stone reinforcements at corners and openings—may have strongly influenced their work. Whether by intent or fortunate outcome, their highly successful adaptation of a Native American pueblo to "NPS rustic" architecture certainly stretched the guiding concept of providing a "pioneer" experience for the park visitor.[25]

The Politics of Park Development

Rapidly increasing activity of state park development during the third period caused the State Parks Board and its federally sponsored personnel to outgrow State Capitol quarters. The board's latest space assignment, noted one report in early 1934, "placed headquarters in the rotunda of the Capitol on the third floor." Fortunately, recent stamps of approval for parks board activities from both the attorney general and governor boosted Colp's status in state government. So with unusual help from the Board of Control and the Game, Fish and Oyster Commission—both ironically Colp's closest rivals for public recreation management in Texas—the State Parks Board moved in mid-April to new quarters in the Walton Building, a converted church northeast of the Capitol at 106 East 13th Street, alongside the larger game commission operation.

At the same time, Maier decided to dismantle his NPS central design office with the parks board in Austin. This left at the Austin office the park service procurement clerks and R. O. Whiteaker, parks board engineer now paid by the state, as well as a desk for Colp. Architects and landscape architects leaving Austin received various assignments at state park projects underway across the state, with Olin Smith transferring to Stephenville and Palmetto, Olin Boese to Corpus Christi and Goose Island, and "Mr. Hanson" to Big Bend.[26]

Maier approved the hiring of additional professionals at other sites, including local architects David Castle at Abilene and Charles Page at Zilker in Austin, where Page had worked with the Civil Works Administration. Equally accomplished architect Samuel Charles Phelps Vosper, former design teacher at Texas A&M College, moved to the Longhorn Cavern encampment. "Mr. Vosper is a man of considerable varied experience in architecture; of mature age, and I believe," inspector Nason speculated, "will give us some design with real character in the cavern and in the surrounding buildings. . . . Mr. Vosper has had experience in stage lighting, and I am hoping that he will develop some very interesting flood lighting effects, and bring out the beauties of the cave." Nason also dispatched Vosper on temporary assignments to rescue stalled designs and construction at both Grayson and Bonham state parks.[27]

At the 13 June meeting of the State Parks Board, Colp announced official receipt of Governor Ferguson's deficiency appropriation of $25,000. Nason submitted a policy letter to the group under his emerging status as senior representative of the NPS with Texas state park developments. Expressing pride in recent architectural accomplishments, Nason told the board that "in some matters—particularly the buildings—we have probably excelled any states in the Union. I have that information from very good authority."

Colp and the host communities of most park projects barely contained their enthusiasm over this "harvest," as Colp put it, of construction and park system development. But when Colp and Whiteaker approved a number of flattering cornerstones for new park buildings, and then sanctioned premature park openings throughout June and on the July 4th holiday, Nason pronounced a severe breech of professional decorum. First, Nason disapproved of commemorative cornerstone installations in concession buildings at Abilene, Meridian, and Palo Duro and accused the parks board of suffering from a "cornerstone complex." Then Nason attended the "so-called opening of Palo Duro Park . . . the finish of a series of State Park openings at Bastrop, Blanco, Longhorn, Abilene, Lampasas, Stephenville, Meridian and Palo Duro." He reported to Maier that "These celebrations were not, to my mind, in keeping with the dignity of the Texas Parks, nor were any of the parks except Blanco and Lampasas, ready for opening ceremonies." [28]

While Colp's concept of state parks clashed with that of the NPS engineer's vision, the success of these celebrations served a tremendous public relations purpose. In fact, with a July 4th visitor count of more than 7,000 at Palo Duro Canyon and perhaps more thousands driving to the other park openings, Colp could point to solid evidence that Texans wanted state parks. [29] Federal park officials, by contrast, in 1934 understood outdoor recreation only in the sense of promoting a passive experience in the wilderness areas of national parks. The NPS looked upon itself as primarily an agency of natural resource protection, and its acknowledged success had not prompted any questioning of its visitors about their own needs and interests. Nason, who had spent twelve years managing a large *city* park system with an active-recreation patronage, should have been able to bridge the gap between the subtle federal approach and the greater variety of services needed at state parks. He chose instead the most parsimonious national park strategy and thus failed to understand the populist-progressive (and New Deal!) attitudes of Colp, Neff, and most mobile middle-class Texans during the depression.

The Politics of Drought

Depression's reality, especially for descendants of western pioneers who had neither time nor money for driving off to a state park vacation, redoubled with the drought of 1934. An agricultural imbalance that had been building since the late 1920s, resulting from overproduction and poor conservation practices, rose to crisis proportions in the spring as dust storms blew across the prairie states. Newspaper reporters dubbed the eerie combination of boiling clouds of airborne topsoil, coupled with defenseless farms and cities in their path, as "The Dust Bowl," and this name and image came to symbolize the 1930s on the Great Plains.

The Dust Bowl's effects created "a desperate need for immediate government action," observes CCC historian John Salmond, and the president turned to his existing relief empire for response. "Roosevelt decided to use the CCC," Salmond explains, "as one of the agencies to implement drought policy and asked Congress for an additional $50,000,000 for Corps work in the drought areas." The special enlistment began on 1 July 1934, expanding the CCC by 50,000 men, including 5,000 war veterans, recruited from twenty-two drought-stricken states, including Texas. With intent to relieve farmers and ranchers of their damaged land and improve specific tracts for public use, FDR's action included additional funds for outright purchase of real estate.[30]

ECW inspectors in early 1934 had already begun investigations of "sub-marginal lands," to identify property that could be stabilized and converted to new uses. The new federal drought initiative quickly sharpened this focus on land rehabilitation, as Interior's Soil Erosion Service and Agriculture's Forest Service dispatched the majority of new CCC "drought" companies across the Great Plains. Interior's park service received a small quota of these camps and created a special "DSP," or Drought State Park, category for projects that could combine soil retention with park development. Texas benefited immediately in July with a second CCC company, DSP-1, for the Big Bend, followed by camps to begin state park work at Big Spring, Hereford, and Balmorhea, DSP-2, -3 and -4 respectively.

Federal drought-relief funds purchased all or parts of these sites, including the 1,160-acre Ira and Leona Hector ranch in the Big Bend, acquired for $3,840 and partial donation. The State Parks Board met on 28 July at Alpine to accept the Hector tract and review the board's immense new holdings in Brewster and Presidio counties. With the crucial Hector ranch purchase Big Bend State Park now totaled 385,120 acres, Colp optimistically claimed, from 158,960 acres of school lands acquired with a $1,948 state transfer appropriation and many private tracts seized for tax debts.[31]

The Politics of Patronage

Texas farmers remained a traditional constituency of Ferguson Populism, but their Dust Bowl plight did not inspire Governor Miriam in 1934 to run again for public office. Instead, according to historian Seth McKay, the year's Democratic primary forecast "the first biennial election year since 1912 in which there was no Ferguson up for a choice." Seven men entered the primary, including Lieutenant Governor Edgar Witt, Attorney General James Allred, and Senator Clint Small of Amarillo, all familiar with the State Parks Board and, perhaps including longtime Colp-antagonist Witt, supportive of its growing recreation system. James Burr V. Allred won the Democratic nomination by little more than 40,000 votes of just less than a million cast.[32]

Mindful of elections for their own congressional seats and those of their Democratic colleagues, Texans in Washington drifted home following their regular spring session. NPS inspector Nason, who recently had visited in the Washington Capitol with John Nance Garner, stopped in late June at the vice president's home in Uvalde. "Apparently [Garner] had a fine impression of work the National Park Service Civilian Conservation Corps is doing," Nason recorded. "Believe he wanted me to report favorably on projects in his [former] district though he would not commit himself to any recommendations." As he had in Washington, Garner showed particular interest, Nason admitted, "in knowing progress that had been made on his list of appointees," meaning his list of friends available for jobs in state park development.[33]

In July, Nason visited with Sam Rayburn at the congressman's home in Bonham, and they discussed the progress of Grayson State Park in Rayburn's district. "He did not seem to be aware that Bonham [State Park] had been definitely set up," Nason commented on Rayburn's careful distance from the largest federal project near his hometown. "He apparently was quite satisfied with the work that is being done [by the CCC], and I believe he has a very good feeling for the National Park Service, and can be counted on to stay with them in an emergency." A few days later Nason had a conference with Congressman Tom Blanton in his office at Abilene, acutely aware that this particular official cared very deeply about who obtained federal jobs in his district. "He now apparently has seen enough of what we are doing in the Abilene Park," Nason granted, "to feel that the National Park Service is sincere."[34]

In August, new NPS inspector Donald D. Obert took his turn at these political housecalls, visiting with U.S. Senator Morris Sheppard in Texarkana. The senator displayed open interest in Caddo Lake State Park and had encouraged the Army to collaborate fully with the parks program to reestablish a CCC camp there. As "dean of the Congress" with thirty-two years continuous service, and chair of the Senate Military Affairs Committee, Sheppard "was obviously the cause of the Army's highly cooperative tendencies," Obert observed. Based on recent authorization from CCC director Fechner to explore lasting use of Army barracks at park sites following development, and now with Sheppard's support, Obert and his Army colleagues anticipated further Caddo Lake work in the fourth period. He and architect Boese worked with the Army "to design and lay out the C.C.C. camp in a location and manner which would make it possible to utilize some of the buildings for the park when the camp was withdrawn."[35]

Preparing for the Fourth Period

On 1 October 1934, the new list of state park projects added Brownwood, Lake Sweetwater, and—at long last—Mother Neff. In addition, well-practiced CCC Co. 857 launched new development at Caddo Lake State Park, which lost its "SP-1" status to be reclassified as SP-40. Soon after Co. 857 headquarters departed Grayson County, its commissioners court notified the State Parks Board of a new name for their leased lake and woodland: Loy State Park, in honor of sitting County Judge Jake Loy. Here and elsewhere improvements continued, with both short-term side camps and new six-month commitments, at seventeen state parks and metropolitan parks already under development. But with a total of fifty-two CCC camps of all types in Texas, only eighteen CCC companies performed state park work in this winter period.

Congressman Blanton of Abilene kept Co. 1823(V) of war veterans within his district, as camp headquarters was transferred a few miles west to begin work on Lake Sweetwater, a large municipal reservoir. The NPS declared Zilker Park complete and its Co. 1814 moved from Austin to the piney woods near Groveton to reoccupy an abandoned U.S. Forest Service camp. Talented, though temporarily divided, Co. 817 officially moved to Mother Neff State Park but continued to provide side camps for completion of both Mineral Wells and Meridian. Lake Brownwood, with 538 acres accepted more than a year before by the parks board and partially improved by Civil Works Administration labor the previous winter, obtained Co. 872 from its completed city park project in Ada, Oklahoma. Strangely, Co. 896 transferred from Big Bend across the state to Lindale as a soil erosion camp, although many of its members reenlisted in drought-program Co. 1855 and continued their work in the Chisos Mountains.[36]

Big Spring, Hereford, and Balmorhea also retained their "DSP" status through the winter of 1933–1934. The far-reaching drought caused a tragic and tremendous surge in nationwide unemployment, dispatching homeless families in their rattletrap automobiles onto the nation's new highways and funneling countless individuals into the government category of transients. With no specific winter public works program in place this fiscal year, Harry Hopkins directed his Federal Emergency Relief Administration to establish "transient bureaus" in the states to round up drifters and assign them to temporary work projects. The recently abandoned CCC barracks

TABLE 4
State Parks of the Fourth-Period ECW
October 1934 – March 1935

NPS Number	Official Name	CCC Company
SP-3	Stephenville State Park	Co. 817[1]
SP-4	Davis Mountains State Park	Co. 879
SP-8	Mineral Wells State Park	Side Camp[1]
SP-10	Palisades State Park	Side Camp[2]
SP-12	Meridian State Park	Side Camp[1]
SP-14	Palo Duro Canyon State Park	Co. 1828(V)
SP-16	" " " " "	Co. 1821(V)
SP-18	Bonham State Park	Co. 894
SP-21	Bastrop-Buescher State Park	Co. 1805
SP-22	" " " "	Co. 1811
SP-24	Loy State Park	Side Camp[3]
SP-26	Lake Abilene State Park	Side Camp[4]
SP-29	Palmetto State Park	Co. 873
SP-31	Lake Worth Metropolitan Park	Co. 1816
SP-32	Lake Corpus Christi State Park	Co. 886
SP-35	Longhorn Cavern State Park	Co. 854
SP-36	Brownwood State Park	Co. 872
SP-37	Goose Island State Park	Co. 1801
SP-38	Mother Neff State Park	Co. 817[1]
SP-40	Caddo Lake State Park	Co. 857[3]
SP-41	Lake Sweetwater Metropolitan Park	Co. 1823(V)
DSP-1	Big Bend State Park	Co. 1855
DSP-2	Big Spring State Park	Co. 1857
DSP-3	Hereford State Park	Co. 1862(V)
DSP-4	Balmorhea State Park	Co. 1856

[1] Co. 817 continued to provide a side camp of more than 100 men at Mineral Wells and in October 1934 dispatched another side camp of 25 men for completion of work at Meridian State Park. The headquarters camp of Co. 817 moved on 26 December 1934 from Stephenville State Park to Mother Neff State Park, yet both side camps remained at their remote assignments.

[2] With a side camp from companies at Palo Duro Canyon, work continued through winter on the Palisades concession building and roads.

[3] A side camp of Co. 857 remained to complete work at Loy (formerly Grayson) State Park.

[4] Co. 1823(V) returned a 25-man side camp in November to Abilene to complete concrete work and other small tasks, preparing the park for summer opening.

at Stephenville State Park became in late December temporary housing for transients who continued landscape development at the park.[37]

With continual prodding from the NPS for the State Parks Board to spend part of its new budget on a design office, D. E. Colp finally assembled a staff in the fall of 1934. He secured Roy E. Lane as "State Parks Architect" on 12 October and, by late November, named M. C. Coney "Landscape Architect for the State of Texas," both the first such salaried positions in Texas state government.[38]

Parks for the Centennial

Nearing the end of their two-year terms, Governor Ferguson and the 43rd Legislature met from August through November 1934 in two more special sessions. They accomplished the primary assignment of issuing another $5 million round of relief bonds and agreed on some details such as again reorganizing the Texas Relief Commission, making it a subdivision of the Board of Control. The relief commission continued, under assistant director Neal Guy, to enroll all CCC volunteers from Texas in cooperation with the federal Department of Labor. Guy "worked heroically attempting to manage the largest state [CCC enrollment] program in the nation," notes historian Ken Hendrickson, "on the smallest budget."[39]

Prolonged and frustrated debates deadlocked lawmakers, unfortunately, over several issues, including control and financing of the Centennial celebration. The state's Centennial Commission, developing a plan since March, voted on 9 September to hold a central exposition during the summer of 1936 in Dallas, with other events and monuments distributed throughout the state. Governor Ferguson recommended in October that state government subsidize the event with $5 million, declaring, "[n]o matter how you figure the Centennial it means a Hundred Million Dollars new money turned loose in Texas. I am for it."

A major vehicle of dispersing these Centennial benefits, recommended State Parks Board chairman Colp, should be the state park system. To this end Colp and friends dug out yellowing stationery for the "Texas State Parks Association," a lobbying moniker dating back to 1923, and prepared a news release picked up by the *San Antonio Express*. "It is the purpose of the parks board," Colp broadcast, "to make full use of the 258,405 acres of land contained in these 72 parks during [the] Centennial year . . . to provide accommodations for visitors and tourists to Texas." He also noted that $6,000,000 in federal funds was being spent "in improvement work on these parks, in addition to other millions for better highways to reach these parks." The Texas State Parks Association, he said, planned to mail a million illustrated folders containing directions to state parks and an invitation from the governor "to join in the celebration and visit Texas during 1936."[40]

Legislators adjourned without specifically funding the Centennial, trusting for the moment that the Texas Highway Department literally would pave the way for automobile tourists. Certainly many of the state's seven historical sites—Fannin, Goliad, Gonzales, King's, San Jacinto, and Washington state parks, plus the Alamo—would benefit from this focus on highway tourism. But neither their oversight agency, the Board of Control, nor Colp showed any interest in organizing improvements at these sites for 1936. Thus in an odd proclamation—and with no funding—lawmakers authorized Colp's parks board "to locate, designate and suitably mark the historic grounds, battlefields and other historic spots in Texas," in anticipation of the Centennial.

When the legislative smoke cleared near the end of the year, Governor Ferguson—as a small concession to Colp's million-folder proposal—issued her own press release for out-of-state visitors. "Texas has much of natural beauty and of historic interest," she cooed in the *New York Herald Tribune,* "which we would gladly share with our friends from other sections of the country." [41]

The Election of 1934

In the November 1934 election, with fewer than a half million votes cast in the governor's race, Jimmie Allred handily defeated his Republican opponent, D. E. Waggoner. Replaced as lieutenant governor by Walter F. Woodul, Edgar Witt now accepted a presidential appointment as chairman of the federal Mexican Claims Commission. Witt's departure might have delighted state-park promoters, but unfortunately faithful parks- and Centennial-supporter Margie Elizabeth Neal also left the Senate for a New Deal job in Washington, to work with the "Blue Eagle" National Recovery Administration. [42]

The midterm vote in Texas and across the nation affirmed widespread popularity of the New Deal by returning most members of Congress, including Senator Tom Connally, to Washington's Capitol. "The 1934 election strengthened the presidential influence on the Hill," concludes historian Arthur Schlesinger, "by bringing into Congress a new breed of New Deal Democrats—men like . . . [Harry S.] Truman of Missouri in the Senate and the more responsible members of the Maury Maverick group in the House—who combined the party regularity of the older Democrats with the liberal fervor of the older progressives."

Fontaine Maury Maverick had earned his credentials in the early 1930s as Bexar County tax collector, brokering relief funds to support colonies of transient workers in San Antonio. The enthusiasm of Maverick and other Bexar County leaders for federal relief funds stimulated significant road construction and improvements at the San Antonio missions, including the

Alamo downtown. Anticipating the Centennial and its boost to local tourism, relief-funds restoration of Mission San Jose had begun in 1932 under the supervision of architect Harvey Smith. During the same period relief-labor development of newly acquired state land around the Alamo created a dignified, four-acre stone-walled compound embellished by landscape architect H. E. Kincaid and architect Henry Truman Phelps.[43]

Congressman Marvin Jones saw his enormous Panhandle district scaled back by redistricting, with George Mahon winning the new 19th District stretching from Lubbock to his home in Colorado City. But Jones lost no enthusiasm for the Palo Duro Canyon State Park project, despite continued apprehension from federal officials over the state's ability to pay off its parkland liens. Although the half-finished park already drew a respectable number of visitors, in 1934 the "gate receipts, concessions, and pasture rentals amounted to $6,426," according to historian Peter L. Petersen, "of which $3,243.37 was applied by the State Parks Board to the park's indebtedness." Alarmed at the park's dismal failure to produce some $40,000 annual income to service its debt, NPS authorities Herb Maier and Conrad Wirth in late 1934 prepared to "withdraw all the CCC camps at Palo Duro Park, and stop all construction work there," recalled lienholder Fred Emery.

"Eventually, after the intercession of Congressman Marvin Jones," Petersen explains, "a compromise was agreed upon." Still betting on the success of the state park, Emery on 30 November 1934 released to the state "free and clear" 120 acres containing the park entrance, Coronado Lodge construction, and campground areas. Emery proved even more generous, he claimed, by providing an additional 100-foot-wide road right-of-way and by paying his own first-lien holders $1,200.00 to grant releases from the 15,104-acre tract.[44]

NEW LEGISLATURE, NEW CONGRESS, AND THE SECOND NEW DEAL

Votes of Confidence from the 1935 Legislature

As the new legislature convened on 8 January 1935 and Jimmie Allred delivered his inaugural speech on the 15th, state government focused mainly on how to coordinate federal government in Texas. Governor Allred successfully proposed the Texas Planning Board to coordinate federal aid among state agencies and local communities and to produce a conservation plan for the state's natural resources.[45]

The day after Allred's inauguration the State Parks Board met to plot its legislative strategy, review fifth-period CCC camp applications, and plan for the coming summer tourist season. With an apparent flash of awareness that the board held power of acceptance and rejection of park sites, Chairman Colp presented a long list of parks for approval, including many of the 1920s donations that had missed the 1927 legislature's brief window of acceptance. The board in turn voted other lands "re-conveyed," including many never-developed 1920s sites that donors demanded returned.[46]

With the previous governor's deficiency appropriation of 1934 almost exhausted, the State Parks Board needed additional operating cash from the legislature immediately. First, lawmakers approved a treasury reimbursement for deficiency appropriations granted in the previous biennium, thus covering the State Parks Board's $25,000 rescue advance from Governor Ferguson. Then representatives E. Harold Beck of Texarkana and William E. Clayton of El Paso successfully underwrote the parks board for the current fiscal year, through August, and persuaded the governor to sign their measure promptly on 27 February.

Chairman Colp's office received a whopping $36,550 for salaries and a good deal of equipment for both administration and field operations. These funds financed R. O. Whiteaker as chief engineer and placed on state payroll one architect, one landscape architect, one construction superintendent, six stenographers, four "technical assistants," three draftsmen, one chief clerk, and one bookkeeper, and covered the expenses of "Two Field Parties —Topographic Survey." The board could now purchase "Two light automobile station wagons for Field Parties, [and] three light sedans for Board and Inspectors, each not to exceed $700." Travel allotments for the board and field personnel (enabling the state to reimburse Colp's out-of-pocket expenses for the first time since 1924!) amounted to $3,000. Another $5,000 outfitted the growing sawmill and maintenance shop inside Bastrop State Park and authorized purchase of "Lumber, hardware, paints and miscellaneous supplies for constructing furniture and park equipment."

With this long-hoped-for match for federal funds and personnel, the State Parks Board reestablished the central design office in Austin and shouldered a much larger burden of system operations. Its chief clerk prepared the board's first-ever regular budget for the coming 1936–1937 biennium— minus automobiles and shop supplies—and submitted it to the legislature. Colp and company received little criticism for their proposal, except for a protest from Amarillo senator Clint Small that the Panhandle parks— Hereford, Palisades, and Palo Duro—appeared in the budget with amounts too low for adequate operations. In defiance, Small introduced legislation to establish a single, separate board to manage those parks, and both houses passed the measure. Governor Allred vetoed Small's secession bill but fortunately signed the appropriations bill, including $29,620 for the State Parks Board in each of the next two years.

Over at the parallel universe of the Board of Control, its six scattered historical parks received an unremarkable total of $13,084 for the Centennial year of 1936 and $10,454 for 1937. While most of these funds represented standard operation and maintenance of Fannin, Goliad, Gonzales, King's, San Jacinto, and Washington state parks, two surprises appeared in this schedule. First, a one-time 1936 appropriation of $2,100 funded a "suitable memorial" for Republic of Texas heroes buried at Monument Hill near La Grange. Then at the end of this "State Parks" category within the Board of Control's budget appeared a "Keeper's salary" of $720 per year for "Palo Duro State Park" plus annual "Contingent expenses" of $250. This salary compared to an annual low of $528 for the keeper at Washington State Park and a high of $1,134 for Andrew Jackson Houston, superintendent of San Jacinto State Park. The Board of Control schedule offered no explanation for this unusual accommodation of Palo Duro Canyon and the rival State Parks Board.[47]

Allred threw considerable weight behind the Centennial movement, having "evolved as the celebration's greatest supporter and most visible asset," says the event's biographer Ken Ragsdale. The governor made no memorable speeches on Texas history during the session, but he did remind legislators of a 1932 state constitutional amendment supporting the Centennial plus recent endorsement from the Democratic party platform, and he promised to sign Centennial legislation.

Dallas Representative Jeff Stinson's subsequent bill bumped through the legislative process but successfully assigned more than $3 million to various components of the celebration. These included further improvements at the state-owned Alamo grounds, and "a permanent memorial at the San Jacinto battlefield," according to a report, each budgeted at an incredible appropriated figure of $250,000. To match the state's $3 million endorsement of its Centennial, the 74th U.S. Congress soon awarded an equal amount to be administered by the United States Texas Centennial Commission, headed by Vice President John Nance Garner.[48]

CCC Parks of the Second New Deal

In January 1935 President Roosevelt approved a doubling of enrollment in the CCC, with a consequent increase in ECW projects across the nation. Reauthorization and expansion of the CCC joined the extension and addition of many other New Deal programs in early 1935, forecasting a movement for reform and relief measures that so surpassed Roosevelt's introduction of the New Deal in 1933 that observers dubbed the results a "Second New Deal."

The NPS secured a moderate percentage of the new CCC camps, and partly in response reorganized its CCC district system into new "regions." Herb Maier's directorate became Region VII, still based in Oklahoma City and still including Texas. But the Department of Agriculture continued to dominate ECW projects: not only did its U.S. Forest Service command a large number of camps—twenty-eight during the fifth period in Texas—but with a major insider coup in early 1935 Secretary Wallace convinced the president to transfer Interior's successful Soil Erosion Service to Agriculture. Under its new name, the Soil Conservation Service beginning 1 April captured thirty-eight CCC companies for its Texas program.[49]

In related federal business, Vice President Garner and Texas congressmen huddled to support their state's coming Centennial celebration and, not coincidentally, a new national park. With Interior secretary Harold Ickes's support, on 1 March 1935 El Paso congressman Robert Ewing Thomason and senators Tom Connally and Morris Sheppard introduced concurrent bills to transform Big Bend State Park into a federal preserve and to join with Mexico in creating an international park for the region. Their bill became law later in the session and "authorized the Secretary of the Interior to designate boundaries within an area of approximately 1,500,000 acres in Brewster and Presidio Counties," remembers Big Bend park geologist and historian Ross Maxwell, providing that private lands checkered within these boundaries could be obtained. Since inspector Nason calculated that the Texas parks board controlled only about 800 acres in the Chisos Mountains—instead of the 225,000 frequently claimed for the present state park—land acquisition proved a staggering, and for the moment insurmountable, obstacle.[50]

By the end of March the parks board had assumed a number of completed state parks from their NPS developers, including Loy (Grayson), Meridian, Mineral Wells, and Stephenville. Colp made informal agreements with Grayson County and each of the cities near these parks to prepare their openings and arrange concession operations during the summer. The board soon issued one of its first standard rules for park operations, declaring that in July and August "visitors can stay no longer than one week per park." With a number of additional CCC camps expected for the coming fifth-period CCC, Colp's staff submitted several new project applications to Washington, including two closely related to Centennial development: Goliad State Park, designated since 1931, and Fort Parker, which would combine a lake and recreation park in Limestone County with the long-proposed reconstruction of the old fort itself.

Since the Board of Control administered Goliad State Park through a local park commission, the State Parks Board acted only as liaison with this application. The parks board likewise assisted Lubbock city and county

TABLE 5
State Parks of the Fifth-Period ECW
April–September 1935

NPS Number	Official Name	CCC Company
SP-4	Davis Mountains State Park	Co. 879[1]
SP-14	Palo Duro Canyon State Park	Co. 1828(V)[2]
SP-16	” ” ” ” ”	Co. 1821(V)[2]
SP-18	Bonham State Park	Co. 894
SP-21	Bastrop-Buescher State Park	Co. 1805
SP-22	” ” ” ”	Co. 1811
SP-26	Lake Abilene State Park	Co. 1823(CV)[3]
SP-29	Palmetto State Park	Co. 873
SP-31	Lake Worth Metropolitan Park	Co. 1816
SP-32	Lake Corpus Christi State Park	Co. 886
SP-33	Big Bend State Park	Co. 1855
SP-35	Longhorn Cavern State Park	Co. 854
SP-36	Brownwood State Park	Co. 872
SP-37	Goose Island State Park	Co. 1801(C)[4]
SP-38	Mother Neff State Park	Co. 817
SP-40	Caddo Lake State Park	Co. 857
SP-41	Lake Sweetwater Metropolitan Park	Co. 1823(CV)[3]
SP-42	Garner State Park	Co. 879[1]
SP-43	Goliad State Park	Co. 3822(V)
SP-44	Fort Parker State Park	Co. 3807(C)
SP-45	Big Spring State Park	Co. 1857
SP-46	Hereford State Park	Co. 1862(V)
SP-47	Balmorhea State Park	Co. 1856
SP-49	Daingerfield State Park	Co. 2891
SP-51	Lockhart State Park	Co. 3803
SP-52	Mackenzie State Park	Co. 3820(V)
SP-53	Cleburne State Park	Co. 3804
SP-54	Tyler State Park	Co. 2888
SP-55	Bachman–White Rock Lake Metropolitan Park	Co. 2896
F-16	Mission State Forest	Co. 888[5]

[1] Co. 879 transferred on 20 July 1935 from Davis Mountains to Garner State Park.

[2] In midperiod both Palo Duro camps changed occupants: on 17 August 1935 CCC Co. 2875(C) took over SP-14, and on 19 August Co. 2876(C) assumed SP-16. Both Veterans companies became soil conservation camps elsewhere in the Panhandle.

[3] "(C)" joined the ECW numbering system to indicate segregated "Colored" CCC camps of African American enrollees, in this case, black war veterans, "(CV)." Co. 1823(CV) began the fifth period as an all-black company at Lake Sweetwater but retreated in mid-June to Abilene for the remainder of this period.

[4] As with Co. 1823, the army replaced white members of Co. 1801 with African Americans to begin the fifth period. After vehement objections from the nearby community of Rockport, the CCC company moved out on 15 June, ending work at the Goose Island State Park project.

[5] While Co. 888 worked under supervision of the U.S. Forest Service as camp F-16, enrollees built this recreation park on state-owned Texas Forest Service land.

officials with a CCC camp application for extension of their old public park in Yellowhouse Canyon, and the city of Dallas for a chain of developments at its municipal Bachman and White Rock lakes.[51]

Newly segregated CCC companies for African Americans, 1801 at Goose Island and 1823 for war veterans at Abilene, reflected changes in ECW management for Texas in the fifth period. Unfortunately, severe criticism of these camps by host communities caused both state park projects to close in mid-June, stalling development of recreation facilities and also killing important local sources of depression cash. Yet after a nationwide realignment of camp enrollments ordered in July by CCC director Robert Fechner, and simultaneous introduction of more new companies during his expansion program, Texas gained a large number of camps as the new federal fiscal year began on 1 July. "The high-water mark in the growth of the CCC" nationwide, recalled NPS official Wirth, "was reached with a total of 2,916 camps on June 30, 1935." As CCC recruitment proceeded in earnest, several new Texas park projects received two-hundred-man companies in midperiod, during July at Cleburne, Garner, Lockhart, and Lubbock, and in August at Daingerfield, Dallas, Goliad, and Tyler.

Former "Drought State Parks" at Balmorhea, Big Bend, Big Spring, and Hereford received regular budgets and "SP" designations, but not because of any decline in the national Dust Bowl crisis. In the spring of 1935 federal drought-relief strategy shifted dramatically to the Prairie States Forestry Project, a combined effort of the U.S. Forest Service and the Soil Conservation Service to create natural windbreaks throughout affected states.[52]

For the State Parks Board, events during the spring and summer of 1935 spotlighted many of the parklands identified in the earliest attempts to create a park system. As CCC work in the fifth period began, Mother Neff State Park enjoyed the full complement of Co. 817 as its side camps returned from Mineral Wells and Meridian. The state parks at Caddo Lake and Big Spring, also proposed in the 1920s, moved forward with CCC development during the fifth period. And Palo Duro Canyon development continued two companies strong, even though the national realignment of segregated CCC units caused its two Veterans camps to be replaced in midperiod by two new "Colored Junior" companies.

On 14 May 1935 the greatest booster of the Palo Duro Canyon park, Phebe Kerrick Warner, passed away. Her charter membership in the State Parks Board had expired in 1933, then her husband, Dr. William Arthur Warner, died in July 1934. These two events coincided with Phebe's curtailment of a long writing career promoting women's issues, as well as the Panhandle and its own state park. Almost eleven years before her death, on 7 April 1924, Warner wrote on newly issued parks board stationary from her home in Claude to Chairman Colp: "The people are beginning to talk Park considerable out this way, asking scores of questions and wanting to know when their turn is coming. . . . I am keeping the subject before the West Texans in about 15 papers. It seems so hard for them to believe we are planning to have a system of parks all over the State instead of just a few that one can get to." [53]

Ten years earlier, Phebe Warner had lamented in her newspaper column that no Texans attended the National Conference on State Parks in Shenandoah National Park at Skyland, Virginia. In 1935, with the group's fifteenth national conference coincidentally being held again at that location, Colp and Pat Neff set off in late June to gain knowledge for Texas. Participation by these two parks board members in the 1935 conference meant that Texas at last directed both a state park system to brag about with its peers and a healthy budget to pay for travel to such meetings.

About the time of that Shenandoah meeting, NPS officials unveiled a new, 246-page guidebook on park design, *Park Structures and Facilities,* pointing with pride to their recent accomplishments in Texas and other regions. "For some years," wrote NPS director Arno Cammerer in his foreword to the guidebook, "the National Park Service, State Park authorities and other agencies which administer natural park areas have been attaining a constantly improving technique of design."

Cammerer's staff—including Herbert Evison, who continued to nurture the NCSP—compiled an exhaustive inventory of park facilities, from rustic culverts and campfire circles to cabins and concession buildings. Inserted here and there as state-of-the-art designs, a number of architect Maier's buildings from the 1920s spotlighted his particular fondness for rough boulder foundations and heavy timber framing. Texas examples built since 1933 under Maier's influence abounded in the new book, including stone entry pylons at Caddo Lake and Lake Brownwood, trail steps at Palo Duro Canyon and Palmetto, bridges and culverts at Bastrop and Lake Corpus Christi, and picnic tables at Clifton and Lampasas. The designs of Texas state park architects guided by Maier, particularly Guy Carlander's rim-hugging Coronado Lodge at Palo Duro and Arthur Fehr's mushrooming cabins at Bastrop, received praise and prominent illustrations. [54]

Parks of a Different Nature

Two of the newly organized state park CCC companies in the spring of 1935 included a camp of white Veterans at Goliad and a unit of African American "Juniors" at Fort Parker. Prior attempts by the State Parks Board to develop parks of primarily historical interest, including Fort Parker, had been rejected for ECW projects. But with success of the Goliad and Fort Parker proposals, the NPS—which in 1933 had become steward of numerous federally owned historic landmarks—finally acknowledged that historic sites could be a suitable medium for state park development. An obvious compromise on these projects allowed CCC development of recreation facilities —now, in fact, the emphasis at Fort Parker—in association with historic building reconstructions. Also, the NPS ultimately viewed Goliad, designated a state park but under management of local park commissioners, as a metropolitan park without the natural landscape emphasis of state parks. No doubt a Congressional push for assistance with the coming Centennial celebration influenced the approval of these projects as well.

Considerable preparation at Goliad State Park preceded assignment of the CCC company there. In May the NPS reassigned architect Sam Vosper from Longhorn Cavern to serve as project superintendent at Goliad. Vosper set off immediately on an approved trip into Mexico to study examples of eighteenth-century Spanish architecture. He was accompanied by young architect Raiford Stripling and sculptor Hugo Villa, both employed by the park service, and Goliad County Judge James Arthur White. "It was suggested to The National Park Service officials," wrote the U.S. consul on 20 May from Matamoros, "that they might wish to photograph the Casa Mata (an old fort), the old chapel, and the interiors of one or two of the better-type old residence buildings at Matamoros. It was also suggested that they visit the old city of Mier, Tamaulipas, the best example in northeastern Mexico of the old Spanish-Mexican city, as no changes have taken place at Mier in several generations." The consul conveyed to Secretary of State Cordell Hull that "Superintendent Vosper informed me that La Bahia [mission] was being reconstructed and restored as a form of work relief and also because of its historical interest. The Texas Centennial is to be celebrated during 1936 and the city of Goliad . . . will be a point of interest to the thousands of visitors expected in Texas next year." [55]

Mission Tejas State Park

At the exact time Vosper and his Goliad entourage searched for authentic examples of Spanish design in Mexico, yet another mission reincarnation— based on considerably less research—rose to quick completion. Near the Houston County village of Weches, the 1928 discovery of a Spanish cannon barrel led to speculation that it marked the site of 1690 mission San Francisco de los Tejas, the first Spanish outpost in East Texas. Coincidentally, in June 1933 the Texas Forest Service stationed CCC Co. 888 in the area as camp P-58-T, to stabilize abandoned timber cuts on private land.

Then in September 1934 a group of history-conscious Texans— including Adina De Zavala and Pat Neff—dedicated two granite markers at the presumed mission site. By early 1935 the federal government had acquired most of the area's adjoining tracts along the Neches River's west bank for development as the new Davy Crockett National Forest, but in January local citizens secured a 117-acre inholding to preserve the mission site. ECW project P-58 officially ended with the national forest acquisitions, and in the spring of 1935 CCC Co. 888 prepared for a move elsewhere.

Congressman Nat Patton of Crockett and U.S. Senator Morris Sheppard pressed the U.S. Forest Service for retention of Co. 888. Patton, arguing that the camp helped offset impacts of the new 200,000-acre national forest, appealed to the chief forester: "We feel that in all justice we should have, at least, some local projects to help us counteract the burden placed on us by the removal of these lands from our tax rolls." Then some Centennial-conscious person proposed that this CCC camp could remain in Weches through the summer 1935 period and create a recreation park around the mission site. Thus in April, Co. 888 changed its status to F-16-T, a CCC camp under direct U.S. Forest Service control, and began improvements at the site, including roads, a small dam and spillway, ornamental plantings, and picnic facilities. As a centerpiece for the new park, CCC enrollees built a log chapel—complete with gabled roof and small belfry, stone fireplace, and shuttered windows—quickly dubbed a "replica" of the original Spanish mission. On 4 July 1935, during a ceremony attended by about 5,000 people including De Zavala, the Texas Forest Service accepted donation of this tract and agreed to maintain its "new State park" officially as "State Forest No. 5." Soon the site acquired an easier name for Centennial tourists: "Mission State Forest." [56]

The Anatomy of Patronage

Another Washington politician carefully denied arranging a CCC company for park development near his hometown, but no one seemed surprised by—nor objected to—the new camp for Garner State Park. Former Uvalde County Judge C. P. Spangler later told the story that "the 'County Fathers' had long recognized the need for such a vacation spot and the scenic wonderland which [the north] part of the county afforded." Ironically the earliest efforts of Colp and Neff had secured a 26.5-acre site in this area when "Mayhew State Park" on the "Alto Frio" River became one of the first park donations in 1924 and one of those accepted by the state in 1927. But in early 1933, on the eve of federal park assistance in Texas, the Mayhew donors wanted their land back and legislators granted that wish. That same year, Judge Spangler claimed, with news of ECW projects and state park development—and no doubt an appreciation of John Nance Garner's leverage as vice president—his commissioners court and others "picked their spot and . . . bargained with Fritz Streib to purchase 478 acres of his ranch land at $12 per acre," on the Frio River.

Spangler unfolded his tale, as he later recounted to Mrs. John H. Burns, of a subsequent "informal call he made on V.P. Garner who happened to be at his home on North Park St." in Uvalde. "I found him and Mrs. Garner in their back yard. I explained what the Court had in mind and told him directly that we wanted some federal money to carry out our plan," Spangler remembered.

"His answer was 'No, No! As long as I am in Washington no such funds will be spent in Uvalde County'," the story continued. Mrs. Garner, well known as the vice president's career-long office manager in Washington, then interrupted, countering, "'But the Judge says the people of the county want and need such a park. I think they should have it.' Then, turning to me, she said, 'Judge Spangler, go ahead and put in your application for the necessary funds. I will personally see to it'."

Spangler did not offer the exact date of his deal with Mariette Elizabeth Rheiner Garner, but CCC Co. 879 arrived on 21 July 1935 from Davis Mountains State Park at its new Frio River camp.[57]

Public Works and the Second New Deal

Congress had convened in early 1935 largely to support President Roosevelt and his New Deal, but also to review his report cards after two years of relief experiments. With 20 percent unemployment lingering into spring, members of Congress as well as FDR's consultants divided into fierce debates on the best approaches to stimulate jobs and rebuild the nation's public services. Ideological battle lines appeared between Harold Ickes's approach to systematic planning through large-scale public works and Harry Hopkins's proven approach to quick relief through small but labor-intensive projects.

Roosevelt, in a typical compromise favoring the approaches of both Ickes and Hopkins, asked Congress for authority to extend and create more agencies for conquering the lingering depression. As part of a $4.8 billion plan to create 3.5 million jobs, the president enlarged Ickes's Public Works Administration (PWA) and expanded enrollment in the widely supported CCC to 600,000 in 2,916 potential camps nationwide through the next two years.[58]

Bending to Harry Hopkins's insistence on a public works program that provided short-term jobs everywhere, Roosevelt on 6 May 1935 created the Works Progress Administration (WPA). Strangely named but strikingly similar to previous winter relief programs, WPA received for the coming fiscal year $1.26 billion of the new federal funds. Eventually with substantial funding in place for their rival programs, Ickes and Hopkins agreed to separate project applications by cost, with construction projects exceeding $25,000 assigned to PWA.

By comparison to the ECW program, the CCC could construct no buildings with material costs of more than $1,000. In further contrasts to the CCC's six-month recruitment of single young men (or any war veterans) for a minimum $30 a month, WPA aimed its employment at heads of households, for as long as the worker could not find private employment. Moreover, the CCC remained a remote encampment experience for its enrollees, while WPA workers reported to day jobs near their homes and earned $60 to $100 per month.[59]

Since the CCC had proved itself so popular for the fortifying of young men, first-lady Eleanor Roosevelt suggested a modified program to include young women. The president listened to warnings of government stepping too far into creation of youth policies, but he also paid attention to statistics that showed a 30 percent unemployment rate for young Americans between the ages of sixteen and twenty-four. Thus, to the growing list of New Deal bureaus, on 26 June 1935 FDR added an agency to employ students— female and male—already in school, and to further train graduates who could not find jobs. The resulting National Youth Administration (NYA) received start-up funding from the WPA.[60]

Clamoring for the job of NYA state director in Texas, twenty-seven-year-old Lyndon Baines Johnson—just ejected from his job as secretary to Congressman Richard Kleberg—envisioned his next career move. Such a "Federal directorship of a state-wide agency," writes LBJ biographer Robert Dallek, "was perfect for a politically ambitious young man whose goal was to represent Texas in Washington." Johnson "approached the job with ferocious energy," summarizes Dallek, and quickly arranged a contract with the Texas Highway Department to employ some 15,000 youths on its two-year-old road beautification program.

This arrangement led in mid-1935 to NYA construction of hundreds of roadside parks across the state to accommodate automobile tourists during the 1936 Centennial celebration and after. One of these sites, composed of fifty acres in Crosby County on the upper Brazos River, originated as Crosbyton State Park, accepted in 1927. This donated land now transferred from the State Parks Board to the highway department in roundabout fulfillment of its original purpose as a motorist wayside. That summer as NYA workers proved their skills in creating outdoor picnic areas, and as WPA laborers assumed those ideal labor-intensive jobs in parks and playgrounds, two more New Deal relief agencies entered the arena of park development, just one step short—for now—of state park work.[61]

Texas Inspires Segregation of Entire CCC

While expansion of the CCC in early 1935 opened more positions for African American enrollees, their placement inspired a number of problems and unfortunate resolutions. Prior to 1935, CCC units in Texas and the Eighth Corps Area—where the Army determined camp rosters—consisted of many "mixed" race companies, each fielding up to thirty black enrollees. ECW director Fechner claimed in mid-1935, however, in a letter to Texas Governor Allred that such integration "was done without my knowledge or consent in the early months of this work, but I corrected it as quickly as possible, after it came to my attention." Yet not until 1 April 1935 with the CCC expansion program did segregated camps of all-black units appear in Texas. And two existing companies, 1801 and 1823(V), ended the fourth period in March as "mixed" camps but entered the fifth period as "Colored" camps after exchanging all their white members for black enrollees.

Responses of local communities to "Colored" CCC camps assigned to nearby projects revealed differing attitudes in Texas toward African Americans, some tolerant and others downright mean. Groesbeck and Mexia expressed satisfaction over Co. 3807(C)'s assignment to Limestone County's Fort Parker project. But Congressman Tom Blanton, who had managed to retain former Abilene Co. 1823(V) in his district with a new assignment at Lake Sweetwater, fumed over conversion of this "mixed" war-veterans company to an all-black camp. Claiming to convey the alarm of his Sweetwater constituents, Blanton complained loudly to Fechner, Vice President Garner, and Governor Allred about the change. Officials in Rockport (population 1,140), where nearby Goose Island's Co. 1801 became an all-black camp after 1 April, reacted to the change with even more hateful rejection. "We do most respectfully request and demand," Aransas County Judge B. S. Fox telegraphed Governor Allred on 29 April, "early removal this colored outfit[;] . . . civic and commercial reasons demand early action[;] on or before June first would satisfy." [62]

Allred's role in the controversy evolved from a new federal strategy of deferring to state officials for assignments of African American CCC camps. "Since the day-to-day struggle to place Negro companies devolved principally on the Army," military historian Charles Johnson summarizes, "the War Department (with Fechner's cooperation), applied pressure on state Governors to designate possible locations if attempts to persuade community leaders failed." Allred "preferred to remain entirely neutral in this matter," explained none other than State Parks Board chairman Colp on 13 June to Vice President Garner. CCC director Fechner, summoned on 14 June to Garner's office in Washington, described Allred's participation differently, telling the vice president, "I am glad to state that every Governor has been glad to . . . give us cooperation . . . except the Governor of Texas."

In fact, Allred's secretary had assured Aransas County Judge Fox in early May that "the Governor is doing everything in his power to get this camp removed." Garner's immediate intervention assured swift resolution, for on 15 June 1935 CCC Co. 1801(C) struck camp at Goose Island State Park and retreated to Fort Sam Houston at San Antonio. "[W]e do not endeavor to force any community to accept a Civilian Conservation Corps company against its will," Fechner explained a few days later to Allred. "However, we have to find a location for these negro companies and failing to work out the problem in a satisfactory manner . . . the War Department has always expressed its willingness to accept a negro company and place it on an Army reservation. Where this is done it means, of course, that the state loses an approved Civilian Conservation Corps camp."

Thus the promising Goose Island project halted abruptly, and Texas park planners lost one of their hard-won state-park CCC camps. The Lake Sweetwater project also closed upon removal of Co. 1823(CV), but fortunately this single company in Texas of black war veterans moved back to Abilene State Park to work the fifth-period balance.

Ironically, both Colp and Allred had suggested to Fechner the retention of mixed camps as a compromise to the new all-black companies introduced early in the year. Unfortunately, the Texans' inadvertent advertisement of such camps already thriving in Texas pushed Fechner over the edge of his separationist philosophy. "It is astonishing to me," Fechner railed at Allred in early July, "that . . . Mr Colp would suggest that white and colored Texas boys be enrolled in the same Civilian Conservation Corps company and domiciled in the same [CCC] camp." Fechner clarified his new policy: "Every negro enrollee in Texas is a Texas negro. No out of state negroes are sent into Texas and in conformity with that practice no Texas negroes will be sent to any other state." Further, all CCC companies in all states henceforth would be segregated as either "White" or "Colored," and necessary reassignments took place immediately.[63]

The great shuffle of enrollees between Texas CCC camps occurred during July and August, moving any black enrollees from mixed-race camps to segregated all-black companies. At Palo Duro Canyon where until reassignment in April some sixty black veterans had worked successfully in two mixed camps, park officials replaced the remaining white veterans with two new Junior Colored companies. Suddenly "a caravan of white-robed Ku Klux Klan members," relates historian Petersen, "visited Canyon [City] and paraded around the square in their cars." Evidently during the CCC racial realignments no park authorities calculated that Major E. A. Kingsley, Palo Duro project supervisor since January 1934, had been an avowed and enthusiastic KKK participant in the 1920s![64]

Fechner's sweeping policy not only invited such indignities, but also condoned the heretofore unofficial African American enrollment at less than 10 percent of the total CCC. This now meant absolutely no expansion of black enrollment: new enrollees would be accepted only to replace departing enrollees. The policy not only defied the Congressional non-discrimination document creating the CCC, it stonewalled the Labor Department's valiant attempts to increase African American enrollment through state and county recruitment agencies. With depression unemployment for blacks in Texas cities at more than 35 percent, and likewise much higher than whites in rural areas, Fechner's "foggy logic," as military historian Johnson describes it, proved considerably more tragic than expedient. President Roosevelt backed away from the controversy, calling it "political dynamite," and quietly approved Fechner's policy.[65]

Perhaps the greater tragedy by 1935, with black employment statistically at 65 percent, resulted from a failure of the State Parks Board to address outdoor recreation for African American Texans. No state parks and apparently none of the New Deal urban parks provided even "separate but equal" facilities for black citizens and, ironically, parks under construction by "Colored" CCC camps—such as Palo Duro Canyon, Fort Parker, and Kerrville—were off limits to local black citizens. As the Texas governor and sponsoring agencies failed to find enough communities that would accept African American camps, by summer fully four 200-man Colored CCC companies lapsed their enrollment periods inside Texas Army posts, unavailable to the Texas park system or for other conservation tasks elsewhere in the state.[66]

Preparing for the Centennial Year

By October Texas public officials focused on the coming Centennial celebration, to be launched early in 1936 and highlighted in the summer by a "Central Exposition" at Dallas. At the second called session of the legislature, members instructed the highway department to complete the Davis Mountains State Park Highway through use of any federal unemployment program available. "It is highly important that the thousands of Centennial visitors from other states," they explained, "shall have the opportunity of visiting and inspecting this great Texas Mountain Area."[67]

Centennial officials also announced plans from their $6 million jackpot for impressive monuments and public buildings at all the state's "historical" parks. In addition a $10,000 Centennial allocation would bring the wooden stockade of 1834 Fort Parker to life, supposedly on its original site, with CCC assistance from nearby Fort Parker State Park.[68] Centennial fever had already prompted reconstruction of eighteenth-century Spanish mission Espiritu Santo at Goliad State Park, but this enormous undertaking by CCC Co. 3822(V) projected well beyond the coming year. With separate initiatives at Fort Parker, Goliad, and Mission Tejas, the State Parks Board and the CCC still played only a small role in Centennial support. Yet all new recreation parks joined ambitious highway revitalization efforts, including NYA work on roadside parks, to prepare visitor accommodations for the coming tourist boom.

TABLE 6

State Parks of the Sixth-Period ECW

October 1935–March 1936

NPS Number	Official Name	CCC Company
SP-14	Palo Duro Canyon State Park	Co. 2875(C)
SP-16	,, ,, ,, ,, ,,	Co. 2876(C)[1]
SP-18	Bonham State Park	Co. 894
SP-21	Bastrop-Buescher State Park	Co. 1805
SP-22	,, ,, ,, ,,	Co. 1811
SP-31	Lake Worth Metropolitan Park	Co. 1816
SP-32	Lake Corpus Christi State Park	Co. 886
SP-33	Big Bend State Park	Co. 1855
SP-35	Longhorn Cavern State Park	Co. 854
SP-36	Brownwood State Park	Side Camp[2]
SP-38	Mother Neff State Park	Co. 817
SP-40	Caddo Lake State Park	Side Camp[3]
SP-41	Lake Sweetwater Metropolitan Park	Co. 1857
SP-42	Garner State Park	Co. 879
SP-43	Goliad State Park	Co. 3822(V)
SP-44	Fort Parker State Park	Co. 3807(C)
SP-46	Hereford State Park	Co. 872[4]
SP-47	Balmorhea State Park	Co. 1856
SP-49	Daingerfield State Park	Co. 2891
SP-50	Tyrrell Metropolitan Park	Co. 845
SP-51	Lockhart State Park	Co. 3803
SP-52	Mackenzie State Park	Co. 3820(V)
SP-53	Cleburne State Park	Co. 3804[2]
SP-54	Tyler State Park	Co. 2888
SP-55	Bachman–White Rock Lake Metropolitan Park	Co. 2896
SP-56	Paris State Park	Co. 857[3]
SP-58	Kerrville State Park	Co. 1823(CV)[2]

[1] Co. 2876(C) shipped out on 12 January 1936, leaving 2875(C) as the single CCC unit at Palo Duro Canyon.

[2] Upon departure of Co. 872 for Hereford, a 40-man side camp from Co. 3804 at Cleburne occupied the Lake Brownwood barracks between 1 November and 5 December; later in this period a side camp from Co. 1823(CV) at Kerrville installed an electric power plant and wiring at Brownwood.

[3] Co. 857 retained a 30-man side camp at Caddo through 6 March 1936, to convert the army barracks to park visitor accommodations, as envisioned in their original design.

[4] Hereford State Park's newly assigned Co. 872, replacing depleted Veteran Co. 1862, worked only from 2 November to 11 December 1935, then moved to New Mexico.

President Roosevelt's authorized doubling of CCC enrollment to 600,000 never reached its goal, and for the sixth period he capped the organization's strength at 500,000. As a result, ECW technical agencies lost some camps and could not occupy many approved assignments for new ones. Texas recreation parks retained a total of twenty-five CCC companies after 1 October 1935, losing two camps from the previous period. And recreation work at "Mission State Forest" near Weches ended as the U.S. Forest Service and the Army disbanded both camp F-16 and Co. 888.[69] As if to balance this particular loss, however, seasoned foresters of Co. 845 moved from Kirbyville to Beaumont, to begin work on that city's Tyrrell Metropolitan Park.

Work continued in the fall at Hereford State Park after disbanding of Co. 1863(V), but its new Co. 872, White Juniors fresh from substantial work at Brownwood State Park, remained little more than a month before abandoning the Hereford project. Also, the Palmetto project shut down on 28 October pending further land acquisitions within the proposed park boundary. Palo Duro Canyon lost one CCC company in midperiod, probably due to reenlistment problems at this remote assignment for young African Americans. Lake Abilene State Park halted development once again, as its Co. 1823(CV) moved to Kerrville to begin one of two new state parks for the period. The other new site, at the municipal reservoirs of Lake Crook and Lake Gibbons northwest of Paris, hosted a majority of Co. 857, which left a side camp at Karnack to continue work on Caddo Lake. The State Parks Board could not reactivate Goose Island in the fifth or sixth periods, but in July Colp accepted the completed "Indian Village" at Davis Mountains. In October he received a complete park at Big Spring, as its Co. 1857 moved to occupy the barracks at Lake Sweetwater Metropolitan Park.

Changes in Command

Adding to the autumn confusion of CCC enrollment cutbacks and the disrupting shuttle of CCC companies, Governor Allred decided at the same time to shake up the State Parks Board. The second full six-year term for Chairman Colp ended in October, whereupon his friends and associates, including board members Pat Neff and Tom Beauchamp—whose first six-year term also expired—lobbied the governor to reappoint Colp to a third term. On 12 October, however, Beauchamp passed to Colp the ominous news that a contact in the governor's office signaled Allred's doubts about Colp. "[H]e said that without being able to know why he has the impression," Beauchamp relayed, "it is in his mind that the Governor had intended to make some other appointment."

Then on the heels of more rumors predicting Colp's exit, the state auditor released a bombshell report to the governor, accusing Colp of "careless and reckless spending." On 4 November, the audit outlined how Colp had exhausted the 1934–1935 deficiency appropriation early in 1935, then had continued to approve purchases by the State Parks Board. "He advised me," the auditor told Allred of his interviews with Colp, "that on February 3, 1935, he asked you for additional appropriation and you told him at that time you could not give him a deficiency appropriation while the Legislature was in session." By then, the auditor revealed dramatically, Colp "had already spent $3,701.00 in excess of his appropriation."[70]

The technical accuracy of this report certainly exposed Colp's lax method of business: a seat-of-the-pants management style based on verbal promises and handshakes. The auditor neglected to explain, however, that before the end of February the legislature and Governor Allred had not only covered the original deficiency funds, but provided the State Parks Board immediate access to a handsome budget for the remainder of the fiscal year. Nevertheless this financial criticism provided an excuse Allred evidently sought, and on 14 November he reappointed Beauchamp but named Brownwood newspaper publisher Wendell W. Mayes to fill the appointment Colp had held for twelve years. Moreover, Allred sought to place his new candidate in the specific role Colp had dominated since 1923, naming Mayes chairman of the State Parks Board to boot.

In response the parks board met on 26 November at its Walton Building office in Austin, and vice chairman Neff launched the counterattack. First the board agreed to offer Colp a paid position managing the state park system full time, with the title "general director of the park work." Then, evidently with no offense to their new colleague—everyone seemed to like Mayes—the entire board encouraged NPS inspector George Nason to ask the Texas attorney general for an opinion on who should be addressed as chairman.[71]

Colp did not answer the job offer with immediate acceptance, but letters of support for him quickly poured into the parks board office. "The change in your position came to our people like a clap of thunder out of a clear sky," declared Cleburne's chamber of commerce manager on 27 November. "We all know that even as late as 1933," Palo Duro Canyon State Park superintendent Louis Bryan offered on the 29th, "the Parks Board was being kept alive by you when its total assets were probably nothing more than some mimeographed letterheads and no money with which to buy." Similar letters came from virtually all the active state park project managers and from officials of their host communities. Only Abilene and Lampasas, whose park development expectations exceeded the scope of recent CCC work for their communities, maligned Colp's record.

Editorials in the Brownsville, Canyon, and Temple newspapers expressed acceptance of Mayes but also hope that Colp would assume the park system management position. "Mr. Mayes is editor of County Progress, the official publication of the County Judges and Commissioners' Association of Texas," long-time Cameron County Judge Oscar Dancy wrote Pat Neff with the same divided emotions, "and we all think the world of him. But I was dumbfounded that Jim [Allred] would kick Mr. Colp out. I really think it is outrageous. Nobody knows any better than you and I what Mr. Colp has done for State parks, and he ought to have had the office just as long as he lived and wanted it."[72]

Attorney General William C. McCraw issued his opinion on 13 December, ruling that "Governor Allred was without authority to appoint a chairman of the state parks board," newspapers declared. The attorney general added, according to the parks board's 15 December press release, "that the board had not 'organized' and elected a chairman since the retirement of D. E. Colp." The initial press statement also explained McCraw's interim solution to leadership on the State Parks Board. Until its members could "organize" in early 1936, "[t]he ruling advanced former Governor Pat M. Neff of Waco, vice chairman, to the chairmanship vacated by Mr. D. E. Colp of San Antonio." Twelve years after Neff as governor created the Texas parks board, he now assumed direct control of its destiny.[73]

PARKS AND LIFE IN THE CCC

Encampments for CCC barracks conveyed all the order and discipline of military life. On Mothers Day, 12 May 1935, a crowd of ten thousand gathered at Mother Neff State Park for open house and Pat Neff's usual program of rousing oratory. *The Texas Collection, Baylor University, Waco, Texas.*

The progressive forty-hour work week observed by CCC units left time for camp commanders to encourage off-hours refinements. Near Lake Corpus Christi State Park, enrollees put their ironwork and landscaping skills to good use. *National Park Service, National Archives.*

Three square meals a day greeted CCC enrollees, even if cooks prepared sandwiches for lunch on work projects. For Thanksgiving dinner 1933, these young men at Lampasas State Park enjoyed an extra ration of fresh apples. *Don Brice Collection, Archives & Information Services Division, Texas State Library.*

In July 1934 Pat Neff (standing at right) and fellow parks board members journeyed deep into the Trans-Pecos to visit the new Big Bend State Park CCC tent camp, established in the Chisos Mountains basin by companies 896 and 1855. *Don Brice Collection, Archives & Information Services Division, Texas State Library.*

Automobiles would carry all visitors into the new Big Bend State Park, so its Green Gulch Road became an impressive necessity with stone-arch culverts built by members of CCC Co. 1855, including enrollee Don Brice (in jaunty hat). *Don Brice Collection, Archives & Information Services Division, Texas State Library.*

Above: Each CCC enrollee sent most of his $30 monthly pay to a destitute family back home. Lucky to be assigned in 1935 to Big Bend State Park (from left), Roscoe Bowers, Irwin Schmidt, O. E. Talkington, and Red Smith strike confident poses.
W. B. ("Red") Smith Collection.

Left: Bastrop State Park's lumber mill produced durable furnishings for parks across the state. Talented Bastrop carpenter "Uncle Joe" Pfeiffer worked as a Local Experienced Man and taught woodcraft in the park's CCC furniture shop.
Harpers Ferry Center, National Park Service.

Although Congress forbade discrimination in the CCC, the Army mixed Latinos and whites in border regions while assigning blacks—until segregating camps in 1935—to domestic duties, as with Co. 879 at Davis Mountains State Park. *E. O. Goldbeck photograph, Texas Parks and Wildlife Department.*

Some improvements had been made at Longhorn Cavern State Park before CCC Co. 854 arrived in 1934, but six years of hard work lay ahead, primarily removal of 2.5 million cubic yards of silt, debris, and bat manure from the cave. *National Park Service, National Archives.*

The summer 1936 Centennial Exposition at Dallas offered CCC enrollees and all their supervising agencies—including the Army, the NPS, and the State Parks Board—a rustic exhibit building and opportunity to tell their New Deal success story. *Harpers Ferry Center, National Park Service.*

Extensive revival of pioneer crafts became a hallmark of CCC work in parks, including the art of trimming shingles. Bastrop enrollees pulled drawing knives along split-cedar planks, safely braced on pine-log "horses." *National Park Service, National Archives.*

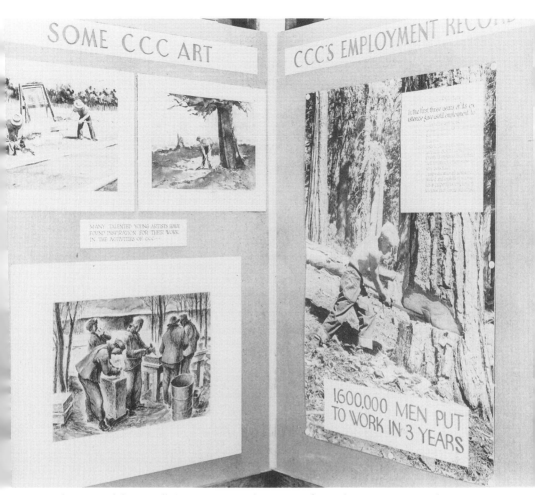

The CCC exhibit at Dallas's 1936 Centennial Exposition featured project statistics and art produced by enrollees during leisure time. These images became hallmark portraits of New Deal social and environmental landscapes. *Harpers Ferry Center, National Park Service.*

In one whirlwind day, 11 June 1936, Franklin D. Roosevelt attended ceremonies at San Jacinto State Park near Houston, at the Alamo in San Antonio, and in downtown Austin as his train halted briefly at 10:15 P.M. The president made no secret of his immediate campaign for reelection—including kind words for his "helpmate," Vice President Garner of Texas—but also lavished compliments on all Texans celebrating their Centennial. An impressive entourage of New Dealers and Texans joined FDR on his private car's rear platform: Jesse Jones, the president's chief government banker (standing left on platform); U.S. Senator Morris Sheppard, also up for reelection (on Jones's left); First Lady Eleanor Roosevelt; and Governor Jimmie Allred, also running for a second term (on Mrs. Roosevelt's left). University of Texas president Harry Y. Benedict handed FDR an electrical switch that activated a dynamite charge on campus several blocks away, commencing construction of the university's Texas Memorial Museum. *Austin History Center, Austin Public Library, #PICA 07071*

Chapter 4

1936–1938

Celebrating a Century of Progress

Texas gradually is becoming a parks state. It should have been long, long ago.
But it took a salesman like D. E. Colp to get the idea over.

Now, with the Centennial coming on, visitors to Texas are going to find
many beautiful parks in Texas to visit and enjoy.

And this state will benefit mightily from its parks development.—*Temple*
Daily Telegram, 29 November 1935 [1]

THE CENTENNIAL COMING ON

Dirt flew and dollars flowed across Texas during the winter of 1935–
1936, as the Centennial celebration singlehandedly created a multi-
million-dollar public works program for the state. The previous fall
an Advisory Board of Texas Historians, made up of James Frank Dobie, the
Rev. Paul Joseph Foik, and Louis Wiltz Kemp—an energetic good-roads
advocate and old friend of D. E. Colp—approved hundreds of applications
for Centennial projects. Wielding some $775,000 of special state and federal
funds, this advisory board recommended an ambitious statewide historical
marker program plus a number of museum projects, including monumental
buildings and commemoratives on state-owned lands at Fannin, Goliad,
Gonzales, and Washington state parks.

Combined state and federal Centennial projects also enabled reconstructions and restorations of a number of historic buildings on lands of
various ownerships throughout Texas. Old forts reemerged at Fort Parker
under State Parks Board direction and under local committees at Bonham
(Fort Inglish), Jacksboro (Fort Richardson), Menard (Presidio San Saba),
Nacogdoches (Old Stone Fort), Newcastle (Fort Belknap), and San Angelo
(Fort Concho). Federal depression-relief programs not only continued restoration of the church at Mission San Jose in San Antonio, but removed a

recent highway intrusion from its adjacent compound and reconstructed the serenity of its walled courtyard.

Meanwhile Centennial-induced construction swelled a new complex of buildings at the old Dallas state fairgrounds, where in June the 1936 world's fair would introduce Texas to its neighbors. All these projects and many others, such as substantial improvements at the Alamo and San Jacinto, enjoyed a total budget of more than $6 million provided by Congress and the state legislature. Texas Centennial undertakings received still more federal support from the Civilian Conservation Corps (CCC) and Public Works Administration (PWA), plus the new Works Progress Administration (WPA) and National Youth Administration (NYA).[2]

An equivalent construction boom in 1936 upon most lands managed by the State Parks Board demonstrated how public-works opportunities of the New Deal distributed federal resources far and wide. "Exact figures are not available," analyzed state parks engineer Bob Whiteaker in early January, "but an approximation of expenditures [from June 1933] up to December 31, 1935, on our Park System, shows the State of Texas has been out about $40,000.00 and the Federal Government $7,759,120.00, for construction and equipping of the several Parks involved." Currently, Whiteaker continued, "we have 18 CCC Camps engaged in building a like number of Parks, with 176 Federal employees in charge of the work, all of whom are under the direction of this office. The State is maintaining a force of Eighteen (18) employees at this date, and in addition, there are seven (7) Inspectors of the National Park Service assigned to the Texas Program."

Whiteaker described to his board membership a far-flung system of complete parks, idle for the winter but most under concession contracts for summer operations, 1 May through 30 September. The state park system ready for Centennial tourists consisted of Abilene, Blanco, Brownwood, Clifton, Hereford, Lampasas, Meridian, Mineral Wells, Palisades, and Stephenville. State parks boasting almost completed facilities included Big Spring, Caddo Lake, Davis Mountains, Goose Island, Loy (Grayson County), and Palmetto. Whiteaker noted that major construction projects continued under Emergency Conservation Work (ECW) sponsorship with CCC camps at Balmorhea, Bastrop and Buescher, Big Bend, Bonham, Cleburne, Daingerfield, Fort Parker, Garner, Kerrville, Lake Corpus Christi, Lockhart, Longhorn Cavern, Mackenzie, Mother Neff, Palo Duro Canyon, Paris, and Tyler. The State Parks Board planned additional applications for CCC development of thirteen more sites.

Several WPA projects already had been approved to supplement CCC work in state parks, Whiteaker reported, and more WPA applications awaited endorsement. Swimming pools no longer allowed by federal park planners, for example, instead could be added to state park facilities with WPA labor. Golf course proposals prompted similar rejections from federal authorities, but fairways could be built inside state parks through WPA assistance. Bastrop State Park managers already directed WPA workers on both a nine-hole golf course and a 75-by-160-foot swimming pool project, and Whiteaker hoped to build similar concrete reservoirs at Caddo Lake, Hereford, and Palo Duro Canyon. A new WPA-sponsored water and sewer system at Bastrop likewise would serve as a model for other parks with overnight cabins and dining facilities.[3]

Death of a Salesman

Following expiration in November 1935 of his twelve-year service on the State Parks Board, David Edward Colp faced what his friends considered a crisis of enormous proportions. Would he fight accusations of failed promises for park development and, worse, charges of "careless and reckless spending" by the state auditor? Would he accept a paid position with the parks board? Would he quit park work altogether?

No one—least of all sixty-nine-year-old Colp—seemed to consider retirement for this self-styled public servant. Sure enough, with optimism and determination to begin the next phase of his busy life, he had accepted by late December the position of Bexar County park superintendent in his longtime home of San Antonio. He agreed to continue consultation with the State Parks Board as well, a fortunate concession for its members and staff because much of its institutional history, including details of land acquisitions, existed only in Colp's memory.

On 30 December 1935 in his capacity as state parks consultant, Colp drove to Bastrop State Park to review its progress and to visit his young friend and park architect Arthur Fehr. While at the park Colp collapsed with influenza symptoms, and the CCC camp doctor placed him in the new park-keeper's lodge for observation. The next day CCC enrollees drove Colp to Scott and White Hospital in Temple, agreeing to a detour stop at the State Parks Board office. "The ambulance just passed through Austin enroute to Temple," state parks engineer Whiteaker wrote to Pat Neff after a curbside visit with Colp. "While he is[,] as usual, most cheerful and unwilling to admit there is anything wrong, I am afraid he will be in the hospital for sometime."

Even from his infirmary room in Temple, Colp remained obsessed with state park business, writing Whiteaker on 1 January "to push W.P.A. projects." His wife Ada dutifully penciled this dictation, but added a note of her own: "Well, the Dr's say . . . . he must absolutely rest, from any annoyance or worry. Of course he is a sick man, but does *not* know it." That day Colp developed "double pneumonia," and henceforth issued no more orders to the Texas state parks staff. On Sunday, 12 January 1936, Arthur Fehr noted in his daybook simply: "Mr. Colp died this morning at 2 a.m."

The next day the commanding general of the Army's Eighth Corps Area at Fort Sam Houston ordered flags "flown at half-mast Monday from noon to sunset in all CCC camps in State parks." State Parks Board workers, on signal from Acting Chairman Neff, closed their Austin office and traveled to San Antonio for Colp's funeral. "Texas has lost a great citizen," Neff eulogized to the crowd that "overflowed a local mortuary," as reported by Colp's frequent critic, the *Dallas News*. Neff recalled that he and Colp had driven twenty thousand miles together, most during Neff's second term as governor, 1923 through 1925, after he appointed Colp to the new State Parks Board. Brought together again in 1933 to direct federal assistance in Texas parks, Neff and Colp at last witnessed their dream of a state-supported "chain of parks" come true. "I know of no one man," Neff concluded, "who has done more to contribute to the lasting happiness of future generations by his work for better roads and parks."

Condolences from across the state and nation soon arrived at both the parks board office in Austin and Ada Colp's residence in San Antonio. "The news was very depressing," wrote NPS assistant director Conrad Wirth, "to all of us in Washington who knew and worked with Mr. Colp." Federal inspector George Nason, with whom Colp frequently disagreed on park development policy, reported that "Colp's never defeated optimism is irreplaceable. The great good that he did in making Texas park-conscious will last for centuries." Cameron County Judge Oscar Dancy, Colp's good-roads protégé, called him a "combination older brother and father to me. . . . I say that he has done more for Texas than the overwhelming majority of its governors, and should have a place in Texas' written history. I hope he does."

An aging good-roads compadre, Hugh Odle of Meridian, penned a memorial in the local newspaper about losing "one of my best friends and Texas one of its best citizens." Odle compared Dave Colp to Will Rogers, whose death the previous August stunned a world that relied upon Rogers's piercing assessments, on radio and in the newspapers, of politics and the depression. "We all loved Will Rogers," Odle related, "because he was true, honest and gave his time freely for the uplift of humanity, and likewise, all who knew D. E. Colp loved him because no better and truer man ever lived. Rogers was to the Red Cross [his favorite humanitarian cause] like Colp was to our State Parks. We shall never forget him for his good deeds, and the result of his very successful career will live forever as a monument to his memory."[4]

The Turn of a New Leaf

The day after Colp's funeral in San Antonio, Neff called attending board members Wendell Mayes and Gus Urbantke into "active session" at Austin. The board and assembled staff observed appropriate ritual for their departed leader, then Neff moved quickly to the realization that Colp had departed with a startling degree of knowledge about the Texas state park system. "Mr. Colp, having been from the creation of the Board, in charge of the entire organization as to the development of the Parks and Superintendency of them," Neff revealed, "left at his death, the Parks Board unfamiliar with the detailed work of the Organization." The board asked state parks engineer Bob Whiteaker to assume "general supervision of the Parks Board organization, until the next meeting of the Board," and to prepare an extensive report on the state of the Texas park system.[5]

Whiteaker's report, mailed to State Parks Board members on 18 January, provided a great deal of information and revelations on sixty-one "separate park areas, aggregating 329,024 acres." The assessment confirmed the unkempt nature of Colp's business, particularly with land titles. In Colp's files Whiteaker stumbled across papers labeled as deeds for parklands ranging from the first donations of 1924, such as Beeville, to the most recent acquisitions, such as Brownwood, but found no legal recording of these land transfers. Eleven of the various "small parks" accepted by the legislature in 1927 "were said by Mr. Colp, to belong to the State, but only on one of them," 69-acre Robinson State Park in Llano County, Whiteaker continued, "is there a record of ownership available."

To his credit, Colp had arranged numerous concession agreements at completed parks built since 1933 by the NPS and the CCC. These agreements—granting a percentage of entry-fees, rentals and other sales within the park to either private managers or city and county governments—guaranteed operation of Blanco, Clifton, Lampasas, and Mineral Wells state parks. The Panhandle Advisory Committee, made up of local officials, had arranged to operate Hereford, Palisades, and Palo Duro Canyon parks, but with an undetermined percentage of receipts paid to the state. The concession contract at Lampasas would expire in February, and Meridian State Park apparently functioned under verbal agreement between Colp and his friend Hugh Odle. Complete parks stood ready for visitors at Abilene and Stephenville but no operators had been identified.[6]

State Parks Board members returned on 25 January for an organizational meeting in Austin. Neff's clearheaded leadership, and manifest devotion to the organization's mission, made him the obvious choice for chairman. Mayes, deprived in November of Governor Allred's appointment as chair, dutifully accepted the vice chairmanship. Urbantke, as the resident Austin member, continued as secretary of the board. Katie Welder, now the only remaining original member of the board, and Tom Beauchamp pledged support for the new order.

After a discussion of the Bastrop State Park furniture shop, Neff decreed that it produce no more "stock furniture," but only custom designs as requested by "individual park Superintendents and Architects." The Bastrop shop soon received an order to build two cedar filing cabinets for board members Beauchamp and Mayes and an allocation of $500 in lumber to build cabin furniture and forty boats for rental at state park lakes.[7]

Managing a Far-Flung System

Following authorization by Congress in June 1935 of a Big Bend National Park, Washington officials pursued establishment of an international park in the Big Bend of the Rio Grande. At subsequent meetings that year in El Paso, conservation planners from the United States and Mexico explored possibilities, recalled Big Bend geologist Ross Maxwell, of "either an international park, wildlife refuge, plant reserve, or forest plantation." An international commission assembled on 17 February 1936 at Alpine and proceeded south to survey the vast river, desert, and mountain formations of the region on both sides of the Rio Grande.

The commission, joined by State Representative Everett Ewing Townsend and Big Bend State Park CCC camp officials, spent a full week exploring the charted and uncharted areas of the territory. As a result of this investigation, and growing publicity that followed progress of the CCC state park camp in the Chisos Basin, the national park idea came ever closer to reality in Texas. In a 14 March 1936 *Texas Weekly* article, author P. J. R. MacIntosh explained for adventurous readers exactly how to drive from the main highway and railhead at Alpine into the Big Bend. He advised, "[i]t is well to keep a watchful eye on the gasoline on this trip. . . . Such a [round] trip is about 250 miles in length."

With sensitivity to the value of other parks and potential acquisitions that together represented the incredible contrasts of Texas landscapes, MacIntosh further enticed his readers. He outlined current state park and highway improvements at the Davis Mountains and Palo Duro Canyon, and mentioned the "well cared for" plain of "the Battle Ground at San Jacinto." He also encouraged future park developments from Padre Island to the Guadalupe Mountains, including "beautiful McKittrick Canyon, close to the New Mexico line and not far from Carlsbad Caverns."[8]

The would-be managers of this far-flung system soon set better financial policies for the State Parks Board's Austin office and clarified various concession agreements for park operations. The board met in February and twice in March, discussing Texas Highway Department assumption of road maintenance in all the operational state parks. Members also authorized payment of $24.50 to Ada Colp for her late husband's mahogany desk, table, and two chairs in the office, and pledged to reimburse her upon discovery of any other items that Dave Colp had purchased with his own funds.[9]

Late in March, board member Beauchamp traveled to Washington, D.C., for extensive meetings with NPS officials and the Texas congressional delegation. Beauchamp encountered severely strained relations between state-park coordinator Herb Evison and the state of Texas, lingering in part from disagreements between Colp and inspector Nason, who had recently left Texas for a job at the Omaha regional office. Evison's "first criticism," Beauchamp reported on 31 March to Chairman Neff, "was that our parks presented an impossible situation; that we have too many little parks which have been taken in and improved and which the Legislature had shown no disposition to maintain."

The blame, Evison and Beauchamp agreed, fell squarely on "our Congressmen [who] are continually fighting for [CCC] camps in their district[s] without any thought of a park system." Shuttling between the offices of Evison, Texas congressmen, and Vice President Garner, Beauchamp ultimately assured federal park planners of congressional cooperation and that "we really do want a park system."

The parks board staff in the meantime prepared applications for the seventh period of ECW projects. Beauchamp and Neff pursued long-term objectives of a recreation park near Huntsville, plus acquisition and restoration of the abandoned military post at Fort Davis. For the immediate CCC period federal authorities agreed, based on Beauchamp's recent arguments, to continue development of eighteen state parks—including historic Goliad and national park–prospect Big Bend—with a total of nineteen CCC companies. Officials also authorized continued work at four "Metropolitan" parks for the cities of Beaumont, Dallas, Fort Worth, and Sweetwater.[10]

Moderate cutbacks of federal funding resulted in a reduction in number of camps per state, and Texas lost two CCC companies—Hereford and one at Palo Duro—from the total assigned previously. The biggest blow to productivity in state park development came with Conrad Wirth's announcement in early April, repeating a new order from CCC director Robert Fechner, that company strengths would be reduced from an average of 200 to 160 men each. Further, the professional staff at each camp fell from ten to six foremen and one superintendent. CCC recruitment for many reasons, including the frustrating low quotas on African American enrollees, fell short of filling the number of authorized camps nationwide.

Still, Texas recreation park applicants received most of their CCC camp

TABLE 7

State Parks of the Seventh-Period ECW

April–September 1936

NPS Number	Official Name	CCC Company
SP-14	Palo Duro Canyon State Park	Co. 2875(C)
SP-18	Bonham State Park	Co. 894
SP-21	Bastrop-Buescher State Park	Co. 1805
SP-22	” ” ” ”	Co. 1811
SP-31	Lake Worth Metropolitan Park	Co. 1816
SP-32	Lake Corpus Christi State Park	Co. 886
SP-33	Big Bend State Park	Co. 1855
SP-35	Longhorn Cavern State Park	Co. 854
SP-38	Mother Neff State Park	Co. 817
SP-41	Lake Sweetwater Metropolitan Park	Co. 1857
SP-42	Garner State Park	Co. 879
SP-43	Goliad State Park	Co. 3822(V)
SP-44	Fort Parker State Park	Co. 3807(C)
SP-47	Balmorhea State Park	Co. 1856
SP-49	Daingerfield State Park	Co. 2891
SP-50	Tyrrell Metropolitan Park	Co. 845
SP-51	Lockhart State Park	Co. 3803
SP-52	Mackenzie State Park	Co. 3820(V)
SP-53	Cleburne State Park	Co. 3804
SP-54	Tyler State Park	Co. 2888
SP-55	Bachman–White Rock Lake Metropolitan Park	Co. 2896
SP-56	Paris State Park	Co. 857[1]
SP-58	Kerrville State Park	Co. 1823(CV)

[1] Co. 857 provided 56 enrollees from 13 March through June for a side camp at Dallas to build a CCC exhibit for the Centennial Exhibition.

requests for the summer period, although no new park projects opened after 1 April. Compared to twenty-three companies in the state under NPS supervision, Texas also received twenty-seven CCC units under the U.S. Forest Service and thirty-two camps directed by the Soil Conservation Service.

As the state park system opened on 1 May, Centennial-year visitors found signs posted with "Rules and Regulations" issued personally by State Parks Board chairman Neff. "Picking of wild flowers," the rules warned, "is positively prohibited," along with defacing "any building, fixture, tree or other park feature." In June, Neff and fellow board members Mayes and Beauchamp set off with engineer Whiteaker on a week-long visit to a dozen state parks, "from the Rio Grande to the Palo Duro Canyon," according to accounts. "We hope to visit others in the state soon," Neff told officials in

Abilene, "as well as in West Texas, where the state park idea had its first loyal support."[11]

CCC Celebrates the Centennial

While the NPS and CCC already prepared indirectly for the Texas Centennial, until the spring of 1936 their officials seemed unaware of an otherwise huge federal boost to the celebration. Awakening to the fact that federal support equaled federal politics, federal park developers finally agreed to offer direct promotion of the Centennial in the form of educational exhibits. When University of Texas faculty in Austin prepared early in the year for a campus-wide series of Centennial exhibits on display from June through December, NPS officials approved the assistance of nearby Bastrop State Park through its furniture shop and architect Arthur Fehr. "It seems to me," university architect W. W. Dornberger appealed, "that a most interesting exhibit could be built out of and around some of the furniture which is manufactured at the mill in the Bastrop Park, and we hope that we may enlist you to cooperate toward setting up such an exhibit, stressing the utilization of native materials in true Texas style."

Fehr began design work by early April, and in early May, he recorded, received from his superiors an "OK for 5 boys to sleep and eat at University during construction of exhibit." Inside huge Gregory Gymnasium these CCC enrollees, directed by Fehr and master carpenter Joe Pfeiffer, constructed a half section of a "typical pioneer home, built as the early settlers of Texas had to build their homes," according to a university press release.[12]

Fehr and his Bastrop wood mill meanwhile assisted a more ambitious exhibit planned for the Centennial's mammoth central exposition at Dallas, also to run from June through December 1936. "A recreational area in a forest of Texas trees, containing two permanent buildings," an April news release announced, "will feature the Centennial Exposition exhibit . . . of the National Park Service and the Texas State Parks Board." Assigned a generous lot at the south corner of the world's fair grounds on Fine Arts Drive, a coalition of all ECW agencies planned "a week-end cabin of the type being placed in Texas recreational areas," plus "a rustic one-story structure for the display of exhibits."

Texas State Parks Board officials solved the problem of constructing the Dallas exhibit when they agreed to dispatch a side camp from Co. 857 at Paris State Park. Federal park planners had run into trouble at Paris by proposing a facility open to all the town's citizens, including African Americans, whereupon the city council stalled development by refusing to approve the park's master plan. Determined to keep the CCC enrollees "usefully employed" as the president directed, district officer Maier ordered a third of the camp's complement, fifty-six men and superintendent Leslie Fowden

Crockett, trucked to the Dallas fairgrounds. Experienced CCC workers of Co. 857 labored from March through June and steadily assembled this impressive "quadrangle enclosing a patio," reported the CCC weekly newspaper *Happy Days,* "constructed of logs and rough lumber in attractive rustic style."

To staff the building and interpret flora displays as well as the work of the CCC, boys from camps across the state signed up for temporary duty at the Dallas exhibit, twenty-four of them at a shift. "Texas enrollees of high character, intelligent and who are good conversationalists," *Happy Days* announced in June, "are getting the rare opportunity of acting as guides at the Texas Centennial Exhibit." Visitation records at this admittedly far corner of the world's fair showed a slow start as the summer began. But when enrollees added an "Admission Free" sign to the entrance, according to *Happy Days,* "attendance jumped to more than 2000 per day." [13]

FDR Celebrates the Centennial

Journeying to Dallas to preside over the grand opening of the Centennial Exposition, President Franklin D. Roosevelt stopped along the way at a couple of Texas historic sites to amplify the celebration. Just a few weeks before on 21 April, Roosevelt's colleague and Houstonian Jesse Jones broke ground at San Jacinto with a hundred-year-old plow pulled by oxen, thus beginning construction on a long-envisioned monument to Sam Houston's decisive victory a century before on this field. On 11 June 1936 at San Jacinto State Park, FDR expressed his appreciation of the site. "There are very few spots in the United States," he dramatized, "which have witnessed events equal in significance to that which took place at San Jacinto."

FDR then warmly greeted the park's superintendent, last living child of the hero of San Jacinto, Colonel Andrew Jackson Houston. "What a magnificent combination of names that is!" the President exclaimed as he told a story of how their respective fathers encountered one another in pre-Civil War Washington, D.C. Referring to nearby fabrication of the San Jacinto obelisk, he noted that "I have seen a glimpse of the future, for I have in my office at the White House a model that Jesse Jones gave me, a model of the beautiful memorial that you are to erect here as an everlasting reminder of the bravery of Sam Houston and his men." [14]

Continuing by train the president later that day sat in front of the Alamo in San Antonio. Yet another grand Centennial project under way at Alamo Plaza, creating a park and support buildings around the old mission church and convento walls, demonstrated the exciting clamor resultant from a mixture of New Deal public works programs and the Centennial jubilee. "We are not lacking in many monuments of noble needs," FDR told Governor Jimmie Allred and a huge crowd in the downtown plaza, "but the Alamo stands out in high relief as our noblest exemplification of sacrifice, heroic and pure." [15]

Disembarking at Dallas on a second day in Texas and motoring through a jubilant crowd to the Cotton Bowl, the president keynoted the world's fair greetings to "my friends of Texas." He spoke to a packed stadium about the progressive evolution of American democracy, and complimented Texas for building a great empire based on "constructive reform." Implying that his policies had reversed the depression—without naming this lingering economic despondency—Roosevelt credited his understanding of the American continent to his travels through it. "During these past three years," he said, "with the return of confidence and the great increase in prosperity, the excellent custom of getting acquainted with the United States has asserted itself. We see a great tide of travel by rail, by plane, by ship and by automobile. We Americans are indeed seeing things at first hand. May the habit spread." [16]

Expecting the president to see the CCC exhibit first hand, Maier scrambled to finish the facility and arrange a suitable reception. "Have just been informed the President will visit Civilian Conservation Corps exhibit building," the regional director wired Dallas exposition officials a week earlier, "and company enrollees will be lined up for review." The CCC, Maier telegraphed as he demanded removal of commercial radio speakers from the exhibit's front lawn, "is in many ways favorite undertaking of President." But Roosevelt's schedule prevented even his familiar convertible back-seat drive-by, and Maier's preparations provided added excitement only for exhibit visitors, and CCC enrollees, that day.[17]

More Publicity for Texas State Parks

As anticipated by mass infusion of public funds into the statewide Centennial celebration, private investors joined this bonfire of prosperity in the middle of the depression. One interesting result of both public and private influence came in June 1936 with the debut of *Texas Parade* magazine, without apology speaking "for the motorists of Texas," especially "the 25,000 members of the Texas Good Roads Association." As "the *only* State magazine for Texas," the new publication promoted a dual agenda of public construction of highways and personal inspiration for Texas motorists in using their good roads during work and pleasure.

The first issue featured an illustrated article entitled "Texas: A State Of Beautiful Parks," spotlighting the "miraculous creation of a state parks system for Texas . . . in three depression years." Due credit appeared for the late D. E. Colp, cofounder in 1910 of the Texas Good Roads Association and longtime advocate of state parks. "From 15,000-acre Palo Duro Canyon to 35,000-acre Caddo Lake on the upper Louisiana line," the magazine bragged, "and from little Goose Island Park on the Gulf Coast at Rockport to the 5,700-acre Davis Mountain Park, a mile above sea level, facilities of astonishing beauty and appropriateness are being built." [18]

Fueling this growing publicity for the Texas State Parks Board, patrons at the NPS frequently issued press releases from their Oklahoma City regional office. A detailed statement in September proudly revealed improvements available in state parks, as well as their visitation figures from the Centennial summer. "Nearly 500,000 people, during the past three months" park officials calculated, "have taken advantage of recreation facilities in eighteen State Parks of Texas." Lubbock's Mackenzie State Park, with its large swimming pool and expansive golf course, both rare attractions for the high plains region, counted an incredible three-month record of 237,000 visitors, "ranking it as the leading State park, in point of attendance." Balmorhea State Park just north of the Davis Mountains placed second in state parks with 27,000, less than 10 percent of Mackenzie's total. But Balmorhea's huge spring-fed swimming pool, also rare in the vast Trans-Pecos region, attracted enough business to inspire "development of tourists' camps and stores, in close vicinity of the park," the press release noted.

Aware that the coming Texas legislative session would review a more aggressive land-acquisition effort for the proposed Big Bend National Park, the release covered this development thoroughly. "A trail through rugged country to the south rim of the Chisos Mountains," opened by CCC workers at the current Big Bend State Park, "has unfolded a view that is somewhat comparable to the Grand Canyon—almost straight down 5,000 feet to the Rio Grande, and over mountain ranges into the Mexican States of Chihuahua and Coahuila." Crediting a three-year cooperative effort of the park service and State Parks Board, the statement summarized that the Texas system had created "a chain of recreational areas that State officials believe will go a long way toward solving the problem of what people can do with their leisure." [19]

Enter Executive Secretary

When State Parks Board member and ambassador Tom Beauchamp visited early in 1936 with officials in Washington, D.C., he received several suggestions on running a more efficient system. "I was assured," Beauchamp reported to Neff, "that the greatest need was for us to make provision for about a $5,000.00 a year man to head our system." While Col. R. O. Whiteaker had accepted the assignment of day-to-day operations after the January death of Colp, the seasoned state parks engineer preferred a less visible profile. Now as the legislative session approached with growing budget requests and a planned push for Big Bend land purchases, the need for a salaried park system director became obvious.

At its September meeting, one day into the new state fiscal year, the board hired thirty-five-year-old William Jennings Lawson as its first executive secretary, at a part-time annual salary of $2,400. Lawson served as private secretary to State Senator John W. E. H. Beck of DeKalb, and in prior endeavors had published a weekly newspaper in Center and managed chambers of commerce in Center, Mount Pleasant, and Huntsville. Lawson either could not devote full time to the parks board or its limited budget could not pay him a full salary, but he possessed perfect credentials for the growing park system. He understood the needs of local communities, perceived the value of favorable publicity for state parks, and comprehended the inner workings of the Capitol in Austin.[20]

Lawson joined the parks board staff just in time to help put finishing touches on CCC camp applications for the eighth period beginning in October. Again, based on federal advice for the board to concentrate development on existing parks rather than enter new sites into their relatively stable CCC camp quota, the staff aimed at maintaining existing development projects with nineteen CCC companies at eighteen state parks (including Goliad, under the Board of Control) plus the established four metropolitan parks.

"Now's the time of year when picnicking in the Texas out-of-doors is at its best," announced an NPS press release urging visits to state parks, shortly after the 1 October approval of CCC camps. "There's a zip in the air that makes you feel like going places." Motoring Texans this autumn would find that Bonham and Lake Corpus Christi state parks now offered completed facilities, as their CCC companies moved respectively to Palo Duro Canyon and the reopening of Palmetto's work camp. Development at Brownwood State Park also resumed with the arrival of Co. 849 from Wyoming, shifted to Texas for the winter. Still unable to obtain approval from city authorities of the master plan for Paris State Park, officials ordered Co. 857 to resume work at Caddo State Park, 157 miles away.[21]

By the fall of 1936 extensive new facilities, just completed or under construction, attracted visitors to numerous state-owned sites commemorating the events and personalities of 1836. Federal and state appropriations for Centennial projects resulted in impressive permanent museums at the Alamo, Gonzales State Park, and the "Sam Houston Shrine" at Huntsville; public auditoriums at Goliad and Washington state parks; other improvements at Fannin State Park, the State Cemetery, and Washington; extensive restoration work at Goliad State Park and San Jose Mission; and monuments at Goliad and King's state parks, Monument Hill, and Stephen F. Austin's home at San Felipe. Construction had begun in April on the towering monument at San Jacinto State Park, which would feature a museum

TABLE 8
State Parks of the Eighth-Period ECW
October 1936–March 1937

NPS Number	Official Name	CCC Company
SP-14	Palo Duro Canyon State Park	Co. 894[1]
SP-21	Bastrop-Buescher State Park	Co. 1805
SP-22	" " " "	Co. 1811
SP-29	Palmetto State Park	Co. 886
SP-31	Lake Worth Metropolitan Park	Co. 1816
SP-33	Big Bend State Park	Co. 1855
SP-35	Longhorn Cavern State Park	Co. 854
SP-36	Brownwood State Park	Co. 849
SP-38	Mother Neff State Park	Co. 817
SP-40	Caddo Lake State Park	Co. 857[2]
SP-41	Lake Sweetwater Metropolitan Park	Co. 1857
SP-42	Garner State Park	Co. 879
SP-43	Goliad State Park	Co. 3822(V)
SP-44	Fort Parker State Park	Co. 3807(C)
SP-47	Balmorhea State Park	Co. 1856
SP-49	Daingerfield State Park	Co. 2891
SP-50	Tyrrell Metropolitan Park	Co. 845
SP-51	Lockhart State Park	Co. 3803
SP-52	Mackenzie State Park	Co. 3820[3]
SP-53	Cleburne State Park	Co. 3804
SP-54	Tyler State Park	Co. 2888
SP-55	Bachman–White Rock Lake Metropolitan Park	Co. 2896
SP-56	Paris State Park	Co. 857[2]
SP-58	Kerrville State Park	Co. 1823(CV)

[1] Co. 2857(C) apparently disbanded at the end of the seventh period, probably due to low reenlistment numbers, and was immediately replaced by Co. 894 from Bonham State Park.

[2] Co. 857, still officially assigned to Paris, moved the majority of its enrollees to resume work once again at the Caddo Lake side camp.

[3] Co. 3820(V) assigned to Mackenzie State Park converted at about this time from its complement of white war veterans to a camp of "White Junior" enrollees, likely due to declining veterans enlistment after their June 1936 "bonus" payments.

in its base, an observation deck at its 570-foot pinnacle, and sprawling improvements to the surrounding battleground landscape.[22]

The Federal Presence

The general ballot of 3 November 1936 presented for reelection Franklin D. Roosevelt and Texans John Nance Garner and U.S. Senator Morris Sheppard, in addition to Governor James V. Allred. During the preceding summer campaign at the national Democratic convention in Philadelphia, Allred had nominated Vice President Garner for reelection on the Roosevelt ticket, and Senator Tom Connally seconded nomination of the president himself. Interestingly, FDR's Republican opponent, Kansas governor Alfred Mossman Landon, "specifically endorsed the CCC," according to historian John Salmond, and "claimed credit for an amendment to the original [Emergency Conservation] bill, namely the one permitting work on state lands."

Throughout Allred's first two-year term, as historian Seth McKay summarizes, "[h]e had received the fullest recognition from the Roosevelt administration at Washington." The Texas governor thus shared the public's overwhelming approval of the New Deal in the nation and in their state. Allred and Connally encountered only marginal opposition in the summer primary, McKay continues, "and the press explained that fact by saying that business had increased, farming was at its height, and the Centennial absorbed the interests of the people." Garner and Roosevelt won reelection handily, as did Allred and Sheppard.[23]

One day after the reelection of the president, NPS director Arno Cammerer set off on a whistle-stop tour of the Southwest, with primary destinations at El Paso and Carlsbad Caverns. Cammerer's train ticket first took him straight to San Antonio, and from there his party drove on the afternoon of 6 November to Bastrop State Park. "[T]his park was favored," reported inspector Donald Obert, "by a visiting group from Washington and Oklahoma City including Director Cammerer, Regional Officer Maier, Ex-Governor Neff and other officials. All seemed impressed by activities and accomplishments in the area." Following an evening meeting in Austin on land acquisition in the Big Bend, and an overnight stay at the Driskill Hotel, Cammerer motored back to San Antonio for a train to El Paso.

There Cammerer met in conference with Mexican officials to emphasize his support for a Big Bend international park on both sides of the Rio Grande. He also "spoke in El Paso before a partisan group of representatives from Texas chambers of commerce, city and county officials," according to historian John Jameson. "Another NPS official calculated that park visitors to Big Bend," Jameson continues, "would spend at least $2,388,000 annually in the state." Cammerer assured the assembled officials that the federal government would invest several more million dollars in the future national park, "[y]et all the Texans would have to pay was approximately one and one-half million dollars," Jameson relates. Thus the NPS director revealed the price Texas legislators would be expected to pay for their long-proposed national park.[24]

Substantial attention came to state park activity in the next few weeks following Cammerer's swath through Texas. Bastrop State Park architect

Arthur Fehr recorded in late December that a park service photographer visited his site, collecting images for a design manual update. And inspectors reported that Tyler State Park architect Joe Lair "is in New York assisting on the new Park Structures book." Just before Christmas park service assistant director Wirth, in company with Evison, Maier, CCC director Fechner, and Frederick J. Morrell of the U.S. Forest Service, flew to El Paso for their entry into the Big Bend for a new inspection trip.

Wirth criticized the CCC camp's version of eggnog—made from goat milk and tequila—served at their Chisos Basin dinner, but gathered information for yet another report on Big Bend's potential. And Fechner's firsthand observation of the future national park, Wirth presumed, would ensure ECW support for continued CCC development of the area.[25]

FEDERAL RETRENCHMENT

The 1937 Legislature

To meet tightening federal guidelines, and to prepare for the coming legislative session, State Parks Board secretary Bill Lawson produced in late December his system's first "master plan." This effort coincided with the beginning of what the NPS called its Park, Parkway, and Recreational-Area Study, an attempt at central planning and direction for a nationwide program. At this early stage, Lawson's Texas contribution to the study really consisted of individual site development plans, covering 36 parks and "14 approved sites," according to his corresponding press release. Using somewhat inflated visitation figures—compared to federal counts—to contrast a meager state contribution to the park system, Lawson hoped his master plan would inspire a much larger budget in the coming biennium.[26]

Lawson's parks board and all state agencies witnessed tremendous increased demands for their many New Deal–spawned services. But all these bureaus now constituted a large crowd lining up to request budget increases from the state legislature. Highway construction boomed as automobile and truck usage continued to climb, while public schools and colleges filled beyond capacity. At the same time prisons also crowded with record numbers of inmates after recent law enforcement and pardon reforms took hold. And the state's recently approved old-age assistance program, though matched by the federal government, rapidly exceeded all funding estimates. In response Governor Allred recommended numerous new funding sources, primarily through tax increases on sulphur, petroleum products, and liquor sales.

Faced with a legislature that "did exactly nothing in the way of solving the fiscal problems of the state," says historian McKay, the State Parks Board nonetheless obtained an adequate budget. Lawson's operation received

$40,000 for each fiscal year, 1938 and 1939, which granted the executive secretary a raise to $2,750 per year and sustained his current staff and expense accounts.

Citing "some question under the present [1923] law as to the length of terms of the five (5) members heretofore constituting the State Parks Board," a new bill clarified the board's staggered six-year terms. This law also added a sixth position on the board, and as charter-member Katie Welder's appointment expired, on 18 May Governor Allred appointed two new members to guide Texas state parks: J. V. Ash, a Ford automobile dealer and Coca-Cola bottler from Bastrop, and Kennedy N. Clapp, a cotton buyer from Lubbock. With Welder's departure, no woman served on the board, and Texas women's clubs, among the earliest supporters of Texas state parks, lost their traditional representation here as well.

In other personnel matters, the State Parks Board received instructions from the legislature to "employ a keeper in each of the State Parks." These permanent employees, the bill required, "shall be clothed with all the powers and authority of a peace officer of the county, for the purposes of caring for and protecting the property within said parks." At its March meeting the board "released" its informal local and regional park commissions that formerly served as community contacts, in favor of service through the new "keeper" system. The same bill authorized the board to investigate potential parklands statewide, especially the feasibility of a "great park" and even a "National Park" in the Davis Mountains. Indeed, in early 1937 federal officials investigated the Madera Canyon area of Jeff Davis County, but for potential state park expansion, not with higher intentions.

Another act in the session returned 100-acre Lampasas State Park in April to city officials who had donated the site four years earlier. Presumably for political expediency, the bill claimed that "no improvement [had been] made thereon by the State of Texas," although the federal government sponsored more than a year's worth of substantial CCC improvements there in 1933 and 1934. The NPS, however, had encouraged the parks board, through meetings the previous year with Tom Beauchamp, to discard the state's "little parks," and Lampasas appeared on the "deed away" list they compiled together.

In contrast to their Lampasas gesture, state legislators granted a $4,500 emergency appropriation, oddly through the State Department of Agriculture, to repair the spillway at 500-acre Normangee State Park in Leon County. The town of Normangee had donated this site to the parks board after a 1933–1934 Civil Works Administration project built its municipal lake, but neither city nor state had since constructed additional recreation facilities.[27]

Lawson's real victory from the confusing legislative session came with his authority to retain "local fund receipts" from concession percentages at the recreation parks. Although the Palo Duro Canyon and Longhorn Cavern note payments absorbed most profits from those state parks, as other new parks opened and as each summer season attracted more visitors, the "special park fund" by 1937 had grown to a few thousand dollars. This cash enabled his fledgling park system to pay keepers and to buy supplies and initiate small construction jobs not subsidized by federal projects or funded by the legislature.[28]

Lipantitlan State Park

The state historical parks—Fannin, Goliad, Gonzales, King's, San Jacinto, and Washington—all had benefited during the past year, in large measure from special Centennial expenditures. To match new facilities and their greatly increased visitation, these parks overseen by the Board of Control received from the legislature substantially expanded caretaker budgets totaling $32,820 for fiscal years 1938 and 1939. Now smitten with romantic sentiments persisting from the Centennial year, legislators in the 1937 regular session accepted a seventh historical park, the site of 1831 Fort Lipantitlan about thirty miles northwest of Corpus Christi, from the J. C. Bluntzer family of Nueces County. Without establishing a supervising local park commission but appropriating $120 per year for "general maintenance," lawmakers assigned to the Board of Control five-acre "Lipantitlan State Park."[29]

Warm Springs in Texas

The legislature also officially endorsed a new rehabilitation center in Gonzales County at Ottine, adjacent to Palmetto State Park, for children stricken with infantile paralysis (polio). Founded on 2 March 1937 and propelled by a $250,000 Easter-seal fund drive, the Gonzales Warm Springs Foundation for Crippled Children launched its campaign for an initial 100-patient physiotherapy hospital. "Gonzales people were convinced," an article explained of the local mineral waters, "that the warm springs near Palmetto Park held possibilities of developing a project that might rival famed Warm Springs, Ga.," the retreat supported since 1924 by polio-victim and now president Franklin Roosevelt.

Unusual federal enthusiasm for Palmetto State Park likely stemmed from the movement to develop this hospital, as Co. 886 from Corpus Christi moved the previous fall to reoccupy CCC barracks in Ottine. "Forty acres of land have been set aside," the foundation explained, "adjoining the 360 acre Palmetto State Park[, together] which form an ideal recreational and playground area."

Indeed, CCC development of Georgia's 1,550-acre Pine Mountain State

Park next to FDR's Warm Springs compound offered obvious inspiration for such therapeutic recreation in Texas. Visiting parents could relax at the nearby park, where recovering children could also enjoy field trips. "Any movement whose aim is to brighten the lives of handicapped children," wrote President Roosevelt to the Gonzales foundation as its development began, "enlists my sincere sympathy and has my hearty commendation."[30]

CCC Cuts Camps

But, at the same time, federal curtailments that spring further reduced CCC expenditures as ECW neared the end of its two-year authorization and funding. The president, optimistic that Washington's relief budgets could now be safely reduced, asked Congress to fund the Corps from April 1937 through the end of the federal fiscal year in June with an enrollment cap at 300,000, down dramatically from 500,000. FDR had no intention of phasing out the Corps; rather, this enrollment figure seemed suitable for the CCC as a permanent agency of the government, and he prepared to ask Congress to make it so. During this crucial interim the Texas State Parks Board could not expect to maintain its complementary workforce of nineteen CCC companies, officials warned, and certainly could not hope to add new state park developments in the coming ninth period.

When state park CCC camp assignments for the ninth period commenced on 1 April 1937, the Texas allotment fell from nineteen to eighteen, although the four metropolitan areas maintained their companies. Development at Kerrville State Park then halted in May, but the talented and highly mobile Co. 1823(CV) of African American war veterans remained in state park work as it changed places with Co. 886 at Palmetto.

Bastrop State Park, which had hosted two CCC units for three and a half years, on 24 May lost Co. 1805 as its enrollees boarded a train for Wyoming and their new U.S. Forest Service assignment. Congressman J. P. Buchanan of Brenham since 1933 had "absolutely demanded both camps for his pet project," Tom Beauchamp claimed, but following Buchanan's death in February the park service wasted no time in reducing Bastrop to the now-standard single-camp complement.[31]

The Bid for a Permanent CCC

The movement of "White" CCC camps out of state while "Colored" camps received only new in-state assignments characterized the byzantine administration of Emergency Conservation Work. Yet, even at reduced enrollment for the ninth period, the program remained enormously popular throughout the country, as President Roosevelt encouraged a federal bill to make his CCC a permanent agency. Congressional sponsors cited in early 1937, notes historian John Salmond, "a recent public opinion poll which indicated that

TABLE 9

State Parks of the Ninth-Period ECW

April–September 1937

NPS Number	Official Name	CCC Company
SP-4	Davis Mountains State Park	Side Camp[1]
SP-14	Palo Duro Canyon State Park	Co. 894
SP-22	Bastrop-Buescher State Park	Co. 1811
SP-29	Palmetto State Park	Co. 1823(CV)[2]
SP-31	Lake Worth Metropolitan Park	Co. 1816
SP-33	Big Bend State Park	Co. 1855[1]
SP-35	Longhorn Cavern State Park	Co. 854
SP-36	Brownwood State Park	Co. 849
SP-38	Mother Neff State Park	Co. 817
SP-40	Caddo Lake State Park	Co. 857[3]
SP-41	Lake Sweetwater Metropolitan Park	Co. 1857
SP-42	Garner State Park	Co. 879
SP-43	Goliad State Park	Co. 3822(V)
SP-44	Fort Parker State Park	Co. 3807(C)
SP-47	Balmorhea State Park	Co. 1856
SP-49	Daingerfield State Park	Co. 2891
SP-50	Tyrrell Metropolitan Park	Co. 845
SP-51	Lockhart State Park	Co. 3803
SP-52	Mackenzie State Park	Co. 3820
SP-53	Cleburne State Park	Co. 3804
SP-54	Tyler State Park	Co. 2888
SP-55	Bachman–White Rock Lake Metropolitan Park	Co. 2896
SP-56	Paris State Park	Co. 857[3]

[1] Co. 1855 from Big Bend State Park in April 1937 began extensive repairs and improvements to the adobe Indian Village lodge at Davis Mountains.

[2] Co. 1823(CV) replaced Co. 886 on 5 May 1937 at Palmetto.

[3] Co. 857, still officially assigned to Paris, apparently continued to put the bulk of its efforts into the large side camp at Caddo Lake.

87 per cent of all Americans, including a majority of registered Republicans, favored the Corps." Nevertheless an unexpected and complicated debate in Washington scrutinized the very nature of this "emergency" relief program and harshly questioned its proposed changes if made permanent.

As these hearings proceeded from April through June, CCC director Fechner endured considerable criticism from powerful members of Congress. Over the past four years he had earned the scorn of many lawmakers through contrary rejections and approvals alike of CCC camps for their districts. Worse, Fechner now supported a change in management that would place all his employees under Civil Service protection, thus ending vast patronage opportunities for congressmen who directly influenced sala-ried positions at CCC projects.

In a further complication, Roosevelt himself had recently alienated many in Congress with his attempt to increase appointments to the U.S. Supreme Court and sway judicial decisions in his favor. Fechner openly supported the president on this controversial issue, further exasperating congressmen over the CCC director's political imprudence. As a result of these and perhaps other considerations, Texas Senator Tom Connally and Congressman Fritz Lanham of Weatherford both directly amended the president's permanent CCC bill. They cut Fechner's salary from $12,000 to $10,000 per year and reauthorized the CCC for only three more years.

Thus the CCC, despite, or more likely because of, its widespread popularity, appeared for renewal before Congress at an inopportune time. The legislative branch chose a debate over this "pet project of the Presi-dent," as members called it, to send a statement of independence to the White House. In the end the pragmatic president accepted a three-year extension of the Corps and pigeonholed his desire to create a permanent CCC for another day. On 28 June 1937 he signed the reauthorization bill that maintained its complicated organization, but which dropped the al-ways-confusing Emergency Conservation Work name in favor of simply Civilian Conservation Corps.[32]

Good News and Bad News for Big Bend

In the spring legislative session, NPS and State Parks Board officials launched their campaign to obtain funds for purchases of about 563,000 acres in the Big Bend. The parks board had secured most of the state-owned 225,000 acres within the proposed Big Bend National Park boundary, but the state's nineteenth-century system of granting or selling alternating sec-tions of public land left a checkerboard pattern on the map, and such a fragmented public park would be impossible to manage. On behalf of the parks board, director Lawson drove in April to Alpine to host some forty members of the House and Senate for an inspection trip of the Big Bend.

As part of the federal strategy, a "major coup for the NPS," according to historian John Jameson, "was the appointment of Walter Prescott Webb as historical consultant on the Big Bend." A renowned history professor at the University of Texas, Webb spent much of the spring in the Trans-Pecos and quickly produced two articles on the Big Bend that were nationally circulated in April by the park service.

"The proposal to create the Big Bend National Park," Webb penned in his first release, "and a corresponding Mexican National Park just across the Rio Grande, has at last focused public attention on the most isolated, and probably the most interesting, spot in Texas." Webb noted in his second

article that "[h]ardly a year goes by that scientists do not come from institutions all over the United States and from Europe to study the Big Bend,
to help unravel or to deepen the mysteries that are a part of the area."[33]

Webb and Lawson stirred sufficient drama to convince the legislature
gathered in Austin to support the national park enterprise. True to their
overall generosity in appropriation, coupled with reluctance to authorize
adequate funding sources in the regular session, lawmakers approved a
$750,000 bill to purchase private lands in the Big Bend. Herb Maier at the
park service regional office rejoiced at this success, even though it represented half his recommended $1.5 million to secure holdings of private land
within approved park boundaries. But then Governor Allred, already inun-
dated with this session's red ink flowing from the Capitol, in June vetoed
the appropriation in an undeniable economy move.[34]

Following the Master Plan

Chairman Pat Neff called the new six-member State Parks Board together
in June for its biennial organizational meeting. Neff and members Beauchamp, Urbantke and Mayes met for the first time with recent appointees
J. V. Ash and Ken Clapp, and with Neff's support elected Mayes their new
chairman. Ash, professing self-interest in his hometown Bastrop State Park,
agreed to hold the vice chairman position. With an adequate stenographic
staff at the board's Austin office and with Bill Lawson's title of executive
secretary, board members omitted their former "secretary" position. The
board accepted the resignation of Robert O. Whiteaker, its first staff engineer and, throughout much of the recent year, its system manager.

Board members also entertained offers from the Lower Colorado River
Authority (LCRA), created in 1934, to develop state parks near two new
dams in Llano and Burnet counties. One future park would be built on
a peninsula at Lake Buchanan, named in 1935 for Congressman J. P. Buchanan. The congressman, who died in office in February 1937, had provided PWA construction funds for the LCRA. The other new park would
be built downstream on unfinished Roy Inks Lake, named for a deceased
LCRA board member. These offers likely originated from Congressman
Buchanan's replacement, the new U.S. Representative who entered Congress on 14 May, Lyndon Baines Johnson.[35]

The parks board, shortly after its June meeting, received good news
from the Texas Highway Department: its commission voted on 22 June to
make park roads "part of the State Highway System." Highway agency staff
identified existing roads to and within eight state parks, totaling about
thirty-six miles, that would be "taken over for maintenance immediately."
As proposed by Neff and Colp as early as 1923 with their founding of the

State Parks Board, such a maintenance agreement with the state's largest agency freed park management from one of its greatest costs. Now the CCC-built byways at Bastrop, Big Bend (already benefiting from a new eighty-five-mile highway to convey motorists from Marathon to Green Gulch), Big Spring, Caddo Lake, Davis Mountains, Longhorn Cavern, Meridian, and Palo Duro Canyon state parks would enjoy good-roads status outside the small park system budget.[36]

On 1 August 1937 the NPS settled on a new national field organization, placing its 337 state park CCC companies and its 83 national park camps under common regional supervision. Texas now fell under a smaller Region III shared with Arizona, New Mexico, Oklahoma, and Arkansas. Anticipating the reorganization, district officer Maier and his chief architect Cecil Doty finished their fabulous Pueblo Revival-style office building in Santa Fe, New Mexico, and transferred the regional staff from Oklahoma City for this closer proximity to many national parks and national monuments. In a compromise with career managers, park service director Cammerer agreed to fill new regional director positions by seniority, so Maier—although he had worked with the service off and on since 1920—became only "acting director" of Region III.[37]

As Maier prepared his move to Santa Fe, he notified the State Parks Board that Texas would lose two more CCC companies in the forthcoming tenth period. Maier urged holding most camps at their present development projects but suggested the closing of two mature projects, at Lake Sweetwater, "Gonzales-Palmetto," or Lockhart. The board chose Sweetwater—an easy elimination of a metropolitan camp—and Palmetto for closing, but at the same time strongly urged the park service to provide a CCC camp for the state's well-studied park site at Huntsville. After exhaustive negotiations with the U.S. and Texas forest services, the forestry project at Huntsville, P-74, transferred to the park service as SP-61, the first new Texas state park project in two years. In return the Paris State Park CCC allotment, SP-56, switched to a tenth-period forest service assignment outside Texas, no great loss to the parks board since the Paris project had remained inactive for months.[38]

Just before approving camp assignments for the tenth period, corps director Fechner announced a nationwide "retrenchment program" from his Washington office. "The Civilian Conservation Corps will abandon nearly 250 camps Oct. 1," his 9 September 1937 press release confirmed, "reducing the number to the lowest [1,604] since 1933." Although the corps fielded its authorized 300,000 enrollees, Fechner justified the cutbacks "because of budgetary limitation, completion of work programs and a desire to [return] the enrollee strength of each camp at 200." In Texas as the tenth period

TABLE 10
State Parks of the Tenth-Period CCC
October 1937–March 1938

NPS Number	Official Name	CCC Company
SP-4	Davis Mountains State Park	Side Camp[1]
SP-14	Palo Duro Canyon State Park	Co. 894[2]
SP-22	Bastrop-Buescher State Park	Co. 1811
SP-31	Lake Worth Metropolitan Park	Co. 1816[3]
SP-33	Big Bend State Park	Co. 1855[4]
SP-35	Longhorn Cavern State Park	Co. 854
SP-36	Brownwood State Park	Co. 849
SP-38	Mother Neff State Park	Co. 817
SP-42	Garner State Park	Co. 879
SP-43	Goliad State Park	Co. 3822(V)
SP-44	Fort Parker State Park	Co. 3807(C)
SP-47	Balmorhea State Park	Co. 1856
SP-49	Daingerfield State Park	Co. 2891
SP-50	Tyrrell Metropolitan Park	Co. 845
SP-51	Lockhart State Park	Co. 3803
SP-52	Mackenzie State Park	Co. 3820
SP-53	Cleburne State Park	Co. 3804
SP-54	Tyler State Park	Co. 2888
SP-55	Bachman–White Rock Lake Metropolitan Park	Co. 2896
SP-61	Huntsville State Park	Co. 1823(CV)

[1] Co. 1855 continued to provide a side camp for repairs at Indian Village in Davis Mountains State Park (see note 4).

[2] The Palo Duro Canyon project closed on 20 December 1937.

[3] Lake Worth Metropolitan Park development ended on 31 December 1937.

[4] The Big Bend State Park Project, including Co. 1855 side-camp assistance to Davis Mountains, ended on 15 December 1937.

began, the NPS controlled nineteen CCC companies (sixteen state park and three metropolitan park camps), the Soil Conservation Service twenty-eight camps, and the U.S. Forest Service thirteen camps.[39]

Years of patchwork improvements at Caddo Lake finally ended as Co. 857 terminated its paper assignment to Paris State Park and its actual labors at Caddo. The Palmetto project also closed, probably because of the community's and state's continued failure to secure additional parklands at Ottine, yet with a considerable investment in facilities ready for visitor use.

Palmetto's CCC Co. 1823(CV) once again dutifully transferred elsewhere, to Huntsville in Walker County to begin 2,044-acre Huntsville State Park, surrounded by the new Sam Houston National Forest. This unique Texas company of African American war veterans now camped at their fifth park construction assignment, having developed substantial parts of Abilene, Kerrville, and Palmetto state parks, as well as Lake Sweetwater Metropolitan Park. The Sweetwater project, with extensive CCC-built facilities around the lake, also finished at the end of September 1937.

CCC Retrenchment in Texas

Although Texas at first hosted sixteen state park camps in the fall of 1937 as promised by the NPS, the retrenchment program cut several projects off early in the new period. In December, CCC camps withdrew from Big Bend and Palo Duro, and the city-park project around Lake Worth also closed, but with a virtually complete park ready for use. In reality, the CCC program had been scaling back for some time, affecting enrollee recruitment under the Texas Relief Commission as well. Still frustrated by the unkind limits on African American selection and an inadequate state budget, Neal Guy, relief commission enlistment officer, "[t]oward the end of 1937 . . . gave up in disgust," writes historian Ken Hendrickson, "resigned, and went to work for the CCC Selection Division in Washington."[40]

Regardless of nationwide retrenchment, CCC cutbacks in Texas obviously accelerated during the winter of 1937–1938, and for more reasons than those given by Fechner in the newspapers. The two greatest supporters of state park development in Texas, Congress and the NPS, throughout 1937 signaled fundamental attitude adjustments that ultimately lowered their priorities for certain New Deal programs in the state. In Congress a growing rift between President Roosevelt and Vice President Garner affected the entire Texas delegation. After the spring Supreme Court "packing" attempt by FDR and disagreements with Garner over labor strikes, "[r]elations between the two men were never the same," notes Garner biographer Lionel Patenaude. Wishing to slow down "this New Deal spending orgy," as resurgent-conservative Garner called it, the vice president "began to use his influence in the House and Senate to create opposition to the relief programs."[41]

At the same time, NPS officials clearly lost patience with Texas on at least three troubling issues. First, the State Parks Board still could not operate its federally built park system, officials asserted, on the moderate $40,000 annual budget recently received from the legislature. Further, the park service puzzled over the Texas habit of closing its state parks each fall for more than half the year, with resulting loss in revenue. The compromise concession/lease solution for park operations could not guarantee appropriate care for millions of dollars in new facilities, federal officials added.

Second, after abundant investment at the Big Bend CCC camp with the expectation that Texas would complete essential land purchases, Governor Allred had vetoed the needed appropriation. Park service and even

CCC authorities revealed their intentions of closing the Big Bend camp shortly after the veto, when they allowed a large side camp to work on Indian Village at distant Davis Mountains State Park. One last push by Big Bend interests in hopes the fall special session of the legislature would restore the money—and Allred would approve its use—kept Co. 1855 assigned to the Chisos Basin as the tenth period began. When Interior secretary Harold Ickes appeared on 16 October in Burnet County for dedication of two federal-project dams, he "devoted much of his speech to Big Bend National Park," notes historian John Jameson. "Besides mentioning the unique, scenic, and international possibilities of the area," Jameson adds, Ickes "chided Texans for doing nothing about it." [42] To no avail; Texans in the legislature and the Governor's Mansion faced bigger problems and failed Big Bend again.

Finally, other land problems at state parks drove federal officials to allow closure of their favored Palmetto State Park project, and to act on their perpetual threat to leave Palo Duro Canyon. At a November meeting in Amarillo, State Parks Board officials Lawson and Clapp met with local and federal representatives on the alarming Palo Duro situation. With second- and third-party liens on state park land due in 1942 and 1947, Lawson recorded, "[t]he citizens from both Amarillo and Canyon agreed that it would never be possible to pay for the park out of its revenues."

The CCC camp at Palo Duro Canyon not only continued the site's development but, unlike other CCC projects, actually operated this 15,000-acre park year-round. If the NPS closed its CCC camp, Lawson noted, "gross revenue of the park will probably decrease from around $12,000.00 a year, to $2,000 or $3,000 a year." He failed to add that the note payments to Fred Emery required about $40,000 annually. The meeting ended with a parks board pledge to discuss with lienholder Emery a new deal on Palo Duro Canyon land. But before the parks board and Emery could arrange a discussion, on 20 December 1937 CCC Co. 894 emptied its barracks, and four and one-half years of NPS guidance ended at Palo Duro Canyon State Park. [43]

1938: OPERATIONS AND INDEPENDENCE

Responding to Recreation Needs

As Congress decreased relief programs for financial and social reasons and the NPS moved away from relief for professional purposes, even President Roosevelt joined the chorus. "[I]t is vitally important that each state should make adequate arrangement," he implored in a message to governors, "to maintain the physical improvements that have been accomplished by Civilian Conservation Corps camps on state property. This is with special reference to state parks and state forests. . . . It seems to me that the time has come for each state to make proper provision for taking over this part of the work."

Even Interior secretary Ickes entered this public appeal for states to carry their part of the load, promoting his favorite topic of conservation but emphasizing that federal assistance must be seen as a partnership, not an endless subsidy. To emphasize Ickes's other favorite topic of comprehensive planning, the NPS had instructed state park authorities in the previous year to study recreation patterns. In response the Texas State Parks Board issued in January 1938 its first compilation of visitor activities. With similar studies from other states the park service began to compile national recreation statistics.[44]

"A complete analysis," wrote Lonnie C. Fuller, a seasoned project superintendent and author of the Texas report, "of all the data relating to all the parks is not attempted." But simply the attendance figures for the previous summer—1,573,026 at fifteen state and five metropolitan parks built by the CCC—showed a 60 percent increase compared to 1936, "undoubtedly due to the advance in the state of development of the various parks," Fuller explained. The metropolitan parks accounted for practically all this increase, but the state parks held their own one year after the boom of Centennial visitation.

"The Texas State Park program is now advancing," he continued, "into the field of *operation* of the parks." Texas state parks offered a variety of activities, with 61 percent of participation classified as passive: picnicking, sightseeing, and driving. Active pursuits—swimming, fishing, and boating—would increase with appropriate facilities in future developments, the report speculated. As executive secretary Lawson and his board digested this information, they prepared applications for the coming eleventh period of CCC assignments.

On 22 February, Lawson and board chairman Mayes traveled to Washington "for the purpose of protesting the further loss of any CCC Camps working in the Texas State Parks," they reported. "The large number of visitors at the State Parks as revealed by this Study," they no doubt displayed to congressmen and NPS officials through Fuller's study, "is considered as conclusive evidence that the State Park program . . . has the enthusiastic support and appreciation of the people of Texas."[45]

Following the midwinter closings of CCC camps at Big Bend, Lake Worth, and Palo Duro Canyon, the Texas allotment stabilized through approvals for the eleventh period beginning 1 April 1938. If one camp moved, another took its place, as with the midperiod exchange of companies at

TABLE 11

State Parks of the Eleventh-Period CCC

April–September 1938

NPS Number	Official Name	CCC Company
SP-4	Davis Mountains State Park	Side Camp[1]
SP-22	Bastrop-Buescher State Park	Co. 1811
SP-35	Longhorn Cavern State Park	Co. 854
SP-36	Brownwood State Park	Co. 849
SP-38	Mother Neff State Park	Co. 817[2]
SP-42	Garner State Park	Co. 879
SP-43	Goliad State Park	Co. 3822(V)
SP-44	Fort Parker State Park	Co. 3807(C)
SP-47	Balmorhea State Park	Co. 1856[1]
SP-49	Daingerfield State Park	Co. 2891[3]
SP-50	Tyrrell Metropolitan Park	Co. 845
SP-51	Lockhart State Park	Co. 3803
SP-52	Mackenzie State Park	Co. 3820
SP-53	Cleburne State Park	Co. 3804
SP-54	Tyler State Park	Co. 2888
SP-55	Bachman–White Rock Lake Metropolitan Park	Co. 2896
SP-61	Huntsville State Park	Co. 1823(CV)
SP-62	Ascarate County Park	Co. 2873(C)[4]

[1] With the departure of Big Bend Co. 1855, Co. 1856 from Balmorhea State Park took over side-camp work at nearby Davis Mountains.

[2] Work at Mother Neff State Park ended in mid-period on 30 June 1938.

[3] On 30 June 1938 Co. 2891 at Daingerfield yielded its barracks to Co. 1801(C), which had been confined at Fort Sam Houston since last working on Goose Island State Park in June 1935.

[4] To fill the camp allotment slot vacated by Mother Neff, work on El Paso's Ascarate County Park—first local park in Texas so designated—began on 1 July 1938 with transfer of Co. 2873(C) from nearby Fort Bliss.

Daingerfield. Even the former Big Bend side camp's work at Indian Village in Davis Mountains State Park—including renewed roof, wiring, plumbing, fireplaces, and a "coat of some type of water proof paint or wash over the entire building"—continued under CCC Co. 1856 from about thirty miles away at Balmorhea.[46]

In May, Big Bend supporters launched "a hard campaign to raise by popular subscription the necessary $1,000,000 to purchase the land outside the present State park in the center of the larger park area." This assessment from the *Dallas News* added that a businessmen's committee—headed by John W. Carpenter of Dallas, Amon G. Carter of Fort Worth, Jesse H. Jones of Houston, and others, including parks board chairman Mayes—decided to "acquaint many Texans who are ignorant of the beauties of the park site with its possibilities." Speaking to the committee of one hundred gathered on 23 May in Austin, Governor Allred pleaded his own ignorance: "I didn't know of the National Government's interest in the park site when I vetoed a defective piece of legislation appropriating money for its establishment." Already holding $25,000 toward their goal, the group vowed to make, as both NPS regional officer Maier and Allred now described, "the greatest investment the State could have." [47]

As CCC balancing acts continued in this eleventh period, on 30 June Co. 817 pulled out of Mother Neff State Park and the next day, far to the west in El Paso, Co. 2873(C) commenced work on Ascarate County Park. Developed around a Rio Grande resaca, or oxbow lake, remaining after straightening of both the river and the international boundary with Mexico, Ascarate began as the first example of direct NPS recreation assistance to a county government in Texas. Both federal and state park officials admitted that this project opened at the insistence of Congressman Ewing Thomason, as exchange for earlier cooperation in closing the Big Bend CCC camp in his district.[48] The unit assigned to Ascarate, Co. 2873(C) of "Colored Juniors," emerged from the confines of Fort Bliss after several years of work on that sprawling installation in both Texas and New Mexico. A similar shift in this period involved Co. 1801(C), which left Fort Sam Houston for fresh assignment to Daingerfield State Park.

Lodging for Distinguished Guests

Mother Neff State Park did not lose CCC Co. 817 without a fight, as Pat Neff traveled in May "to present the Texas situation to the Washington authorities." Neff had enjoyed the privilege of a CCC camp developing his favorite park for almost four years, a lengthy stay compared to other projects long since completed. But on behalf of this park, as well as the entire Texas park system, Neff pleaded for a halt to CCC retrenchment in the state. The Mother Neff project "will require several months more of work for completion," he asserted in the *Waco Tribune,* referring particularly to an unfinished project that would create a Gatesville entrance to the park and a scenic byway along the Leon River.[49] But Co. 817 had finished its approved master plan facilities, and the NPS granted only a three-month extension on its already planned 1 April 1938 closing.

One of the last projects at Mother Neff State Park, its "caretakers cottage," brought criticism from federal officials and might have killed Neff's attempts to retain Co. 817 at the park. "The geographic location of this park," parks board manager Lawson had recently argued with a federal inspector, "makes it necessary to have lodge accommodations for . . . distinguished guests." Lawson explained that the park's traditional summer Chautauqua programs relied on a series of "noted speakers, lecturers, ministers, Evangelists and statesmen." NPS officials deduced, without stretching their imaginations, that Neff himself would be the most frequent "noted statesman" to enjoy the extra bedroom, bath, and garage added to the keeper's house.[50]

Lawson got his expanded caretaker's cottage at Mother Neff, in effect winning the battle but losing the war, once CCC Co. 817 received its marching orders. This large Neff-inspired cottage might have stood out as an elaborate non-visitor facility, but in fact the New Deal philosophy of the State Parks Board, at first accommodated by the NPS, envisioned year-round "keepers" whose state-provided dwellings constituted the greatest compensation for their duties. At this time other facilities were drawing similar reproach, but they nonetheless had attracted desirable keepers at Bastrop, Cleburne, and Lockhart. Goliad State Park, while not under parks board supervision, featured an impressive custodian's complex as well.

Though criticized by a regional inspector, the "Custodian's Dwelling" at Lockhart State Park enjoyed praise as a featured example in the park service's own publication of 1938, *Park and Recreation Structures.* More than a reprint of *Park Structures and Facilities* from three years before, this greatly expanded guidebook to park development recommended hundreds of new examples, including dozens crafted by the CCC in Texas state parks. With "refectories" shown in photos and floor plans from Bastrop, Goose Island, Lake Corpus Christi, and Palmetto, the new book explained this odd term, and others, for newcomers to NPS-designed parks.

> It is difficult to fix the stages of development at which the concession building becomes a refectory and the latter in turn becomes a lodge, and it may be pointless to attempt it. However, it seems logical to catalog them as park counterparts of familiar urban institutions—the concession, the store, dispensing food supplies and snacks; the refectory, the restaurant, serving meals; the lodge, the hotel, adding overnight accommodations to the serving of meals.[51]

Also in the new publication, stone cabins at Brownwood, Longhorn Cavern, and Palo Duro Canyon demonstrated a variety of floor plans, building materials, and adaptations to each park's unique landscape. Two pages of "Stone Pylons In Texas" illustrated entry signs at nine parks; water towers at Bonham, Mother Neff, and Palmetto showed how such utilitarian necessities could be disguised as rustic outcrops; whimsical wrought-metal silhouettes pointed the way to restrooms at Bastrop; even service-entrance gates displayed unusual craftwork at four Texas parks. Of architect Sam Vosper's "Service Group In Extenso" at Goliad, the author noted "the nice attention here lavished on detail is as welcome as it is startling." And of architect George Walling's custodian house at Lockhart, author Albert Good praised his "masterful molding" and "satisfying results."[52]

Respectful Distance

Mixed signals over caretaker's dwellings symbolized the growing distance between Texas and federal park officials, in hindsight an inevitable evolution of their depression-born relationship. Yet Lawson's hearty justification for the state's own choice of park facilities represented a positive maturity as well, and an appropriate venture into independent supervision and operation of its still-growing park system.

By summer 1938 the Santa Fe regional office looked from its own elaborate new dwelling primarily toward development and operations of the national parks under its jurisdiction. While the region's chief architect Doty and chief landscape architect Harvey Cornell continued to review major developments in Texas state parks, the roving inspector system—once vanguard of federal control at CCC projects—had been turned over to the state.

The NPS continued to pay for inspectors and designers in the Austin office through a percentage of site development budgets, but with decreasing oversight from the regional office. This recent change in procedure created some problems, as Cornell pointed out in June when he diplomatically urged the State Parks Board to dispatch its federal-salary inspectors on more frequent park visits. "Occasional mistakes in the field were nearly always traceable to the lack of technical supervision by the Central Design Office," he wrote in June after visiting a dozen of the Texas parks still occupied by CCC development camps.

Cornell's mission clearly intended to mend a few fences with Texas and to clarify the new federal role of greatly diminished, but certainly not severed, relations with the State Parks Board. He visited and wrote brief and constructive site reports on state parks at Balmorhea, Bastrop and Buescher, Brownwood, Daingerfield, Fort Parker, Garner, Lockhart, Mackenzie, Mother Neff, and Tyler. He also traveled to the Dallas metropolitan parks and the extensive mission restoration work at Goliad. "It is a real privilege," he ultimately complimented, "to observe commendable park development. . . . Marked improvement in design and execution was apparent everywhere. It is doubtful if those directly associated with the work fully appreciate the degree of accomplishment in connection with a park program starting from little or nothing only a few years ago."[53]

In late August the summer visitation figures, still compiled by federally

TABLE 12
State Parks of the Twelfth-Period CCC
October 1938–March 1939

NPS Number	Official Name	CCC Company
SP-22	Bastrop-Buescher State Park	Co. 1811
SP-35	Longhorn Cavern State Park	Co. 854
SP-36	Brownwood State Park	Co. 849
SP-38	Mother Neff State Park	Side Camp[1]
SP-42	Garner State Park	Co. 879
SP-43	Goliad State Park	Co. 3822(V)
SP-44	Fort Parker State Park	Co. 3807(C)
SP-47	Balmorhea State Park	Co. 1856
SP-49	Daingerfield State Park	Co. 1801(C)
SP-50	Tyrrell Metropolitan Park	Co. 845
SP-51	Lockhart State Park	Co. 3803
SP-52	Mackenzie State Park	Co. 3820
SP-53	Cleburne State Park	Co. 3804
SP-54	Tyler State Park	Co. 2888
SP-55	Bachman–White Rock Lake Metropolitan Park	Co. 2896
SP-61	Huntsville State Park	Co. 1823(CV)
SP-62	Ascarate County Park	Co. 2873(C)

[1] A side camp from Co. 3804 at Cleburne State Park worked at Mother Neff early in the twelfth period.

. employed project superintendents at state parks under development, appeared in a release from the regional office. "A twenty-two percent increase over 1937," the article boasted, "was reported in total number of visitors at eleven Texas State Parks during the first ten weeks" of the summer. Mackenzie State Park in Lubbock recorded a decline from the previous year to 156,200, but still topped the chart among all state parks. "Tyler State Park jumped to second place in popularity," the release continued, "visitors there numbering 39,000 as compared with 6,675 for the June-August period of last year. Daingerfield State Park . . . advanced to third place this year with a count of 33,800." [54] Enthusiasm for each of these sites compelled their inclusion on the Texas application for continued CCC development in the coming twelfth period, to begin on 1 October 1938.

Parks board appeals earlier in the year for the NPS to maintain the Texas CCC camp allotment apparently showed results as the winter period commenced. Pat Neff even secured a side camp from Cleburne for a few final details at Mother Neff State Park. The park service approved no new assignments, but all sixteen CCC companies from the summer period continued development into winter at their state, metropolitan, and county park projects. Likewise the Agriculture Department in the fall of 1938 maintained in Texas a consistent allotment of thirteen forest camps and twenty-seven soil conservation units.

Pass the Biscuits, Pappy!

While state park development proceeded smoothly through the most recent work-period transitions, this election year's campaign for governor threw the course of Texas politics for a confounding loop. Earlier in the year no fewer than thirteen candidates announced intentions for the Governor's Mansion, describes historian Seth McKay, and three experienced hopefuls rose quickly to the top: four-time runner Tom Hunter, who proposed to "abolish duplicating and overlapping departments of the state government"; Attorney General William McCraw, who had favored the State Parks Board in 1935 when Governor Allred attempted to appoint its chairman; and Ernest Thompson, now a member of the powerful Texas Railroad Commission, who included soil conservation as part of his platform for his drought-ravaged Panhandle home and all of Texas.

Then a fourth candidate from outside the Texas Democratic Party, Fort Worth flour merchant Wilbert Lee O'Daniel, began an unorthodox campaign through his own promotional radio program. Like his fellow candidates, O'Daniel had nothing to say about recreation or parks and declined to join debates on the New Deal, state agencies, or natural resource conservation. But he quickly bewildered traditional opponents with his small- and large-town automobile rallies (a technique perfected by Neff in 1920) combined with the mass appeal of radio (the enormously successful medium of Franklin Roosevelt) and his evangelistic rhetoric (the proven wavelength used in 1934 by Jimmie Allred). In the July primary, O'Daniel defeated all other candidates with a new record of votes cast at 1,114,885.

On 1 November, O'Daniel easily defeated his Republican opponent, San Antonio oil executive Alexander Boynton, and promised to fulfill his campaign pledge of a $30 per month old-age pension. Coke Robert Stevenson, rancher and state legislator from Kimble County since 1928 and House Speaker since 1933—the first to hold that office in two successive sessions—won the election for lieutenant governor. Most Texas congressmen reappeared in Washington after the election, with the notable exception of Maury Maverick, who returned to his San Antonio home and immediately won its election for mayor.[55]

In strategic preparation for the coming legislative session, the December 1938 issue of one-year-old *Texas Geographic Magazine* featured a lengthy article on state parks by Bill Lawson. The State Parks Board executive secretary presented a detailed summary of the system, based primarily on figures gathered in the preceding summer. "The most popular feature in the parks at the present time," Lawson revealed, "is driving through them in a car or picnicking. These more or less passive activities outnumber all others."

Thus the first Texas park-visitor survey justified all the intuitions of Stephen Mather, Pat Neff, and D. E. Colp after a twenty-year push to orient state parks thoroughly toward the automobile. Placement of state parks near major highways, and careful engineering of scenic lanes and loop drives within each park, provided for urban dwellers quick access to the outdoors. The exhilaration of quietly dashing beneath forest canopies on rubber tires and smooth roads now proved the most fashionable use of state parks! Modern Texans soundly demonstrated their appetite for this peculiar industrial-age phenomenon labeled by historian Leo Marx as the "machine in the garden."

"[A]mong the more active sports," Lawson continued to detail summer park activities, "water recreation has been outstandingly popular." He confirmed an abundance of wildlife in these sanctuaries from hunting, and added that "[o]ut-of-state visitors are always delighted and amazed by their first sight of an armadillo." To obtain a CCC camp for development, Lawson explained, "a state park was [now] defined as having a minimum of 500 acres." His further definition of "state park" became the first offered by the State Parks Board since 1925.

> In the future, no state park should be designated which does not contain some outstanding or unusual feature which makes it of interest to visitors from all over the state or nation. It should also contain adequate water facilities and except in rare cases, should provide for water sports and recreations. It should contain enough acreage so that many different forms of park use could be in progress at the same time without crowding or congesting the park.
>
> The term "state park" should be applied only to those areas which meet all of these minimum requirements, and should not be applied to roadside or highway parks or to small areas which are of interest chiefly to the immediate locality, and which serve only as county or municipal parks.[56]

Lawson concluded this definition with further policy that revealed how far the State Parks Board had traveled in thirteen years. Neff and Colp's original concept had been simply that "parks be near the main highway, that they have trees and water, and that where possible, the spot have some historic significance." Such "camping parks" along the state's highway system now seemed a distant (and somewhat embarrassing) legacy, especially since the Texas Highway Department had developed its own extensive roadside park program since 1933.[57]

Parting Reports and Shots from the NPS

NPS landscape architect Cornell devoted the last week in November and most of December to an extensive inspection trip through all Texas parks occupied by CCC camps. At most sites CCC enrollees still labored on landscape features in heavy visitor-use areas, as Cornell observed in the state parks at Bastrop, Brownwood, Daingerfield, Fort Parker, Garner, Lockhart, Longhorn Cavern, and Tyler. Overwhelming interest shown in swimming by park visitors during previous summers, he noted, caused several park managers to propose new bathhouses at Daingerfield, Fort Parker, Garner, and Lockhart. With these observations, Cornell produced one last detailed federal report on progress at each Texas site, the conclusion of a series of records that began with the first federal inspector, Fred Dale, in June 1933.

- At Balmorhea, Cornell recommended formal plantings, even non-native cedar and cypress, for its bathhouse and pool area.
- At Bastrop, he concluded that the "major development is now complete" and from "the standpoint of public use and appreciation, Bastrop State Park has every justification for existence."
- At Brownwood, a major entrance road realignment followed earlier recommendations, and a new "Game Warden's Residence" with garage exhibited "excellent work."
- At Buescher, stone construction work continued on the "combination building" and a picnic shelter.
- At Daingerfield, "the decision had finally been made to revise the present hazardous entrance to the park."
- At Garner, "[r]ough lap siding on a number of the cabins was not being carefully matched and represented inferior workmanship."
- At Goliad, visited only in June, Cornell reported that the "custodian's residence will, of course, be one of the finest in any state park. . . . The restoration work on Unit No. 1 [a five-room mission school and quarters], virtually completed, and on Unit No. 2, the church, reflected careful attention to details and finesse in workmanship."
- At Huntsville, tree clearing for its planned lake neared completion.
- At Lockhart, Cornell cautioned "[l]imited CCC participation . . . with the completion of the golf course now under construction through WPA."
- At Longhorn Cavern, "construction now underway on the new road connecting . . . with Inks Dam represents excellent work."
- At Mackenzie, Cornell agreed to "CCC participation in relation to the existing golf course," and recommended that "bent grass is preferred over bermuda" for the greens.

- At Mother Neff, where Pat Neff finagled extended help from a CCC side camp, "[t]he recently completed entrance reflects highly commendable design and workmanship. It was explained that a NYA project might be approved for this park following abandonment of the CCC side camp. It was suggested that any park work attempted should be in accordance with the plans approved by the Parks Board."
- At Tyler, Cornell praised the "black-top pavement . . . established over the entire length of the main park road, thus completely eliminating the problem of dust. It is hoped that other Texas State Parks may receive the benefit of a similar program of road maintenance."[58]

For unexplained reasons, Cornell avoided the 508-acre Cleburne State Park project during both his June and December inspection trips through Texas. At Cleburne that fall, CCC Co. 3804 had completed the handsome caretaker and maintenance complex and placed the finishing touches on a large earthen dam to impound a 116-acre spring-fed lake. Park service inspectors continually awarded high praise to these enrollees, and in October the CCC's own inspector J. S. Billups noted an "exceptionally high class camp" during his visit.[59]

Washington official Conrad Wirth's appraisal of Texas state parks, on the other hand, produced a rather pessimistic report on 19 December for CCC director Fechner. "[I]n order to give you certain statistics and information to use when you write to the Governors" about "the future CCC program," Wirth wrote, "we have attempted to analyze each individual State and give you our opinion of what the State should do in order to participate properly." In a scathing summary of all states where the NPS had cooperated to build park systems, few ranked with "good" or "fair" against Wirth's simple yardstick of funding. "We feel that the States should contribute at least two or three thousand dollars per camp for materials and supplies, besides furnishing sufficient technical assistance to prepare detailed plans for their parks."

But in this audit that at first seemed to focus only on active CCC development, Wirth made sweeping comments about all parks, both finished and unfinished. Texas "has a number of fine State park areas," he admitted, "which unfortunately are not being operated or maintained at all satisfactorily because of lack of funds." He ranked Texas as "Poor," and charged that its state parks suffered from administration by "six separate agencies" that should either be unified or achieve "better coordination." Wirth failed, however, to total the combined budgets of these six agencies—unnamed but probably meaning the parks board, the Board of Control plus Goliad's local park commission, the Reclamation Board, the Board of Water Engineers, and perhaps the State Planning Board—for a more accurate total of funds devoted to state parks in Texas.

"Unless there is a great improvement in this State in the very near future," Wirth warned Texas ominously, "we feel that we will have to recommend the cutting down of the CCC participation here." [60]

Some of the earliest and most ambitious CCC projects in Texas state parks moved mountains of earth and concrete to create dams and lakes on small streams and a few rivers. Stephenville State Park's dam took shape in 1934. *Harpers Ferry Center, National Park Service.*

Construction of a rim-to-floor road became the first task assigned to the four CCC companies at Palo Duro Canyon State Park. With only dump trucks for mechanization, most earth and rock was moved by way of dynamite and hand tools. *National Park Service, National Archives.*

For Bastrop State Park's refectory, CCC enrollee James Taylor modeled fireplace mantel brackets in clay, later to be carved of walnut in the images of an Indian and a "tree army boy," as instructed by architect Arthur Fehr. *National Park Service, National Archives.*

Park designers at Bastrop-Buescher State Park found suitable stone for buildings and landscape embellishments at an outcrop a few miles from the project. CCC enrollees cut, shaped, and lifted boulders with simple tools. *National Park Service, National Archives.*

Entry signs, such as this 1935 gem in Hereford, represented crowning achievements at each state park development, directing motorists into the park and signaling their expected transformation into a more relaxed world. *National Park Service, National Archives.*

A cautious policy of CCC supervising agencies required that projects be completed within six months. Thus the large undertaking of El Coronado Lodge at Palo Duro Canyon proceeded in distinct sections, never fully completed. *National Park Service, National Archives.*

Finding no supply of stone for buildings, CCC workers at Goose Island State Park revived a pioneer technique of making tabby blocks from gravel and seashells, casting units in random sizes to resemble chiseled stone. *National Park Service, National Archives.*

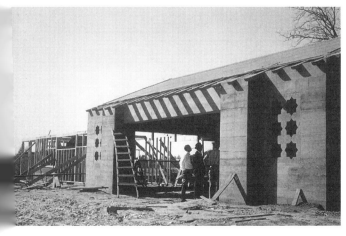

Daingerfield State Park planners rejected a local abundance of red sandstone for their major park building and prescribed a cast-concrete shelter with wood-frame roof and wings. The park entry pylon followed this same variation. *National Park Service, National Archives.*

Construction from sun-dried mud bricks (adobe) had long been a Southwest Texas tradition when CCC workers commenced Balmorhea State Park. Here, they assembled a bathhouse, refectory, shelters, and San Solomon Courts lodging of the earthen material. *National Park Service, National Archives.*

Caddo Lake State Park, beset like its West Texas counterpart at Palo Duro Canyon with land acquisition problems, realized only a fraction of its planned development. It nevertheless featured scenic walks and this latrine along Cypress Bayou. *National Park Service, National Archives.*

Abilene State Park featured one of the few concrete swimming pools—with adjacent concrete patios—approved by the NPS for a Texas state park. The pool was finished in summer 1935 by CCC war veterans from Co. 1823(CV). *National Park Service, National Archives.*

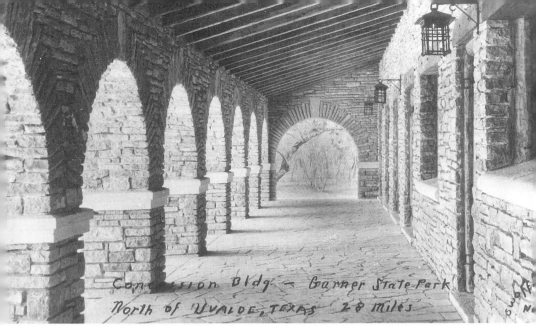

Architect John Morris directed construction of Garner State Park's massive and rambling refectory, where one arcade demonstrates the handiwork of CCC enrollees in stone piers, concrete sills, wood beams, and iron lanterns. *Swofford postcard, Author's Collection.*

Bastrop State Park's refectory interior exhibited the depth of skills and time devoted to art and craft at this project. Paneling, massive beams, furniture, and a wagon-wheel lamp highlighted stone carvings and iron fireplace tools. *National Park Service, National Archives.*

The State Parks Board long presumed that appropriations would never finance park operations and hoped that resident managers would accept first-class dwellings in partial exchange for their services, as at Cleburne State Park. *National Park Service, National Archives.*

CCC enrollees in spring 1936 built, and then staffed, this exhibit at Dallas for the Centennial Exposition, showing thousands of visitors the charm of a weekend cabin at a state park; the building survived only through the 1950s. *Harpers Ferry Center, National Park Service.*

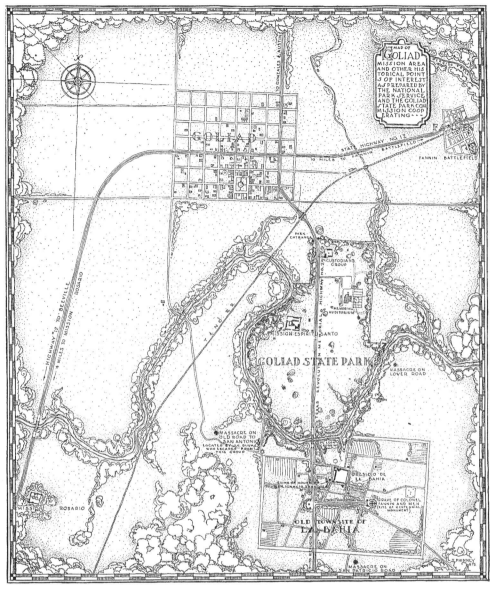

Goliad State Park development utilized NPS design assistance and CCC labor, but site management fell to the local park commission, reporting to the Board of Control. This magnificent map illustrated greater Goliad's attractions. *Archives & Information Services Division, Texas State Library.*

One of the CCC's most impressive feats in Texas rose not as a recreation facility, but as a full-blown reconstruction of Mission Espiritu Santo at Goliad State Park; camping facilities extended along the nearby San Antonio River. *Texas Historical Commission.*

Ft. Parker Restoration
Groesbeck, Texas

Limestone County citizens proposed reconstruction of Fort Parker even before they donated enough land in 1935 for a recreation park. Timber cleared by the CCC for Lake Fort Parker provided ample material for these palisade ramparts. *Author's Collection.*

Built in 1935 by a CCC camp assigned to East Texas reforestation, "Mission State Forest" at Weches featured a conjectural log church representing 1690–1693 Mission San Francisco de los Tejas, first Spanish outpost in the region. *Monuments Commemorating the Centenary.*

The Alamo received one of the largest single Centennial project fundings, at $250,000. San Antonio architect Henry Phelps's Alamo Museum (now a gift shop) cost $128,000, and the balance of the funds were used for improving unofficial "Alamo State Park." *Monuments Commemorating the Centenary.*

In 1936 Gonzales boasted one of the oldest state parks, a forested mall east of the court-house square, which received this imposing limestone-clad museum, reflecting pond, and amphitheater entrusted to the local park commission. *Monuments Commemorating the Centenary.*

Always compared to the Alamo in importance but not benefiting from a populous urban site, San Jacinto State Park in 1939 solved its recognition problem with New Deal completion of this 567-foot monument of concrete and limestone. *Author's Collection.*

The "world's largest spring-fed swimming pool," completed in 1936 by the CCC at Balmorhea State Park, centered a 200-foot stone-lined circle (middle left in aerial photo) over San Solomon Spring to capture its daily 23-million-gallon flow of artesian water. Placement of the pool along US 290, long designated as the transcontinental highway Old Spanish Trail, ensured access for much of the population of West Texas, including soldiers on maneuvers from Fort Bliss outside El Paso. In 1938 mounted troops of the U.S. Army's First Cavalry Division camped on a convenient plain adjacent to the new state park, foreshadowing the state park system's role of providing crucial recreation facilities for servicemen and families in the coming global conflict. *Howard's Studio, Pecos*

Chapter 5

1939–1942

New Priorities

I wish to ask you as donor, benefactor and sponsor of Mother Neff State Park, for permission to use the park in case our town should suffer from enemy air raids.—Eugenia Sheppard Lee, chairman McGregor housing committee, civilian defense program, 3 March 1942

. . . when life, for any reason, becomes hazardous in the town of McGregor, Mother Neff State Park will gladly open her gates to all McGregorites. —Pat Morris Neff, 7 March 1942 [1]

CENTENNIAL AFTERGLOW

Executive secretary William Lawson relayed recent threats of federal cutbacks in a 4 January 1939 letter to his State Parks Board members. The National Park Service had just broadcast—between Christmas and New Year's Day—to Lawson that "it will become necessary . . . to participate in a concrete way with funds if [you] are to receive continuing benefits from the CCC on State park development." He calculated for his board that the current CCC camps operated on a $2300 per month federal appropriation, totaling $27,600 in contribution per camp per year for overhead and operating expenses.

The State of Texas, Lawson explained, matched few if any of these dollars, but would soon be required by the park service to guarantee "not less than $8500.00 per year for materials and supplies." In addition, Washington had warned, the Austin central design office, presently subsidized through a percentage of CCC camp federal budgets, would be the total responsibility of the state after 1 July. [2]

To meet this sobering challenge, the State Parks Board inadvertently

TABLE 13

State Parks of the Thirteenth-Period CCC

April–September 1939

NPS Number	Official Name	CCC Company
SP-22	Bastrop-Buescher State Park	Co. 1811
SP-35	Longhorn Cavern State Park	Co. 854
SP-36	Brownwood State Park	Co. 849
SP-42	Garner State Park	Co. 879
SP-43	Goliad State Park	Co. 3822(V)
SP-44	Fort Parker State Park	Co. 3807(C)
SP-47	Balmorhea State Park	Co. 1856
SP-49	Daingerfield State Park	Co. 1801(C)
SP-50	Tyrrell Metropolitan Park	Co. 845
SP-51	Lockhart State Park	Co. 3803
SP-52	Mackenzie State Park	Co. 3820
SP-53	Cleburne State Park	Co. 3804
SP-54	Tyler State Park	Co. 2888
SP-55	Bachman–White Rock Lake Metropolitan Park	Co. 2896
SP-61	Huntsville State Park	Co. 1823(CV)
SP-62	Ascarate County Park	Co. 2873(C)

fielded an immediate and highly experienced ally. W. Lee O'Daniel, as one of the first appointments announced in preparation for his new job as Texas governor, named ten-year State Parks Board member Tom L. Beauchamp as secretary of state. Beauchamp had established an excellent rapport with Washington officials and moved with knowledge and respect among legislators. Furthermore, with fortunate intuition in the past year, he stood out as one of few Democratic Party faithfuls who supported O'Daniel's unusual path to the Governor's Mansion. On 17 January James V. Allred vacated the executive mansion for a federal judgeship granted by President Roosevelt, and O'Daniel took the oath of office. Shortly after the governor's unusually flamboyant inauguration, the State Parks Board met to plan its strategy for the new legislature.

The board debated renewed legislative pressure to designate a new state park at San Felipe to commemorate colonizer Stephen Fuller Austin. Board members, however, showed little patience with this deviation from outdoor-recreation plans and recorded "much discussion upon the advisability of taking any more small parks of historical value only." They concluded this agenda item by noting that board member Ken Clapp "made a strong argument against it but no action was taken."

Members considered more favorably their latest offer in the Guadalupe

Mountains, giving landowner Judge Jesse Calhoun Hunter "and his associates a twenty-five year lease of the concessions," but again reached no decision. Following a report on winter activities at the state parks and CCC camps, the board settled on a substantial budget request for the legislature and on plans for reporting to the Capitol the threat of federal cutbacks. Lawson and his staff then began work on CCC camp applications for the approaching thirteenth period, to begin 1 April.[3]

Despite federal grumbling and threats of CCC cutbacks, the State Parks Board again maintained its thirteen active projects as the summer period began. Work continued, as well, on the three active local parks in Beaumont, Dallas, and El Paso. Only the side camp at Mother Neff abandoned its barracks, which board member Pat Neff now struggled to obtain from Army ownership and convert to park visitor use or a National Youth Administration encampment.[4]

And despite the frustrating and well-publicized financial troubles of Texas government that spring, the Texas park system won large funding increases from an increasingly park-minded legislature. Well beyond its roughly $40,000 budget in the current fiscal year, the State Parks Board received $68,800 for 1940 and $68,500 for 1941, plus authority to spend its visitor receipts held in the Special Park Fund. Line-item construction budgets for parks under development attempted to match federal demands, but these figures—ranging from $1,000 annually for Balmorhea, Bastrop, Brownwood, Fort Parker, Garner, Mackenzie, and Tyler, to $2,500 at Caddo Lake and Huntsville—could not adequately supplement federal development. A single two-year appropriation of $12,500 specifically for future parks at Buchanan and Inks lakes came closer to what the NPS demanded.

Also below federal expectations, the central design office obtained salaries only for an "Inspector-Architect," two technical assistants, and a draftsman. But keeper's salaries now appeared for most parks, usually at $300 per year with housing. And a central "Director of Concessions" at $1,800 annual salary would ensure consistent services throughout the system's operating parks. Finally, executive secretary Lawson gained another raise to $3,600 per year, effective 1 September.[5]

In related matters, the struggling Texas Relief Commission still administered enrollment for the CCC plus a host of other underfunded state relief programs. This legislature, acting on earlier proposals and now Governor O'Daniel's pledge of old-age assistance, created the State Department of Public Welfare to absorb all relief duties, administer O'Daniel's program for the elderly and child welfare offices, and process federal Social Security and surplus commodities distribution programs. The new agency also continued recruitment for the CCC, primarily through county welfare boards.[6]

Triumph at San Jacinto

The Board of Control in 1939 returned to caretaker budgets for its seven state historical parks: Fannin, Goliad, Gonzales, King's, Lipantitlan, San Jacinto, and Washington. Down from a post-Centennial high of $32,820 in the current year, the new budgets of about $25,000 per year for 1940 and 1941 included few capital improvements. But with keepers' annual salaries ranging from $720 to $1,800 plus free dwellings, these parks still offered much higher management benefits than those of State Parks Board custodians. One of the highest-paid employees at any Texas state park at $1,500 per year, eighty-five-year-old Andrew Jackson Houston now drew a thinly disguised legislative pension as "Advisory Superintendent" for San Jacinto State Park. His battleground park also received for the new biennium by far the largest individual state park appropriation at $17,410 per year, primarily for maintenance of its vast new formal landscaping and just-completed concrete and limestone memorial tower.[7]

On 21 April, Superintendent Houston joined Governor O'Daniel in dedicating this inspiring obelisk and associated museum, under construction since the Centennial year of 1936. Houstonian and New Deal banking czar Jesse Jones had arranged for several federal agencies to supplement the state's budget of $250,000, and a federal Centennial contribution of $385,000, to complete the monument and battleground improvements. The Public Works Administration added $225,000, and by 1939 the Works Progress Administration had completed fourteen projects at the site adding up to $876,375, for a total effort costing $1.8 million. "The shaft towers 570 feet above the famous battlefield where Texas won its independence," the Centennial commission's final report described, "to give the memorial eminence as the tallest as well as one of the most distinctive stone monuments in the world."

Indeed, Jones and architect Alfred Charles Finn defied PWA director Harold Ickes's insistence that his funds should not contribute to a structure taller than the Washington Monument. Before Ickes calculated the Texans' resolve to break a world's record, their San Jacinto Monument soared about twelve feet higher than its marble counterpart in Washington, D.C., completed in 1885. The new record breaker utilized a number of modern construction techniques worked out by project engineer Robert Cummins and contractor Warren Bellows. To match the Washington surroundings as well, landscape architect Mrs. C. B. Whitehead designed monumentally scaled walkways and formalized terrain around the tower, including a 200-by-1,800-foot reflecting pool stretching along the path of Sam Houston's victorious army toward the base of the tower.[8]

In preparation for the 1939 dedication, sculptor William M. McVey carved shallow-relief scenes from Texas history into the Cordova-shell lime-stone surrounding the shaft's base. And the newly formed San Jacinto Museum of History Association outfitted massive rooms inside the monument base with displays interpreting early Texas settlement and the 1836 revolution.

Finally, Louis Kemp, energetic leader of Centennial historians, wrote for inscription a six-hundred-word account of the background and events of the revolution. McVey's crew incised this narrative around the museum base in eight huge paragraphs and a giant alphabet. "The lettering is large enough to permit its being read from the driveway which encircles the monument," observed Rosa Todd Hamner a few months before the dedication. "In this streamlined age of ours, it is not enough to write our history so plainly that he who runs may read," she deduced, "we must write it so that he who rides in his automobile may read."[9]

Stephen F. Austin State Park

Disregarding emphatic arguments by the State Parks Board not to acquire commemorative parkland, lawmakers on 15 May accepted fourteen acres of the old San Felipe townsite in Austin County. In 1823 Stephen Austin, seeking to fulfill his father's colonization charter, and Baron de Bastrop, representing the Mexican government, chose this crossing on the Brazos River as the capital of Austin's new colony. For many years the village served as headquarters for his far-ranging agricultural venture and as the site of important events leading to the Texas Revolution. Almost a century later, in 1929, parkland donation offers began, but the legislature declined to budget development funds for the site. The idea for a state park resurfaced in 1936 as the state's Centennial commission placed a $14,000 statue of Austin at San Felipe, along with a replica of his log cabin. Now the legislature assigned responsibility to the State Parks Board because, in addition to the small historic landscape deeded by the San Felipe Park Association, a nearby tract of 657.3 acres came from the San Felipe city council, "provided the state would take it over and the federal government would locate a CCC camp there," its donors stipulated.

In addition, they also envisioned development of the small tract by a "federal CCC camp" and "possible restoration of the old town as in the days when Stephen F. Austin lived there." Indeed, legislators provided the parks board an appropriation of $2,500 for San Felipe in each of the coming two fiscal years, a top-dollar amount shared only with Caddo Lake and Huntsville, "to match local or Federal funds" for park development. An additional $500 per year appeared for a keeper's salary, but Governor O'Daniel vetoed that specific contribution to Stephen F. Austin State Park.[10]

Big Bend National Park

In early May the dormant Big Bend project enjoyed a dusting off with the legislature's approval of the Winfield-Cauthorn Bill, taking great strides to create by name a Big Bend National Park. Senator H. L. Winfield of Fort Stockton, author of the Big Bend funding bill vetoed two years before, and cosponsor Representative Albert R. Cauthorn of Del Rio this time cleverly sidestepped any land-purchase issue. Their new measure instead jumped ahead to the ultimate goal, detailed an article in *The Texas Weekly,* "by authorizing transfer to the Federal Government of State-owned lands in the area." Winfield and Cauthorn "now think no State money will be needed," the story explained, "inasmuch as it is hoped that donations sufficient to buy land needed for the proposed park will be obtained from various sources."

Governor O'Daniel, already deadlocked with the legislature over his promised old-age pensions and other enormous obligations, fully supported this largely symbolic gesture. "I have before me," he told lawmakers as they considered the bill, "information based on actual experience of the National Park Service. . . . It is estimated that the Federal Government would spend $225,000 annually for maintenance and protection of the park." Then projecting 120,000 out-of-state visitors spending an average $4 per person per day over seven days, O'Daniel quoted, "it would bring to the State $3,360,000 expenditure every year. Not only would the park prove valuable from this standpoint, but it, of course, would add much to the enjoyment of citizens throughout the State."

O'Daniel signed the bill on 12 May, no doubt at advisor Beauchamp's urging, and no doubt pleasing NPS advocates for the park. "Some further action," *Texas Weekly* admitted, "may turn out to be necessary, of course." [11]

Changes in Management

The State Parks Board convened in July at its Austin office to consider results of the legislative session and a larger but far from adequate budget to maintain all CCC development camps. Fully half of those attending this organizational session came as new members, since Governor O'Daniel early in the year had named Raymond L. Dillard of Mexia to replace Beauchamp, then appointed Jake D. Sandefer of Breckenridge and H. G. Webster of Huntsville to fill the expired terms of Pat Neff and Gus Urbantke.

Neff's departure ended a fascinating, roller-coaster era for the parks board. It began in the early 1920s when, as governor, he first proposed a state park system, and continued through his recent chairmanship of the board during the peak of New Deal development. "I would, of course, have been happy to remain on the Board," Neff wrote current Chairman Wendell

Mayes, "but being left off the Board will not decrease in any way my interest. . . . I shall serve it in every way to the best of my abilities and my opportunities." Mayes soon accommodated Neff by naming him official custodian of Mother Neff State Park!

O'Daniel's board appointments followed a trend begun in 1935 with Mayes of Brownwood, favoring businessmen from communities near large new state parks. Dillard, an "oil operator" from Mexia, showed particular interest in Fort Parker State Park, according to an internal memo from the NPS regional director. The same document painted Webster as "a shrewd, keen minded banker" from Huntsville, with an "immediate local interest" in Huntsville State Park. Sandefer, from Breckenridge in Stephens County, also was noted as an "oil operator" and "great football fan and poker player." He had secured a position on the State Parks Board to ensure a major new park development on the shores of Possum Kingdom Lake, under construction in adjacent Palo Pinto County. Further, these men no doubt came to the governor's attention through Secretary of State Beauchamp, in private practice a prominent oil attorney and former resident of Huntsville.[12]

The board agreed at the July meeting, after reviewing its new budget, to expand the executive secretary's position to full time. Upon reelecting Mayes chairman and J. V. Ash vice chairman, members then tackled a multitude of business, including CCC camp assignments for the forthcoming winter period.

Since the legislature awarded an approaching biennial budget below that desired by the NPS for its current program in Texas, federal officials issued notice that five CCC state park camps would close in the fall. Board members further learned that the crucial sawmill and furniture shop at Bastrop State Park, one of the sites slated for discharge, already had ceased operation. In addition, only two CCC camps from the park service–supervised Texas allotment would receive new park assignments, at metropolitan developments on Lake Austin and Fort Worth's Eagle Mountain Lake, neither for improvement of state parks.

Attempting to balance the unpleasant news, executive secretary Lawson proudly informed the board that profits from Longhorn Cavern, acquired in 1932, recently retired the park's $6,567 debt on schedule. The parks board would henceforth receive 20 percent of revenue from the concession operation at this popular Burnet County park. Finally, armed with authority from the recent legislature—courtesy of Lawson's old boss, Senator J. W. E. H. Beck—to release any state lands deemed "not suitable" for park operation, the board voted on 10 July to return quitclaim deeds for several difficult sites. They also instructed the owners to discontinue use of the title "state park" at the released areas:

- Jefferson [Jeff] Davis State Park near Hillsboro, a 35-acre reunion grounds, had been donated in 1927 by the Old Settlers Association but "never operated or developed" by the parks board.
- Hereford State Park, 540 acres initially developed by the CCC as a Panhandle drought-relief project, had since been operated by the city and never legally deeded to the state.
- Ochiltree State Park, a 647-acre proposal in extreme northwest Texas, had been repeatedly turned down by the NPS for CCC camp development, to the frustration of local donors.
- Palisades State Park, whose CCC-developed 320 acres in upper Palo Duro Canyon apparently had never been donated to the state, proved to be a flood-prone site encroached by private development.[13]

A New Executive Secretary

At their 30 August meeting, parks board members accepted the resignation of William Jennings Lawson after three years' service as the park system's first executive secretary. Former board member Beauchamp had recommended Lawson earlier in the year for the job of personal secretary to Governor O'Daniel, but Lawson declined. The governor and his secretary of state repeated their offer during the summer, and Lawson accepted the job effective with the new fiscal year on 1 September.

For Lawson's replacement, the board found forty-four-year-old Frank David Quinn, an accountant and most recently manager of the Seguin and Guadalupe County Chamber of Commerce. A native of Mississippi, Quinn moved in 1931 from Tennessee to Tyler to start a new career in the booming East Texas oil business. There he no doubt encountered Tyler attorney Beauchamp, and after 1934 in Seguin developed friendships with power brokers in the San Antonio region. Quinn would receive the executive secretary's newly raised full-time salary of $3,600 per year.[14]

Prompted by a recent attorney general's opinion that the board should revise its park lease agreements, Quinn acted immediately to negotiate new contracts with concessionaires. The board soon adopted a form of concession or lease contract, the state auditor recorded, "which provides that the Board shall receive 85%, and the concessionaire 15%, of the net profit from operations." This new approach basically transposed previous arrangements —demonstrated by the recent Longhorn Cavern change in which the parks board received a straight 20 percent of revenue—into a much better deal for the state. Partly as a result, the Palo Duro Corporation—concession manager at Bastrop, Bonham, Caddo Lake, and Palo Duro Canyon state parks—withdrew from the first two sites, alarming park personnel by taking with it the Bastrop cabins' bed springs and mattresses.

TABLE 14
Texas Parks of the Fourteenth-Period CCC
October 1939–March 1940

NPS Number	Official Name	CCC Company
SP-35	Longhorn Cavern State Park	Co. 854
SP-36	Brownwood State Park	Co. 849
SP-42	Garner State Park	Co. 879
SP-43	Goliad State Park	Co. 3822(V)
SP-44	Fort Parker State Park	Co. 3807(C)
SP-47	Balmorhea State Park	Co. 1856[1]
SP-49	Daingerfield State Park	Co. 1801(C)[2]
SP-51	Lockhart State Park	Co. 3803[3]
SP-52	Mackenzie State Park	Co. 3820
SP-53	Cleburne State Park	Co. 3804
SP-54	Tyler State Park	Co. 2888
SP-61	Huntsville State Park	Co. 1823(CV)
SP-63	Fort Griffin State Park	Co. 3803[3]
CP-1	Ascarate County Park	Co. 2873(C)
CP-2	Eagle Mountain Lake County Park	Co. 1801(C)[2]
MA-1	Tyrrell Metropolitan Park	Co. 845
MA-2	Bachman–White Rock Lake Metropolitan Park	Co. 2896[2]
MA-3	Lake Austin Metropolitan Park	Co. 1805
NP-1	Big Bend National Park	Co. 1856[1]

[1] Co. 1856 finished its work at Balmorhea and on 2 January 1940 reoccupied the Chisos Basin camp as NP-1-T.

[2] A cadre from Co. 2896, MA-2 at Dallas, helped set up the new CCC camp at Azle, but on 30 January 1940 Co. 1801(C) arrived from Daingerfield to begin work on CP-2, Eagle Mountain Lake.

[3] Lockhart's Co. 3803 transferred on 5 January 1940 to Fort Griffin State Park.

Undaunted, Quinn arranged new concession contracts for the coming year at Daingerfield, Davis Mountains, Lake Corpus Christi, Meridian, Normangee, and Tyler state parks. The parks board then elected to operate most of its other parks, including Bastrop and Bonham, directly through its Austin office and immediately authorized replacement furnishings for Bastrop's lodgings.

Quinn also compiled and submitted CCC camp applications for the coming fourteenth period. Notwithstanding recent federal promises of camp reductions, the State Parks Board wished to place a camp at Normangee and to reestablish CCC development at Meridian. Quinn and his board also hoped to have several new sites approved, although they held no deeds to their proposed parklands at Buchanan Lake, McKittrick Canyon in the

Guadalupe Mountains, Possum Kingdom sites on both sides of the future lake, and San Augustine.[15]

As the NPS had warned three months before, CCC camps moved out of Bastrop and Lockhart in October, and from Balmorhea and Daingerfield in January. Only the threatened Longhorn Cavern camp obtained a reprieve as its resident Co. 854 continued road development there. About the time Bastrop's Co. 1811 abandoned its long-occupied barracks, its former companion Co. 1805 returned on 9 December from Wyoming to Texas for the winter period, now assigned to a new metropolitan park project on Lake Austin. Lockhart's experienced Co. 3803 moved to the Brazos River valley in Shackelford County to begin work on Fort Griffin State Park, a 519-acre county donation encompassing ruins of the 1867–1881 frontier fort and part of its companion townsite.

In slow but positive response to the legislature's promise of transferring Big Bend land to the federal government, the park service in January reopened its Chisos Basin CCC camp by moving Balmorhea's Co. 1856 into the old barracks there. Later in January, Co. 1801(C) moved from its completed job at Daingerfield to begin a new county park on Eagle Mountain Reservoir northwest of Fort Worth.

A significant change appeared in the park service classification of local park projects as the fourteenth period began. Since the beginning of the CCC program, all federally sponsored projects had received a "State Park" number for project approval and budget coordination. But with reduction in funding for traveling inspectors and central design offices, the park service moved away from close control of state programs in favor of more local management of projects. For the State Parks Board this new policy meant considerably less contact with the Santa Fe office and no further board assistance to local parks, previously included each six months with the state's CCC applications. For local park authorities, however, this meant increased contact with the NPS for project applications and management of associated CCC camp expenses.

Thus "County Parks" now displayed a CP- designation, and "Metropolitan Areas" received an MA- prefix, both followed by numerical assignment within the state as a whole. For examples, Ascarate County Park, formerly SP-62 as the sixty-second "State Park" designation in Texas, now became CP-1 as the first county park project. Tyrrell Metropolitan Park, formerly SP-50, now became MA-1, and so forth. And for the first time in Texas, a genuine "National Park" project appeared, to resume CCC development in the Big Bend with Co. 1856 carrying the corresponding designation of NP-1.

As the shuffled CCC companies of the fourteenth period settled into their new assignments, Texas actually retained its previous parks allotment of sixteen camps. Congressmen Sam Russell, Lyndon Johnson, Fritz Lanham, and Ewing Thomason apparently threw their political muscles behind the newest camps, and many colleagues worked to continue their own highly favored CCC projects. Other technical-agency camp retentions also showed a distinct shift to the state's western districts, as U.S. Forest Service camp numbers in East Texas dropped to ten in this winter period, and the Soil Conservation Service—deeply involved with erosion control on the high plains of West Texas—maintained its previous allotment of twenty-seven CCC companies. Such congressional control of the CCC camp selection process certainly benefited particular districts, but it came with a price for Texas authorities attempting to manage a statewide program.

The frustrated State Parks Board, for example, lost control of three CCC companies as its own allotment fell to ten active camps by the middle of the fourteenth period. Further, the NPS approved none of the new state park developments actually applied for, yet opened a project at Fort Griffin, plus a city park for Austin and a county park for Fort Worth. For all its amazing benefits, the CCC with its park service supervision remained a frustrating program for Texas park planners. "The State Parks Board does not have full control, by any means, over the CCC program," an exasperated Quinn explained to board members at their 9 December meeting.[16]

Seeking Relief Elsewhere

The parks board now realized it should look beyond sagging relationships with the NPS and CCC for relief-labor assistance in park building. Departed parks board chairman D. E. Colp had led the way to such diversity in 1935 by securing Works Progress Administration labor to build swimming pools, golf courses, and other visitor amenities outside the CCC list of allowed projects. Then in 1937 Pat Neff secured the first park-system road-maintenance agreement with the Texas Highway Department.

Retired from the board but determined to obtain additional development at Mother Neff State Park after its CCC camp left, Neff found his old good-roads contacts willing to help. He arranged in early 1939 for the highway department to construct a scenic byway west from the park along the Leon River, as an entrance road for park visitors from the Gatesville area. In return, Neff's friends on the parks board in August granted an "unrestricted right to the State Highway Department" to extend this road through the park as a general purpose thoroughfare. As president of Baylor University in nearby Waco, Neff also realized that the institution's National Youth Administration–supported students could assist with park improvement, and late that year he established an NYA resident camp at Mother Neff in the park's old CCC barracks.

The parks board likewise turned to the NYA for assistance after the

CCC abandoned its furniture shop at Bastrop. Executive secretary Quinn contracted in late 1939 with NYA wood shops in Bowie, Vernon, and Wichita Falls to fabricate twenty sets of furnishings for the new San Solomon Courts housekeeping cottages at Balmorhea State Park. "All materials such as paint, pine lumber, sandpaper, etc.," the *Texas NYA Digest* announced, "were furnished by the Texas State Park Board." Congressman Johnson, former state director of the NYA, in the meantime established a huge NYA resident crafts center for fifteen hundred students at Inks Lake. With Bastrop State Park in Johnson's district, the parks board likewise thought of creating an NYA resident center at the old CCC barracks for operation of that park's own extensive but idle shop.

Furthering the Colp and Neff legacy of diversity in partnerships, board members in December finalized yet another, broader, agreement with the highway department. Naming additional park roads on a list expected to grow as the system matured, the parks board arranged for state highway crews "to maintain all standard roads in our present park system." This priceless boost to park operations not only relieved the board of tremendous expenses, it ensured that all park roads would meet the high standards of the Texas highway system, itself widely advanced through federal New Deal programs.[17]

Federal Changes in Management

Early in the year at President Roosevelt's urging, Congress passed the Administrative Reorganization Act of 1939, effective with the new fiscal year in July. Citing several reasons for a new federal management structure, including economic recovery and threats of war from Asia and Europe, historian Charles Schilke emphasizes that "the ad hoc group of alphabet agencies created during the hundred days and the burst of legislation in 1935 required rationalization into a structured welfare state."[18] In other words, the NPS exercises of the past two years—balancing the resources of a number of agencies, dispersing leaders and budgets to the park service regions, encouraging partner states to plan and participate to a greater degree—hinted at this development through Interior secretary Harold Ickes's own experiments in rationalization. Now all of Roosevelt's executive departments began a government-wide shifting and balancing of resources that particularly affected the multiple New Deal relief agencies.

Hoping to create large new cabinet agencies, Roosevelt instead compromised with Congress on umbrella organizations, including the Federal Security Agency and the Federal Works Agency. Now, terms such as "security" and "welfare"—in sight of a new decade and with hopes that the depression would end as the 1930s closed—replaced the term "relief" in federal parlance. Both the CCC and the NYA, because they benefited the welfare of their enrollees, fell under the Federal Security Agency. The new Federal Works Agency coordinated FDR's existing Public Works Administration and its rival WPA, renamed Work Projects Administration on 1 July for the new bureaucracy.

The resulting placement of authority other than the president over the CCC actually caused little alteration in its administration, for better or worse, despite loud objections from Director Fechner. A far more important change came when, because of disability costs for CCC camp commanders, Roosevelt reduced the number of armed-services reserve officers at those posts. The War Department continued to supply and administer CCC camps, and at first the replacement "civilian" commanders actually came from military reserve-officer lists. But when a new European war broke out on 1 September, the U.S. military shifted in attitude and function—followed slowly by the federal government and the American people—toward the possibility of involvement. The regular Army began a deliberate mobilization within its meager force of 174,000 enlisted men, compared to 300,000 enrollees in the CCC. Fewer and fewer reservists chose the CCC for their company-command experience, as more and more military assignments became available.[19]

Fechner weathered a rough year in 1939 with unwelcome attacks on his authority, arguments over the military role in the CCC, and more trouble from Congress on local camp jobs and expenditures. According to historian John Salmond, Fechner missed the point of federal decentralization and forgot a critical basis of support for the CCC—the operational money that each camp spent in its host congressional district. Fechner's first act after placement under the Federal Security Agency, Salmond notes, was to "set up a huge chain of central machine repair shops directly under his control." Individual CCC camps could no longer hire Local Experienced Men as truck and auto mechanics, and no miscellaneous vehicle supplies could henceforth be purchased from local businesses.

"The plan was implemented almost immediately [in November], a signal triumph for Fechner's centralization policies," Salmond explains. "It was also his last official act. His health had been poor throughout 1939, and in December he suffered a severe heart attack. He died at Walter Reed Hospital on New Year's Eve, after a three-week struggle for life."[20]

1940: END OF THE DEPRESSION

The Struggle to Maintain Programs

President Roosevelt appointed CCC deputy director James J. McEntee, a New Jersey native and longtime machinist union colleague of Fechner, to head the corps soon after Fechner's death. McEntee made no course changes in the CCC and pressed on, even more stubbornly than his inflexible predecessor, with the unwieldy centralization plan. McEntee immediately faced a turbulent Congress in January 1940 with reauthorization plans in one hand and more proposals for huge cutbacks in his other. Again, Roosevelt had no intention of eliminating the CCC but recognized the political necessity of reducing the organization himself before Congress acted more drastically. As Texas parks manager Quinn learned during a March visit to Washington, FDR proposed to cut the CCC in October by $56 million, reducing nationwide enrollment to 230,000 in 1,227 camps.

"Texas naturally will have to stand her part," Quinn warned parks board members at their March meeting in Austin. But he also relayed good news with the Texas Highway Department's plans for some eight hundred signs "to be placed 1 to 1 1/2 mile from the entrance to each park" before the coming summer visitor season. Then reviewing a new list of parkland deeds proposed for release, the board agreed to return three more:

- Beeville State Park, 128-acres donated by the city in 1927 and leased since 1933 to the local American Legion post, whose release would clear the way for WPA construction on the site of a city auditorium and recreation center.
- Robinson State Park, 69-acres near Llano, also a 1927 donation and apparently the only "small park" deed actually recorded by the late D. E. Colp.
- McKittrick Canyon, a conditional deed of unsurveyed magnitude, returned because it received no CCC camp assignment in the last period.

Members deliberated the usual list of "new areas" for park developments at which they held no deeds, but added speculation on coastal sites at Brazos Island and Brazoria County. Holding either insufficient acreage or no titles on these parklands for future CCC developments, and mindful of further cutbacks from Washington, Quinn struggled to sustain even the current level of work at Texas state parks with his CCC camp applications for the approaching fifteenth period.[21]

When the new CCC period commenced on 1 April, Texas's park allotment remained stable, a notable political accomplishment for the congressional delegation and the State Parks Board. Following this positive CCC trend in mid-April, Congress rejected even the president's proposed cuts to the corps, voting to restore more than $50 million to its budget and reauthorizing it at current levels for another two years. With elections looming for all parties this year, Roosevelt had staged his requisite economy stance, and Congress had acted to disturb the economies in its individual districts as little as possible.[22]

TABLE 15
Texas Parks of the Fifteenth-Period CCC
April–September 1940

NPS Number	Official Name	CCC Company
SP-35	Longhorn Cavern State Park	Co. 854
SP-36	Brownwood State Park	Co. 849
SP-42	Garner State Park	Co. 879
SP-43	Goliad State Park	Co. 3822(V)
SP-44	Fort Parker State Park	Co. 3807(C)
SP-52	Mackenzie State Park	Co. 3820
SP-53	Cleburne State Park	Co. 3804[1]
SP-54	Tyler State Park	Co. 2888
SP-61	Huntsville State Park	Co. 1823(CV)
SP-63	Fort Griffin State Park	Co. 3803
CP-1	Ascarate County Park	Co. 2873(C)
CP-2	Eagle Mountain Lake County Park	Co. 1801(C)
MA-1	Tyrrell Metropolitan Park	Co. 845
MA-2	Bachman–White Rock Lake Metropolitan Park	Co. 2896
MA-3	Lake Austin Metropolitan Park	Co. 1805
MA-4	Franklin Fields Metropolitan Park	Co. 3804[1]
NP-1	Big Bend National Park	Co. 1856

[1] Cleburne State Park's project closed on 16 August, and Co. 3804 transferred to San Antonio's Olmos Basin to begin work on Franklin Fields Metropolitan Park.

"Security" Assumes New Meaning

During the winter of 1939–1940 the war in Europe seemed to Americans as finished, since Germany's conquests in the East appeared to measure the extent of its aggression. Then this "phony war" resurged in March 1940 with a Russian victory in Finland, followed on 9 April by German invasions of Denmark and Norway. Suddenly on 10 May the German armies pushed west into the "low countries" of Holland and Belgium, routing British and French defenders and shocking the U.S. Congress with news too close to home. Lawmakers in Washington nervously debated the consequences to U.S. defensive security, and asked the War and Navy departments for reports on the condition of their forces.

By 15 May Britain's prime minister Winston Churchill cabled Roosevelt for immediate assistance. Amidst a "hurricane of events," as he labeled these rapid developments, FDR on 16 May "drove up to Capitol Hill and asked a cheering Congress for almost a billion dollars for increased defense," writes Roosevelt biographer James MacGregor Burns. "An alarmed Congress," details historian Robert A. Devine, "acted with amazing speed," and forthwith smothered the depression—and perhaps the New Deal—under massive deficit defense spending. Additional requests for funding reached $5 billion after the fall of France in July and achieved an astonishing total of $10.5 billion by September.[23]

The CCC, long caught between conflicting arguments to reduce or increase its military potential, now fell under the glaring spotlight of national defense. Congress had dismissed attempts early in 1940 to move the CCC toward military training but seemed interested in its potential role as a "noncombatant auxiliary to Army troops," according to historian Salmond. During the summer uproar in Washington, such an amendment to the coming fiscal year's relief appropriation passed with "the full support of the Federal Security Agency, the War Department, and the Administration," Salmond adds. Through enhancement of the educational programs already offered in CCC camps, after July all enrollees participated each week in twenty hours of "general defense training," ranging from map and plan reading to simple engineering and mathematics, as well as operation of field kitchens, first-aid stations, and communication equipment.[24]

Meeting on 11 July at the Brownwood State Park refectory in the shadow of CCC Co. 849's barracks, the Texas State Parks Board discussed the implications of recent world and national events. With federal mobilization planned for the Texas National Guard, and a site near Brownwood selected for its autumn training exercises, board members patriotically volunteered their convenient state park for anticipated military recreation needs. And forecasting a possible role for other parks in the Texas system, they generously offered the use of any state park facilities necessary "for military training."

Texas park authorities learned in August of more changes with their federal partners as NPS director Arno Cammerer, in ill health for some time, announced his retirement. During Cammerer's directorship, which began with the New Deal seven years earlier, "the areas under the Service tripled in number," credits historian Edwin C. Bearss, "and facilities for public use increased notably. Visitation [at national parks] jumped from approximately 2 million to 16 million persons a year." Cammerer fervently backed the national park proposal for Big Bend and clearly facilitated for Texas one of the largest state-park assistance programs in the nation. His replacement on 20 August, Newton B. Drury, came to the park service not from the bureau's insular line of succession but from a closely associated preservation effort, California's Save-the-Redwoods League.

About the same time Herbert Maier, park service emissary for Texas and another seven-year veteran of New Deal development, left his acting-regional-director position at Santa Fe for California. As Maier moved to a job in the western regional parks office at San Francisco, Minor Raymond

Tillotson, superintendent at Grand Canyon National Park, became director of NPS Region III.[25]

Yet another federal "security" bureau, the NYA, like the CCC, saw its mission shifted to a supportive role for national defense. Radio training and repair soon dominated coursework at NYA resident centers, and its furniture shops tinkered with manufacture of gunstocks and other military craftwork. Without anticipating their coincidental defense alliance, the State Parks Board by midsummer had forged a major agreement with the NYA to occupy the old CCC barracks at Bastrop State Park and staff the furniture mill. About forty-five NYA boys now processed pine lumber from forest-thinning operations at the park, and with select walnut, cedar, and oak logs turned out furniture orders for state parks across Texas.[26]

Unfortunately, the large warehouse and lumber mill at Bastrop burned to the ground on 22 August from suspected spontaneous combustion fueled by the mill's finishing room. Reporting to fellow board members on the incident, Vice Chairman J. V. Ash of Bastrop explained that "both the warehouse and the mill were a total loss, together with all supplies and equipment stored therein." NYA authorities in Austin promised Ash, however, that their program "is willing to furnish the labor with which to rebuild the mill and will replace their woodworking machinery and equipment, which was installed in the mill at the time of the fire."[27]

In September, the War Department and Congress accepted, in a fashion, the parks board's offer of counting on its Texas facilities for defense work. Acting on a politically bold suggestion from organizers of Citizens Military Training Camps—an obscure but persistent summer-soldier group that included the new Secretary of War, Henry Lewis Stimson—Roosevelt proposed the nation's first peacetime conscription. On 14 September with bipartisan support and greatly diminished opposition from isolationists, Congress passed the Selective Training and Service Act. The next day House Speaker William Brockman Bankhead died, and as extra-continental mobilization of the U.S. Army began, Samuel Taliaferro Rayburn of Bonham, Texas, ascended by unanimous vote to succeed Bankhead as Speaker of the House.

The immense strength of the Texas congressional delegation—led by John Garner as vice president and now Rayburn as Speaker—once again emerged in the form of federal patronage. The Army quickly staked out major training camps for the National Guard and draftees near several Texas communities, all incidentally with adjacent state parks ready to perform recreation duties: Abilene (Camp Barkeley), Brownwood (Camp Bowie), Mineral Wells (Camp Wolters), and even Palacios (Camp Hulen) where the CCC had built "Tres Palacios State Park" at the New Deal's beginning in 1933.[28]

Election Season

Texas Democrats convened in September at Mineral Wells to regain their composure after Governor O'Daniel once again required no runoff following the primary vote. Ernest Thompson and Miriam Ferguson—each running one last time—failed to dent O'Daniel's hold on the electorate, despite his first term's short list of accomplishments. Debates focused instead on the proposed third-term candidacy for FDR, particularly in light of the short-lived presidential bid by Garner that ended at the July national convention.

The vice president's recent support of the Selective Service Act came wholly from his interest in national defense rather than harmonious alignment with his president. After their falling out in 1937 over the Supreme Court, labor unions, and relief spending, Garner's "obstructive and behind the scenes tactics were a source of constant concern to Mr. Roosevelt and the New Deal establishment," summarizes Garner biographer Lionel Patenaude. Thus for the 1940 reelection contest Roosevelt and the Democratic Party rejected Garner, who vehemently opposed FDR's unprecedented third-term attempt anyway. On 17 July at the Chicago convention Roosevelt accepted the nomination, joined on the ticket by his long-time Agriculture secretary, Henry Agard Wallace.[29]

Few Texas congressional races in 1940 attracted attention outside the invincible candidacy of U.S. Senator Tom Connally, but few congressmen displayed the ambition of the 10th District's representative Lyndon Johnson. Taking full advantage of the federal Park, Parkway and Recreational-Area Study initiated just as he entered Congress, Johnson persuaded the NPS to assist the Lower Colorado River Authority (LCRA) with a comprehensive analysis of its huge new reservoirs in his district. The resulting sophisticated publication, *The Highland Lakes of Texas,* detailed vast possibilities for Central Texas water recreation, backed by an introduction from President Roosevelt describing similar benefits realized by the Tennessee Valley Authority. The Highland Lakes booklet appeared in the fall, just in time to create a wealth of positive publicity inside—and outside—Johnson's district. It clearly took aim, as well, at the coming Texas legislative session and appropriations for the State Parks Board and Big Bend land purchases.

With grandiose sentences projecting the potential of recreation for the entire state, not just these Colorado River lakes, the report described untold resources waiting for use and improvement. "Not until a large portion of the countryside had been won from a total wilderness," it related, "could [Texans] really enjoy the wilderness of the remaining part." Then reminding readers that their new state recreation system resulted primarily from federal funding, the report pictured a large penny with the caption declaring:

TABLE 16

Texas Parks of the Sixteenth-Period CCC

October 1940–March 1941

NPS Number	Official Name	CCC Company
SP-36	Brownwood State Park	Co. 849
SP-42	Garner State Park	Co. 879
SP-43	Goliad State Park	Co. 3822(V)
SP-44	Fort Parker State Park	Co. 3807(C)
SP-52	Mackenzie State Park	Co. 3820
SP-54	Tyler State Park	Co. 2888
SP-61	Huntsville State Park	Co. 1823(CV)
SP-63	Fort Griffin State Park	Co. 3803
SP-64	Inks Lake State Park	Co. 854
CP-1	Ascarate County Park	Co. 2873(C)
CP-2	Eagle Mountain Lake County Park	Co. 1801(C)
MA-1	Tyrrell Metropolitan Park	Co. 845
MA-2	Bachman–White Rock Lake Metropolitan Park	Co. 2896
MA-3	Lake Austin Metropolitan Park	Co. 1805
MA-4	Franklin Fields Metropolitan Park	Co. 3804
NP-1	Big Bend National Park	Co. 1856

"(ONE CENT) represents the actual amount that each person in Texas was called upon to contribute" two years earlier to the state parks program.

In probable coordination with Johnson's publicity effort, on 2 September Roosevelt registered yet another advance for Texas, while he dedicated the new Great Smoky Mountains National Park in Tennessee and North Carolina. "Here in the Great Smokies we meet today to dedicate these mountains, streams, and forests to the service of the American people," FDR advised. "We are living under governments which are proving their devotion to national parks. . . . the Secretary of the Interior has today ready for dedication two more parks—Kings Canyon, in California and the Olympic National Park, in the State of Washington—and soon, I hope, will have a third, the Big Bend Park, in Texas."

Such language and quality of presentation from both Johnson and the president greatly boosted the movement for all recreation parks in Texas. Their timing particularly benefited the State Parks Board as Quinn submitted winter period CCC camp applications and prepared his budget for the coming legislative session. "If dollars are to be expected in return, ONE CENT is not a very generous yearly capital outlay," Johnson's booklet continued. "If the Highland Lakes Region is added to the State's system of recreational facilities, it will be obvious that appropriations must be substantially increased." [30]

Like magic the proposed 816-acre Inks Lake State Park project appeared on the assignment list of 1 October 1940 for NPS-supervised CCC camps. The Lake Austin project, also in Johnson's district on one of the Highland Lakes, was similarly approved for continuation of the development started there a year earlier. Longhorn Cavern work finally closed with completion of its last effort, a northerly access road connecting its visitor complex to State Highway 29 along Inks Lake's shoreline. This neat transition proceeded with further ease through transfer of Longhorn Cavern's experienced Co. 854 directly to the Inks Lake project, without requiring relocation of its barracks on the road near Inks Dam. Moreover, the previous legislature through special appropriation provided a handsome $12,500 contribution to match federal expenditures for this new park. Additionally, Congressman Johnson's pleasure with the State Parks Board also materialized in a $30,000 federal contribution through the NYA to rebuild the furniture mill, and add a dormitory complex for resident NYA workers, at Bastrop State Park! [31]

Cleburne State Park's CCC camp closed a few weeks before the sixteenth period began, frustrating State Parks Board staff who judged this project unfinished. But other political forces in Washington likely intervened with that effort, as Interior Department undersecretary and Texan Alvin Jacob Wirtz needed a CCC camp to begin work for his friend Maury Maverick, at San Antonio's Franklin Fields Metropolitan Park. As instigator of, then general council for, the LCRA, Wirtz developed through the 1930s impressive political influence based on dam construction and resulting electric power cooperatives. He brokered much of Lyndon Johnson's political and financial support, and in January 1940 obtained the Interior appointment from President Roosevelt. [32] Since Wirtz's earlier law career in Seguin overlapped with Frank Quinn's residence there, the State Parks Board executive secretary—like Maverick and Johnson—no doubt orbited within the gravity of Wirtz's influence as well.

Another project drawing Wirtz's support came to Quinn and his parks board late in 1940, as the NPS helped arrange for preservation of Mission San Jose in San Antonio. Unlike the recent CCC restoration of Mission Espiritu Santo at Goliad, San Jose remained in part an active Roman Catholic parish church, and none of its adjacent lands had been acquired as a state park. Wirtz now proposed that the State Parks Board assume title to San Jose properties acquired by Bexar County and the San Antonio Conservation Society to facilitate recent extensive restoration work at the mission. Then the parks board, the NPS, and the Catholic diocese would manage the complex through a "three-way cooperative agreement," Quinn explained to the board at a fall meeting, hoping to complete negotiations by the spring legislative session.[33]

The election of 5 November 1940 brought more than one million Texans to the polls and a resounding victory for Governor O'Daniel and the Roosevelt–Wallace ticket. Republican Wendell Lewis Willkie obtained 23 percent of the Texas presidential vote, but his Lone Star colleague George C. Hopkins of Dallas conducted a quiet campaign for governor and registered only 6 percent of the vote. Lieutenant Governor Coke Stevenson also won his second term in office. Senator Connally never left Washington during election season yet drubbed his Republican opponent George Shannon of Amarillo about sixteen to one. As with most of his Democratic fellows, Congressman Johnson returned to Washington with a vote of confidence from his 10th District and a growing statewide exposure through his unwavering support for Roosevelt's successful but diminishing public works programs.

1941: TEXAS PARKS GO TO WAR

O'Daniel and the 1941 Legislature

An increased budget for the popular recreation parks system occupied the State Parks Board in January 1941 when lawmakers returned to Austin, but the Big Bend issue promised greater headlines. A two-year-old private campaign to raise money for land purchases for the authorized national park "had planned an intensive drive last spring," related the *Dallas News,* "but this was postponed because of the German blitzkrieg" the previous May. Almost a year later federal defense budgets stimulated the national economy and benefited Texas directly through military training camps and industrial revitalization. Legislators no doubt considered whether to offer a similar defense-emergency deferral for Big Bend or to fund the private land purchases from obviously increasing tax revenues.

As the Big Bend campaign intensified, work progressed through the winter at the park service's CCC camp in the Chisos Basin. "Attractive stone cottages for tourists are now being built on the small, wooded flats of the basin," the *Dallas News* advertised. "After the national park is established, a large lodge or tourist hotel will be added. A water supply has been provided, and roads and trails are being improved." Proving the regional community's support for the measure, Sul Ross State Teachers College president Horace Wilson Morelock announced his "Big Bend Trail [on] U.S. Highway 67, which will carry tourists from Northeastern and Midwestern States through Dallas to the Big Bend." Reminding readers that "Virginians subscribed $1,250,000 for the Shenandoah National Park, [and] their legislators voted an equal sum," the article concluded that Texans would need $1.5 million to make Big Bend National Park a reality.[34]

Senator Winfield of Fort Stockton introduced, for the third legislature in a row, a Big Bend acquisition bill with Representative Cal Huffman of Eagle Pass as House cosponsor. Winfield's first Big Bend measure had successfully drawn $750,000 from the legislature for land purchases, but Governor Allred vetoed the appropriation. The senator's second proposal again met success, but that bill authorized only eventual transfer of state-owned parklands in Brewster County to the federal government. Now his effort called for the full $1.5 million long identified as the amount that would meet NPS demands for acceptance and management of the proposed national park.

On 25 February, Governor O'Daniel elevated his personal secretary Bill Lawson to the position of Secretary of State. Tom Beauchamp, former State Parks Board member and Secretary of State in O'Daniel's first term, had moved in August 1939 to the Texas Court of Criminal Appeals through another O'Daniel appointment. Lawson, the parks board's first executive secretary, fortunately continued his support for state parks at the highest levels of state government.[35]

As the legislative session moved into spring with few tax and funding issues settled, lawmakers at least received the brightest financial reports in more than twelve years. This meant that Texans anticipated a prosperous year ahead and many would indulge in extended summer vacations at parks in their growing state park system. Park keepers throughout the system prepared their facilities for anticipated record-breaking late spring openings. CCC camps still labored at nine state park developments, plus six local parks and the Big Bend National Park project. And the parks board's generously funded mill reconstruction continued at Bastrop State Park. Inspired by all this prosperity, Texas parks manager Quinn received positive signals from the governor and lawmakers for his biennial budget. Meanwhile he busily prepared the seventeenth-period CCC camp applications, hoping to maintain as many projects as possible after 1 April.

Unfortunately, when CCC officials in Washington announced their summer camp assignments, Texas lost four state park development projects and three CCC companies. Tyrrell Park in Beaumont also lost its metropolitan-area CCC company. Units at Garner, Fort Parker, Mackenzie, and Tyler state parks received their marching orders, and Goliad's experienced Co. 3822(V) of war veterans moved in May to continue city park development at San Antonio's Franklin Fields. The Soil Conservation Service also lost four camps, down to twenty-three, and the U.S. Forest Service lost two companies, down to eight for the seventeenth period.

The State Parks Board retained from these cuts only Co. 2888 as it

TABLE 17

Texas Parks of the Seventeenth-Period CCC

April–September 1941

NPS Number	Official Name	CCC Company
SP-36	Brownwood State Park	Co. 849
SP-44	Fort Parker State Park	Co. 3807(C)
SP-61	Huntsville State Park	Co. 1823(CV)
SP-63	Fort Griffin State Park	Co. 3803
SP-64	Inks Lake State Park	Co. 854
SP-65	Possum Kingdom State Park	Co. 2888
CP-1	Ascarate County Park	Co. 2873(C)
CP-2	Eagle Mountain Lake County Park	Co. 1801(C)
MA-2	Bachman–White Rock Lake Metropolitan Park	Co. 2896
MA-3	Lake Austin Metropolitan Park	Co. 1805
MA-4	Franklin Fields Metropolitan Park	Co. 3822(V) [1]
NP-1	Big Bend National Park	Co. 1856

[1] Co. 3822(V) moved on 2 May 1941 from the completed Goliad project and replaced Co. 3804 at Franklin Fields.

transferred from Tyler to the single new state park project for the period, on Possum Kingdom Lake in Palo Pinto County. This new assignment pleased board member Jake Sandefer, especially when the Army agreed to establish its CCC barracks on U.S. Highway 180 at Caddo in Stephens County, just a few miles east of Sandefer's home at Breckenridge. The Brazos River Conservation and Reclamation District, builders of the Possum Kingdom reservoir, presented a deed to the parks board for 6,969 acres, enough land to build a two-unit park on both sides of the impounded Brazos River. The $8.5 million dam, funded in part with federal New Deal monies, had been completed on 20 March and officials estimated that the lake would fill in about three years, allowing CCC workers access for several months to both future park units from their west-shoreline encampment. Tremendous rainfall in late April, however, filled the reservoir to capacity, inundating the river crossing and preventing removal of vegetation from the lake bed near the park development area.[36]

Coincidentally, sixty-five-year-old Senator Morris Sheppard, for whom the Possum Kingdom dam had been named, died on 9 April in Washington, after thirty-nine years in Congress, including twenty-eight in the Senate. As "dean of Congress," notes historian Seth McKay, Sheppard "had been an especial favorite in the Senate, in Texas, and over the nation; and Texans were sobered by a desire to see a suitable man selected to succeed him and serve in the period of critical international relations."

Governor O'Daniel, compelled to appoint a replacement immediately, then to call a special election, kept his choice secret until a 21 April San Jacinto Day speech at the battleground state park, on a platform before its massive new monument. After a lengthy speech on Sam Houston, emphasizing his service almost a hundred years before in the U.S. Senate, O'Daniel dramatically pointed to Houston's last surviving son—and "advisory superintendent" for San Jacinto State Park—eighty-six-year-old Andrew Jackson Houston, naming him the new Senator from Texas. After the shock, then nervous applause, then howling from Texas Democrats, everyone realized that the governor had chosen someone who would not oppose an O'Daniel candidacy in the special election.[37]

April camp closings at Garner, Mackenzie, and Tyler state parks proved that the CCC company political shell game, as always, created winners as well as losers. All three park developments arguably could have continued for some time. But park-insider Beauchamp could not sustain his now-distant influence on the parks board for retaining the Tyler camp, although the Huntsville project—near his alma mater of Sam Houston State Teachers College—remained a favorite, he admitted. O'Daniel's April reappointment of Wendell Mayes to the board ensured continuation of his Brownwood hometown project. At the same time, Lubbock board member Ken Clapp's replacement by T. C. Ashford of Maud (in Bowie County) coincided exactly with the discontinuation of Lubbock's Mackenzie State Park CCC camp. Clapp made the most of his retirement by following the Pat Neff model, obtaining from his former colleagues the title of Mackenzie "custodian and manager."

Garner State Park's loss in April loomed as obvious as its namesake's return from Washington three months before. After thirty-seven years in Congress, John Nance Garner retired as "the most powerful Vice President in the history of the United States," estimates biographer Patenaude. "[W]hen Garner packed his bags and crossed the Potomac for the last time, he left behind a political legacy that few politicians in Washington will ever match." Yet Garner authored very few bills and took pride in the presence of very few federal projects in his district. One local official remembered when, in 1934, he proposed Garner State Park and a CCC camp for its development, the vice president exclaimed, "No, No! As long as I am in Washington no such funds will be spent in Uvalde County." Yet Garner certainly condoned the resulting state park throughout its federal development between 1935 and 1941. And perhaps he had quietly condoned all CCC work in Texas as well, for after Garner's departure the state lost a number of other CCC camps in the seventeenth period. Yet the corps suffered from no nationwide cutbacks at the time.[38]

Jim Hogg Memorial Park

About 1937 when fire destroyed an old home in Rusk, local citizens noted with curiosity the impressive stone-lined basement revealed after the wreckage was cleared. Stories from the town's oldest citizens linked with deed records to confirm this had been the homestead of Joseph Lewis and Lucanda McMath Hogg and thus the 1851 birthplace of their son James Stephen Hogg, first native-born Texas governor. Interest grew in commemorating the site.

Governor Hogg's family had long since sold the property, so in 1940 his surviving children, Ima and Mike, and their cousin Thomas Elisha Hogg acquired the site and donated it to the city of Rusk. Then in April 1941 the legislature passed a bill for the state to accept this 177.36-acre tract. The measure placed the land "under the care and direction of the State Parks Board . . . as a public State Park in commemoration of the birth of James Stephen Hogg, said park to be known as Jim Hogg Memorial Park." [39]

San Jose Mission State Park

By May 1941 all landowners at the restored 1768 Mission San Jose y San Miguel de Aguayo on the San Antonio River had assented to a proposed cooperative agreement for common management as a public park. Following recommendations of NPS historian Ronald Lee in his 1935 examination of San Jose, the federal agency moved for congressional designation of the mission grounds—about six acres, including the imposing stone granary restored in 1932–1933—as a National Historic Site. Interior undersecretary Wirtz supported the common management idea and left negotiations to State Parks Board director Quinn.

Congratulating Quinn on his success, park service regional director Tillotson exclaimed that upon official completion "quite a precedent will have been set. Not only will it be the first national historic site created in cooperation with a State Park Agency, but, also, it will be the first national historic site established in cooperation with the Catholic Church." Eclipsing the Big Bend endeavor momentarily, Tillotson noted, San Jose "will be the first permanent National Park Service area established in Texas, as well as the first national historic site west of the Mississippi River." [40]

On 8 May through joint action of Congress and the Department of the Interior, Secretary Ickes declared San Jose a National Historic Site. In formal ceremony the same day with all members of the State Parks Board present at the San Antonio mission, the San Antonio Conservation Society and Bexar County officials signed their deeds over to the state, represented by board chairman Mayes and executive secretary Quinn. Then with further "colorful ceremony," Quinn's news release recounted, Mayes, Wirtz, and Archbishop Robert E. Lucey signed their "three-way agreement" for long-term management of the site. Each original participant, including the conservation society and the county, appointed representatives to a new advisory board, with Quinn serving as secretary. In its first action two days later, the advisory board appointed Ethel Harris as both custodian and concessionaire of the site, and visitor operations commenced.[41]

A Park-Minded Summer

Poor Andrew Jackson Houston, oldest individual thus far to serve in the U.S. Senate, arrived in Washington, D.C., on 2 June, checked into a Baltimore hospital on the 20th, and died on the 26th. Two days later the special election for his Senate seat fielded twenty-nine candidates—including congressmen Martin Dies and Lyndon Johnson—and Governor O'Daniel squeaked by Johnson with a 1,300 vote lead that took several days to count statewide.[42]

Texas state parks fortunately provided summer readers some relief from the headlines of politics, as a number of periodicals featured the park system for vacation destinations. These June and July articles played their own political role, however, in supporting the State Parks Board budget, which was then under consideration by the legislature in Austin. "Vacation time is upon us," the *Texas Digest* announced on 21 June. "One drawing card that is helping to make Texas one of the greatest recreational States in the nation is the system of State Parks." The June issue of *Texas Parade* printed a number of photos from state parks, noting that "[n]o pity need be wasted on the Texas vacationer with only two weeks to spend at his favorite recreation. No, because Texans need lose no time traveling to far-off spots to find it."

In July, *East Texas* magazine pictured "Speed Boats in line for start of race at Dedication of Tyler State Park," on 14 June. The author focused, however, on moving his readers west for vacations in the Big Bend and the Davis Mountains, where he had recently taken part in a travel writers' tour led by parks board manager Frank Quinn. "In spite of the lack of tourist accommodations," he reported, "Big Bend is already attracting great numbers of venturesome tourists." The *Texas Almanac* in its new edition listed thirty-five state parks—including Big Bend—and their features and facilities, from scenic drives to boating, golfing, and dancing. "Now that the period of great expansion has progressed far enough and the Parks Board administrative organization has had time to begin functioning smoothly," the almanac article concluded, future plans called for new equipment in the present system and new sites to be developed in "suitable areas of the state."[43]

The unusually long legislative session ended on 3 July, and W. Lee

O'Daniel chose to remain governor long enough to sign its resulting laws. The appropriations bill revealed a greatly increased budget for the State Parks Board, once again a substantial accomplishment from a session that witnessed long and bitter arguments over taxes and which programs to fund. Administrative costs for the Austin office alone remained about $25,000, interestingly the same as the board's first substantial appropriation in 1934. But now with thirty-seven parks to manage, operating budgets added more than $65,000, for a 1942 total of $91,000 and a slight reduction in 1943 to $89,000.

Keepers' salaries under the State Parks Board increased in most cases to $600 per year, double their typical wage provided in the closing biennium. Parks with active CCC camps and a few others—utilizing WPA and NYA assistance—received construction budgets for matching federal funds, ranging each year from $1,000 at Garner, Goose Island, Brownwood, Mackenzie, Tyler, and Stephen F. Austin; $1,200 at Possum Kingdom; $1,500 at Inks Lake and San Jose Mission; to $2,500 at Caddo Lake, Cleburne, and Huntsville. Bastrop received a special appropriation of $2,000 in 1942 to rebuild the park system warehouse that burned the previous August along with the NYA furniture shop. No appropriation appeared for the new Jim Hogg Memorial Park.

The astonishing figure in the parks board appropriation appeared under the line item "Big Bend State Park," with a staggering $1.5 million for fiscal year 1942. "For the purchase of land for National Park by the Texas State Parks Board," began the instructions substituted within the appropriation schedule for Senator Winfield's bill. The board "shall first use the moneys herein appropriated," it continued, "in reimbursing and paying into the State Public School Permanent Fund the moneys due it for the public school land acquired for park purposes, together with the mineral rights underlying said property." The balance would be applied to purchases of private land inside authorized park boundaries, exclusive of condemned properties acquired long ago from the state but now delinquent in payments.

Historical parks under the Board of Control—Fannin, Goliad, Gonzales, King's, Lipantitlan, San Jacinto, and Washington—received a modest increase over the previous budget. With paint for the Gonzales keeper's cottage, sidewalks around the King's Centennial monument in Refugio, and a "band stand" for Lipantitlan, the 1942 budget totaled $29,160, dropping to conventional operations in 1943 at $26,260.

The lingering governor signed these appropriations for the State Parks Board, as well as one other bill that clarified once again board authority to "operate or grant concession" at its recreation parks. Thirty-one days after the session ended, on 4 August O'Daniel at last resigned to accept the U.S.

Senate seat, and Lieutenant Governor Coke Robert Stevenson took his oath of office to become the new Texas chief executive.[44]

Mr. Quinn Goes to Alpine

Following the successes of the past legislative session, the parks board met in July and elected Bastrop's J. V. Ash chairman and Mexia's Raymond Dillard vice chairman. The newly organized board immediately reviewed disturbing news from the NPS in Santa Fe. "Washington has advised that due to drastic curtailment of CCC funds," Regional Director Tillotson wired Quinn, "it will be necessary to discontinue the operation of all central design offices by this service not later than July 31." While the park service had gradually reduced its subsidy to the board's Austin office over the previous four years, it still maintained a monthly contribution of $500 for operating costs plus the salaries of two field inspectors.

The latest cutbacks came not from overall CCC budget reductions, for Congress on 1 July had funded the corps at a level similar to its previous year, but from more companies being reassigned directly to military support. More Soil Conservation Service units, for example, shifted to work at military training camps, and the park service found itself playing a diminishing role in the national defense effort. Nevertheless, at this July meeting of the State Parks Board, Tillotson's representative optimistically assured Texas park planners that "he was inclined to feel that the present program would go through for the balance of the fiscal year."[45]

Park service officials in Santa Fe and Washington still failed to calculate the proposed extension, and most importantly *expansion*, of the year-old Selective Training and Service Act. On 12 August at the bustling House of Representatives inside the Washington Capitol, Speaker Rayburn confronted the most important hurdle to extending the draft, which President Roosevelt deemed urgent. But FDR at that moment sailed aboard the cruiser U.S.S. *Augusta* off the coast of Newfoundland, Canada, in a secret meeting with Winston Churchill arranged by special U.S. envoy Harry Hopkins. The president, therefore, could not participate in a crucial personal lobby of Congress for expansion of selective service. With a skillful combination of persuasion, strong-arming and parliamentary maneuvering, Rayburn hammered his gavel to close proceedings after he tallied a favorable 203 to 202 vote. "So the draft was saved," writes Rayburn biographer Alfred Steinberg. "The eight hundred thousand young men in army camps remained in training, and an additional eight hundred thousand were soon on their way into military life."[46]

CCC enrollment plummeted as a result of the expanded draft, the recent increase in jobs, and even growing competition with the NYA. "With employment rising," figures historian John Salmond, "and the armed forces expanding, the CCC had lost its main function. . . . [Y]ouths were leaving at the rate of six thousand monthly to take jobs in industry as war conditions closed the unemployment gap. There was no chance of replacing these men."[47]

Any danger of losing the Big Bend CCC camp seemed inconsequential to the Texas parks board, at last fortified with $1.5 million to create a bona fide national park in Brewster County. At its 22 August meeting, the board instructed Quinn to open an office on 1 September in Alpine "to take charge of the purchasing of 675,775 acres necessary for the development of Big Bend National Park," the *Dallas Morning News* reported. The present state park at Big Bend totaled 112,907 acres, this article stated, assembled since 1933 from state school lands, repossessed ranches and farms, and certain tracts purchased with federal drought-relief funds. Quinn quickly hired local resident Everett Ewing Townsend—former Texas Ranger, sheriff of Brewster County, and state representative who facilitated the national park idea—to assist in the huge task ahead. "Mr. Townsend was one of the first persons to envision the huge, rugged and colorful area as a park." the *Dallas News* recapped. "That was more than forty years ago, Mr. Townsend said." Quinn's and Townsend's new mission "brought the dreams of thousands of Texans—that of making the rugged and picturesque area into the fifth largest national park—nearer completion."[48]

Park Planning for an Uncertain Future

Quinn's title changed temporarily to director of the Big Bend project, and the board appointed its manager of concessions, B. Glenn Link, as acting executive secretary in Quinn's absence. Quinn retained, curiously, his "state park authority" title for approval of federal cooperative transactions. As Link and the parks board staff prepared applications for the uncertain eighteenth period of CCC camp assignments, summer visitation figures arrived from the state park system. "Reports show that this year's patronage of the state parks of Texas," the board's press release bragged, "has been more than double that of two years ago. . . . They indicate that Texas vacationists appreciate what is being done to give then entertainment in outdoor settings."[49]

At about this time, the NPS issued results of its five-year Park, Parkway, and Recreational-Area Study that compiled information on park systems in thirty-four states. The document also served, with its companion 1941 NPS yearbook, *Park and Recreation Progress,* as a plea for centralized federal recreation planning, in order to coordinate the efforts of the park service, the U.S. Forest Service, and other agencies, including the War Department. The report highlighted Texas parks of all types, principally those developed with federal assistance since 1933, through a map, graphs, and listing by acreage. With a population of 5.8 million inhabiting 168 million acres, Texas provided just over one million acres of parkland, although national forests represented two-thirds of that figure. "The State has developed parks within 50 miles of 57 percent of the population," 1941 statistics revealed for Texas. "Future park planning should include consideration of recreation areas for the un-served portion of the population with particular attention to the creation of day-use areas near urban communities and local areas for the State's 850,000 Negroes," the report projected. "Consideration should also be given to the setting aside of outstanding scenic, historic, and scientific areas before they are injured by the rapidly advancing development of the State." [50]

The summer season ending 15 September at thirty-four Texas state parks entertained a total of 1,510,943 visitors, according to the parks board's own figures. Once again, Mackenzie State Park topped the list in visitation figures, now compiled by park manager and former board member Ken Clapp. Sustained popularity of facilities at Tyler, Daingerfield, and Bonham proved that East Texans also embraced their new state parks. "Other especially popular parks," the board's press release added, "include Lake Brownwood, Bastrop, Fort Parker and Caddo Lake." And the parks board hoped to realize further improvements at Brownwood and Fort Parker by holding on to those CCC camps after 1 October. [51]

Incredibly the State Parks Board retained all its previous federal development camps as the CCC announced assignments for the coming six-month winter period. But in Washington the corps soon confronted its growing crisis over recruitment and national defense priorities. At the beginning of this eighteenth period the CCC could muster only 160,000 enrollees, drastically below its authorized 300,000, to fill only nine hundred camps nationwide. By October, Director McEntee had implemented a number of desperate measures: recruitment doors opened full-time instead of periodically on the six-month cycle, African Americans could join in expanded quotas, enrollees could leave camps for short periods to help farmers with their fall harvest, and $47 million of the CCC budget could be returned for other uses. Meanwhile a congressional committee authorized to review all federal agencies for national security functions, and to declare obsolete any that did not contribute to defense, zeroed in on the CCC and orchestrated unflattering testimony against its continuation. [52]

The first Texas casualty of the faltering CCC came with closure on 1 December of the Fort Griffin camp. "Although the Texas State Parks Board can do little toward dictating to the National Park Service and the Army as to what disposition is made of camps," acting park system manager Glenn Link explained to the board, "nothing was left undone in attempting

TABLE 18
Texas Parks of the Eighteenth-Period CCC
October 1941–March 1942

NPS Number	Official Name	CCC Company
SP-36	Brownwood State Park	Co. 849[1]
SP-44	Fort Parker State Park	Co. 3807(C)[2]
SP-61	Huntsville State Park	Co. 1823(CV)
SP-63	Fort Griffin State Park	Co. 3803[3]
SP-64	Inks Lake State Park	Co. 854[2]
SP-65	Possum Kingdom State Park	Co. 2888
CP-1	Ascarate County Park	Co. 2873(C)
CP-2	Eagle Mountain Lake County Park	Co. 1801(C)
MA-2	Bachman–White Rock Lake Metropolitan Park	Co. 2896
MA-3	Lake Austin Metropolitan Park	Co. 1805
MA-4	Franklin Fields Metropolitan Park	Co. 3822(V)
NP-1	Big Bend National Park	Co. 1856

[1] Brownwood's Co. 849 moved out on 28 February 1942.
[2] Fort Parker and Inks Lake CCC camps closed in January 1942.
[3] Development at Fort Griffin continued until 1 December 1941, when the army moved Co. 3803 out of state.

to retain the CCC camp in the Fort Griffin State Park." The Department of Agriculture took a harder hit in Texas, losing three Soil Conservation Service camps and three U.S. Forest Service companies early in the eighteenth period.[53]

The United States Enters the War

On Sunday morning, 7 December 1941, State Parks Board members met at the Texas Hotel in Fort Worth and received critical news that the CCC might not long survive. Detecting no similar decline in operations of the WPA, the board concluded that future state park development might rely on increased WPA assistance. Applications had been forwarded to San Antonio and Washington for a "state-wide WPA project," Glenn Link told the board, to "improve park areas, including constructing cabins, latrines, bath houses, and pump houses; installing sewer and water facilities; and performing demolition, and appurtenant and incidental work." Such flexible deployment of WPA workers would be matched through a fiscal year total of $15,000 provided by the recent legislature through individual park budgets.[54]

As the parks board sat down to lunch, four time zones away in the Pacific Ocean, Japanese aircraft attacked U.S. Naval, Army, and Air Corps installations in Hawaii. In Washington, President Roosevelt and Harry

Hopkins finished their leisurely meal and heard the news at 12:47 P.M., Texas time. "Throughout the afternoon," historian Robert Devine chronicles, "reports came in to the President and his advisors. The Pacific fleet at Pearl Harbor was crippled; 2400 Americans had lost their lives." One of U.S. Senator Tom Connally's Foreign Relations Committee staff, Edith Parker, hastily researched proper language for a declaration of war. FDR incorporated her notes into his response to the attack, and the next morning he asked Congress to confirm open hostility with Japan.

This immediate U.S. entry into the Second World War "transformed Roosevelt into a global leader," asserts his biographer Nathan Miller. In FDR's own simple words, "Old Dr. New Deal was replaced by Dr. Win-the-War." Indeed the president's New Deal relief programs, including the CCC, faced a new volley of criticism for their vague connections to defense and as outdated reminders of the vanished depression. On Tuesday, 9 December, Congressman Johnson with the president's consent introduced a bill to combine the CCC and the NYA into a new Civilian Youth Administration for training young defense-plant workers. Two days later when Germany declared war on the United States, realization of a two-front war dashed such hopes and galvanized the federal government to command all resources toward nothing less than winning the war.[55]

1942: RECREATION FOR THE HOME FRONT

Hail and Farewell the CCC

After the nation's December entry into the Second World War, CCC administrators in Washington hastily saddled even more two-hundred-man companies with duties related to military posts. For example CCC Co. 3818(V), a Soil Conservation Service camp near Brownwood, Texas, moved onto the Army's Camp Bowie reservation to assist with expansion of its training area. Enrollees of NPS-directed Co. 849 remained at their Brownwood State Park barracks but now turned to a previously undeveloped section of the state park for "construction of facilities for a 1,000 man army recreation camp," according to a newspaper account. For exclusive use of the 36th Division's 27,000 soldiers from nearby Camp Bowie, "[t]he campsite . . . already has sewer line, electric lights and a water supply," and would be the "largest of three to be constructed in the 8th Corps Area, [t]o provide a place where enlisted men may spend week end and other leaves at little cost."[56]

One by one, remaining CCC park camps closed as their enrollees left to bring other CCC companies up to strength, to enlist in the armed forces, or to take new jobs created by the booming economy. Fort Parker and Inks Lake camps vacated in January, and Brownwood State Park's company finally dissolved at the end of February. Even the NYA wood shop at Bastrop

TABLE 19

Texas Parks of the Nineteenth-Period CCC

April–July 1942

NPS Number	Official Name	CCC Company
SP-61	Huntsville State Park	Co. 1823(CV)[1]
SP-65	Possum Kingdom State Park	Co. 2888
NP(D)-1	Ascarate County Park/Fort Bliss	Co. 2873(C)[2]
NP(D)-2	Franklin Canal/Fort Bliss	Co. 2872(C)[3]
NP(D)-3	Franklin Fields Metropolitan Park/	
	Duncan Army Air Field	Co. 3822(V)[4]

[1] Co. 1823(CV) continued after 1 April to work at Huntsville but left the park sometime after 11 April. The CCC's official roster does not indicate that Huntsville's camp survived into the nineteenth period after 1 April. However, at the State Parks Board meeting of 10–11 April, members reviewed the CCC assignment list, which included both Huntsville and Possum Kingdom. A January 1943 inspection of the abandoned barracks at Huntsville listed the CCC departure date as 14 July 1942, but this late date is unlikely.

[2] A new "NP(D)" prefix signaled a National Park (Defense) camp, as part of a quota of companies assigned to the direction of the NPS.

[3] Co. 2872(C) had been assigned since 1935 to Interior's Bureau of Reclamation as BR-4, signifying the "fourth" company working on all irrigation waters controlled by Elephant Butte Reservoir on the Rio Grande in New Mexico.

[4] Co. 3822(V) shifted to Duncan Field, a part of Kelly Army Air Field, yet maintained its MA-4 "Metropolitan Area" prefix in subheadings to its new assignment.

State Park received orders from Washington in February to "cease operations immediately." Big Bend National Park's Co. 1856 abandoned its barracks on 20 March, just before the eighteenth period ended. Only Huntsville and Possum Kingdom remained active state park projects through March, the former attempting to repair its dam and spillway knocked out a year earlier, and the latter developing recreation facilities accessible to rapidly expanding Camp Wolters at Mineral Wells. "In a period of strain like the present one, relaxation and recreation are more important than normally," as one newspaper article described the changes taking place. "The state parks of Texas, whose development has been phenomenal in the last few years, offer convenient and inexpensive means for physical and mental refreshment at nominal cost. Their use by an even larger number of people will be in the interest of strength and stability."[57]

In a more official response to the nation's defensive preparations, in March the parks board staff signed "permits" for the military to use any remaining CCC barracks at state parks. Those compounds at Brownwood, Garner, Fort Griffin, Longhorn Cavern, and Tyler remained in top condition and would be ideal "for use by the War Department for any purpose it may be deemed advisable." However, as the parks board staff cautiously applied for another round of CCC development applications, its patriotism stopped short of volunteering CCC barracks at Fort Parker, "due to the fact that the location of this camp is such that if it should be used as an alien jail, as reported, it would seriously interfere with the operation of the Park." [58]

New CCC camp assignments announced on 1 April for the nineteenth six-month period clearly revealed the nine-year-old conservation program's shift to military duties. Texas hosted a total of seventeen CCC companies, but a majority of their duties reflected the state's ballooning number of military posts resulting from the nationwide buildup for war. Seven Soil Conservation Service camps now carried "Army SCS" prefixes to reflect their postings to vast cantonment constructions at Camp Barkeley (2 camps), Camp Bowie, Camp Hood (2 camps), Camp Wolters, and Waco Army Flying School. In addition, three camps remained under Interior Department supervision but worked directly on recreation projects for Fort Bliss —incorporating El Paso's Ascarate County Park camp plus a former Bureau of Reclamation company—and Duncan Army Air Field in San Antonio, utilizing Co. 3822(V) from the Franklin Fields city-park project.

For the moment, three soil conservation companies continued their private-land erosion control work at Morton, Wolfe City, and Yoakum, and two forest service camps worked in Sabine and Angelina national forests. One other forest camp worked on private timber from its base in Nacogdoches. Huntsville State Park's unique Co. 1823(CV) of veterans from earlier wars lasted but a few weeks past 1 April. Only one park development camp under NPS direction survived the drastic CCC cuts and reorganization for the summer period, as Co. 2888 hustled to finish its access road in Stephens County between Caddo and the west shore state park on Possum Kingdom Lake. [59]

Fortunately the parks board received anticipated assistance from its "state-wide" WPA project, particularly to take up spillway repair at Huntsville. Other WPA jobs, members heard at their April meeting, continued development work at Caddo Lake, Cleburne, Normangee, and San Jose Mission at a state cost of $15,000. At this meeting the board approved a call for all park managers to "gather up all scrap iron and other items which have been discarded but still may be of benefit to the National Defense Program." At their next meeting in May, members traveled to the Big Bend CCC barracks (perhaps flaunting their privilege as state officials to drive on otherwise tightly rationed tires) to meet with NPS director Newton Drury and his assistant director Conrad Wirth. Parks board executive secretary and Big Bend land-office manager Quinn detailed his progress on purchasing hundreds of private land tracts within the proposed national park boundary. [60]

Despite CCC cutbacks and new wartime priorities, the president hoped to retain the corps and instructed its advisory council to further clarify a defense contribution. By mid-April, CCC director McEntee and his council proposed a "victory program," historian Salmond recounts, "in which Corps work would be limited to fire protection, the development of Army camps, and the maintenance of military reservations, as well as supplying partially trained men to the Army. All camps which could not qualify under one of these categories were to be closed." Roosevelt backed this plan with a 4 May request to Congress for $49 million to operate 150 camps nationwide.

The House Appropriations Committee on 3 June denied the president's request. For old New Deal colleagues at the NYA and WPA, however, Congress agreed to fund these agencies during the coming fiscal year based on the NYA's value to defense training and the WPA's ability to provide day laborers on military reservations. For the CCC in June 1942, "[t]he fight then went to the [House] floor," writes historian Ken Hendrickson, where "friends of the Corps fought a final desperate battle to preserve it, losing on June 5 when the House voted 158–151 to provide $500,000 for liquidation." Hendrickson further reports, "At first the Senate balked at this abrupt move, but on June 30 House-Senate conferees agreed on a compromise providing $8 million for the phase-out program. The Civilian Conservation Corps was dead." [61]

Since the new federal fiscal year began on 1 July, this final vote of Congress meant the CCC phase-out would begin immediately. The Possum Kingdom State Park CCC camp, last park development company assigned to the Texas State Park Board, abandoned its barracks on 13 July 1942. [62] Thus ended the great nine-year construction episode for Texas state parks, courtesy of the federal government that had declared victory in its progressive war against the depression and now embarked on a shooting war of global proportions.

"WE WILL BE LONESOME UNTIL WE SEE YOU AGAIN"

PALO DURO CANYON STATE PARK

"A Western Way of Saying Goodbye" - Palo Duro State Park, Canyon.

National gasoline rationing, begun in 1942, severely reduced visitation at remote state parks, particularly Big Bend and Palo Duro Canyon. Visitors could enter Palo Duro for 35 cents and have their choice of campsites for an additional 60 cents, or bed down in comfort at El Coronado Lodge for $7.50—until the concessionaire closed the lodge that fall. After a long war and multiplying indebtedness for the park—and one day after victory in the Pacific Theater—on 15 August 1945, gas rationing ended. Texas state government entered this new era free of debt, for the first time since before 1933, but would wait until its next biennial legislative session to consider spreading its wealth to pay more than $300,000 owed to this park's lienholders. *Author's collection*

Chapter 6

1942–1945

The End of the Beginning

. . . it will take 20 years to put this whole thing over.—Phebe Kerrick Warner,
19 June 1924

All Board Members further pointed out that our failure to properly develop
[Possum Kingdom State Park] is due entirely to reasons beyond our control;
namely, an act of God and a world war.—State Parks Board minutes,
17–19 June 1944 [1]

GOING IT ALONE

"It is with regret," Executive Secretary Frank Quinn reported at the
August 1942 State Parks Board meeting, "that we can no longer use
the familiar words, 'The following camps are now engaged in developing State Parks'." The New Deal contract between the State of Texas, the
National Park Service, the Civilian Conservation Corps, and the U.S. Army
spanned nine extraordinary years through July 1942, and developed an incredible forty-three outdoor recreation parks. Of these, the Texas parks
board now independently operated a system of thirty-two sites—including
Big Bend for those tourists who ventured that far—having turned back the
balance of developments for various reasons to communities who originally
donated the lands.

In addition to those eleven "released" parks, the CCC coalition built
nine parks for counties and cities, from Ascarate in El Paso to Zilker in
Austin. Under direction of other federal agencies, the CCC also constructed
several recreation areas in state and national forests and in association with
soil conservation projects.

The state-park benefits of the New Deal spread even farther to include
six Texas parks of historical interest under the Board of Control: Fannin,

Goliad, Gonzales, King's, San Jacinto, and Washington. At these sites—plus the Alamo, Monument Hill, San Jose Mission, Stephen F. Austin, and the State Cemetery—special 1936 Centennial funds along with assistance from the Works Progress Administration, the National Youth Administration, and other federal agencies resulted in a windfall of handsome permanent facilities. Further, the NYA built hundreds of roadside parks, and the WPA improved untold scores of local parks throughout Texas, all in a local-materials, hand-finished tradition inspired during the depression by the trend-setting NPS.

Of roughly $750 million in federal funds spent in Texas throughout the New Deal, some $20 million had been invested in state parks alone, a miraculous sum considering the state matched about 2 percent of that amount. "As we have so often expressed ourselves in the past," Quinn continued in his report to the parks board, "we owe a deep debt of gratitude to the National Park Service for all it has done in constructing our present system of State Parks." Looking toward an end to the world war, he expressed confidence "that when the present emergency is over, this construction program will rise to greater heights than at any time heretofore; and our earnest desire is that we may again become associated with the administrative and construction personnel of the CCC in our joint effort to give the public a greater system of state parks." [2]

Meanwhile in the summer of 1942, without CCC enrollees to count visitors or federal public relations staffs to help advertise Texas parks, the State Parks Board stepped up its own publicity efforts. Quinn wrote a lengthy article for the August *Texas Parade* that blended a little state park history with facility highlights and encouragement for Texans to vacation close to home, since automobile tires had been rationed just after the 1941 attack on Pearl Harbor. "With rubber wearing thin and prospects for more stringent gasoline rationing looming along the Eastern seaboard, Texans can no longer take that summer trek to faraway states," Quinn began. "Already state parks in Texas are a contributing factor in building health, welding unity and upholding morale in these tragic times of war when recreation is more important than ever. They offer the same sort of facilities close to home or close to Army camp where vacationers heretofore have felt they must travel thousands of miles to obtain."

At the August board meeting in Huntsville State Park, Quinn also told members that ever increasing military activity presented the state park system with mixed blessings. While some parks "have high visitation" with "a heavy burden upon recreation facilities," he reported, "some have none." The parks near Brownwood, Bastrop, Caddo Lake, and Mineral Wells catered to overwhelming weekend crowds from nearby training camps and war industries. But Palmetto early in the summer hosted "practically no business . . . due to high water, tire restrictions, and other unsatisfactory conditions." And now the remote Big Bend project found itself with practically no visitors, and more importantly without the great gasoline tax collection anticipated by its promoters.

Quinn compiled this information from regular contacts with all state park managers, he explained in *Texas Parade*. "In most cases these reports are made daily, but some of the small parks are required to report only for the week." One exception interrupted this system, Quinn confided to board members, since he could not relate statistics on Mother Neff State Park. Park custodian Pat Neff would not turn in his concession receipts! In addition, this park had sustained major damage in spring floods and—Quinn could only assume—suffered a severe decline in visitation that summer.[3]

Palo Duro Canyon State Park, by contrast, presented much more disturbing problems in this unbalanced visitation season. Quinn strongly emphasized the ailing Panhandle facility in his *Texas Parade* promotion, noting that an auto and driver could enter the park for 35 cents (plus 20 cents for adult passengers and 10 cents for children), and that overnight rates ranged from 60 cents for a single campsite to a deluxe room in El Coronado Lodge for $7.50 per day. "Few travelers ever forget that first sight of this remarkable gorge," he described, "which, without any apparent geological warning, slaps the unsuspecting motorist accustomed to the level pattern of the Great Plains smack between the eyes as the bottom drops out from beneath his car just off State Highway 217."

But this summer far too few West Texas drivers steered down the dramatic CCC-built access road into Palo Duro Canyon. "Gasoline rationing cut sharply into both tourism and local pleasure driving," notes historian Peter L. Petersen in describing the Panhandle home front, "consequently fewer people visited the park in 1942 than in any year since its opening." Only 7,286 cars entered the park compared to 10,686 in 1941, netting in 1942 only $5,598.72 toward the park's $40,000 annual break-even requirement. As the park's indebtedness continued to mount, park concessionaire Frank Miller soon closed Coronado Lodge, and the State Parks Board faced the maturity of its first liens on the park's mortgage.

For the moment, board members and system manager Frank Quinn scrambled to spend the one-year appropriation of $1.5 million for Big Bend land purchases by the end of August 1942. With this state appropriation spent, the private Big Bend Park Association provided another $8,300 for late purchases at Government Spring. Quinn reported in November to his board that all property within the described national park boundary had been purchased, with the exception of 13,316 acres primarily in the Castolon area, for a total of 691,338.95 acres. Adding existing state parklands, he revised the total proposed Big Bend National Park boundary to include 712,919 acres.

Park supporters throughout Texas rejoiced over the Big Bend success, except for Panhandle citizens who expressed bitterness at the state's failure to pay cash similarly for Palo Duro Canyon. After exploring improbable alternatives for the indebted state park—including a federal or state buyout, or a sale to the city of Amarillo—Quinn and the State Parks Board appealed to lienholder Fred Emery to extend this troubled deal past their due date of 1 November. Emery first responded by enthusiastically suggesting that the board and park manager Miller attract more visitors by reopening the lodge, building more road bridges, offering horseback riding, arranging for bus service from Amarillo, and providing rural electric service. Then, conceding the extenuating circumstances of a world war, Emery quietly arranged to extend his parkland note for the duration of hostilities.

Throughout the year both Palo Duro Canyon and Big Bend parks continued to suffer from severe declines in automobile entries, their only source of customers. This problem quickly became common to most of the country's national parks, exasperated by brutal budget cuts after 1 July for the park service as a whole. And thus the fate of the proposed Big Bend National Park fell under increasing doubt.[4]

The Politics of Rationing

Coke Stevenson easily secured his first full term as governor in 1942, as his cool management style stirred neither controversy nor opposition. His predecessor W. Lee O'Daniel, playing down a dismal freshman record in the U.S. Senate, now carried his own flamboyant style of public service into a contest for a full six-year term. "There ain't gonna be no gasoline rationing in Texas," he proclaimed in a foggy mix of support for defense and opposition to President Roosevelt, "we ain't gonna lose the war; and there ain't gonna be no runoff." The July primary quickly proved O'Daniel wrong on the last count, but in the August runoff he managed to defeat former governor Jimmie Allred in a tight race. Roosevelt waited for the elections to pass before implementing new economy measures and ordered gasoline rationing to begin a few weeks later on 1 December, shattering another of O'Daniel's campaign predictions.[5]

Legislators convened in January at Austin to conduct the considerably diminished business of state government in a wartime economy dominated more than ever by Washington. "Texans accepted with a modicum of grumbling," historian Rupert Richardson remembers, "the austerity that war imposed. . . . In its session of 1943 the legislature cut appropriations to most state agencies."[6]

But in a well-timed assault on the budget sensitivities of lawmakers, the State Parks Board issued an April press release that linked parks directly to the defense effort. "This coming Spring with its atmosphere of War," Quinn soberly announced, "and the grim reality of Defense plants throughout the State attaining a peak production of planes and deadly munitions of war—all have combined to bring an early influx of relaxation-seeking visitors to the State Parks of Texas unequalled in its history." Quinn urged "that citizens take advantage of these thousands of acres encompassed in Texas' system of State Parks and enjoy to the fullest Texas' folk-lore and atmosphere of the southwest, at the same time combining it with all modern facilities for healthy, happy relaxation."[7]

Ultimately the State Parks Board accepted a reasonable cut in its biennial budget, but only because it required no federal-match construction dollars and because federal caretakers now staffed the Big Bend park. Although lower than previous operating budgets that peaked in 1942 with $91,000, the new fiscal year figures for 1944 and 1945—at more than $72,000 each— confirmed the value of state parks to state legislators. Most park-keeper salaries jumped from the old annual compensation of $600 to $720, still with dwelling and utilities provided. Bastrop and Buescher state parks now appeared as separate line items, which boosted support for these extensive combined facilities. Fort Parker and the nearby Old Fort Parker reconstruction also appeared as distinct items, enhancing service at this popular recreation pair. Without the NPS subsidy for central-office design personnel, and with no budgets for construction work anyway, the parks board retained only an engineer (Nottie Lee), an architect (Paul Roesle) and a draftsman in its ten-person office.

The "loss of two maintenance men," Frank Quinn told the board, "is worst blow of all." Quinn's compensation as "executive secretary-director" remained at $3,600 per year, but Governor Stevenson offered some continuity for Quinn's system management in May by reappointing Chairman J. V. Ash and Wendell Mayes to the board.

A bill introduced by Senator Fred Mauritz of Jackson County proposed "placing all historical and other state parks and recreational areas under the control and custody of the Texas State Parks Board." While this logical measure did not succeed, for the first time state-owned Monument Hill received a $400 budget item under the State Parks Board budget, thus passing responsibility to the board for this historic site in Fayette County. For the state's other "Historical State Parks" as the appropriations bill identified, the Board of Control received more than $23,000 in both 1944 and 1945, a slight drop from fiscal year 1943. But keepers' salaries, retaining a now-traditional advantage over the rival parks board's compensations, rose to a new range from $750 per year at King's State Park to $840 at Fannin, $900 at Goliad and Gonzales, and $1,020 at Washington state parks. The superintendent at San Jacinto still received the highest annual salary of $1,800 and, with a total budget of $15,820, commanded the largest park maintenance crew in the state.[8]

The State Parks Board, for all its success in the mixed blessings of wartime service, faced a number of vexing problems caused by the unusual state of life in Texas. An influx of Mexican workers to meet employment demands, for example, and a corresponding emergence of the state's Mexican American population presented conflicts in communities not wishing to share their state parks with any minority population. The swimming pools at Balmorhea and Lockhart state parks had for some time attracted local Hispanics, who frequently found themselves ejected from the parks' recreation offerings. Although the board discussed at length the question of "Latin-American patronage" in its park system, members and staff avoided — or thus created — statewide policy by allowing local communities to make the predictable choice of exclusion.

Pressures to allow commercial exploitation of park resources also increased with the demands, or perceived extenuations, of national shortages. In the Big Bend, recalled geologist Ross Maxwell, "[w]hen landowners sold their holdings to the State for inclusion in the park during 1941 and 1942, they were given free grazing rights until January 1, 1945. Some ranchers therefore increased their herds, thus further depleting the range." The parks board agreed reluctantly in 1943 on a "wartime policy of permitting grazing in State Parks where such grazing does not interfere with normal operations of the facilities of the park." Likewise prospectors for oil presented continuing pressure for exploration in state parks, but the board managed to resist such proposals and to deflect related legislative inquiries, for the moment.[9]

Another Record-Breaking Year

An encouraging legislative year led the State Parks Board in October 1943 to develop "tentative plans . . . for postwar park developments on other sites," according to a winter press release. With abolishment that July of the WPA and the NYA, board members realized that federal assistance, even if available after the war, might assume an entirely new structure. The board looked closely at sites in the Lower Rio Grande Valley, perhaps an outgrowth of its "Latin-American patronage" discussions, and at a "Dogwood Trails" possibility near Palestine. Donation offers at these sites did not exceed 250 acres each, however, and Frank Quinn reminded board members that "none of the small areas in our State Park System have ever proved satisfactory." Encouraged by this discussion at least to release another "small park," the board voted in October to "re-convey" the 128-acre Beeville

State Park—one of the first park donations accepted in 1927—to original land donor Sudie Scott.

Soon the board learned that great crowds of recreation seekers during the previous summer had overcome the limitations of gasoline and tire rationing to balance the losses of visitation at some state parks. "Wartime restrictions on motor travel," the *Dallas News* announced on 29 December, "did not prevent state parks of Texas from having their busiest year in 1943. For the first time, the number of visitors passed the two million mark." Even beleaguered Palo Duro Canyon boasted a 1,011-car and 8,200-visitor increase over the previous year for its entry count. "Although the parks get most of their patronage from May through September, some are equipped through the year for picnics and week-end outings," the press release added, explaining why state parks near military training camps also accommodated large crowds in early spring and late fall.[10]

Big Bend a National Park at Last

The parks board attempted, and failed, in the latest regular session of the legislature to secure an additional $65,000 appropriation for purchasing elusive lands in the Big Bend. Quinn's staff continued to work through the spring consolidating state holdings in the Big Bend to a single instrument and in the summer informed Governor Stevenson of their success. The governor on 24 August officially transferred 691,338 acres—the final tally of state-owned land—to the NPS. Then, a few days later, just as Stevenson prepared a trip to Alpine for formal presentation of title, park service assistant director Hillory A. Tolson repeated the all-or-nothing land acceptance threat. He told the governor that his bureau "did not consider transfer of the deeds would constitute acceptance of the . . . tract nor guarantee that a national park would be established."

Stevenson countered simply that the state would "retain civil and criminal jurisdiction over the Big Bend park area" if federal officials would not accept the land or a development role in the Big Bend. "Whether or not the deeds are transferred Sunday," the *Dallas News* reported of the governor's schedule, "he plans to stop at Alpine en route to El Paso" on other business. The NPS bluff had been called and on 5 September, Stevenson presented the deed to Tillotson.[11]

The next step in this singularly bureaucratic, if not melodramatic, process required provision of a "deed of cession" for Big Bend property from the state to the federal government. State Parks Board staff produced this document and on 30 December Stevenson signed it. For safe transport to Washington, D.C., the governor entrusted the paper to his "special emissary," *Fort Worth Star-Telegram* publisher and Big Bend Park Association founder Amon Gary Carter, Sr. Wartime distractions delayed formalities for months, then incredibly Carter found himself hosted by the business-as-usual commander-in-chief on the evening of 6 June 1944, just hours after Roosevelt's announcement of the greatest U.S. undertaking of the war, the American and Allied invasion of German-occupied France at Normandy.

"Delivery of the deed of cession was made at an informal gathering in the executive offices in the White House," Carter's rival *Dallas News* reported the next day amidst headlines on the pivotal European battle. "The brief ceremony was attended by Carter, Senator Tom Connally, Speaker Sam Rayburn and Representative R. Ewing Thomason of El Paso. . . . The President showed great interest in the park and asked Thomason many questions about the nature of the land and the scenery, the degree of development already attained and plans for future development of a great international park."

Interior secretary Ickes accepted the Big Bend parklands on 12 June, and Congress agreed to a paltry $15,000 budget for the fiscal year beginning less than three weeks later. The park "has not been officially opened to the public," explained *Dallas News* science editor Victor Schoffelmayer on 5 July during a publicity visit. "That will have to wait until the war has been won. There are no tourist accommodations, although some neat cabins, built under direction of the Texas State Parks Board, some day again will be refitted for occupancy. Just now their furniture is gone."

The same day Dr. Ross Maxwell, former geologist with the Chisos Basin CCC encampment and now superintendent of the newest federal park unit, joined four other employees at the abandoned CCC barracks as the first staff for Big Bend National Park.[12]

MOVING TOWARD A POSTWAR FUTURE

Possum Kingdom and Political Conflicts

The State Parks Board met in June at Possum Kingdom State Park, lodging at member J. D. Sandefer's lake house and touring partially developed parklands nearby. By the summer of 1944, with substantial visitation and an acceptable operating budget plus almost $55,000 in its Special Parks Fund, the board radiated confidence from its successes. Board members and Quinn reveled in the conclusion of their Big Bend responsibilities, reviewed several new concession agreements, and discussed a proposal from Pat Neff for his donation of an additional 2,000 acres to Mother Neff State Park.

The board had recently accepted 587 acres of native thickets in the Lower Rio Grande Valley from Edna Ruth and Lloyd Millard Bentsen, Sr. Also the future shorelines of a huge reservoir under federal construction on the Red River in Grayson County beckoned with potential. Parks board property at Possum Kingdom Lake, however, caused considerable distress;

the Brazos River Conservation and Reclamation District demanded its return because no recreation improvements had been made.[13]

In joint meeting with Brazos River authorities, board members and system manager Quinn pleaded their case, noting that in 1940 the board applied for two CCC camps to develop the lake's twin sites. "Only one camp was available and it was located on the west side," Quinn explained. "Second," he continued, "it was anticipated that at least three years would be required for the lake to fill but unprecedented rains came and the lake filled within six weeks' time." Development on the west shore subsequently concentrated on surveys, fences, picnic and swimming areas, latrines, and "park road part 'A'," Quinn added. Following departure in July 1942 of the state's last state-park CCC camp from Possum Kingdom, the parks board staff concentrated on plans for a west-park cabin group and appointed the superintendent of Mineral Wells State Park to "better control and regulate" the isolated east-park tract. Quinn read from a recent letter offered by Conrad Wirth stating that "this project will be among the first to be considered" by the NPS for postwar assistance. Then "both sides calmed down," Quinn recorded, "and the meeting closed amicably but with neither side agreeing with the position of the other."[14]

Retreating on their last evening to dinner at Sandefer's lodge, board members considered Quinn's request for an indefinite leave of absence, "due to some urgent personal business." Privately, Quinn confessed problems with legislators over what he considered wartime abuse of state parks, ranging from pressures to force more grazing and oil exploration to an attempt by the Board of Control to house "adjusted mental patients" at abandoned Longhorn Cavern and Inks Lake CCC barracks. Although Quinn elected to continue his work, he also grew frustrated with his stagnant salary. Probably as a byproduct of his legislative and Board of Control clashes, it had been held at $3,600 per year since he joined the parks board almost five years earlier.[15]

The next month Coke Stevenson handily won the 1944 Democratic primary against eight opponents. The party's national convention in July, however, did not reflect the same satisfaction with the status quo. Texans and other delegates at Chicago divided over a fourth presidential term for Roosevelt and other sectional issues. This disruption helped dislodge Vice President Henry Wallace, placing Senator Harry S. Truman of Missouri on the successful ticket with FDR.[16]

Fortunately in Texas, prospects for the State Parks Board during the coming year held great promise. "For the forty-ninth legislature, which assembled in January, 1945," along with reelected Governor Stevenson, analyzes Rupert Richardson, "the problem of state finance was delightfully simple. Income had outrun expenditures so far that a $42,000,000 deficit had been eliminated by economies and increased revenues, and had been changed to a surplus." The parks board met just after the legislature convened to discuss its proposed biennial budget, and to spend its entire $67,500 Special Park Fund balance before legislators discovered this nest-egg. Projects thus approved in preparation for the summer 1945 season included construction of five cabins at "West Side Possum Kingdom"; roof projects for Caddo Lake cabins, Indian Lodge, and San Jose Mission buildings; replacement of a burned cabin at Garner; and spillway repairs at Fort Parker and Normangee. Members also pondered a renewed proposal from Senator Mauritz, rejected by the last legislature, to transfer the state's historical parks from the Board of Control to the State Parks Board.

Relations between the parks board and the Board of Control deteriorated severely by February, principally over the issue of using state parks for mental patient housing and cattle grazing. Board members unanimously backed Executive Secretary Quinn in opposing the use of CCC buildings at Longhorn Cavern "for the housing of adjusted mental patients (some of them being negroes) which is causing a great deal of dissatisfaction," not all of it local. "[W]e must respectfully state," they added in a letter to control board chairman Weaver Baker concerning disruption at Inks Lake State Park, "that we are convinced that it ruins a park for recreational purposes to permit the grazing of cattle in same."

The conflict boiled over to the issue of historical parks as board chairman J. V. Ash told Baker, "please bear in mind that while we are willing to accept these parks, it was not our idea, and we are not asking for them." The historical parks transfer proposal died again, as did an innovative measure to create a State Recreation Board for coordinating all outdoor recreation sponsored by state government. And the legislature appropriated no funds for the Board of Control to refurbish the Longhorn Cavern CCC barracks for interim patient housing. Unfortunately, a personal attempt by Fred Emery to extract an appropriation for the state's Palo Duro Canyon land debts met the same fate of legislative indifference.[17]

The Curtain Falls

Taking popular advice for war-weary Americans to relax at a favorite recreation spot, President Roosevelt set off on 29 March to a secretive vacation at Warm Springs, Georgia. Pine trees and a rustic setting awaited at both FDR's "Little White House" and at nearby Pine Mountain State Park, built by the CCC as a model recreation facility at the height of his New Deal. "Roosevelt had come down to Warm Springs," writes biographer Nathan Miller, "an exhausted and shrunken figure too tired to even acknowledge the greetings of old friends. . . . But his spirits were revived by the unfailing magic of his second home."

On a morning in mid-April, FDR sat in the knotty-pine living room of his main cottage reviewing bulletins, and signing a bill extending the Commodity Credit Corporation. This agricultural "CCC," governing federal crop loans and harvest storage, had been established in 1933 at the New Deal's beginning but outlasted the better-known Civilian Conservation Corps. While sitting for portrait painter Elizabeth Shoumatoff just before his 1 P.M. lunchtime, the president muttered that he had a terrific headache and slumped forward in his chair. "Franklin D. Roosevelt died of a cerebral hemorrhage," records biographer Bernard Asbell, "on 12 April 1945 at 3:35 P.M." local time.[18]

About 5 P.M. in the Washington Capitol, Vice President Truman finished his day in the Senate and marched over to the House to join Speaker Rayburn at his "Board of Education" sanctum. In this hideaway decorated with a Texas flag, mounted longhorns, and other memorabilia from Rayburn's home state, power brokers of the federal government—dominated by Texans since John Nance Garner appropriated the room in 1931—met to shape the nation over glasses of chilled whiskey. Truman's hosts this evening volunteered that the White House had just rung for him, and after a quick return call the vice president ran out, then motored immediately to the executive mansion. At 7:09 P.M. Washington time Truman took the oath of office as 33rd President of the United States.[19]

The Lights Turn Up

That night in the Austin Capitol, Texas legislators recessed early to solemnize the inevitable passage of Roosevelt and the sudden emergence of Truman. Three weeks later German military commanders surrendered to Allied forces, but President Truman asked that Americans refrain from celebrations, since fighting continued against Japan. "The debt is unpaid," he told his War Mobilization and Reconversion director, "at least until we have finished the war and solved those urgent problems which war leaves in its aftermath."[20] The Texas legislature, not as concerned as Truman with the weight of the world or even a governmental debt, happily adjourned on 5 June with state government well financed for the anticipated postwar biennium.

The State Parks Board met later that month in Mexia, near Fort Parker State Park, and elected Raymond Dillard chairman and Jake Sandefer vice chairman. Governor Stevenson had recently reappointed Sandefer and H. G. Webster to new six-year terms on the board. Texas state recreation parks had received by far their largest budgets ever, awarded $120,571 for fiscal year 1946 and $118,571 for 1947, to operate thirty-seven sites. Recently acquired "Bentsen-Rio Grande State Park" joined the list with a keeper's salary and maintenance allowance, plus a $4,000 construction budget for the first year only. Legislators boosted operations of many sites with annual construction budgets ranging from $2,000 in one year only, to twice that amount over the biennium. Monument Hill did not appear in this appropriation, but a standard operating budget for Jim Hogg Memorial State Park swelled with $2,000 each fiscal year for "post war construction." A rider on the appropriation bill once again allowed park concession profits to be maintained in the Special Park Fund. However, lawmakers now required that all expenditures of the board, as with all state agencies, "be subject to approval of the State Auditing Committee."

The recent legislature authorized yet another commemoration of native-son Hogg in his one-time home of Quitman. But a $2,000 per year total budget for this twenty-six-acre tract, known as the Wood County Old Settlers' Reunion Grounds and now to be called "Governor James Stephen Hogg Memorial Shrine," appeared under the Board of Control's appropriation for its Historical State Parks. The board in addition received an unusual $300 budget for "improvements and repairs" on the state's 1913 monument at the grave of Elizabeth Crockett—David Crockett's widow, who had claimed his Texas Revolution land bounty—at Acton Cemetery in Hood County. Appropriations for all historical parks under the Board of Control totaled $28,319 in 1946 and $26,341 for 1947.

Most state employees, including park keepers, received generous 15 percent raises, with typical state recreation park custodians earning $900 and Board of Control park managers $966 annually. Yet Executive Secretary-Director Frank Quinn, in an obvious slap from the legislature, received no raise and would continue to earn $3,600 for the seventh year in a row.[21]

Following the devastation of two Japanese cities by American atom bombs on 6 and 9 August, the war's last belligerent surrendered on 14 August 1945. Nationwide a "great spontaneous spree that lasted three or four days commenced the moment Truman confirmed the capitulation," writes historian Paul D. Casdorph. "On August 15 rationing was ended for gasoline. Immediately, great lines of fuel-starved automobiles lined up at neighborhood filling stations," Casdorph adds, "for the first fill-up in more than three years."

Recreation facilities lay in the path of this happy rush of Americans to the open road, and at least the Texas State Parks Board faced its postwar visitors with an appreciable budget. The National Park Service by contrast—in a startling inversion of the old New Deal arrangement—now played the poor partner and embarked on a long struggle with pitiful appropriations to rebuild its overworked facilities and serve a tidal wave of visitors. "[U]nder the weight of the vast war debt left by the Second World War," national park analyst John Ise recalls of this ordeal, "Congress was in no mood to spend lavishly, particularly for the protection of natural resources."[22]

State Parks Board director Quinn endured an early encounter in late August with the new State Auditing Committee, as it authorized the board's first expenditures of the new fiscal year. "The committee approved a six-months' budget of $77,710 appropriated funds and an anticipated $33,000 special funds," reported the *Dallas Morning News,* explaining that the parks board "contemplates starting minor improvements in several parks at the first opportunity." But Quinn considered his unchanged salary a failure by his board to win for him a long overdue pay increase, and he judged this the final straw in difficult relations with the legislature. Facing another two years with no boost in compensation and growing restless with the lure of business opportunities at war's end, Quinn invested in a new truck dealership in Austin and prepared to become its general manager. "I expect to become a permanent resident of Austin," he told the board of his planned exit, "and my services will be available to the Board without cost at any and all times." [23]

As a parting gesture, Quinn wrote in August to ex-governor and ex-State Parks Board chairman Neff in Waco requesting a copy of "that picture of the First Texas State Parks Board." Neff quickly sent "all framed and well preserved the picture," and admonished, "to be guarded with your life. It is to be returned to me unharmed and unblemished, or I will not assume any responsibility for what might happen to you." But with the identification of those in the photo he added, "I am unable to figure out from the photograph where it was taken." Neff had not recorded that board members and friends stood for their portrait in July 1924 during their first West Texas park inspection caravan. Neff named all the optimistic park supporters in the photo, including David Edward Colp, whom Neff now misspelled as "D. E. Culp, hired by me as the first Chairman of the Park Board." [24]

Quinn dutifully copied the group portrait and placed it on the parks board office wall between large photos of Colp and Neff, the board's first two chairmen. Quinn also made arrangements to pass his management position to his "inspector-engineer" Nottie Lee, a seasoned veteran of the CCC development era. Just before the board's last meeting of the year—in Houston with a planned inspection visit to San Jacinto State Park—the executive secretary-director submitted his resignation letter effective 1 November 1945.

> I love these parks and the administrative work connected with same. The past six years, though strenuous and trying at times, have been happy ones. . . . My interest in parks and recreation will continue and I feel that the State Parks program of Texas is now well on the road to a great future. [25]

When the first State Parks Board chairman and de facto manager David E. Colp vacated his office in 1935, he generously offered to serve as a consultant to the system. As Pat M. Neff in 1939 finished a term on the board, this former chairman arranged his own appointment as superintendent of Mother Neff State Park. Frank D. Quinn somewhat reversed this tradition after serving a time as consultant, receiving in 1949 appointment to the parks board and quickly extending his participation to the National Conference on State Parks. Thirty years after its first meeting in Des Moines, Iowa, and after many years of proposing an annual meeting in Texas, the Conference in October 1950 followed Quinn's invitation to Bastrop State Park. Some seventy-five participants completed their meeting with a tour of parks across the state, ending at Big Bend National Park, where charter superintendent Ross A. Maxwell (left) hosted outgoing conference president Thomas Morse and his incoming successor Quinn (at right). *Frank D. Quinn Papers, Barker Texas History Collections*

POST-1945

The Road to the Future

Each of us has need to escape occasionally from the noisy world which sur-
rounds us and find refreshment in the grandeur of nature. Yet, year after year,
our scenic treasures are being plundered by what we call an advancing civiliza-
tion. If we are not careful, we shall leave our children a legacy of billion dollar
roads leading nowhere except to the other congested places like those they left
behind.—General Omar Nelson Bradley, quoted in a 1960 report of the Texas
State Parks Board [1]

CONTINUING THE BATTLES OF PEACE

Frank Quinn soon recovered from his somewhat bitter departure in late
1945 as State Parks Board director. Although now engaged in private
business, he quickly accepted from the board the title of "consultant"
and zealously redoubled a personal relationship with Texas state parks ri-
valed only by those of Pat Neff and Dave Colp during the system's formative
years. Neff's and Colp's New Deal windfall clearly would not be repeated,
however, and Texas state parks faced a postwar future with no federal funds,
National Park Service assistance, or Civilian Conservation Corps labor force.

Undeterred and unafraid to work through his differences with the legislature, Quinn pushed state lawmakers for public recreation development
at Padre Island and preservation of nearby Port Isabel's historic lighthouse.
He also supported the board's quest for new state parks honoring Second
World War heroes and native Texans Dwight David Eisenhower and Chester William Nimitz. Most significantly and to the great relief of Quinn's
agency, in 1947 the legislature authorized sale of $300,000 in revenue bonds
to pay off Palo Duro Canyon State Park's long-troubled land notes. [2]

During the 1949 legislative session Quinn motivated transfer to the
board of most state historical parks (but not San Jacinto nor its new neigh-

bor, the retired battleship *Texas*) from the Board of Control. In September that year Governor Robert Allan Shivers appointed Quinn to the State Parks Board, just as the agency came under legal attack for excluding all but white Texans from its forty-four parks. Shivers, Quinn's board, and the legislature repeatedly sidestepped this discrimination issue for several more years, even as crowded Texas state parks deteriorated from inadequate funding and maintenance.

Neff and Colp through the 1920s and 1930s had declined anything more than corresponding association with the National Conference on State Parks. Quinn however, probably on advice from his close relations with U.S. Senator Lyndon Johnson, embraced the connection. In 1950 he brought national recognition to Texas parks by serving as president of the Washington, D.C.–based organization. After guiding its thirtieth annual meeting that year on a tour from Bastrop State Park to Big Bend National Park, Quinn served a long tenure as the conference's board chairman.

The next year he also became chairman of the State Parks Board, as well as chairman of his hometown Austin Park and Recreation Board. In 1952, the year that Pat Morris Neff passed away at the age of eighty, Quinn sought to elevate his own career and his appeal for parks to the state Senate, but he lost in a spirited primary campaign. He thereafter focused his energies on increasing funds for state parks, maneuvering a $25 million bond bill through the legislature in 1955. Shivers signed the measure, but the attorney general would not allow sale of the approved revenue bonds. In desperation, Quinn's board permitted the lease of Tyler State Park for oil exploration and the sale of timber from Huntsville State Park to raise maintenance dollars for the system.

Approaching the end of two terms on the parks board, Quinn observed that "the coming of automobiles and good highways has resulted in an enormous increase of enjoyment of . . . recreational activities." But the "unspoiled outdoors" so desired by park visitors was fast disappearing in the path of those same technologies, creating "a critical need to save the outstanding naturalistic areas in every state," he asserted. "The pending threats, or at least one impending threat," Quinn warned in a speech reminiscent of Neff, complete with references to "battles of peace" was "the development of the large Federal Highway program."[3]

TEXAS PARKS AND WILDLIFE DEPARTMENT

The National Park Service in the 1950s faced a similar competition for both dollars and development priorities associated with highway building and other public works and defense projects. In response, the federal agency launched its ten-year "Mission 66" program to reawaken congressional interest in national parks through 1966. Strongly influenced by its old partner's innovation, the Texas State Parks Board introduced "Operation Ten-Seventy" in 1960. Demonstrating that park attendance two years earlier had topped five million visitors—a number steadily rising in virtually the same system since it first hosted one million in 1940—the board proposed state investment of $10 million in its parks during the coming decade.

Instead, the legislature commissioned through Texas Technological College a major study of state parks, which called for acquisition of 373,000 acres and expenditure of $462 million between 1963 and 2000. Newly elected Governor John Bowden Connally, Jr., in 1963 boldly employed these statistics to press for merger of the parks board and the State Game and Fish Commission, an old and controversial idea opposed by both outdoor sport enthusiasts and park supporters like Frank Quinn. Connally skillfully swayed opinion in his favor, and as a reward his new Texas Parks and Wildlife Department tripled the old parks budget with an annual $1.7 million for maintenance at fifty-eight sites covering 62,000 acres and for development of four new parks. Following passage by Congress of the Civil Rights Act in 1964, Connally, the legislature, and state agencies gradually lifted their racial barriers, and state parks for the first time officially opened to all Texans.

In 1965 San Jacinto Battleground transferred from its separate commission to the state parks agency, and a year later rising visitor receipts paid off the last of Palo Duro Canyon's revenue bonds. Even with increased maintenance budgets, however, by 1966 the system's fifty-nine parks continued to lean heavily upon their thirty-year-old New Deal improvements built mostly by the Civilian Conservation Corps. "[D]evelopments to accommodate visitors," the *Houston Chronicle* reported early that year, "date back to the 1930s in all but three parks." A new Texas Tech master plan in 1967 repeated the need for broad improvement and expansion of the system but cautioned that "[s]tatewide significance of potential scenic and historic parks would be determined by professional scientists in the fields of geology, archeology, biology and history—not by amateurs, politicians, or local 'boosters'." [4]

A $75 million, voter-approved bond issue for land acquisition resulted from this report. Then in 1971—the year that seventy-six-year-old Frank David Quinn died—lawmakers provided additional funding for improvements. Their new cigarette tax, coupled with state bond money and new federal grants, fueled a remarkable decade of expansion that doubled Texas state parkland acres and built a sprawling office complex for the Parks and Wildlife Department on the outskirts of Austin. [5]

THE NEW DEAL LEGACY

A new era of federal participation in environmental issues, coupled with the fiftieth anniversary of the New Deal in 1983, fostered renewed appreciation for the older parks in the state system. Few noticed that this year also marked the sixtieth anniversary of the State Parks Board's creation, and even the one-hundredth anniversary of state acquisition of land at San Jacinto and the Alamo. Fortunately, the Parks and Wildlife Department headquarters staff reverently undertook a system-wide inventory of New Deal artifacts in the agency's thirty-one operating parks constructed by the CCC.

They identified more than *four hundred CCC buildings* built between 1933 and 1942 and surviving in the parks, ranging from the boathouse at Bonham to the pumphouse at Palmetto. A vast majority of these venerable structures—plus roads, bridges, culverts, signs, and monumental landscape improvements not included in the inventory—still served crushing numbers of visitors on a daily basis. While some 130 state parks now constituted a system two generations beyond its origins, senior agency staff began referring affectionately to the aged CCC parks as "the backbone of the system."

As part of the inventory effort, *Texas Parks & Wildlife* magazine in September 1983 published an anniversary story titled "CCC: Fond Memories from a Time of National Hardship." This article chronicled part of the agency's vast New Deal legacy, focusing on CCC enrollees who had assembled a bona fide state park system for Texans in the middle of the Great Depression. Authors also noted that the National Association of CCC Alumni had been formed, to remind new generations of their handiwork and to support a modern reincarnation of the program for disadvantaged youth. Moreover, as the youngest surviving CCC veterans advanced to retirement age and into a period of reflection on formative experiences, the article also solicited their remarks and memorabilia for commemorating the state park agency's heritage.

Werner Schlabach, a member of CCC Company 886 in the mid-1930s building Lake Corpus Christi State Park, responded with memories of hauling cast-stone caliche blocks for the park's Mediterranean-style refectory. "Most of the visitors at the park," when it opened in 1936, he related to author Jim Cox, "told us it would never last through the first hurricane. You can imagine how I felt when I went back to visit the park in 1976—the building was still there!"[6]

Stimulated by anniversaries, retirement, and the CCC alumni organization, other veterans of the program have recounted their days in the New Deal sun. Ezekial Rhodes, Jr., who helped construct Fort Parker State Park in the late 1930s, at a reunion of his CCC cohorts at the park emphasized his satisfaction at making $30 per month in the Great Depression. He described the constant use of hand tools for clearing the lake bottom and building the dam and roads, plus his not-unwelcome regimen of military life in barracks. Rhodes's New Deal experiences now seem an amazing component of a remarkable family history spanning from slavery through emancipation to tenant farming, then to his own service in the CCC, all not far from his home in Mexia. "Everybody was glad to make money . . . people were desperate," Rhodes recalled. The state park development, he acknowledged, though closed at the time to his race, "boosted the economy here in Limestone County."

Roscoe Bowers in 1934 "lacked three months being 18 so [I] moved my birthdate up accordingly" to join the CCC. Assigned to Co. 896 just commencing Big Bend State Park, "I arrived in the Basin in the Chisos Mountains in the dark . . . as a terrific rainstorm was subsiding," he reflected. "As daylight came we . . . found ourselves completely surrounded by rock walls with water streaming and cascading all around—a spectacular sight." Concluding his CCC experience as a mechanic at Garner State Park, Bowers knew that times were changing. "The park was essentially finished by early 1941 as the expansionist aspirations of Japan caused the Federal Government to reassess its priorities," he dramatized. "As a result, Garner State Park was declared complete and the CCC camp was disbanded."

Raymond Rigsby, a First World War veteran and 1933 recruit to Company 1829(V), reviewed a long life affected by war, drought, depression, and then the CCC. From time spent at Palo Duro Canyon, he proudly recalled his ride in the "first truck that ever moved down the road" upon completion of that herculean project from canyon rim to base. Rigsby also recognized the immense importance of New Deal state park endeavors. Settled in Canyon City with his family and employed by the park concessionaire some years after New Deal development, one day Rigsby noticed a college student dumbstruck by his first encounter with Palo Duro Canyon.

"He was just beside himself," Rigsby observed, learning that the young man studied park management at a distant state university. "He said, 'I never dreamed of things like this'," the old veteran repeated in wonder. "'I never dreamed of things like this here in Texas'." [7]

NPS officials familiar with park facilities across the nation, and with the principles of their proper design, acknowledged early that Texas could boast of the finest results from New Deal development. "Although the eye is first attracted by the novel palmetto-thatched roof," of Palmetto State Park's refectory, architect Albert Good wrote in 1938 for *Park and Recreation Structures,* "it lingers on to observe intently and admire the masonry with outcrop base, the adzed timbers, and the vigorous treatment generally." Designer Olin Smith advanced a distracting magical quality to this building, perhaps because of the park's next-door neighbor, a new hospital for children stricken with polio, modeled on President Roosevelt's favorite philanthropy at Warm Springs, Georgia. *National Park Service, National Archives*

APPENDIX A

*Operational parks established through 1945
in alphabetical order of historic names*

> . . . in some matters—particularly the buildings—we have probably excelled
>
> any state in the Union. I have that information on very good authority.
>
> —NPS Inspector George Nason, reporting to the State Parks Board
>
> on site development in Texas, 13 June 1934

In this alphabetical appendix of state parks and their features developed through New Deal agencies, generally each park appears under its name of the 1930s and 1940s. For example, Fort Griffin State Park has since been reclassified as Fort Griffin State *Historical* Park but is readily found under its original name below. If a park's first name changed after 1945, cross-reference generally is provided; for example, a cross reference to Lake Abilene State Park appears under the park's current name Abilene State Park. In some cases, details are provided under the most easily recognizable name for a facility, such as Stephen F. Austin State Park rather than Austin State Park.

Park locational information provides enough direction for finding the facility on any detailed travel map of Texas. Each listing includes the county and nearest community, followed by the connecting state-maintained highway or farm/ranch road with the state-maintained Park Road. Of historical interest, low-number Park Roads provide a clue to the hierarchical importance, not necessarily chronological accession, of these parks to early system managers.

A full explanation of Civilian Conservation Corps nomenclature appears in the concluding section of chapter 1. Unless noted as war-veteran (V) or African American (C for "colored") units, CCC company numbers indicate enrollment of predominantly young white men before April 1935 and segregated white companies thereafter. Some CCC companies chose a distinct name for their Army-controlled encampment, apart from the park project number and name, and when known this title appears in the park's descriptive details below.

Outstanding designers and artisans—architects, carpenters, etc.—are listed when their association with a particular park development is known. In park statistics where no individuals are credited for buildings and landscape designs, these facilities likely were planned by parks board employees at the Central Design Office in Austin.

See the List of Terms and Abbreviations for full names of New Deal programs cited below.

Abilene State Park (see Lake Abilene State Park)

Acton State Park
Hood County in Acton Cemetery, FM 208 to FM 1190.

Parkland consists of the burial plot of .006 acre within Acton community cemetery, for Elizabeth Patton Crockett (1788–1860), second wife and widow of Alamo hero David Crockett, and her family. Through a 1911 appropriation, the state in 1913 erected a 28-foot-tall, gray-granite monument topped by a pioneer woman in marble; the plot is owned by the cemetery association but maintained as Acton State Historical Park by TPWD.

The Alamo
Bexar County, downtown San Antonio on Alamo Plaza.

State property includes parts of 1724 Mission San Antonio de Valero, managed by the Daughters of the Republic of Texas since 1905. State-owned parkland totals 4.162 acres: the church purchased in 1883, convento property optioned by DRT representatives in 1903 and purchased by the state in 1905, and the balance purchased in 1930–1933 by the state and Clara Driscoll to create unofficially labeled "Alamo State Park."

State- and DRT-financed development took place between 1913 and 1933, then county- and federal-relief funds paid laborers to clear later buildings and develop the site as a park. In 1933–1934 the Texas Relief Commission brokered state and federal funds for further renovations, then in 1935 additional government funds for celebrating the 1936 Centennial allowed major improvements to state-owned Alamo property. The DRT in 1950 completed its library building within the compound.

The 1844–1858 Alamo church, with its prominent carved-stone facade on Alamo Plaza, is credited to Spanish master builder Hieronimo Ybarra; its 1850 curvilinear parapet resulted from tenant improvements of the U.S. Army, credited to architect John Fries; architect E. Palmer Giles in 1920 designed the church's concrete-vault roof; landscape architect H. E. Kincaid oversaw 1930s landscape improvements and stone perimeter wall construction; and architect Henry Truman Phelps designed the 1936 museum/gift shop.

Austin State Park (see Stephen F. Austin State Park)

Balmorhea State Park
Reeves County outside Toyahvale, US 290 to Park Road 30.

Development on donated land began in July 1934 as DSP-4, a federal drought project, redesignated SP-47 in April 1935; property was listed as 980 acres in 1935, then 504 acres in 1938; TPWD currently manages 43.1 acres.

CCC Co. 1856 established camp here in July 1934; with the exception of a 45-man side-camp assignment to nearby Davis Mountains State Park in 1937 and 1938, this company improved Balmorhea State Park through January 1940, when its members moved south to reoccupy the barracks at newly designated Big Bend National Park.

CCC work includes the formal, concrete-rimmed, 1.75-acre swimming pool that captures water from San Solomon Springs, as well as entry portals, combination building, "San Solomon Courts" lodging, bridges, and other improvements of adobe and local limestone.

Bastrop State Park
Bastrop County near Bastrop, SH 21 and Loop 150 to Park Road 1.

New Deal development began in 1933 at combined Bastrop-Buescher State Park (see also Buescher State Park) as SP-21/SP-22; Bastrop unit development began with 753 acres (including a 1914 dam and lake on Copperas Creek) donated by the city of Bastrop and others; more land was donated in the mid-1930s and in 1966. A forested lane (Park Road 1C) developed in 1935 and totaling 112 acres connects Bastrop and Buescher state parks. The Bastrop unit is now 3,503 acres managed by TPWD.

CCC companies 1805 and 1811 arrived in late 1933 and early 1934, respectively, camped on private property near the park entrance, and developed a "flagship" state park for the Texas system through 1937 and 1939, respectively.

With exception of initial designs from the State Parks Board's Austin office for entrance portals and refectory exterior, architect Arthur Fehr designed all 1930s buildings in the park and directed their construction. Landscape architects H. L. Scogland, Rufus Hirsch, and Norfleet Bone contributed to the extensive rustic design esthetic here; local stonemasons and master carpenter "Uncle Joe" Pfeiffer directed the CCC labor resulting in exceptional facilities. CCC-built work includes the entry structures, refectory, cabins, overlook shelters, and stone erosion-control and beautification work, all in red sandstone from a nearby quarry, with carved-wood details. Other New Deal programs built the original nine-hole golf course (FERA, CWA, WPA) and the swimming pool and bathhouse (WPA), and operated the wood mill and furniture shop (NYA) after CCC departure.

TPWD added in 1995–1997 an additional nine holes to the golf course but designed these alterations with sensitive respect for the original master plan. As a result of Bastrop State Park's extensive original development and sensitive maintenance over 60 years, the federal government in 1997 designated the park a National Historic Landmark.

Beeville State Park
Bee County in Beeville.

Of many "firsts" in the Texas state park system, this site may have been the first accepted by the State Parks Board; the park was presented in 1924 by the city of Beeville at the board's first stop on its first park-promotion caravan. The state in 1927 officially accepted this 128-acre site, but in 1933 the board signed a lease with local American Legion members for operation.

Some CWA work took place in the winter of 1933–1934; to qualify for WPA improvements including an auditorium and recreation center, parks board members on 19 March 1940 voted to return the site, voting again in March 1943 to reconvey the land to Sudie Scott.

Bentsen–Rio Grande State Park
Hidalgo County near Mission, FM 2062 to Park Road 43.

Land for this park was acquired in 1943 through donation from the Bentsen family; TPWD currently manages 588 acres of surviving woodland habitat on the Rio Grande. No New Deal development occurred here.

Big Bend National Park
Brewster County south of Marathon, US 385; south of Alpine, SH 118.

Texas's first national park was initially named in 1933 Texas Canyons State Park and then Big Bend State Park. Development began in spring 1934 as SP-33; the project later that year also briefly carried designation DSP-1, a federal drought project; between 1940 and 1942 it became NP-1, the state's single national park project. Development began with up to 158,960 acres from state school lands; other property increased the park through foreclosed ranches, then through purchase with federal drought funds and, in 1941, $1.5 million in state appropriations. Texas in 1944 transferred 691,338 acres to the federal government; Big Bend National Park is currently 801,163 acres managed by the NPS.

CCC Co. 896 camped in the Chisos Basin from May through October 1934; Co. 1855 arrived in July 1934 and remained through December 1937;

Co. 1856 moved here from Balmorhea State Park in January 1940 to resume development through March 1942.

In addition to dramatic Green Gulch Road to the basin, with its stone bridges and erosion control, CCC work includes four cottages of stone and adobe, and initial trail work, particularly evident on Lost Mine Trail. The Second World War curtailed extensive planned development of lodge and resort facilities, and these were not resumed until the 1950s.

Big Spring State Park
Howard County near Big Spring, FM 700 to Park Road 8.

This park originated in 1924 with a 200-acre donation from the Big Spring Federation of Women's Clubs to the State Parks Board, accepted by the state in 1927 and briefly named Edwards Monument Park and Big Spring Mountain Park. In 1934 it became Big Spring State Park, designated DSP-2, a federal drought project, then SP-45 with 335 acres adding Scenic Mountain's crest; TPWD currently manages 382 acres.

CCC Co. 1857 arrived in July 1934, completed the day-use park, and departed in October 1935.

CCC facilities include the park road with impressive boulder curbing, mountaintop pavilion and nearby latrine, concession building converted to headquarters (with unfinished observation tower), caretaker's house, and other landscape features.

Blanco State Park
Blanco County in Blanco, US 281 to Park Road 23.

Blanco hosted one of the first New Deal state park projects in Texas, designated SP-7 in the early summer of 1933; local citizens donated 105 acres along the Blanco River, still managed by TPWD.

CCC Co. 854 established "Camp Crist" in June 1933 and remained through May 1934.

CCC work includes two dams and low-water crossings, an impressive stone-arch bridge, entry station and keeper's residence, pavilion, and elaborate picnic facilities.

Bonham State Park
Fannin County near Bonham, FM 271 to Park Road 24.

Development began in late 1933 as SP-18, originally on 532 acres donated by the city of Bonham. TPWD currently manages 261 acres, including the 60-acre lake built by CCC.

CCC Co. 894 arrived in December 1933 and camped on the south limits of Bonham for city water access. Enrollees completed day-use park development and departed in November 1936.

CCC work includes the dam and lake, roads and bridges, entry portals, the concession/bathhouse, an abandoned water tower of local limestone, an unusual wooden boathouse, and lake pavilion.

One of the few visible federal projects in small, rural congressional District Four, Bonham State Park represented the subtle patronage of powerful Congressman Sam Rayburn. A companion New Deal park on Fannin Lake north of Bonham near the Red River (FM 273 to Park Road 34) featured more extensive public facilities—lodge and overnight cabins—constructed with WPA labor under the Rural Resettlement Administration; that site is now managed by the USDA Forest Service, but only its fishing lake remains open to the public.

Brownwood State Park

Brown County near Brownwood, SH 279 to Park Road 15.

Floodgates on Lake Brownwood, completed in 1933, closed the first era in Texas of locally financed municipal reservoirs. The State Parks Board that fall accepted the water district's reservation of a 538-acre peninsula; this parkland received CWA improvements that winter, and in 1934 was designated SP-36 for CCC development. The prefix "Lake" applied to the park by 1935; parks board members in October 1944 renamed the facility "Thirty-Sixth Division State Park," in honor of the Texas National Guard unit that assembled at Brownwood, used the park for training and recreation, then distinguished itself in the Italian Campaign. In the 1950s the name changed back to Lake Brownwood State Park, managed today by TPWD.

CCC Co. 872 arrived in November 1934 and picked up where CWA workers had finished the previous winter, remaining through October 1935. One year later Co. 849 reoccupied the barracks and settled for a long tenure through February 1942.

CWA and CCC work here is exceptional and denotes one of the major New Deal park developments in Texas. The CWA-built native stone refectory, designed by Waco architect Roy E. Lane (appointed in late 1934 the first "State Parks Architect"), became the centerpiece for CCC work directed by superintendent Nottie H. Lee (later parks board executive secretary) that added 16 stone cabins, a monumental boat dock stairway with shelter overlook, a "fisherman's lodge," 2 residences, and a stunning portal ensemble, plus numerous lakeside and trailside features.

Brownwood publisher Wendell Mayes joined the parks board in November 1935 and served through 1961, at times occupying secretary, vice chairman, and chairman positions, and always serving as chief publicist for Texas state parks. While he pressed for continual development of Brownwood State Park, he unselfishly promoted the whole system, writing numerous feature articles on parks for regional and statewide periodicals.

Buescher State Park

Bastrop County near Smithville, FM 153 to Park Road 1.

This park originated in 1924 with 150 acres offered by Emil Buescher of Smithville to the State Parks Board, accepted by the state in 1927 and called Smithville State Park. The board, at its second meeting of 1933, accepted additional acreage donated by the city of Smithville, based on recent enabling legislation, and the tract became part of Bastrop-Buescher State Park, jointly designated SP-21/SP-22, with additional acreage donated through 1936. The park includes CCC-built 30-acre Buescher Lake and connects to a forested lane (Park Road 1C) developed in 1935 and totaling 112 acres between Bastrop and Buescher state parks. The Buescher unit is currently 1,017 acres managed by TPWD.

CCC companies 1805 and 1811 arrived in late 1933 and early 1934, respectively, camped on private land near the entrance to Bastrop State Park, and developed this facility in conjunction with the Bastrop unit through 1937 and 1939, respectively.

Architect Arthur Fehr designed all 1930s buildings in the park and directed their construction. Landscape architect Norfleet Bone contributed to the extensive rustic design esthetic; local stonemasons and master carpenter "Uncle Joe" Pfeiffer directed CCC labor. CCC-built work includes the entry bridge and wing walls, group pavilion (originally Boy Scout shelter), extensive residential complex, the lake, and drainage structures.

Caddo Lake State Park

Harrison County near Karnack, FM 2198/134 to Park Road 2.

State park origins at Caddo Lake date from the earliest proposals in 1923 by the State Parks Board for a handful of "large parks" in the state, or possibly from the 1926 donation of 120-acre "Marshall State Park," accepted by the state in 1927; 1929 and 1931 legislation dedicated the state-owned lakebed and adjacent lands for recreation purposes.

Donated land became SP-1-T in 1933 (and later SP-27 and SP-40) with 468 acres from several landowners, including Thomas Jefferson Taylor. The 1930s park fronts on the Cypress Bayou channel leading to Caddo Lake proper with its 1910–1914 (improved in 1971) dam in Louisiana. The park is currently 484 acres managed by TPWD, along with additional lands in and around the lake.

CCC Co. 889 arrived on 7 June 1933 to develop this first official state park with federal New Deal assistance; the camp moved that November but work resumed from October 1934 through March 1937 under Co. 857, alternating from assignments at Paris State Park and the Centennial Exposition at Dallas.

CCC work includes massive entry portals of red sandstone, road and drainage work, active and abandoned latrines, and abandoned pavilion. Enrollees converted their CCC barracks to the original park concession building and log-veneered guest cabins.

While Caddo Lake received the first official New Deal state park project designation, its development through the 1930s proved intermittent, probably because of land acquisition questions raised by its NPS sponsors. Through the political support primarily of powerful U.S. Senator Morris Sheppard of Texarkana (who years earlier had facilitated the Caddo Lake dam in Mooringsport, Louisiana), CCC enrollees periodically returned to Caddo Lake to complete substantial recreation facilities.

Cleburne State Park
Johnson County near Cleburne, US 67 to Park Road 21

City of Cleburne officials in the 1920s frequently discussed donations to the State Parks Board; not until 1935 did the city contribute 508 acres for the development of SP-53. The park's present 529 acres include spring-fed 116-acre Cedar Lake built by the CCC, all currently managed by TPWD.

CCC Co. 3804 arrived in the spring of 1935 and continued development in the park for more than five years, through August 1940.

CCC work includes the dam and lake, an apparently frustrating and incredibly labor-intensive project that reportedly would not fill with water through most of the camp's long tenure. CCC enrollees also completed a fine limestone residence and maintenance area, entrance portals, and outdoor fireplace units; additional work in 1941 through WPA labor finished a bathhouse and concession building, plus a water and sewer system.

Clifton State Park
Bosque County in Clifton, off SH 219.

The City of Clifton tried to donate 80 acres along the Bosque River to the state in spring 1933 to secure a CCC camp for park development; however, the State Parks Board, upon resumption that fall of New Deal park development control, refused to accept the property, and it remains a city park.

CCC Co. 878 arrived on 18 June 1933 to establish "Camp Clifton" and began work on one of the first New Deal state parks in Texas, remaining only through early January 1934.

CCC work of river-washed limestone is exceptional and perhaps the most advanced from the "first period" assignments in Texas; included are entry portals, concession building, picnic and fireplace units, a semicircular seating area, and abandoned latrine.

Daingerfield State Park
Morris County near Daingerfield, SH 49/11 to Park Road 17.

The park developed as SP-49 on 580 acres of donated land, including the 900-foot CCC-built dam impounding 80-acre Little Pine Lake (later named Lake Daingerfield). Current boundaries managed by TPWD are reduced to 551 acres, probably for construction of new SH 49/11 across the northeast property corner.

CCC Co. 2891 arrived in August 1935, following a nationwide boost in CCC enrollment and project budgets, and remained through June 1938; Co. 1801(C) then moved from Fort Sam Houston's Camp Stanley into the Daingerfield barracks and continued work on the park through January 1940.

CCC work utilized much machinery and includes the dam and lake, fences, 500-foot water well, pine reforestation, and pavilion with unusual concrete walls (despite local abundance of red sandstone); the entry road was improved with WPA labor in 1936. A concrete entry pylon, moved to the lake area, once marked the original entrance to the park from the old highway alignment.

Davis Mountains State Park
Jeff Davis County near Fort Davis, SH 118 to Park Road 3.

Supporters in the 1920s of a state park in the Davis Mountains claimed that their efforts to establish public recreation grounds began in 1903, probably inspired by the Bloys Cowboy Camp Meeting, dating from 1890, and by President Theodore Roosevelt's well-publicized creation of national parks and monuments for outdoor recreation. Despite a 1921 legislative committee visit and primary assignment in 1923 for the new State Parks Board to secure a Davis Mountains park, land acquisition proved difficult. Following instruction of the 1927 legislature, the Texas Highway Department supervised construction of the Davis Mountains State Park Highway upon donated right-of-way.

Finally, in the spring of 1933 several landowners donated about 560 acres, along Keesey Creek and the new "State Park Highway" (now SH 118/166), for development of SP-4/SP-5 with a projected 2,130 acres; further land donations were received in 1937. The park currently encompasses 1,321 acres managed by TPWD.

CCC Companies 879 and 881 arrived on 15 June 1933 to pitch a 400-man tent camp on Keesey Creek; Co. 881 departed in November and Co. 879 worked through July 1935; Co. 1856 at Balmorhea State Park then performed frequent "side camp" work at Davis Mountains, even after that company's assignment from January 1940 through March 1942 at Big Bend National Park.

CCC work resulted in the resort-class adobe-walled Indian Lodge (originally called "Indian Village Hotel"), designed by architect William Calhoun Caldwell; CCC work also includes roads and stone erosion structures, the mountaintop pavilion, and a latrine (now abandoned). The highway department finished its SH 118/166 Scenic Loop after the war, fulfilling the 1927 promise of admitting motorists deep into the Davis Mountains, accommodated with nine rustic roadside picnic areas.

Fannin State Park
Goliad County at Fannin, US 59 to Park Road 27.

Hugh B. and Lizzie Hanley in 1913, and Sol Parks in 1918, donated some 13 acres to the state, in commemoration of the Battle of Coleto Creek, which took place on 20 March 1836 near here. From the beginning the park was unofficially known as Fannin State Park in honor of Col. James Walker Fannin, who died with his defeated Texian troops in infamous execution near Goliad a few days following the battle. The park transferred in 1949 from the Board of Control to the State Parks Board, and today TPWD manages Fannin Battleground State Historical Park of some 14 acres.

Landscape improvements to the grounds—including an elaborate entry of iron gates surplussed from the State Capitol, since removed and now displayed elsewhere, and a caretaker's cottage—took place through the 1920s, sponsored by local park commission members. With $5,000 the Centennial Commission in 1936 added a water system and commissioned architects Samuel Charles Phelps Vosper and Raiford Stripling to design a classical visitors shelter and improvements for a two-story bandstand. A stone obelisk honoring the battle stands at the center of the small park (a similar 1885 obelisk in Goliad anchors a quarter-block city park northeast of the courthouse square).

Fort Griffin State Park
Shackelford County near Albany, US 283 to Park Road 58.

County government donated the fort ruins in 1935 and additional land in 1940 for recreational use, totaling 519 acres for development as SP-63. The park is now surveyed as 506 acres and designated a State Historical Park managed by TPWD.

CCC Co. 3803 transferred here in January 1940 from Lockhart State Park, with promises to reconstruct the 1867–1881 fort and develop recreational grounds along the Clear Fork of the Brazos River. National defense priorities cut short these elaborate plans, and the company moved on 1 December 1941.

Impressive CCC work nevertheless includes the park roads and stone drainage structures and numerous stone picnic cookers.

Fort Parker State Park and Old Fort Parker
Limestone County between Mexia and Groesbeck, SH 14 to Park Roads 28 and 35.

Growing interest in the approaching centennial of Texas independence inspired county citizens in 1933 to request a CCC camp for reconstruction of Old Fort Parker. After the State Parks Board held its October 1934 meeting at the site, a donation of land totaling 1,496 acres to the board also secured recreational development as SP-44. The resulting CCC-built, 750-acre Lake Fort Parker (originally named Lake Springfield) on the Navasota River dominates the recreation component, still 1,459 acres and managed by TPWD. The old fort site consists of 37 acres on Park Road 35 owned by the state but now managed through agreement with local governments.

CCC Co. 3807(C), a unit of young African American recruits, established "Camp Mexia" here in July 1935 as part of a national increase in CCC enrollment. These enrollees moved in January 1942 to a forest assignment after completing their substantial park development.

CCC work includes the concrete dam and lake, road and drainage system, and Meridian architect Jay P. Dunlap's concession building and former bathhouse, both of caliche bricks, red clay bricks, and wood. The current park headquarters, a small wooden building, is said to have been the CCC camp infirmary. The elaborate one-acre palisade-wall fort, designed in 1936 by Mexia architect J. F. Denning (and since rebuilt), employed $10,000 in Centennial Commission funds and possibly other labor sources, although the CCC is credited with the fort's original water and electrical systems and artifact display cases.

Each of the handful of all-black CCC companies helping build Texas state parks suffered the irony of creating recreation facilities for whites only. The Fort Parker project, in addition, placed such improvements atop the old townsite of Springfield, a thriving African American community in the late 19th and early 20th centuries.

Garner State Park
Uvalde County near Uvalde, US 83 to Park Road 29.

Numerous recreation sites along the Frio River, particularly in scenic spots accessible to San Antonio, attracted much interest for state-park status after 1923. Donations in 1927 of Mayhew—or Alto Frio—State Park, 25 acres near Leakey on the upper Frio (returned in 1933), and Tips State Park, still a 31-acre park at Three Rivers on the lower Frio, did not qualify for CCC camps. In 1935 Uvalde County purchased more than 600 acres on the Frio for donation to the state and development as SP-42, adding 531 acres in 1936; today the park totals 1,456 acres managed by TPWD.

CCC Co. 879 transferred here on 21 July 1935 from Davis Mountains

State Park and remained through April 1941. Though classified as a "white junior" unit, according to an inspector's report in 1940 the company consisted of "74% Mexican" enrollment.

Long tenure here by a productive CCC camp resulted in a well-developed park with a wide range of recreation facilities. Architect John H. Morris and landscape architect Ewart Gladstone Carney directed facility design for one of the premier parks of the state system. Their work includes a massive stone refectory with riverside dance terrace, elaborate residence and service complex, 16 stone and wood cabins, road system highlighted by original entry portals on US 83, and numerous stone features at riverside and trailside.

As with Bonham State Park in Congressman Rayburn's district, this park is one of few visible federal projects supported by Vice President John Nance Garner in his old district and home county. Departure in early 1941 of CCC Co. 879 from the project just after Garner left office was no coincidence.

Goliad State Park
Goliad County near Goliad, US 183 to Park Roads 6 and 71.

Preservation and reconstruction of 1749 Mission Espiritu Santo (and of nearby Presidio La Bahia) had been proposed since at least 1913, when landowners unsuccessfully offered some of this property for sale to the state. In 1931, with the urging of County Judge James Arthur White, Goliad County and the city of Goliad donated to the state 207 acres within a horseshoe bend of the San Antonio River, including the mission ruins, plus some 2.6 acres containing the burial site of James Walker Fannin and his command, massacred on 27 March 1836.

Developed as SP-43, the New Deal park consisted of 237 acres under joint administration of the Board of Control and the local park commission. The northeast corner of the park, containing a large Centennial auditorium, was later returned to the county and city, excluding the park residence there; remaining land transferred in 1949 to the State Parks Board. TPWD now manages about 183 acres of the original state park.

CCC Co. 3822(V), middle-age war veterans, arrived on 5 August 1935, part of nationwide expansion of the CCC that summer. The unit remained until 2 May 1941, when it transferred to Franklin Fields Metropolitan Park in the Olmos River basin in north San Antonio.

Early improvements at this site resulted from federal work relief projects —RFC and CWA, including reconstruction of the mission granary by San Antonio architect Atlee Bernard Ayres—from 1932 through 1934. The Texas Highway Department built its "Texas Revolution Memorial Highway" (now US 183) through the park, and later assistance by WPA workers included roads, fences, and landscaping. Extensive CCC accomplishments at the park resulted in the park residence and maintenance complex, plus reconstructions of the mission church, granary, school, and surrounding walls, based on archeological investigation and designed by master architect Samuel Charles Phelps Vosper and his assistants Raiford Stripling and Chester Nagel. The Centennial Commission sponsored a $25,000 granite monument on the Fannin gravesite, designed by architect Donald Nelson. The CCC also cleared and fenced the 5-acre site of Mission Rosario southeast of Goliad.

Obtaining a CCC unit for the primary task of restoring a large Spanish mission complex was testimony to the persistence of Judge White, the powerful influence of Congressman Joseph Jefferson Mansfield, and the general appeal at all levels of government for a major Centennial commemorative project.

Gonzales State Park
Gonzales County in Gonzales, SH 146 and SH 97.

Inspired by the 75th anniversary of Texas independence in 1911 and hoping to attract the new breed of automobile tourists, the city of Gonzales in 1913 presented to the legislature a 150-acre section of its municipal parkland. This wooded "mall" took its place with the first handful of state parks overseen by the Board of Control through 1949, when it transferred to the State Parks Board. The board reconveyed the property in 1953 to the city, which maintains part of the land as a city park.

Lawmakers appropriated $7,500 in 1913 for improvements, and in 1936 a major Centennial project, including PWA assistance for a total of $64,045, erected a substantial museum, amphitheater, and landscape improvements designed by San Antonio architects Phelps & Dewees and others.

Goose Island State Park
Aransas County near Lamar, SH 35 to Park Road 13.

Independent of State Parks Board requests, the 1931 legislature transferred title to a 150-acre island in Aransas Bay off Lamar Peninsula from the General Land Office to "control and management" of the board for a "public park and playground." With additional peninsula land acquired after 1935, including roadway access to and land around the "Big Tree," development under SP-37 included about 177 acres; now 314 acres managed by TPWD.

CCC Co. 1801 arrived on 28 May 1934 with 178 white and 4 African American enrollees. In April 1935 the company became an all-black unit, and continued the project until transfer on 15 June 1935 to Fort Sam Houston.

Surviving CCC improvements include a "shellcrete," or cast concrete block, concession building and road and drainage systems.

Local residents and the Aransas County Judge objected loudly in the spring of 1935 over conversion of the Goose Island CCC camp to an all-African American company. Following demands for removal by Governor Jimmie Allred and then an incident that purportedly involved a murder in the camp, the company retreated to safe haven at the army post in San Antonio. Co. 1801(C) reemerged in June 1938 as a state park unit with assignment to Daingerfield State Park.

Governor James Stephen Hogg Memorial Shrine
(see Hogg Memorial Shrine)

Grayson State Park
Grayson County near Denison, FM 131 to Loy Lake Road.

This park was established as SP-24 on 350 acres "leased" but never deeded from the county to the state, including CCC-built Loy Lake. Upon departure of the CCC camp, county commissioners renamed the facility "Loy State Park," in honor of County Judge Jake Loy, and assumed operations; the county still operates this local park.

CCC Co. 857 arrived on 7 November 1933 and completed the day-use park by their departure on 15 October 1934 for Caddo Lake.

Surviving CCC work includes the dam and lake plus a massive stone water tower, picnic tables, and other features designed by architect Rollin M. Rolfe and landscape architect Joe W. Westbrook.

Hamilton State Park
Hamilton County near Hamilton, US 281.

This proposed 70-acre park began optimistically as SP-6 on land promised, but never deeded, to the state, as one of a group of parks along new SH 66 (now US 281). Following the departure of CCC workers, the land reverted to private ownership.

CCC Co. 882 arrived at the Hamilton city fairgrounds on 20 June 1933, one of the first half dozen units assigned to state park work in Texas. Unfortunately, due to an outbreak of typhoid fever, according to the local newspaper—but for disruptive behavior according to other memories—the company moved on 8 August to quarantine at the U.S. Army's Camp Bullis near San Antonio. Co. 882 never returned to Hamilton, but was reassigned from October 1933 through April 1937 to soil conservation projects near Taylor.

Hereford State Park

Deaf Smith County in Hereford, US 60 to Park Avenue.

Deaf Smith County and the city of Hereford in 1934 answered a call for special drought-relief CCC camps assigned to the infamous "dust bowl" region of the high plains. "DSP-3," a "drought state park" project, developed some 540 acres of land along Tierra Blanca Creek; the project received designation as SP-46 in April 1935, but its land apparently never transferred to the state. The State Parks Board voted in March 1940 to release all claim to CCC improvements, and in 1947 the county sold its parkland interest to local Veterans of Foreign Wars members. Today this section, downstream from the city-operated golf course and Jaycee Park, is called Veterans Park.

CCC Co. 1862(V) arrived on 31 July 1934 and worked through 2 November 1935, when it traded its barracks with Co. 872 fresh from Brownwood State Park. The "junior" company worked only through 11 December 1935, when it transferred to New Mexico.

Exceptional CCC work at this park included, foremost, the planting of 10,300 trees, many from Fort Sumner, New Mexico. An NPS-textbook-quality sign and a concession building of Palo Duro Canyon stone now mark Veterans Park; a bathhouse of local limestone, converted to a pro shop, is headquarters for the city park.

Hogg Memorial Park

Cherokee County in Rusk, US 84 to Park Road 50.

Descendants of Texas's first native-born governor, James Stephen Hogg, in 1940 purchased his 1851 birthplace and presented 177 acres to the city of Rusk. In April 1941 the legislature accepted title and charged the State Parks Board with the care of Jim Hogg Memorial Park; the site received no New Deal development. TPWD operates the same acreage today, with recent improvements, as Jim Hogg State Historical Park.

Hogg Memorial Shrine

Wood County in Quitman, SH 37 to Park Road 35.

Not to be outdone by J. S. Hogg's birthplace of Rusk, citizens of Quitman arranged commemoration of Hogg's 1874 marriage to resident Sarah Ann Stinson and his early law career and elected positions in Wood County. In 1945 the community presented this 26-acre site—the Wood County Old Settlers Reunion Grounds since 1902—to the legislature, which named it Governor James Stephen Hogg Memorial Shrine and placed it in custody of the State Parks Board; no immediate development occurred. TPWD operates the same wooded acreage today, with a collection of historic buildings, as Governor Hogg Shrine State Historical Park.

Houston State Park/Sam Houston Memorial Museum
Walker County in Huntsville, US 75 at 19th Street.

Sam Houston Normal Institute between 1905 and 1910 acquired 15 acres of Sam Houston's 1847–1858 homeplace through an initiative of students and faculty. This "park" occasionally appeared on lists of other state historical parks, but responsibility for operation and maintenance of the 18-acre Sam Houston Memorial Museum has remained with what is now Sam Houston State University. Texas Department of Transportation county maps through the 1980s labeled this site "State Park."

Funds raised by 1911 "reproduced the dwelling, kitchen, and law office as they were before Houston's [1863] death," according to a later study. The legislature in 1927 appropriated $15,000 for improvements, and by 1936 the Centennial Commission had provided $35,300 for construction of a rotunda museum designed by architect Harry D. Payne. An additional Centennial allocation paid for moving the "Steamboat House," Sam Houston's last residence, to the site.

Huntsville State Park
Walker County near Huntsville, US 75 and IH 45 to Park Road 40.

Long-favored plans in the 1930s by the State Parks Board for a facility near Huntsville culminated with project SP-61 and acquisition of 2,044 acres of cutover timberland, including construction of 210-acre Lake Raven, in the midst of Sam Houston National Forest. The park now consists of 2,083 acres managed by TPWD.

CCC Co. 1823(CV), the single unit of African American war veterans in Texas, transferred here on 2 October 1937 from Palmetto State Park for its last of five park-project assignments, and worked from barracks in south Huntsville until disbanding in early April 1942.

CCC work includes the original dam (utilizing an abandoned railroad grade), concrete spillway and lake, reforestation throughout the park, road and drainage systems, stone concession building, and lakeside dance terrace. The park master plan called for extensive development, including overnight cabins, but war preparations diverted funds and CCC assistance. The dam failed during a heavy rain on 24 November 1940 and was not rebuilt for many years.

Indian Lodge (see Davis Mountains State Park)

Inks Lake State Park
Burnet County near Burnet, SH 29 to Park Road 4.

Development of SP-64 began on 676 acres provided by the Lower Colorado River Authority, which had just completed its 803-acre Inks Lake in 1938. The park now encompasses 1,202 acres managed by TPWD.

CCC Co. 854, working on nearby Longhorn Cavern since 1935, shifted its efforts on 1 October 1940 to this new recreation park, remaining through 5 January 1942.

Ambitious plans for the park were curtailed by the Second World War, but the CCC completed an elaborate road network highlighted by dozens of stone culverts, plus the boathouse (converted to concession building). The Texas Highway Department completed much of Park Road 4 connecting to SH 29.

Jeff (or Jefferson) Davis State Park
Hill County near Hillsboro, FM 3267 to County Road.

This 1925 donation to the State Parks Board of 35 acres from the Old Settlers Association was accepted by the legislature in 1927. The land, leased for operation to American Legion members, was returned by the board on 10 July 1939.

The CWA sponsored improvements in the winter of 1933–1934.

Jim Hogg Memorial Park (see Hogg Memorial Park)

Kerrville State Park
Kerr County near Kerrville, FM 534 to Park Road 19.

During one of the first calls by the State Parks Board for donations, in 1924 Kerrville's Schreiner family offered some 42 acres on the Guadalupe River, and the state accepted that property in 1927; however, through initiative of Representative Coke Stevenson, that property reverted to the donors in 1931.

In 1934 the city of Kerrville donated a different 500-acre tract—once owned by Schreiner interests—to the State Parks Board for development as SP-58 along the river. In 1990 Texas Parks and Wildlife commissioners voted to change the 517-acre facility's name to Kerrville-Schreiner State Park, still managed by TPWD.

CCC Co. 1823(CV), the state's single unit of African American war veterans, arrived on 12 January 1935 and remained until 5 May 1937.

CCC work includes the road and drainage system, park residence, water tank, stone terrace work and riverside picnic units.

King's State Park
Refugio County in Refugio, US 77 to FM 774.

Spurred by an early-20th-century wave of interest in the Texas Revolution and the potential of automobile tourists, the city of Refugio in 1915 donated its central plaza to the state. King's State Park encompassed this town square where Captain Amon Butler King and his command were imprisoned by the Mexican army before execution on 16 March 1836.

In 1886 the city erected an obelisk on the square to commemorate the 50th anniversary of these events. In 1936 with placement of a $7,500 Centennial monument designed by Raoul Josset, officials moved the old "King's Men Monument" to nearby Mount Calvary Cemetery. The park transferred in 1949 from the Board of Control to the State Parks Board, which thereafter returned the land to the city of Refugio.

Lake Abilene State Park
Taylor County near Buffalo Gap and Tuscola, FM 89 to Park Road 32.

Project SP-26 began in 1933 with the name Lake Abilene State Park to develop 507 acres, donated that August to the State Parks Board, adjacent to the city's 1921–1922 Lake Abilene on Elm Creek. TPWD currently manages 621 acres with no lake frontage.

CCC Co. 1823(V), a mixed-race unit of war veterans, established "Camp Abilene" here in fall 1933; the company moved in fall 1934 to Lake Sweetwater, where in spring 1935 it became an all-black war veterans company; Co. 1823(CV) returned to Lake Abilene in June 1935 but transferred to Kerrville that fall. CCC work includes concession building, swimming pool, water tower base and other facilities constructed of local red sandstone and designed by Abilene architect David Castle.

Lake Brownwood State Park (see Brownwood State Park)

Lake Corpus Christi State Park
San Patricio County near Mathis, SH 359 or FM 1968 to Park Road 25.

Project SP-32 developed this park on an initial 288 acres leased in 1934 for 99 years from the city of Corpus Christi. The original nearby Mathis Dam, constructed by the city concurrent with park development, served until replacement in 1959 by a new dam and higher lake levels. The current park covers 365 acres managed by TPWD.

CCC Co. 886 on 27 April 1934 established "Camp Kleberg"—named for Congressman and King Ranch heir Richard Mifflin Kleberg—and remained until transfer to Palmetto State Park on 31 October 1936.

The CCC concession building atop a rocky peninsula above the lake, designed by architect Olin Boese and built of cast caliche blocks laid in a random ashlar pattern, is one of the extraordinary architectural gems of the Texas park system. Associated CCC work included a dance terrace and cast-stone staircase to water's edge, the road system and bridges, and formerly two boathouses, a bathhouse, and the residence.

Lake Sweetwater State Park

Nolan County near Sweetwater, RM 1856.

Officials in Sweetwater during the 1920s frequently discussed land donations with State Parks Board chairman D. E. Colp, and in 1926 accepted
his recommendation of graduate engineer Dewitt Carlock Greer to design
a tourist camp for the city. Then in summer 1933 Sweetwater joined a number of communities offering parkland to the state in exchange for New Deal
development. The Texas Relief Commission responded first with CWA assistance that winter on the city's 760-acre lake built in 1929; then in fall
1934, project SP-41 commenced development of the complete shoreline. A
land transaction never took place and the NPS designated the project a
"metropolitan park," which it remains today.

CCC Co. 1823(V) arrived in October 1934 with 200 white and 12 black
enrollees; six months later this unit became the state's only all–African
American war veterans company, 1823(CV). Congressman Tom Blanton
thereupon demanded removal of the camp and in June 1935, Abilene—
ironically Blanton's hometown—accepted the black veterans to revive work
on that city's nearby state park.

The CWA refectory is now the park keeper's residence, adjoining a golf
course with extensive 1930s improvements. CCC work around the lake is
extensive and exceptional, but these shelters, overlooks, and other features
were observed in the early 1990s to be sadly suffering from neglect and
vandalism.

Lampasas State Park

Lampasas County near Lampasas, US 190 to County Road.

In 1924 residents of Lampasas and San Saba counties briefly fielded the
Central Texas State Park Association to promote a new park somewhere
along their shared Colorado River boundary. In late spring 1933 as the Texas
Rehabilitation and Relief Commission solicited parklands for CCC camps,
the city of Lampasas donated 142 acres elsewhere along a scenic bend of
Sulphur Creek near the "Temple highway" (now US 190) and new SH 66
(now US 281); project SP-2 became the second official New Deal state park
in Texas. The legislature in April 1937 returned this small park to the city,
which later sold the land. Ironically, TPWD in the 1980s established Colorado Bend State Park in the original area promoted unsuccessfully in the
1920s.

CCC Co. 896 established Camp Miriam—named for Governor Miriam
Ferguson—on 17 June 1933 and worked through 20 May 1934, when the
company was transferred to the Chisos Mountains for Big Bend State Park.

CCC work, now on private land, included a number of limestone
buildings, shelters, picnic units, and drainage structures.

Lipantitlan State Park
Nueces County near Orange Grove, FM 70 to County Road.

The J. C. Bluntzer family in 1937 donated this five-acre tract, a tardy commemoration of the Centennial celebrated a year earlier. This presumed site of 1831–1835 Fort Lipantitlan features a standard gray-granite Centennial historical marker and received no other New Deal improvements. TPWD still maintains the site as Lipantitlan State Historical Park.

Lockhart State Park
Caldwell County near Lockhart, FM 20 to Park Road 10.

The city of Lockhart in November 1933 donated some 200 acres for a state park, but not until the summer 1935 CCC expansion did SP-41 begin development on 265 acres drained by the Clear Fork of Plum Creek. Today TPWD manages the same acreage.

CCC Co. 3803 on 28 July 1935 established Camp Colp—in honor of onetime Lockhart resident and parks board chairman D. E. Colp—on private land opposite the park entrance. This day-use facility was complete when, on 5 January 1940, the company departed for Fort Griffin State Park.

Austin architect George Walling designed a remarkable keeper's residence and maintenance compound of native stone; other CCC-built facilities include the Olin Smith–designed hilltop refectory, swimming pool, roads, and drainage system.

Longhorn Cavern State Park
Burnet County near Burnet, US 281 to Park Road 4.

After almost a decade of failing to receive funds or permission to operate state parks, State Parks Board chairman D. E. Colp in 1931 finally obtained legislative authority to acquire land through promissory notes and to negotiate contracts with private park developers. His single success with this approach came in July 1932 with acquisition of 457 acres covering "Sherrard's Cave," near Burnet and new SH 66, for $6,567 from Dr. J. L. Williamson, to be repaid with visitor fees. With help from a San Antonio concessionaire and convict labor, the park opened on Thanksgiving weekend that year.

In 1934, project SP-35 brought a CCC camp for more extensive development of 676 acres; the parks board in July 1939 proudly paid off the land note. A contract concessionaire still operates 639 state-owned acres.

CCC Co. 854 arrived on 18 May 1934 and completed extensive development on 1 October 1940 when, without moving barracks, it switched its work to nearby Inks Lake State Park.

Remnants of 1932 development and landscaping may survive, but CCC work is extensive and impressive, particularly the massive excavation of debris, and theatrical cave lighting by architect Samuel Charles Phelps Vosper. More visible work includes distinctive entry portals on US 281 and many Park Road 4 drainage structures, plus the unusual refectory of local stone and quartz formations from the cave, water tower and shelter, and a single prototype tourist cottage (mistakenly labeled "CCC officer's quarters"), all designed by Austin architect George Walling.

Mackenzie State Park
Lubbock County in Lubbock, US 87 to Park Road 18.

Taking advantage of a progressive 1915 state law allowing local governments to develop parks through their own taxes, the city and county of Lubbock soon established a joint public park along Yellow House Canyon along the Brazos River. The State Parks Board in 1935 accepted donation of 547 acres here, arranging designation as SP-52 and a long-term operation contract with the city of Lubbock. The park was named Mackenzie State Park, for U.S. Army adventurer Ranald Slidell Mackenzie. The state's long-term operation contract with the city of Lubbock for Mackenzie State Park continued until 1993, when the state traded its land for property at Lubbock Lake Landmark State Historical Park.

With nationwide expansion of the CCC in 1935, Co. 3820(V) encamped here on 25 July 1935. Probably because few veterans re-enlisted after their $500 "bonus" payments of June 1936, in an unusual procedure this company converted that fall to a "white junior" unit, which remained through the fall of 1941.

CCC work includes stone entrance portals on US 87, roads and bridges, a small refectory and other shelters, plus the large and once extremely popular concrete swimming pool, now closed.

Lubbock cotton buyer and State Parks Board member (1937–1941) Kennedy N. Clapp strongly supported development of this park and received appointment as "custodian and manager" by the board upon his return to private life.

Meridian State Park
Bosque County near Meridian, SH 22 to Park Road 7.

Parks board chairman D. E. Colp's friend and good-roads associate Hugh C. Odle lived in Meridian and in 1922 made the first move toward a state park in the area. Just as Pat Neff crafted his proposed state parks bill, Odle suggested a nearby donation from former Governor Jim Ferguson, who owned 1,000 acres on the Bosque River. Nothing came of this idea, but in 1933, during Ferguson's wife's second term as governor, the city of Meridian donated 542 acres elsewhere on Bee Creek for designation as SP-12, one of the state's first CCC-developed parks. The facility now encompasses 502 acres, including CCC-built 70-acre Meridian Lake, managed by TPWD.

CCC Co. 1827(V) arrived on 1 July 1933 and immediately began the difficult task of dam building; upon completion of the lake and day-use facilities, this unit disbanded on 9 October 1934.

CCC stonework here—in addition to the dam, lake, and road—is exceptional and supports the lakeside refectory, entry portals, retaining walls, and bridges.

Mineral Wells State Park
Palo Pinto County in Mineral Wells, North Oak Avenue (old US 281).

As a resort destination since the 1880s, greater Mineral Wells featured a number of parklike landscapes, particularly along nearby bends in the Brazos River. As a popular stop in the 1920s along the transcontinental Bankhead Highway, the community hoped to establish a state park where this highway crossed the river. In spring 1933, however, the town simply offered its existing 70-acre city park, previously known as Millings Park after donor Dr. H. H. Milling, for early designation as SP-8. No land transaction took place and the city eventually reclaimed the park, later called Lions Club Park and now Pollard Creek Park.

CCC Co. 1811 arrived on 17 June 1933 and divided its time between the park and improvements to National Guard facilities at nearby Camp Wolters. This unit remained until 2 January 1934, when it was reassigned to the Bastrop-Buescher State Park project, and side camps later that year from Co. 817 completed additional work here.

CCC work is largely hidden in this undermaintained city park, but original portals, roads, and stone steps lead to refectory and latrine ruins, and a splendid arched footbridge crosses over stone-lined Pollard Creek.

Relief commission chief Lawrence Westbrook, as first state director of CCC work and a lieutenant colonel in the Texas National Guard, maneuvered this camp's dual mission of park work and army training-ground improvement. Other New Deal park work completed in 1933–1934 by the CWA at the city's 1920 reservoir east of town became in 1974 Lake Mineral Wells State Park.

Mission State Forest (Mission Tejas State Park after 1957)
Houston County at Weches, SH 21 to Park Road 44

The uncovering in 1928 of a buried cannon near this site prompted historians to declare discovery of the site of 1790 Mission San Francisco de los Tejas. This pronouncement, combined with heightened interest in the approaching Centennial and New Deal development of huge Davy Crockett National Forest, led in 1935 to acquisition by the Texas Forest Service of these 117 acres on San Pedro Creek near the Neches River. Designated F-16, a prefix that normally signaled CCC forestry work on federal land, the project concentrated on development of a state-owned recreation site and timber preserve within the vast national forest. In 1957 legislators transferred Mission State Forest (or State Forest No. 5) to the State Parks Board, and TPWD still operates 118-acre Mission Tejas State Historical Park.

CCC Co. 888 began its work on 18 June 1933 as project P-58 (forestry work on Private land), changing in April 1935 to F-16 as newly acquired federal lands became Davy Crockett National Forest; the company remained through 31 October 1935 at Weches.

CCC work included a timber lookout tower (since removed), small pond, the log-cabin allegory of Mission Tejas, road and drainage structures, and reforestation.

Mission Tejas State Park (see Mission State Forest)

Monument Hill
Fayette County near La Grange, US 77 to Park Road 92.

The 1905 legislature authorized acquisition of .36 acre on this Colorado River bluff, the burial site for members of the 1842 "Dawson Massacre," 1843 Mier Expedition, and others. Local members of the Daughters of the Republic of Texas paid $350 in condemnation costs and offered long-term maintenance of the 1848 tomb here. The property was transferred in 1949 from Board of Control oversight to the parks board, and local citizens in 1956 donated some four additional acres. These earlier acquisitions are now part of 40-acre Monument Hill-Kreische Brewery State Historical Park managed by TPWD.

The DRT in 1933 sponsored improvements with a new vault, and in 1936 a $10,100 Centennial project added a 48-foot-tall stone shaft designed by Austin architects Page & Southerland, supporting artwork by Pierre Bourdelle and Raoul Josset.

Mother Neff State Park
Coryell County near Oglesby, FM 236 to Park Road 14.

Pat Morris Neff, governor of Texas from 1921 to 1925, steadfastly credited the beginnings of this facility as his inspiration for a state park system, and through his long life never corrected the title "first state park" for his mother's gift. Yet several "state parks" existed before 1923, when Neff fathered the State Parks Board, and his mother upon her death in 1921 had simply directed that about six acres be dedicated to "public service." Not until 1934 did Neff transfer this Leon River clearing to the state, along with some 250 additional acres to secure a CCC camp. Thereafter project SP-38 developed a model recreation ground, still managed by TPWD.

CCC Co. 817 arrived on 28 December 1934 in a "mixed" camp of young white and black enrollees, becoming all-white in April 1935 and remaining through 30 June 1938.

Architect Guy Newhall, landscape architect Stewart King, and engineer W. K. Adams directed CCC work that included massive earth fill and underground drainage in the flood-prone river bottom; limestone entry portals, tabernacle, refectory, residence, and water tower; the road and drainage system; and numerous picnic and trail features throughout the park. Some NYA work occurred after 1938, and the Texas Highway Department in 1939 built the "river road" as a west entrance into the park.

Normangee State Park
Leon County near Normangee, FM 3.

Answering the April 1933 call from state relief director Lawrence Westbrook for parklands, the city of Normangee offered some 500 acres surrounding its municipal lake on Running Creek. State officials in the 1950s reconveyed this land to the community, and it remains a city park.

In the winter of 1933–1934 some CWA work improved the site, but by 1937 the dam needed repairs estimated at $4,500; the parks board unsuccessfully requested CCC camp assignments through 1939 and assigned WPA workers to the site in 1942.

Palisades State Park
Randall County near Canyon, RM 1151 to County Road.

Henry Clay Harding's 100,000-acre ranch directly south of Amarillo in the 1920s routinely opened its Palo Duro Canyon access to seasonal recreation for Panhandle citizens; the owners in 1921 hosted a legislative park-search committee and later inspections arranged by parks board chairman D. E. Colp. In the spring of 1933 Amarillo businessmen bought 320 acres of the ranch and promised donation to the state in exchange for CCC development. Project SP-10 subsequently made too few improvements to suit the donors, and the parks board returned the property on 10 July 1939; the land is now a private residential area.

CCC Co. 856 arrived on 21 June 1933, one of the first camps assigned to Texas state park work, but departed on 2 December. Side camps from units assigned to nearby Palo Duro Canyon State Park performed subsequent work at the park through the winter of 1934–1935; at some point transient workers performed other duties at the ill-fated park site.

CCC work, now on private land, included a stone refectory, check dams, and picnic units.

Palmetto State Park
Gonzales County at Ottine, US 183 and FM 1586 to Park Road 11.

In Caldwell and Gonzales counties in 1933–1934, enthusiastic and "park-minded" citizens, as the NPS called them, offered to donate to the state as much as 500 acres of unusual swamplands along the San Marcos River in Ottine for CCC development. Project SP-29 soon began improvement of 160 acres, but few additional lands could be secured in the 1930s and only a day-use park was completed. Today the park covers 268 acres managed by TPWD.

CCC Co. 873 arrived in early May 1934 and remained until October 1935, when Co. 886 arrived and occupied its cottage-style barracks through May 1937; Co. 1823 (CV) then resumed work on the park until reassignment in October that year.

CCC work in the park includes the outstanding stone refectory and river-terrace overlook designed by architect Olin Smith, the water tower with stone base, US 183 entry portals and road system partly along an abandoned railroad bed, and picnic units. Landscape architects Mason Coney and C. C. Pat Fleming earned particular praise from the NPS for their sensitivity to the rare natural spectacle at Palmetto. Another elaborate stone entry group west of the park remains from onetime expectations for a much larger facility.

Palo Duro Canyon State Park
Randall and Armstrong counties, SH 217 to Park Road 5.

If column-inches of publicity could create a state park, Palo Duro Canyon would have been the state's first grand scenic park, and thereafter its most completely developed facility during New Deal realization. Congressman John Hall Stephens of Vernon in 1906 introduced a bill in Washington to create a national park here, whereupon the *Canyon City News* sponsored a canyon field trip and accelerated its persistent booster campaign. Panhandle resident and roving reporter Phebe K. Warner of Claude by 1920 waged an unrelenting crusade in support of a Palo Duro Canyon park. Her efforts inspired a 1921 legislative committee visit and in 1923 won this famous "clubwoman" a seat on the new State Parks Board. In 1931 Fred A. Emery, owner of an accessible and particularly panoramic section of the canyon, signed a two-year contract with the Canyon Chamber of Commerce for operation of a public park here.

After many years of unsuccessful schemes to acquire Palo Duro Canyon land, in April 1933 parks board chairman D. E. Colp struck a deal with Emery to buy an estimated 15,103 acres for the state, to be paid with highly optimistic estimates in concession profits. That June the park was assigned an unparalleled four CCC camps—with corresponding project designations SP-13, SP-14, SP-15 and SP-16—and development began in earnest. Land payments were concluded in 1966, and today the park consists of 16,402 acres managed by TPWD.

On 12 July 1933 CCC companies 1824(V), 1828(V) and 1829(V) established a huge tent camp overlooking the canyon, and on 1 December Co. 1821(V) joined the project. Companies 1824(V) and 1829(V) departed in April 1934; the two remaining war-veteran units worked through August 1935, then exchanged barracks with companies 2875(C) and 2876(C), both "colored junior" units. Co. 2876(C) worked through January 1936, and in October of that year lone Co. 2875(C) turned its quarters over to Co. 894. These last enrollees essentially operated the park through 20 December 1937.

CCC work once projected extensive development modeled on Grand Canyon National Park, with a headquarters lodge and numerous facilities on the canyon floor. Because of land ownership uncertainties and political diversions, including the host community's unhappiness with African American CCC workers, the park's New Deal improvements fell far short of those planned. The road into the canyon floor remains the CCC's hallmark achievement here, followed by the unfinished stone lodge (now an interpretive center), stone entry complex, four cottages, and three residences.

Paris State Park
Lamar County near Paris, US 271 to County Road.

The city of Paris in 1933 offered for state park consideration about 2,700 acres encompassing its 10-year-old municipal Lake Crook plus some 820 acres holding its 1911 Lake Gibbons, both on Pine Creek. The city's refusal to approve project SP-56 with nondiscriminating swimming facilities caused the NPS to lose interest in the project. In 1955 the city reenacted this scenario and again refused to transfer its land to the state. Today, these remain largely undeveloped municipal estates, although Lake Gibbons hosts the Gambill Goose Refuge.

CCC Co. 857 arrived on 27 November 1935, leaving some 30 men as a side camp through March 1936 at Caddo Lake State Park; from March through June that year, the company detailed 56 men with supervisors to Dallas for construction of the CCC's Centennial exhibit. Thereafter the entire camp, though officially assigned to Paris, apparently returned to Caddo Lake through November 1937.

CWA work, designed by Paris architect Thomas Broad, in 1933–1934 developed fine facilities at Lake Crook, including a concession building, boathouse, road and picnic units; the buildings unfortunately burned in the 1950s. Surviving CCC work appears limited to additional road and drainage work.

Possum Kingdom State Park
Stephens and Palo Pinto counties near Breckenridge, US 180 to Park Road 33.

New Deal construction from 1936 through 1941 of Morris Sheppard dam and 19,800-acre Possum Kingdom Reservoir, and transfer of 6,969 parkland acres from the Brazos River Conservation and Reclamation District, presented the State Parks Board with its largest-ever recreation park opportunity. But in April 1941 the lake unexpectedly filled just as project SP-65 began, halting plans to develop opposite shorelines with west- and east-park units. TPWD today manages 1,529 acres of the surviving west-park unit.

CCC Co. 2888, transferred from Tyler State Park, arrived here on 1 May 1941 and remained through 13 July 1942, the last active CCC state park camp in Texas.

Although the Second World War interrupted the CCC's extensive work program here, enrollees left seven miles of Park Road 33 as a monumental legacy. The parks board, with its growing revenues, completed other facilities by 1945, including five concrete-block overnight cabins.

Sam Houston State Park and Sam Houston Memorial Museum (see Houston State Park)

San Jacinto State Park
Harris County near LaPorte, SH 134 to Park Road 1836.

As with landscapes around the world where epic clashes took place, San Jacinto battleground attracted curious and reverent pilgrims immediately after Sam Houston's momentous victory over Santa Anna on 21 June 1836. At their 20-year reunion on the site, battle veterans initiated a monument fund, but by 1881 only a single grave marker had been placed. However, two years later state legislators appropriated $1,500 to buy the 10-acre cemetery. With assistance from the newly organized Daughters of the Republic of Texas, in 1897 lawmakers committed $10,000 to purchase 336 acres, and in 1907 they approved an additional $25,000 for more land, keeper's salary, beautification, and a master plan, and gave the park an official title. As The San Jacinto State Park, this site became unquestionably the first official state park in Texas. Today TPWD manages 1,003 acres— plus the battleship *Texas* berthed here in 1948—as San Jacinto Battleground State Historical Park.

After 1907 public and private groups sponsored refinements, including ambitious improvements coinciding with the 1928 Democratic National Convention in Houston. New Deal assistance for monumental development, driven by Houston banker Jesse H. Jones, came just in time for the Centennial celebration; federal sources—including PWA, WPA and President Roosevelt himself—contributed more than $1.5 million and the state added about $300,000. Groundbreaking took place on 21 April 1936 for a soaring obelisk designed by Houston architect Alfred C. Finn, and three years later Governor W. Lee O'Daniel dedicated the 567-foot shaft, museum, and extensive landscaping by [Mrs.] C. B. Whitehead.

San Jose Mission
Bexar County in San Antonio, SH 536 (Roosevelt Avenue) to Park Road 39.

This architectural masterpiece, begun in 1768 on the San Antonio River as the Spanish mission San Jose y San Miguel de Aguayo, had fallen to ruin by 1931 when the San Antonio Conservation Society purchased and restored its massive stone granary. The society and Bexar County purchased additional land and in May 1941 donated their property to the State Parks Board, just as the U.S. Secretary of the Interior designated this first National Historic Site west of the Mississippi. An unusual three-party operational agreement—between the Catholic diocese with its own five-acre church site, the state, and the NPS—advanced from 1941 to a 1983 agreement for the park service to operate the state's 16 acres here as part of the San Antonio Missions National Historical Park.

From 1932 local and federal funds helped reconstitute the entire walled compound, culminating in 1937 with restoration of the landmark church building. Local architect Harvey Partridge Smith directed labor sponsored, in succession, by federal RFC, FERA, CWA, and WPA projects, plus funds provided by the Centennial Commission.

State Cemetery
Travis County in Austin, SH 343 (7th Street) to SH 165.

In 1854 the state purchased, for use as its official burial ground, some 20 acres of undeveloped hills east of downtown Austin overlooking the Colorado River. Aside from the nearby Capitol grounds, this constituted the first action by Texas lawmakers to appropriate land for scenic purposes. Few refinements appeared, however, until 1911 when plans were made to move the body of Stephen F. Austin here. This reinterment inspired many more, and development of the cemetery continued through preparations for, and the aftermath of, the 1936 Centennial. The property has been managed since 1919 by the Board of Control and its successor, the General Services Commission.

Periodic placement of statuary, monuments, and other memorials highlighted improvements here until 1932 when considerable grounds improvements, inspired by engineer-historian Louis W. Kemp and directed by landscape architect Jac L. Gubbels, transformed the State Cemetery into a dignified showplace. Probable assistance that year from federal RFC funds was combined with Texas Highway Department construction of SH 165 for vehicle circulation as the "state's shortest highway." The State Cemetery in 1997 received some $4 million in improvements supervised by the General Services Commission, in cooperation with TPWD, Texas Department of Transportation, and the Texas Historical Commission.

Stephen F. Austin State Park
Austin County at San Felipe, FM 1458 to Park Road 38.

"The Stephen F. Austin Memorial Park" of some 14 acres was first offered to the state in 1929 by the San Felipe community, which envisioned reconstruction of their colonial village. The State Parks Board, however, through 1939 adamantly refused to accept "small parks of historical value." That year acceptance by the legislature of village lots plus 657 acres along the Brazos River caught the board's attention and willingness to apply for CCC recreation development. Today TPWD manages 667 acres in both historical and recreational units as Stephen F. Austin State Historical Park.

Centennial contributions in 1936 to the old village included a $14,000 statue of S. F. Austin designed by John Angel and a log replica of Austin's home. No CCC development took place here.

Stephenville State Park
Erath County near Stephenville, US 281.

Answering the April 1933 call from state relief director Lawrence Westbrook for parklands, the city of Stephenville offered 294 acres along new SH 66 (now US 281) and received designation as SP-3 for immediate development. Initially called Garner State Park, in honor of Vice President John N. Garner, the park upon its completion was renamed by the city and initially operated as a day-use facility. State Parks Board members on 11 April 1942 voted to return ownership to the original private land donors, and the property remains posted today.

CCC Co. 817 arrived on 23 June 1933 and remained through 26 December 1934, also supplying side camps to complete Mineral Wells State Park; this company after assignment to Mother Neff State Park in 1935 completed additional work here through side camps.

CCC work, now on private land, included a dam and lake, a limestone refectory, picnic units, and a road system. Following abandonment of CCC activities, a federal transient camp occupied the barracks in winter 1934–1935, with some associated work in the park.

Tips State Park
Live Oak County in Three Rivers, SH 72.

One of the small parks accepted in 1927, this 31-acre donation from local landowner Charles Tips received city improvements in 1931 and benefited from a $1,250 NYA project between May and June 1940. Still state owned, the property has been leased by TPWD since 1965 to the city of Three Rivers.

Tres Palacios State Park
Matagorda County near Palacios, SH 35 to Loop 141

Newly inaugurated President Franklin Roosevelt's interest in posthaste alignment of CCC camps with conservation projects led to a few strange enterprises during the program's first months. Among Texas Governor Miriam Ferguson's initial suggestions to the president for "state park" CCC assignments was 1,300-acre Tres Palacios Camp Grounds. Also known as Camp Hulen, the grounds had served since 1926 as the state's National Guard training field on Turtle Bay for summer infantry bivouacs. Perhaps the guard and the community intended to offer project SP-9 as a public park for use during nonsummer months, but the State Parks Board never asserted control of the site.

CCC Co. 1805 arrived on 10 June 1933 and remained through 20 October upon reassignment to Bastrop-Buescher State Park.

CCC work assignments included "planting trees and other non-skilled labor," according to reports, and these improvements after 1940 likely augmented massive development of the site as an Army training post during the Second World War.

Relief commission chief Lawrence Westbrook, as first state director of CCC work and a lieutenant colonel in the Texas National Guard, maneuvered this improvement of the 36th Division's permanent training grounds.

Tyler State Park
Smith County near Tyler, FM 14 to Park Road 16.

Part of the summer 1935 CCC expansion program, project SP-54 developed 992 acres, including a 65-acre lake on a branch of Hills Creek, of donated property heavily damaged by timber cutting and erosion. Today TPWD manages 983 acres.

CCC Co. 2888 arrived on 1 June 1935 and remained an unusually long time at this project, until transfer on 30 April 1942 to Possum Kingdom State Park.

CCC work includes the dam and lake, extensive reforestation, and a road system, all directed by landscape architect Ben K. Chambers. Architect Joe C. Lair demonstrated knowledge of Frank Lloyd Wright's work plus a prophetic change away from NPS rustic styling with his uncharacteristically modern concession building, bathhouse, boathouse, and residence of wood framing and geometric lines.

Tyler attorney Tom L. Beauchamp served on the State Parks Board from October 1929 through January 1939, often representing its interests in Washington, D.C., and pushing the board toward businesslike management and the hiring in 1936 of its first executive secretary. Beauchamp strongly supported state parks in his "three home towns," as he described Paris, Tyler, and Huntsville; the first and second had both hosted his law practice for many years, and he attended college in the third. He continued to support Texas park interests, including critical Big Bend land purchases, while serving as secretary of state under Governor W. Lee O'Daniel.

Washington-on-the-Brazos State Park
Washington County at Washington, FM 1155 and FM 912 to Park Road 12.

The community known as Washington-on-the-Brazos never developed to the ambitions of its founders, but pivotal events here—the signing in March 1836 of both the Texas Declaration of Independence and the Constitution, and the election of the new Republic's first officers—transformed the Brazos River hamlet into an everlasting shrine. In 1916 Governor Jim Ferguson directed a legislative committee with $10,000 in purchasing 50 acres of the original townsite to create the "State Park at Washington." The Board of Control in 1949 transferred the property to the State Parks Board; today TPWD manages 240 acres here.

In 1900 the county placed a commemorative stone obelisk where a building hosting 1836 events once stood, and the state made incremental improvements after 1916. In 1936 the Centennial Commission provided $34,000 for renovation of the existing auditorium and caretaker's house, a new amphitheater and support facilities, and placement of the historic Anson Jones house on expanded park acreage.

Other New Deal improvements and proposals:

Apparently no lists survive of park improvements sponsored during the winter of 1932–1933 by the Reconstruction Finance Corporation. Nor have records been found for similar park support between mid-1933 and mid-1935 through the Federal Emergency Relief Administration, predecessor to the Works Progress Administration. Fortunately, Civil Works Administration records confirm State Parks Board inventories of winter 1933–1934 improvements at various parks detailed above. Undeniable physical evidence state-wide confirms that between 1932 and 1942 untold numbers of local parks and cemeteries received stone entry portals, perimeter walls, and other improvements through these hometown work-relief programs.

A handful of "small parks," accepted officially or unofficially by the state, passed in the 1930s to the Texas Highway Department for development as roadside parks. These included Love's Lookout on US 69 in Cherokee County, Crosbyton on US 82 in Crosby County, and possibly others.

The NPS allocated several consecutive project numbers to park proposals that ultimately secured no CCC camps and thus do not appear in Tables 1 through 19. In the CCC second period, winter 1933–1934, Meridian was to receive a second 200-man camp as SP-17, and Brownwood was to become SP-25, but both camps were "discontinued," according to NPS records. Unnamed "canceled" camps SP-19, -20, and -23 might have been projected to fulfill state relief director Lawrence Westbrook's applications for Barreda (Brownsville), Indian Hot Springs (Hudspeth County), and Zilker (Austin) parks.

Missing project numbers in the third period, summer 1934, again included SP-25 for Brownwood, where the previous winter CWA workers developed park facilities. Other numbers were: SP-27 to renew work at Caddo Lake but "discontinued"; SP-28 to develop 15-acre "Sam Houston State Monument" on Cedar Bayou in Harris County but "discontinued"; SP-34 reserved for a second CCC company at Big Bend, which became DSP-1 instead; and SP-36, later assigned to Brownwood. The missing number of the fourth period was SP-39, assigned to ill-fated "Smith Memorial State Park" in Harris County.

Missing numbers in the fifth period, summer 1935, included SP-48 for 500-acre Lake Dallas Park as "discontinued," but indeed SP-55 at Bachman Lake and White Rock Lake in Dallas began on 8 August 1935. Missing from this period's sequential order, SP-50 was entered during the sixth period as Tyrrell Metropolitan Park in Beaumont.

Missing numbers from the sixth period, winter 1935–1936, denoted projects probably discontinued because of the nationwide cutback in CCC enrollment. SP-57 was to be Devils River State Park near Del Rio, and SP-59 would have provided recreation facilities for Nocona on its city lake briefly leased to the State Parks Board. SP-60 would have created a much-needed Ochiltree State Park in the northern Panhandle south of Perryton; the parks board accepted this land but returned it on 10 July 1939. That October, all the city and county parks previously assigned federal SP- (state park) project numbers received MA- designations for metropolitan areas and CP- numbers for county parks.

Two independent state-park bills authored by state senator William E.

Stone of Galveston emerged from the 1939 legislature, according to its records. One entrusted title to the State Parks Board for "Brazoria County Park," that county's entire Gulf of Mexico coastline between high and low tides, and the other for "Quintana State Park," 125 acres in the same county on the coast near Freeport.

For further information on the earliest historical parks owned by the state before 1945, look for their entries in the *New Handbook of Texas,* published in 1996 by the Texas State Historical Association. For more information on all state parks in the current system, see Laurence Parent's *Official Guide to Texas State Parks,* published in 1997 by the University of Texas Press.

Typical of parkland donations accepted in 1927 by the legislature, this scenic spot along
the White River (incorrectly listed as the Brazos in 1927 accounts) in Blanco Canyon
came from citizens of nearby Crosbyton. This fifty-acre site met the basic criteria of early
State Parks Board notions of "wayside" parks: on a highway (in this case, new US 82 in
background) with water and shade trees, plus interesting topography for a visual break
in the motorist's long journey. In 1933 the NPS changed this vision of state parks in
exchange for its design services to the state, but at the same time the Texas Highway
Department developed a formal roadside park program. Crosbyton State Park fortunately
was not lost in this shuffle and in 1935 the parks board formally transferred its acreage
here to the highway department for development by the National Youth Administration.
Texas Department of Transportation

APPENDIX B

The First Official State Park "System" of 1927, with brief descriptions provided by Marian Rather Powell, chairman, Parks and Playgrounds Committee, Texas Federation of Women's Clubs *

These parks accepted by the 40th Legislature appeared in Senate Concurrent Resolution 13 and then in the *Dallas News* roughly in the order originally donated. In Senate Concurrent Resolution 13 the parks were listed by the donated name, sometimes different from the name of the host community; in Marian Powell's article they were listed by community name first, often leaving off the donated name. They are listed here in alphabetical order by community for clarity, with donated names in parentheses if not included in Powell's information. Powell's notes in this article on the accepted donations appear to be the only details in one place describing the camping park "system" of 1927. Neither the original deeds nor any comprehensive descriptions survive in D. E. Colp's files or records at the State Archives or Texas Parks and Wildlife Department. While a few of these parks served the public for some time under local management, and still fewer received elaborate facilities in the 1930s, most others claimed the "state park" title only briefly, and Powell's notes represent their only known descriptions.

- Alto Frio (Mayhew State Park)—25 acres, on the Frio River.

- Beeville State Park—128 acres, 95 miles from San Antonio and 60 miles from Corpus Christi, on the main highway.

- Big Spring State Park—200 acres, on the Big Spring Mountain; 3,150 feet above sea level.

- Brownsville (Barreda State Park)—75 acres, with great variety of timber.

- Campbellton (Mary Campbell State Park)—30 acres, fronts the Atascosa River.

- Canadian (Young State Park)—10 acres, containing the only running water and shade in that section.

- Crosbyton State Park—50 acres on the Brazos River.

- Crowell (Fergeson [sic] Brothers State Park)—35 acres.

- Fort Worth (John Henry Kirby State Park)—100 acres, on Sycamore Creek.

- Frio River State Park—50 acres, between Pearsall and Dilley, halfway between San Antonio and Laredo, on the Meridian Highway.

- Hillsboro (Jefferson Davis State Park)—35 acres, the former site of the Old Settlers' Association.

- Kerrville (Schreiner State Park)—44 acres, on the Guadalupe River.

- Laredo (Mackin State Park)—118 acres, on the Meridian Highway.

- Llano (Robinson State Park)—69 acres.

- Lovelady (Abram and Lucy Womack Memorial State Park)—30 acres.

- Marshall State Park—120 acres, a key to the Caddo Lake.

- Palestine (Howard Gardner Memorial State Park)—25 acres.

- San Angelo (Johnson Memorial State Park)—50 acres fronting the Concho River; a wonderful pecan grove.

- Smithville (Buescher State Park)—100 acres, small dam across the creek.

- Sterling City (Foster State Park)—532 acres, on one fork of the Concho River.

- Three Rivers (Tips State Park)—30 acres, on the Nueces [sic, actually Frio] River.

- Van Horn (Thomas State Park)—80 acres, waterfalls and canyon.

- Wayside State Park—120 acres, about 30 miles from Amarillo, on the edge of Palo Duro Canyon; rugged and very beautiful.

* From "State Accepts 24 New Parks / Mrs. Ben Powell, Austin, Presses Resolution in Legislature," *The Dallas News,* 19 March 1927; *House Journal* (1927), pp. 1543–1544.

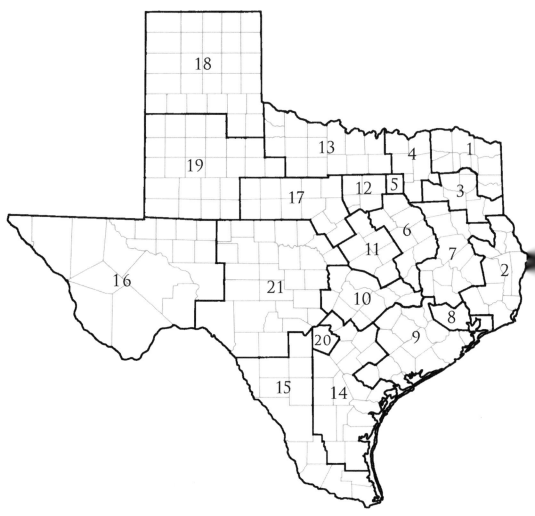

Before the New Deal, when most Texas congressmen enjoyed vague affiliation with constituents back home, the state legislature responded slowly to population shifts and the need to adjust district boundaries. Dramatic growth for Texas in the 1920s resulted in three new congressional seats following the census of 1930, but Austin lawmakers could not agree on twenty-one new district boundaries until 1933, making their first such adjustments since 1917! By 1935, at the peak of New Deal influence, including the highest number of Civilian Conservation Corps companies assigned to Texas parks, the state's powerful members of Congress had crafted very direct relationships with home districts. From Sam Rayburn's small rural Fourth District to R.E. Thomason's sprawling Sixteenth District, CCC camps rescued overworked farm and ranch lands, and pumped into the local economies a large percentage of their $2,300-per-month federal operating costs. *University of Texas Press graphic, based on 74th Congress, 1st Session beginning January 3, 1935, Official Congressional Directory for the use of the United States Congress, Second Edition corrected to March 21, 1935*

APPENDIX C

Texas Congressional Delegation, 1935

District	Congressman	Hometown	Home County
1	Wright Patman	Texarkana	Bowie
2	Martin Dies	Jasper	Jasper
3	Morgan G. Sanders	Canton	Van Zandt
(later)	Lindley Beckworth	Gilmer	Upshur
4	Sam Rayburn	Bonham	Fannin
5	Hatton W. Sumners	Dallas	Dallas
6	Luther A. Johnson	Corsicana	Navarro
7	Nat Patton	Crockett	Houston
8	Joe H. Eagle	Houston	Harris
(later)	Albert Thomas	Houston	Harris
9	J. J. Mansfield	Columbus	Colorado
10	J. P. Buchanan	Brenham	Washington
(later)	Lyndon B. Johnson	Johnson City	Blanco
11	O. H. Cross	Waco	McLennan
(later)	William R. Poage	Waco	McLennan
12	Fritz G. Lanham	Fort Worth	Tarrant
13	W. D. McFarlane	Graham	Young
(later)	Ed Gossett	Wichita Falls	Wichita
14	R. M. Kleberg	Corpus Christi	Nueces
15	Milton H. West	Brownsville	Cameron
16	R. E. Thomason	El Paso	El Paso
17	Thomas L. Blanton	Abilene	Taylor
(later)	Clyde L. Garrett	Eastland	Eastland
(later)	Sam M. Russell	Stephenville	Erath
18	Marvin Jones	Amarillo	Potter
(later)	Eugene Worley	Shamrock	Wheeler
19	George H. Mahon	Colorado (City)	Mitchell
20	Maury Maverick	San Antonio	Bexar
(later)	Paul J. Kilday	San Antonio	San Antonio
21	Charles L. South	Coleman	Coleman
(later)	O. C. Fisher	San Angelo	Tom Green

The ideal recreation park building, according to 1930s National Park Service administrators, would be a small facility, low to the ground with strong horizontal lines, and built of local materials finished by simple tools. Cabin No. 1 at Bastrop State Park, designed in 1934 by Austin architect Arthur Fehr, met these fundamental requirements, and carried a depression-conscious materials cost of $112.34 to boot. This timeless bungalow of stone and timber assembled by Civilian Conservation Corps enrollees symbolized the incredible decade of state park development in Texas between 1933 and 1942.
Ralph Anderson NPS photograph 1935, National Archives

APPENDIX D

State Parks of Texas, 1945*

State Park	New Deal Improvements	Nearest Community
STATE PARKS BOARD:		
Abilene	CCC	Abilene
Balmorhea	CCC	Balmorhea
Bastrop	CCC; CWA; FERA; WPA; NYA	Bastrop
Bentsen–Rio Grande Valley		Mission
Big Bend (National Park after 1944)	CCC	Marathon
Big Spring	CCC	Big Spring
Blanco	CCC	Blanco
Bonham	CCC	Bonham
Buescher	CCC	Smithville
Caddo Lake	CCC	Karnack
Cleburne	CCC; WPA	Cleburne
Daingerfield	CCC; WPA	Daingerfield
Davis Mountains	CCC	Fort Davis
Fort Griffin	CCC	Albany
Fort Parker	CCC; Centennial	Mexia and Groesbeck
Frio		Pearsall
Garner	CCC	Uvalde
Goose Island	CCC	Rockport
Huntsville	CCC	Huntsville
Inks Lake	CCC	Burnet
Jim Hogg		Rusk
Kerrville	CCC	Kerrville
Lake Corpus Christi	CCC	Mathis
Lockhart	CCC	Lockhart
Longhorn Cavern	CCC	Burnet
Mackenzie	CCC	Lubbock

State Parks of Texas, 1945*

State Park	New Deal Improvements	Nearest Community
STATE PARKS BOARD: (*Continued*)		
Meridian	CCC	Meridian
Mineral Wells	CCC	Mineral Wells
Mother Neff	CCC; NYA	McGregor and Gatesville
Normangee	CWA	Normangee
Palmetto	CCC	Luling and Gonzales
Palo Duro Canyon	CCC	Canyon
Possum Kingdom	CCC	Breckenridge
San Jose Mission	RFC; FERA; CWA; WPA	San Antonio
Stephen F. Austin	Centennial	San Felipe
Thirty-Sixth Division (Lake Brownwood)	CWA; CCC	Brownwood
Tyler	CCC	Tyler
BOARD OF CONTROL:		
Fannin	Centennial	Fannin
Goliad	RFC; CWA; CCC; Centennial	Goliad
Gonzales	Centennial	Gonzales
King's	Centennial	Refugio
San Jacinto	Centennial; PWA; WPA	Deer Park
Washington	Centennial	Washington
OTHER:		
Alamo	RFC; CWA; FERA; Centennial; NYA	San Antonio

**Texas Almanac and State Industrial Guide* (1945–1946). Although in 1945 the State Parks Board held title to other lands, its list presented what the board labeled as "major state parks" in the active system.

NOTES

Prologue

1. Pat M. Neff, "State Parks," in his *Battles of Peace* (Fort Worth: Pioneer Publishing, 1925), pp. 127–135.

2. 23rd Legislature, Regular Session, 1893: *Journal of the House of Representatives*, pp. 1099–1101 (hereafter *House Journal*); *General Laws of the State of Texas*, p. 148 (hereafter *General Laws*).

3. 30th Legislature, Regular Session, 1907: *House Journal*, p. 447; *Journal of the Senate*, p. 665 (hereafter *Senate Journal*); *General Laws*, p. 104.

4. "Here, Eighty Years Ago Today Was Signed Texas Declaration of Independence," *San Antonio Express*, 2 March 1916.

5. McLennan County Clerk's Office, Wills, File E/5641; Neff, *Battles of Peace;* Neff, "State Parks for Texas," *Holland's Magazine* 44, no. 1 (January 1925): 14.

6. Henry R. Francis, ed., *Proceedings of the Second National Conference on State Parks. May 22–23–24–25, 1922* (Washington, D.C.: National Conference on State Parks, 1923), pp. 8–84.

7. Frank Freidel, *Franklin D. Roosevelt: A Rendezvous with Destiny* (Boston: Little, Brown, 1990), p. 60.

Chapter 1

1. Seth McKay and Odie B. Faulk, *Texas after Spindletop, 1901–1965* (Austin: Steck-Vaughn, 1965), p. 137.

2. "State Parks Must Not Be Starved!" and "Unemployed Relief Work in the Parks," *State Recreation* 7, no. 1 (January 1933): 5–10.

3. Phebe K. Warner, "Depression Boosts State Parks," *Texas Federation News,* April 1933, p. 9; E. Hamblin, *Rim to Rim* (Quanah and Wichita Falls: Nortex, 1971), pp. 61–63. Armstrong County Commissioner William Henry Hamblin initiated "Hamblin Drive" (now FM 207) about 1930, utilizing in 1932–1933 federal RFC and perhaps, later, CWA, FERA, and WPA labor programs to develop the road. Wayside State Park on the south rim had been returned or sold in 1931 by order of the legislature.

4. D. A. Bandeen, manager of the West Texas chamber, to Walter D. Cline, chamber president, 15 November 1933, Southwest Collection; Robert S. McElvaine, *The Great Depression* (New York: Times Books, 1984), p. 75.

5. R. W. Barry, "Housewife Again Becomes Boss of Lone Star State," *Austin American,* 18 January 1933.

6. Seth McKay, *Texas Politics, 1906–1944.* (Lubbock: Texas Tech Press, 1952), p. 250; *The Government of the State of Texas* ["Griffenhagen Report"] (Austin: The Joint Legislative Committee on Organization and Economy, 1933).

7. 43rd Legislature, Regular Session (1933), *House Journal,* pp. 442–444.

8. Fred C. Croxton (RFC assistant) to Honorable Miriam A. Ferguson, 3 March 1933; "Legislature Remade the Relief Commission," *Amarillo Daily News,* 10 December 1933; "State Board of Control, Texas Relief Commission Division," finding aid and introduction to Record Group 303, Texas State Archives, p. 1; "Guide for Administering of and Accounting for Relief Funds," 21 March 1933, Texas Relief Commission bulletin at State Archives.

9. "Col. L. Westbrook Dies Here Today," *San Angelo Standard-Times,* 24 January 1964.

10. McElvaine, *Great Depression,* p. 137; *Time Capsule, 1933: A History of the Year Condensed from the Pages of* Time (New York: Time Inc., 1967), p. 16; Arthur M. Schlesinger, *The Coming of the New Deal* (Boston: Houghton Mifflin,1988), p. 1; Franklin D. Roosevelt, *The Public Papers and Addresses of Franklin D. Roosevelt* (New York: Random House, 1938), Vol. Two, p. 13.

11. Lionel V. Patenaude, "John Nance Garner," in *Profiles in Power: Twentieth Century Texans in Washington,* edited by Kenneth E. Hendrickson, Jr., and Michael L. Collins (Arlington Heights, Illinois: Harlan Davidson, 1993), p. 49.

12. Rexford G. Tugwell, *Roosevelt's Revolution: The First Year—A Personal Perspective* (New York: Macmillan, 1977), pp. 7, 78–79; John A. Salmond, *The Civilian Conservation Corps, 1933–1942: A New Deal Case Study* (Durham, North Carolina: Duke University Press, 1967), pp. 10.

13. Jesse H. Jones, *Fifty Billion Dollars: My Thirteen Years with the RFC* (New York: Macmillan, 1951), pp. 260, 523; Schlesinger, *New Deal,* pp. 4, 8, 10–11.

14. Schlesinger, *New Deal,* p. 337; Salmond, *Civilian Conservation Corps,* p. 11.

15. Salmond, *Civilian Conservation Corps,* pp. 3–4.

16. Ibid., 11–13; Roosevelt, *Public Papers,* Vol. 2, pp. 80–81.

17. Salmond, *Civilian Conservation Corps,* pp. 13–23, 26, 31; Senate Bill 598 (Public-No. 5-73d Congress [1933]) copy in National Archives, Record Group 35, Civilian Conservation Corps.

18. "Texas Relief Commission Guide for Administering of and Accounting for Relief Funds," 21 March 1933, Texas Relief Commission bulletin at Texas State Archives; Croxton to Ferguson, 3 March 1933.

19. Gib Gilchrist (Texas Highway Department engineer-director) memoranda to agency engineers, 4 and 10 April, 25 May 1933; "Design for Living Real With Gubbels," *Austin American-Statesman,* 30 November 1947.

20. *House Journal,* pp. 1660–1662; 43rd Legislature, Regular Session (1933), *General Laws,* pp. 365–368.

21. C. M. Hammond, "Opportunity for Texas," *Texas Weekly,* 6 May 1933, p. 11.

22. Salmond, *Civilian Conservation Corps,* p. 31; Miriam A. Ferguson to Robert Fechner, 15 April 1933.

23. Miriam A. Ferguson to Robert Fechner, 29 April 1933, with double-page attachment, "Summary of Texas State Park and Flood Control Projects Recommended for Emergency Conservation Work," Texas State Archives.

24. Ferguson telegram to Neff, 28 April 1933.

25. Neff telegrams to Ferguson, 29 April, 1 May 1933; Secretary of State Election Register, 1933, Record Group 307, Texas State Archives; "Urbantke, Gus Frederick," vertical file at Austin History Center.

26. Salmond, *Civilian Conservation Corps,* pp. 31–32; Acting (U.S.) Forester to Robert Fechner, 3 May 1933.

27. Fechner to Ferguson, 8 May 1933; Salmond, *Civilian Conservation Corps,* pp. 29–30; Fechner "Radiogram" to Ferguson, 19 May 1933.

28. Salmond, *Civilian Conservation Corps,* p. 40; "Officers Go To Pick Camp Sites," *San Antonio Light,* 15 May 1933.

29. Conrad L. Wirth, *Parks, Politics and the People* (Norman: University of Oklahoma Press, 1980),

pp. 76–77, 105, 111; Laura Soulliere Harrison, *Architecture in the Parks: National Historic Landmark Theme Study* (Washington, D.C.: NPS, 1986), pp. 317–318; Linda Flint McClelland, *Presenting Nature* (Washington, D.C.: NPS, 1993), p. 99.

30. Ferguson to Fechner, 15 May 1933; Ferguson to "Hon. Sam Rayburn, M.C.," 15 May 1933.

31. Ferguson telegram to Fechner, 16 May 1933.

32. Fechner memo to Albright, 27 May 1933.

33. Sam Rayburn to Fechner, 22 May 1933; various CCC camp rosters from National Archives, Record Group 35.

34. 43rd Legislature, Regular Session (1933), *Special Laws of the State of Texas,* pp. 52–54 (hereafter *Special Laws).*

35. Fred Emery to D. E. Colp, 15 April 1933; Fred Albion Emery, "History of Palo Duro Canyon State Park," manuscript in Guy F. Carlander papers, Panhandle-Plains Historical Museum, pp. 2, 7; Peter L. Petersen, "A Park for the Panhandle: The Acquisition and Development of Palo Duro Canyon State Park," in *The Story of Palo Duro Canyon,* edited by Duane F. Guy (Canyon: Panhandle-Plains Historical Society, 1979), pp. 150–152; *General Laws* (1933), p. 897.

36. *Amarillo Daily News* 1933: "Palo Duro Park Plans Taking Definite Form," 2 May; "Inspect Route Today for Canyon Highway," 3 May; "Proponents of Goodnight Trail Lay Plans To Get Right-of-Way," 4 May; "Action To Obtain Right of Way for 'Goodnight Trail' Is Begun," 5 May; "R.F.C. Officials Hear Canyon Trail Project" and "Guleke Leaves Today for Washington Parley," 20 May; "Point Where Goodnight Entered Canyon Will Be Beginning of Scenic Highway," *Amarillo Sunday News-Globe,* 7 May 1933; *General Laws* (1933), pp. 571–572.

37. *General Laws* (1933), pp. 503–505, 567–570, 761, 1013–1014; *House Journal* (1933), p. 2785.

38. *General Laws,* (1933), p. 503; McKay, *Texas Politics,* pp. 251–254; McKay and Faulk, *Texas after Spindletop,* pp. 134–136; Rupert Richardson, *Texas: The Lone Star State* (Englewood Cliffs: Prentice-Hall, 1958), p. 325.

39. Herbert Maier, "Weekly Report, July 1 1933, Third District, State Park Emergency Conservation Report," typed and illustrated manuscripts at National Archives, Record Group 79 (such reports hereafter referred to as Inspector Report with inspectors' names and dates for specific references).

40. "Frederick Amerman Dale," application for membership in American Society of Civil Engineers, 22 February 1931; "Buchanan Dam and Lake," "Buchanan Reservoir," and "Hamilton Dam, Texas," *The Handbook of Texas,* edited by H. Bailey Carroll and Walter Prescott Webb (Austin: Texas State Historical Association, 1952), hereafter *HOT.*

41. Ferguson telegram to Horace Albright, 7 June 1933; Conrad Wirth telegram to Ferguson, 8 June 1933.

42. "Park Site Gets Approval at Port Caddo," unattributed clipping dated 6 June 1933, from Fred Dahmer scrapbook, Harrison County Historical Commission.

43. Ibid.; various CCC camp rosters from National Archives, Record Group 35; Inspector Report, Victor Brock, 10 July 1933.

44. Barry Scobee in *Alpine Avalanche,* 1933: "Real State Park in the Davis Mountains May Be Reality," 2 June; "Boys from Various Walks of Life Having Big Time in Conservation Camp in the Davis Mts.," 23 June; "Park Work at Davis Starts," 30 June; "Davis Park Developm't Is Started," 7 July.

45. Emery, "History," pp. 7–11; "Roosevelt Approves Palo Duro Park Projects," and "Federal Plans Provide Park Eight Miles Long in Heart of Palo Duro," *Amarillo Daily News,* 2 June 1933.

46. Petersen, "Park for the Panhandle," pp. 153–154; Inspector Report, Fred Dale, 1 July 1933; Governor Ferguson to Robert Fechner, 2 December 1933.

47. Fechner "Cheapest Night Rate" telegram to governors, 5 May 1933; *House Journal* (1933) pp. 2174–2175; Fechner to Governor Ferguson, 7 November 1933.

48. Petersen, "Park for the Panhandle," p. 154; Inspector Report, Dale, 1 July 1933; various CCC camp rosters.

49. Inspector Report, Dale, 1 July 1933; various CCC camp rosters; Petersen, "Park for the Panhandle," pp. 154–155.

50. *Hamilton Herald,* 1933: "Hamilton Gets Conservation Camp: Nearly Two Hundred Men and Officers Are Now Encamped Here," 23 June; "Hamilton Welcomes Reforestation Boys," 30 June.

51. Inspector Reports: Dale, 15 July 1933; Elwood, 22 July 1933.

52. Inspector Reports, Dale, 1 July, 22 July, 28 July 1933. The NPS Austin office architect could have been *Verle* L. Austin, listed in the 1932–1933 Austin city directory as an engineer working with the U.S. Geological Survey.

53. Harold Buckles, "Hard, Constructive Work Is the Lot of Civilian Conservation Youths," *Marshall News Messenger,* 18 November 1934, p. 18.

54. Charles Price Harper, *The Administration of the Civilian Conservation Corps* (Clarksburg, West Virginia: Clarksburg Publishing, 1939), p. 109. Harper uses the term "quasi-military" to describe the nature of CCC "camp administration."

55. William James, "The Moral Equivalent of War," quoted in Harper, *Administration,* p. 5.

56. Captain Francis V. Fitz Gerald, "The President Prescribes—The Organization and Supply of the C.C.C.," in *Quartermaster Review* 13, no. 1 (July–August 1933): 10; Salmond, *Civilian Conservation Corps,* p. 9.

57. Harper, *Administration,* p. 20; *State Recreation,* 1930: "Bills Propose Federal Aid for State Parks," March, pp. 10–11; "Federal Aid for State Parks," June, pp. 11–12.

58. Schlesinger, *New Deal,* p.337; Salmond, *Civilian Conservation Corps,* p. 11; Russell D. Buhite and David W. Levy, eds., *FDR's Fireside Chats* (Norman: University of Oklahoma Press, 1992), pp. 13, 21.

59. Schlesinger, *New Deal,* pp. 341–343; *Alpine Avalanche,* 21 April 1933.

60. Kenneth E. Hendrickson, Jr., "The Civilian Conservation Corps in the Southwestern States," in *The Depression in the Southwest,* edited by Donald W. Whisenhunt (Port Washington, N.Y.: Kennikat Press, 1980), p. 4.

61. Salmond, *Civilian Conservation Corps,* p. 46.

62. Wirth, *Parks,* pp. 75–77, 83–84; Horace Albright as told to Robert Cahn, *The Birth of the National Park Service* (Salt Lake City: Howe Brothers, 1985), p. 289; Herbert Evison to Governor Ferguson, 20 March 1933.

63. Wirth, *Parks,* pp. 76, 111.

64. Schlesinger, *New Deal,* p.338.

Chapter 2

1. State Parks Board minutes, 17 October 1933, at Texas Parks and Wildlife Department and Texas State Archives (hereafter SPB Minutes).

2. Emery, "History," p. 12.

3. SPB Minutes, 7 July 1933.

4. "Ferguson Talks to Cabinet Heads on Texas' Needs," *Dallas Morning News,* 15 July.

5. Maier, NPS District Officer Report, 29 July; Inspector Report, Elwood, 29 July 1933.

6. Emery "History," p. 11.

7. Ibid., p. 12; Petersen, "Park for the Panhandle," p. 153; warranty deed: Fred A. Emery and Millie B. Emery to Texas State Parks Board, 28 July 1933, in TPWD land records.

8. Westbrook to Fechner, 12 August 1933. The Texas Rehabilitation and Relief Commission applied for a total of 64 CCC camps during the coming second period, encompassing "soil erosion" and "flood control" projects.

9. Albright and Cahn, *Birth of National Park Service,* pp. 93, 291–301, 312–314.

10. Tugwell, *Roosevelt's Revolution,* pp. 154–155.

11. Salmond, *Civilian Conservation Corps,* p. 47.

12. Westbrook to Fechner, 19 August 1933; "Report on Administrative Expenses March 1st to September 1st, 1933," Texas State Archives, Record Group 303 (General Services Commission), Entry 4–19, Box 331.

13. McKay and Faulk, *Texas after Spindletop,* pp. 134–136; Richardson, *Texas,* p. 327.

14. SPB Minutes, 11 September 1933; "C.C.C. Camp Typhoid Boys All Recovered," *Hamilton Herald Record,* 29 September 1933.

15. Emery, "History," p. 12.

16. McKay and Faulk, *Texas after Spindletop,* p. 134; Richardson, *Texas,* pp. 324–325; *General Laws* (1933), pp. 118–131.

17. 43rd Legislature, First Called Session, (1933), *General and Special Laws of the State of Texas,* pp. 275–278 (hereafter *General and Special Laws*).

18. Petersen, "Park for the Panhandle," pp. 150–151.

19. SPB Minutes, 30 September 1933; Secretary to the Governor to Colp, 30 September 1933; A. M. Vance, State Reclamation Engineer, to Ferguson, 1 September 1934.

20. *House Journal* (1933, First Called Session), p. 307; Inspector Report, Maier, 30 September, 14 October 1933.

21. Inspector Reports: P. H. Elwood, 12 August 1933; F. A. Dale, 23 September, 9 October 1933; H. H. Cornell, 2 October 1933.

22. Inspector Report, Maier, 14 October 1933; "George Lister Nason" (obituary), *Landscape Architecture,* undated clipping, ca. January 1950, pp. 128–129; Wirth, *Parks,* pp. 6, 39; Raymond L. Freeman, "National Parks," in *American Landscape Architecture* (1989): 172–174; McClelland, *Presenting Nature,* p. 234.

23. Inspector Report, George L. Nason, 14 October, 21 October, 29 October, 15 November 1933; "The Late Hobart Key Was a Constant Advocate for State Park on Caddo Lake," *Marshall News Messenger,* 18 November 1934, p. 5.

24. SPB Minutes, 17 October; J. H. Davis, Jr., Secretary to the Governor, to Governor Ferguson (care of Blackstone Hotel, Fort Worth), 18 October 1933.

25. Inspector Report, Nason, 15 November; Ferguson to Wirth, 13 November; Ferguson to Maier, 15 November 1933.

26. SPB Minutes, 9 November, 16 November; Inspector Reports: Nason, 15 November 1933; Maier, 30 November 1933.

27. Westbrook to Ferguson, 3 November 1933; Fechner to Ferguson, 7 November 1933; Ferguson telegram to Westbrook, 13 November 1933; Ferguson to Fechner, 2 December 1933; Fechner to Ferguson, 11 December 1933; Davis, Secretary to the Governor, to Fechner, 18 December 1933; Fechner to Davis, 23 December 1933.

28. Petersen, "Park for the Panhandle," pp. 156–157.

29. Inspector Report, Nason, 15 November 1933.

30. Inspector Reports: Dale, 9 September 1933; Nason, 14 October 1933; Rayburn to Wirth, 8 September 1933, National Archives, Record Group 79, Wirth files, E620, "Rayburn."

31. Various CCC camp rosters; "Tree Corps To Be Kept in Operation Another 6 Months," *Hamilton Herald-Record,* 25 August 1933.

32. Inspector Report, Nason, 29 October, 30 November, 1933. Martin Dies (1901–1972, son of Martin Dies and father of Martin Dies, Jr.) once practiced law in Marshall; he moved to Orange and entered Congress in 1931 as its youngest member, representing District 2 including Harrison County. With new district boundaries drawn by the legislature's regular session in 1933, effective that August, Harrison County fell within District 1, represented since 1929 by Wright Patman of Texarkana ("Dies, Martin," *HOT; Texas Almanac* [1931], p. 296, and [1933], p. 323).

33. Inspector Report, Maier, 21 October 1933; Petersen, "Park for the Panhandle," pp. 156–157; "Two CCC Units Will Be Moved," *Amarillo Globe,* 4 July 1934.

34. Schlesinger, *New Deal,* pp. 269–270.

35. Ibid.; Inspector Report, Nason, 15 November 1933.

36. Inspector Report, Nason, 30 November 1933; "Application: Civil Works Project" for Lake Brownwood, 12 December 1933, Lake Crook (Paris), 11 December 1933, Lake Mineral Wells, 20 February 1934 (supplemental), Lake Sweetwater "Estes Park," 5 December 1933, all from National Archives on microfilm at Texas Department of Transportation, Environmental Affairs Division; "Countless Citizens Help in Development of Zilker's Gift," *Austin American,* 1 July 1934; Mineral Wells Chamber of Commerce flier in vertical file, Barker Texas History Collections; "Status Report on the Texas State Parks System—January 18th, 1936," in Pat Neff Papers, Texas Collection at Baylor University (hereafter Neff Papers).

37. Alanzo Wasson, "State's Park System Given Federal Help," *Dallas News,* 10 December 1933.

38. Inspector Reports, Maier, 15 December 1933; Nason, 15 November, 30 November, 15 December 1933, 1 January 1934; "Texas Parks Putting on New Dress; Uncle Sam Foots the Bill," *San Antonio Express,* 18 March 1934.

39. Inspector Report, Harry L. Dunham, 30 November 1933.

40. Inspector Report, Nason, 15 November 1933.

41. Wasson, *Dallas News,* 10 December 1933; Inspector Report, Dunham, 31 December 1933.

42. Warner to Colp, 19 October 1923.

Chapter 3

1. Office of State Auditor and Efficiency Expert, "Summary of Audit Report, Texas State Parks Board, April 29, 1933, to August 31, 1934," p. 2, Legislative Reference Library.

2. Fon Wyman Boardman, Jr., *The Thirties: America and the Great Depression* (New York: Henry Z. Walck, 1967), p. 100.

3. Wirth, *Parks,* p. 105.

4. Inspector Report, Nason, 3–4 January, 18–19 January 1934; John R. Jameson, *Big Bend National Park* (El Paso: Texas Western Press, 1980), pp. 9–10.

5. Inspector Reports: Dunham, 15 March 1934; Nason, 23 April 1934.

6. Inspector Report, Nason, 6 December 1933; "Texas Parks Putting on New Dress; Uncle Sam Foots the Bill," *San Antonio Express,* 18 March 1934; Harrison, *Architecture in the Parks,* p. 319; McClelland, *Presenting Nature,* p. 234.

7. "Bonham State Park To Be Planted in a Natural Style," unmarked clipping in NPS Inspector Reports, probably *Bonham Daily Favorite,* 14 March 1934.

8. Inspector Reports, Nason, 20 November, 15 December 1933; Dunham, 20 November 1933; McClelland, *Presenting Nature,* p. 99.

9. Inspector Reports, Nason, 7 December, 16 January 1934; Arthur Fehr's daybook at Austin History Center; personal interview with Mary Jane (Mrs. Arthur) Fehr, 1 March 1985; Inspector Report, Dunham, 15 March 1934.

10. Inspector Report, Nason, 9 January 1934; "Col. L. Westbrook Dies Here Today," *San Angelo Standard-Times,* 24 January 1964.

11. Colp to Fechner, 16 January 1934.

12. Ibid.; 43rd Legislature, Second Called Session (February 1934), *Senate Journal,* p. 189.

13. SPB Minutes, 22 February 1934; Inspector Reports: Dunham, 28 February 1934; Nason, 28 April 1934.

14. Colp to Fechner, 16 January 1933; Inspector Report, Dunham, 28 February 1934; 43rd Legislature, Second Called Session (1934), *Senate Journal,* p. 189; Kenneth Baxter Ragsdale, *The Year America Discovered Texas: Centennial '36* (College Station: Texas A&M University Press, 1987), pp. 32–33.

15. SPB Minutes, 1 March 1934; "Texas Parks Putting on New Dress; Uncle Sam Foots the Bill,"

San Antonio Express, 18 March 1934; "Allred Approves Park Purchases: Deficiency Appropriation Necessary for CCC," *San Antonio Express,* 30 March 1934.

16. Wirth, *Parks,* p. 106.

17. "Allred Approves Park Purchases; Deficiency Appropriation Necessary for CCC," *San Antonio Express,* 30 March 1934.

18. Ibid.

19. "Pat Neff Give[s] Two Hundred and Fifty Acres of Land to State for a Park," retyped press release, ca. 12 May 1934, in Neff Papers.

20. *Proceedings of the Second National Conference on State Parks* (1923), pp. 56 – 60; Robert Shankland, *Steve Mather of the National Parks, 3d ed.* (New York: Knopf, 1970) p. 187; "State Parks Must Not Be Starved!" *State Recreation* 7, no. 1 (January 1933): 5 – 10; "Caddo Site Preserves Ideal Set for State Parks as 'Large, Wild, Natural Unspoiled Areas' Within Easy Reach," *Marshall News Messenger,* 18 November 1934, p. 15.

21. Maier, NPS District Officer Report, 15 December 1933; "State Park Head To Officiate Today at Palo Duro Ceremony," unmarked, undated clipping, c. 12 May 1934, in D. E. Colp Papers, Barker Texas History Collections.

22. Inspectors Reports: Nason, 10 May, 28 May, 6 September 1934; B. Ashburton Tripp, 15 September 1934.

23. Fehr's Daybook, 16 January, 9 May 1934; Albert H. Good, *Park and Recreation Structures* (Washington, D.C.: NPS, 1938) Vol. 3, pp. 50 – 51.

24. Inspector Report, Nason, 15 May 1934; Sam Sterling, "Structure Narrative, Indian Lodge, Ft. Davis, Texas," unpublished report for University of Texas at Austin, 1993.

25. Fehr's Daybook, 19, 26, 29 May 1934; Charles E. Peterson, "The Historic American Buildings Survey: Its Beginnings," in *Historic America: Buildings, Structures, and Sites,* edited by C. Ford Peatross (Washington, D.C.: Library of Congress, 1983), pp. 8 – 9, 20; Peter Nabokov, *Architecture of Acoma Pueblo: The 1934 Historic American Buildings Survey Project* (Santa Fe: Ancient City Press, 1986).

26. Inspector Report, Dunham, 30 April 1934; SPB Minutes, 20 April 1934; *S-PARKS,* January 1940, p. 11.

27. Inspector Reports, Nason, 31 May, 1 September 1934.

28. SPB Minutes, 13 June 1934; Inspector Reports, Nason, 19 June, 4 July 1934; various July 1934 SPB press releases.

29. Petersen, "Park for the Panhandle," p. 158 – 159.

30. Salmond, *Civilian Conservation Corps,* pp. 55 – 56; Inspector Reports: Dunham, 30 June 1934; Nason 15 July 1934.

31. SPB Minutes, 13 June, 28 – 30 July 1934; Office of State Auditor and Efficiency Expert, "Summary" (1934), Exhibit C.

32. McKay, *Texas Politics,* pp. 247 – 288.

33. Inspector Reports, Nason, 11 – 12, 29 June.

34. Ibid., 27, 30 July 1934.

35. Richard Bailey, "Morris Sheppard," in *Profiles in Power,* pp. 36 – 39; Inspector Report, Obert, 15 August 1934; "Army Officials Co-Operate in Caddo Park Building Program; Far-Sighted Plan Is Followed," *Marshall News Messenger,* 18 November 1934, p. 9.

36. Ibid.

37. Steely, James W., "Depression-Era Structures at the 'Q Ranch' in Northwest Travis County," University of Texas at Austin research paper, 10 May 1984, MS, Austin History Center; Inspector Report, Fiddleke, 26 December 1934.

38. Inspector Reports: Nason, 11 October 1934; A. F. Ahrens, 1 December 1934.

39. "State Board of Control, Texas Relief Commission Division," Record Group 303 finding aid,

p. 1, Texas State Archives; McKay and Faulk, *Texas after Spindletop,* p. 134; Hendrickson, "Civilian Conservation Corps in the Southwestern States," p. 9.

40. Ferguson, Miriam, quoted in Ragsdale, *Centennial 1936,* pp. 58–59, 64; "Parks Offered for Centennial," *San Antonio Express,* 2 September 1934.

41. "Centennial Gives Vast Stimulation To Road Building," *Dallas Morning News,* 7 October 1934; 43rd Legislature, Third Called Session (1934), *General and Special Laws,* p. 110; undated, unmarked press release for *New York Herald Tribune,* from Miriam Ferguson papers, Bell County Museum.

42. McKay, *Texas Politics,* p. 289–290; "Lieutenant Governor, Office of," "Neal, Margie Elizabeth," and "Witt, Edgar E.," *HOT.*

43. Schlesinger, *New Deal,* p. 554; "Maverick, Maury," *HOT;* Maury Maverick, *A Maverick American* (New York: Covici-Friede, 1937), pp. 150–151; James E. Ivey and Marlys Bush Thurber, *The Missions of San Antonio: A Historic Structures Report and Administrative History,* ch. 6, pp. 1–3, MS on file, NPS Regional Office, Santa Fe; "Development of Grounds about the Alamo," unpublished 1934–1935 report of the Texas Relief Commission, DRT Library; *San Antonio Express,* 6 December 1936.

44. Petersen, "Park for the Panhandle," pp. 158–159; Emery, "History," pp. 12–13.

45. "Texas Planning Board," *HOT;* Robert A. Calvert and Arnoldo De Leon, *The History of Texas* (Arlington Heights, Illinois: H. Davidson, 1990), p. 312.

46. SPB Minutes, 16 January 1935.

47. 44th Legislature, Regular Session (1935), *General and Special Laws,* pp. 38–41, 67–69, 468–469, 1142–1145; Mrs. Clyde W. Warwick (comp.), The Randall County Story, from 1541 to 1910 (Hereford, Tex.: Pioneer Book Publishers, 1969), p. 276; "Mier Expedition" and "Monument Hill," *HOT.*

48. Ragsdale, *Centennial '36,* pp. 70–74; Harold Schoen, comp., *Monuments Erected by the State of Texas To Commemorate the Centenary of Texas Independence* (Austin: Commission of Control for Texas Centennial Celebrations, 1938), pp. 2, 9; Gould (1992), p. 122.

49. Schlesinger (1958), pp. 342–343 554; Wirth, *Parks,* pp. 118–119, 130–131; Various CCC rosters.

50. Ross Maxwell, *Big Bend Country: A History of Big Bend National Park* (Big Bend National Park, Texas: Big Bend Natural History Association, 1985), p. 56; Inspector Report, Nason, 20 October 1934.

51. SPB Minutes, 29 April 1935.

52. Various CCC Rosters; Wirth, *Parks,* p. 121; Phoebe Cutler, *The Public Landscape of the New Deal* (Yale University Press, 1985), pp. 106–111.

53. Warner to Colp, 6 January and 7 April 1924.

54. Program for 18–21 June 1935 National Conference on State Parks at Skyland, Virginia, in Neff Papers; Albert H. Good, *Park Structures and Facilities* (Washington, D.C.: NPS, 1935); Wirth, *Parks,* pp. 204–207.

55. American Consul Herndon W. Goforth to Secretary of State, 20 May 1935, National Archives, Record Group 79, Entry 37, Box 439.

56. "Original Missions To Be Dedicated, *Dallas News,* 16 September 1934; "Houston County Dedicates New Park," *San Antonio Express,* 4 July 1935; "Replica of First Mission in Texas and 117-Acre Park Near Crockett Dedicated," *Houston Chronicle,* 5 July 1935; Congressman Nat Patton to Acting Chief Forester C. M. Granger, 22 October 1935; Senator Morris Sheppard to Conrad Wirth, 22 October 1935; "San Francisco Mission State Forest," and "Texas State Forests," *Texas Forest News* 16, no. 2 (February 1936): 1–3; Nina Craig and Eliza H. Bishop, "CCC Company 888—Weches Camp P-58-T," application for Official Texas Historical Marker.

57. Mrs. John H. Burns, comp., "Garner State Park," in *A Proud Heritage: A History of Uvalde County, Texas* (Uvalde: El Progreso Club, 1975), p. 69.

58. Arthur M. Schlesinger, *The Politics of Upheaval* (Boston: Houghton Mifflin Company, 1960), p. 270; Salmond, *Civilian Conservation Corps,* pp. 57–58.

59. *Final Report on the WPA Program* (Washington, D.C.: U.S. Government Printing Office,

1946); Schlesinger, *Politics of Upheaval,* pp. 346, 352; Richard D. McKinzie, "Work Projects Administration," in *Franklin D. Roosevelt, His Life and Times: An Encyclopedic View,* edited by O. L. Graham, Jr., and M. R. Wander (Boston, Mass.: G. K. Hall, 1985), pp. 461–463; "Work Projects Administration in Texas," *HOT;* Harrison, *Architecture in the Parks,* p. 419.

60. Joseph P. Lash, *Eleanor and Franklin* (New York: W. W. Norton 1971), p. 537; John Salmond, "National Youth Administration," in Graham and Wander (eds.), *Franklin D. Roosevelt,* pp. 278–279

61. Robert Dallek, *Lone Star Rising: Lyndon Johnson and His Times, 1908–1960* (New York: Oxford University Press, 1991), pp. 123–127; Ronnie Dugger, *The Politician: The Life and Times of Lyndon Johnson.* (New York: W. W. Norton, 1982), p. 186; *Texas Highway Department Tenth Biennial Report* (Austin: Texas Highway Department, 1936), p. xxii.

62. Fechner to Allred, 2 July 1935; Blanton telegram to Allred, 16 April 1935; "B S Fox County Judge" to C. R. Miller, Allred's secretary, 29 April 1935.

63. Charles Johnson, "The Army, the Negro and the Civilian Conservation Corps: 1933–1942," *Military Affairs,* 36, no.3 (October 1972): 82–83; Miller to Fox, 1 May 1935; Colp to Garner, 13 June 1935; Fechner to Garner, 15 June 1935; *Texas Almanac* (1936), p. 387.

64. Petersen, "Park for the Panhandle," pp. 169–170; 1920s correspondence between Kingsley and Colp, D. E. Colp Papers.

65. William J. Brophy, "Black Texans and the New Deal," in *The Depression in the Southwest,* edited by Donald W. Whisenhunt (Port Washington, N.Y.: Kennikat Press, 1980), p. 117; Johnson, "The Army, the Negro," p. 83; Salmond, *Civilian Conservation Corps,* pp. 98–99.

66. "CCC Camps Approved for Fifth Period (1935)," official roster in National Archives; Good, *Park and Recreation Structures,* various references to Boyle Park in Arkansas.

67. 44th Legislature, 2nd Called Session (15 October 1935), *General and Special Laws,* pp. 1790, 1888–1889.

68. Schoen, Monuments, p.46.

69. Salmond, *Civilian Conservation Corps,* p. 63; Acting Chief Forester C. M. Granger to Congressman Patton, 16 October 1935.

70. Beauchamp to Colp, 12 October 1935; State Auditor Orville S. Carpenter to Allred, 4 November 1935.

71. Secretary of State Election Register, 1935; Inspector Report, Nason, November 1935; SPB Minutes, 26 November 1935, 14 January 1936.

72. Cleburne chamber of commerce manager J. T. Webster to Colp, 27 November 1935; Louis J. Bryan to Colp, 29 November 1935; "An Able Official Lost," *Temple Daily Telegram,* 29 November 1935; untitled clipping, *Amarillo Daily News,* 14 December 1935; "Neff Heads Parks Board," *Brownsville Herald,* 15 December 1935; Oscar Dancy to Neff, 17 December 1935.

73. Uncredited clipping datelined 13 December in Colp Papers; "Neff Heads Parks Board," *Brownsville Herald,* 15 December 1935.

Chapter 4

1. "An Able Official Lost," *Temple Daily Telegram,* 29 November 1935.

2. Schoen, *Monuments.*

3. R. O. Whiteaker, "Status Report on the Texas State Parks System—January 18th 1936," copy in Neff Papers.

4. Arthur Fehr, Daybooks, 30 and 31 December 1935, 12 January 1936; R. O. Whiteaker to Pat Neff, 31 December 1935; D. E. Colp and Mrs. D. E. Colp to Whiteaker, 1 January 1936; "Colp Is Praised As Great Texan By Baylor Head," *Dallas News,* 14 January 1936; George Nason to Herbert Maier, 14 January 1936; Oscar Dancy to Mrs. D. E. Colp, 14 January 1936; Conrad Wirth to Mrs. D. E. Colp, 21 January 1936; "D. E. Colp, Road and Parks Builder, Is Pneumonia Victim," n.d., n.p. (from Meridian), in Neff Papers.

5. SPB Minutes, 14 January 1936.

6. Whiteaker, "Status Report."

7. SPB Minutes, 25 January, 15 February, 10 and 18 March, 7 and 18 April 1936.

8. "U.S. Scientists Leave for Alpine To Study Big Bend," *Dallas News,* 16 February 1936; Maxwell, *Big Bend Country,* p. 57; William H. Sontag, ed., *National Park Service: The First 75 Years* (Washington, D.C. [?]: Eastern National Park & Monument Association, 1990), pp. 22–23, 32–35; P. J. R. MacIntosh, "New State Parks for Texas," *Texas Weekly,* 14 March 1936.

9. SPB Minutes, 10 and 18 March 1936.

10. Beauchamp to Neff, with attached "Memorandum Report," 31 March 1936, Neff Papers.

11. Various CCC Rosters; "Notice to the Public," typed "Rules and Regulations" in Neff Papers; "State Board Calls Here, Indicates May Take Over Operation of Abilene Park," *Abilene Reporter,* 30 June 1936.

12. W. W. Dornberger to Nason, c. 17 March 1936, "UT Supervising Architect Office, Centennial—Exhibits" file at Architectural Drawings Collection, UT Austin; Fehr Daybook, 2 May 1936.

13. *Paris News,* 30 January, 2 February, 25 March; NPS Press Releases, 12 April, 4 September, National Archives; Fehr Daybook, 16 April; "CCC Gets Ready for Artistic Display at Texas Exposition," *Happy Days,* 16 May, news item, 13 June, photo caption, 19 September; "CCC Forces Show What Youths Do in U.S. Service," *Dallas News,* 9 June 1936; "History Company 857 SP-56-T Paris, Tex.," in *Official Annual 1936, Tyler District 8th Corps Area, Civilian Conservation Corps* (Baton Rouge: Direct Advertising Company, 1936), p. 19; personal interview with Leslie F. Crockett, Austin, 1 April 1994.

14. Franklin D. Roosevelt, *The Public Papers and Addresses of Franklin D. Roosevelt* (New York: Random House, 1938), Vol. Five, pp. 203–206; Jack T. McCully, "Where Freedom Rang!!" *Texas Parade,* March 1938, pp. 7, 29.

15. Roosevelt, *Public Papers,* pp. 206–207.

16. Ibid. pp. 209–217.

17. Herbert Maier telegram to R. L. Thornton, 8 June 1936.

18. Roscoe E. Wright, "Texas: A State of Beautiful Parks," *Texas Parade,* June 1936, Vol. 1 / No. 1, pp. 2, 14–15, 22. *Texas Parade* featured state parks in a series of articles that spanned from 1936 through 1939, covering the larger sites in the system.

19. NPS Press Release, 27 September 1927, in Neff Papers. Other park attendance figures, June through mid-September 1936, revealed were Bachman-White Rock Lake 172,000, Lake Sweetwater 68,000, Bastrop 24,000, Lake Worth 17,000, and Longhorn Cavern 5,000.

20. Beauchamp to Neff, 31 March 1936, p. 6; SPB Minutes, 2 September 1936; "Faces of the Month," *Texas Parade,* February 1941, pp. 18, 25.

21. "Going Places for that Fall Outing?" *San Antonio Express,* 18 October 1936; Inspector Report, G. T. Patrick, 2 October 1936; Leslie F. Crockett, NPS Superintendent's Progress Report, 1 February 1936, National Archives.

22. Schoen, *Monuments.*

23. Salmond, *Civilian Conservation Corps,* pp. 68–69; McKay, *Texas Politics,* pp. 295, 298, 302, 304.

24. Inspector Report, Obert, 1 December 1936; "Mr. Cammerer's Itinerary, Nov. 4 to 17, 1936," National Archives, Record Group 79, Entry 18, Box 2; Jameson, *Big Bend National Park,* p. 21.

25. Fehr Daybook, 21 December 1936; Inspector Report, Olin Boese, 2 December 1936; Wirth, *Parks,* pp. 119–121.

26. "Texas Park Plan Given Approval," *Kerrville Times,* 31 December 1936; Wirth, "The National Aspect of Recreation," *1937 Yearbook: Park and Recreation Progress* (Washington, D.C.: NPS, 1938), p. v.

27. McKay, *Texas Politics,* pp.306–307; 45th Legislature, Regular Session (1937), *General and Spe-*

cial Laws, pp. 360–361, 431–432, 532, 687, 1446–1450; Ray Miller, *Ray Miller's Texas Parks: A History and Guide* (Houston: Cordovan Press, 1984), pp. 202–203.

28. 45th Legislature, 2nd Called Session (1937), *General and Special Laws,* p. 1790.

29. *General and Special Laws,* pp. 1448.

30. "Site Provided Near Gonzales for Warm Springs Hospital," n.d., n.n., ca. May 1937, and "Gonzales Warm Springs Foundation" fundraising brochure, ca. May 1937, both at "Gonzales Warm Springs" Vertical File, Barker Texas History Collections; Beauchamp to Neff, 31 March 1937, p. 5. Shortly after FDR's death in 1945, Georgia renamed Pine Mountain "Franklin D. Roosevelt State Park."

31. Beauchamp to H. G. Webster, Huntsville, 1 March 1937.

32. Salmond, *Civilian Conservation Corps,* pp. 151–157.

33. Walter Prescott Webb, quoted in Jameson, *Big Bend National Park,* pp. 18–19; Lawson, "Memorandum," 15 April 1937, in Neff Papers; NPS press releases, 23 March, 18 and 25 April 1937.

34. NPS press release, 2 May 1937; 45th Legislature, Regular Session (1937), *Senate Journal,* pp. 1215–1216.

35. "Buchanan, James Paul," "Hamilton Dam, Texas," *HOT;* Dallek, *Lone Star Rising,* p. 178; Jameson, *Big Bend National Park,* pp. 20, 60.

36. Texas Highway Department Minute Order #13841, 22 June 1937, copy in Neff Papers.

37. Wirth, *Parks,* p. 128.

38. SPB Minutes, 4 June 1937; William Lawson to Texas Forest Service E. O. Sieke, 1 March 1937.

39. "Fund To Provide for 65 Camps in Texas' Program," *Austin American,* 10 September 1937; Wirth, *Parks,* p. 149; CCC Camp Rosters, National Archives.

40. Hendrickson, "Civilian Conservation Corps in the Southwestern States," p. 9.

41. Lionel V. Patenaude, *Texans, Politics, and the New Deal* (New York: Garland, 1983), pp. 46–47. See also Hendrickson, "Civilian Conservation Corps in the Southwestern States," pp. 12–13.

42. Jameson, *Big Bend National Park,* pp. 20, 60; Ickes dedication speech, 16 October 1937, National Archives.

43. Lawson, "Report of Meeting Held in Amarillo on November 10, 1937," in Neff Papers.

44. Acting ECW Director J. J. McEntee to Agriculture SCS official J. G. Lindley, including draft of Roosevelt message to state governors, 12 February 1937; Harold Ickes radio address, 17 January 1938.

45. L. C. Fuller, "Report on Twenty Texas Parks Activity and Use Study," 24 January 1938, pp. 7, 9, 37, Texas State Library and Archives; Lawson, "Memo. All Board Members," 7 March 1938, in Neff Papers.

46. Lawson "Memorandum" to SPB members, 15 April 1937.

47. "$1,000,000 Campaign Started To Establish Big Bend Park," *Dallas News,* 24 May 1938.

48. Lawson, "Agenda for the Texas State Parks Board," 29 January 1938; Lawson, "Memo. All Board Members," 7 March 1938, in Neff Papers.

49. SPB Minutes, 29 January 1938; "Neff To Plead for CCC Continuance at Capital," *Waco Tribune,* 6 May 1938.

50. Lawson to NPS Inspector B. A. Tripp, 13 December 1937, in Neff Papers.

51. Albert H. Good, *Park and Recreation Structures* (Washington, D.C.: National Park Service, 1938), Vol. 2, p. 73.

52. Good, *Park and Recreation Structures,* Vol. 1, pp. 14–15, 88, 91, 100–101, 126, 128; Vol. 2, p. 73; Vol. 3, pp. 52–53.

53. Harvey Cornell, NPS Regional Landscape Architect's report, June 1938, National Archives.

54. NPS press release, 28 August 1938, National Archives. Other listed visitation figures for summer 1938 included: Balmorhea 16,800, Bastrop 30,600, Brownwood 9,500, Cleburne 3,800, Fort Parker 12,900, Garner 4,500, Goliad 32,300, Lockhart 9,600 and Longhorn Cavern 5,300. Tyrrell Park in Beaumont recorded 20,900 visitors.

55. McKay, *Texas Politics,* pp. 308–325; Richardson, *Texas,* pp. 333–336; "Maverick, Maury," and "Stevenson, Coke Robert," *HOT.*

56. Wm. J. Lawson with Will Mann Richardson, "The Texas State Park System," *Texas Geographic Magazine,* December 1938, pp. 1–12;

57. Ibid.; Leo Marx, *The Machine in the Garden: Technology and the Pastoral Ideal in America* (New York: Oxford University Press, 1964); Mrs. W. C. Martin to Pat Neff, c. 1925.

58. Harvey Cornell, NPS Regional Landscape Architect's reports, June and December 1938, National Archives.

59. J. S. Billups, CCC Inspector's Reports, 5 May 1937, 28 October 1938, National Archives.

60. Wirth to Fechner, 19 December 1938, pp. 1, 13, National Archives.

Chapter 5

1. Eugenia Sheppard Lee to Pat Neff, 3 March 1942; Neff to Lee, 7 March 1942, in Neff Papers.

2. Maier Memorandum to State Park Authorities, etc., 27 December 1938; Lawson to Mayes, 4 January 1939.

3. "Tyler Jurist Named State Secretary," *Dallas News,* 27 December 1938; SPB Minutes, 16 January 1939.

4. Maier to SPB Inspector W.F. Ayres, 22 October; Lawson to Neff, 26 October; Neff to Lawson, 31 October; Lawson to Neff, 5 November 1938, Neff Papers.

5. 46th Legislature, Regular Session (1939), *Special Laws,* pp. 159–166; *General Laws* (1939), pp. 517–518.

6. 45th Legislature, Regular Session (1937), *House Journal,* pp. 1757, 2316; 46th Legislature, Regular Session (1939) *General Laws;* Hendrickson, "Civilian Conservation Corps in the Southwestern States," p. 9.

7. *Special Laws* (1939), pp. 157–159.

8. Schoen, *Monuments,* pp. 77–80; Alfred Finn to Jesse Jones, 21 March 1938, at San Jacinto Museum of History; *Houston Post,* 21 and 22 April 1939, various articles and photo captions.

9. Rosa Todd Hamner, "The San Jacinto Memorial," 3 November 1938, MS in "San Jacinto Chapter, [DRT]," application for Official State Historical Marker, THC.

10. 46th Legislature, Regular Session (1939), *General Laws,* pp. 527–529; C. P. Kendall to Neff, May 1937; *Real Property Evaluation Report of the Texas Parks and Wildlife Department* (Austin: General Land Office, 1991), Vol. II, pp. 117–120; Schoen, *Monuments,* pp.57, 35; *Special Laws* (1939), p. 165; "San Felipe de Austin," *HOT.*

11. "Texas Park Plan Nears Consummation," *Texas Weekly,* 6 May 1939; 46th Legislature, Regular Session (1939), *General Laws,* pp. 520–525.

12. SPB Minutes, 10 July 1939; Neff to Mayes, 11 July 1939; NPS Region III Director M. R. Tillotson to NPS Director Newton B. Drury, 4 December 1941.

13. *General Laws* (1939), p. 519; SPB Minutes, 10 July 1939.

14. Lawson to Neff, 21 January 1939, Neff Papers; SPB Minutes, 30 August 1939; "Quinn (Frank David) Papers, 1913–1971," finding aid and "Resume," Barker Texas History Collections.

15. SPB Minutes, 30 August 1939; State Auditor and Efficiency Expert, "Report of Examination of the Texas State Parks Board for the Fiscal Years Ended August 31, 1937, 1938, 1939, and 1940," p. 5, Legislative Reference Library.

16. SPB Minutes, 30 August, 9 December 1939.

17. Ibid.; *Texas NYA Digest,* May 1940, p. 22, Barker Texas History Collections.

18. Charles Schilke, "Reorganization Act of 1939," in Graham and Wander (eds.), *Franklin D. Roosevelt,* pp. 355–357.

19. Ibid.; Salmond, *Civilian Conservation Corps,* pp. 174–180; Katie Louchheim (ed.), *The Making*

of the New Deal (Cambridge, Mass: Harvard University Press, 1983), pp. 282–283; Christopher R. Gabel, *The U.S. Army GHQ Maneuvers of 1941* (Washington, D.C.: Center of Military History, 1992), pp. 8–9.

20. Salmond, *Civilian Conservation Corps,* pp. 175–176.

21. Ibid., pp. 29, 200; SPB Minutes, 19 March 1940.

22. Salmond, *Civilian Conservation Corps,* p. 200.

23. James MacGregor Burns, *Roosevelt: The Lion and the Fox, 1882–1940* (New York: Harcourt Brace Jovanovich, 1956), pp. 415, 418–419; Harry C. Thomson and Lida Mayo, *The Ordnance Department: Procurement and Supply* (Washington, D.C.: Office of the Chief of Military History, 1960), pp. 1–32; Robert A. Devine, *The Reluctant Belligerent: American Entry Into World War II* (New York: John Wiley & Sons, 1979), p. 90.

24. Salmond, *Civilian Conservation Corps,* pp. 196–197.

25. Albright and Cahn, *Birth of the National Park Service,* pp. 324–325; Wirth, *Parks,* pp. 47, 233; Edwin C. Bearrs, "Arno B. Cammerer 1883–1941," in Sontag (ed.), *National Park Service,* pp. 38–39.

26. Salmond, "National Youth Administration," p. 279; SPB Minutes, 19–20 September 1940; Victor Schoffelmayer, "Smithville, Bastrop Communities Find New Wealth in Forest, Soil, Team Work," *Dallas News,* 24 February 1941.

27. SPB Minutes, 19–20 September 1940.

28. Graham and Wander (eds.), *Franklin D. Roosevelt,* pp. 384–385; Robert A. Caro, *The Path to Power* (New York: Alfred A. Knopf, 1982), p. 593; H. G. Dulaney and Edward Hake Phillips, comp., *"Speak, Mr. Speaker"* (Bonham: Sam Rayburn Foundation, 1978), p. 74.

29. McKay, *Texas Politics,* pp. 328–338; Patenaude, *Texans, Politics,* p. 51.

30. McKay, *Texas Politics,* p. 340; *The Highland Lakes of Texas* (Washington, D.C.: NPS, 1940), pp. 7, 9–10, 63, Texas State Archives and National Archives; excerpt from FDR's speech in "Big Bend" file of NPS Director Newton B. Drury's papers, Record Group 79, Entry 19, Box 3.

31. SPB Minutes, 9 December 1939; 46th Legislature, Regular Session (1939), *General Laws,* pp. 517–518; Victor Schoffelmayer, "Smithville, Bastrop Communities Find New Wealth in Forest, Soil, Team Work, *Dallas News,* 24 February 1941.

32. "Wirtz, Alvin Jacob," *HOT.*

33. SPB Minutes, 19–20 September 1940; Jake E. Ivey and Marlys Bush Thurber, *The Missions of San Antonio: A Historic Structures Report and Administrative History* (Santa Fe: NPS, 1984), unpublished manuscript, pp. 3–4.

34. Wayne Gard, "Big Bend Park Awaits Developing," *Dallas News,* 20 October 1940.

35. "Former State Official Buried," *Victoria Advocate,* 22 December 1985; "Tom Beauchamp in Court Race," *Austin American-Statesman,* 26 May 1946.

36. SPB Minutes, 19–20 September 1940; "Brazos River Conservation and Reclamation District," "Morris Sheppard Dam," "Possum Kingdom Lake," "Sheppard, Morris," *HOT.*

37. McKay, *Texas Politics,* pp. 342–345.

38. "Tom Beauchamp in Court Race," *Austin American-Statesman,* 26 May 1946; Beauchamp to H. G. Webster, 1 March 1937, Neff Papers; SPB Minutes, 10 July 1941; Patenaude, *Texans, Politics,* p. 51; Patenaude, "John Nance Garner," p. 59.

39. Ima Hogg to Eldridge R. Gregg, 17 June 1969, and associated "Hogg State Park" file from Texas Historical Commission; 47th Legislature, Regular Session (1941), *General and Special Laws,* pp. 266–267; SPB minutes, 29 September 1941. The legislation called for "improvements to include as far as possible a replica of the original Hogg home and grounds adjacent to the residence," fulfilled in 1969, much to the irritation of Ima Hogg who disavowed any resemblance of the replica to the Hogg homestead.

40. SPB Minutes, 7–8 May 1941.

41. Ibid.; Mary Waurine Hunter, "Just Recognition Comes to the Queen," *Texas Parade,* June 1941, pp. 4–5, 20–21. Current Texas Parks & Wildlife Department land records show the state owns 15.76 acres at San Jose, with an additional 6.525 acres "leased to TPWD."

42. McKay, *Texas Politics,* pp. 345–346, 365.

43. "Tyler's New State Park to Be Dedicated," *Dallas News,* 8 June 1941; Ray Roddy, "Tell Tourists About Texas," *Texas Digest,* 21 June 1941; "Trekking on Texas Trails," *Texas Parade,* June 1941, pp. 16–17, 25–26; Hubert M. Harrison, "State Parks Are Great Texas Asset," *"East Texas,"* July 1941, pp. 7–8, 20; Jack Whitehead, "Texas State Parks—Public Recreation," *Texas Almanac* (1941–1942), pp. 276–281.

44. 47th Legislature, Regular Session (1941), *General and Special Laws,* pp. 691, 1206–1214.

45. SPB Minutes, 10 July 1941; Regional Officer Minor Tillotson to Quinn, 8 July 1941.

46. Steinberg (1975), pp. 169–172; Warren F. Kimbell, "Atlantic Conference and Charter" in Graham & Wander (eds.), *Franklin D. Roosevelt,* pp. 11–13.

47. Salmond, *Civilian Conservation Corps,* pp. 208–210.

48. SPB Minutes, 22 August 1941; Ray Osborne, "Quinn Named To Buy Land for Big Park," *Dallas Morning News,* 23 August 1941.

49. John Wagner, "Under the Dome at Austin," *Waco Times-Herald,* n.d. 1941; "Using the State Parks," *Dallas Morning News,* 15 October 1941.

50. *A Study of the Park and Recreation Problem of the United States* and *1941 Yearbook: Park and Recreation Progress* (Washington, D.C.: NPS, 1941).

51. "Using the State Parks," *Dallas Morning News,* 15 October 1941, Section Two, p. 3.

52. Salmond, *Civilian Conservation Corps,* pp. 208–210; Hendrickson, in Whisenhunt, ed. (1980), p. 25.

53. SPB Minutes, 7 October 1941.

54. SPB Minutes, 7–8 December 1941. The minutes fail to mention the larger events of 7 December!

55. Devine (1979), p. 162–163; Miller, (1983), p. 480; Salmond, *Civilian Conservation Corps,* p. 209; Edith Parker papers, Barker Texas History Collections.

56. "Recreation Camp for Bowie Troops Gets Under Way," *Dallas Morning News,* 11 September 1941.

57. SPB Minutes, 7 February, 10–11 April 1941; *Texas Almanac* (1941–1942), p. 317; "Using the State Parks," *Dallas Morning News,* 15 October 1941, Section Two, p. 3.

58. SPB Minutes, 10–11 April, 18–20 May 1942.

59. CCC Roster, "Nineteenth Period 1942," National Archives.

60. SPB Minutes, 10–11 April, 18–20 May 1942; "WPA Participation, 1941–1942," in "Texas State Parks Board Reports, 1939–1944," Texas State Archives, T719 / T311; John Ise, *Our National Park Policy: A Critical History* (Baltimore: Johns Hopkins Press, 1961), p. 381.

61. Salmond, *Civilian Conservation Corps,* pp. 212–215; Hendrickson, in Whisenhunt (1980), p. 25.

62. "Report, Final CCC Camp Site Liquidation Inspection, Possum Kingdom State Park, 23 January 1943, National Archives, Record Group 79, Entry 72, Box 7.

Chapter 6

1. Mrs. W. A. Warner to D. E. Colp, 10 June 1924; SPB Minutes, 17–19 June 1944, at Breckenridge and Possum Kingdom State Park during a joint meeting with the Brazos River Authority. The references are to 1941 rainfall that filled Possum Kingdom Lake within one month of its dam completion, before dedicated parkland could be cleared, and abolishment of the CCC program six months after U.S. entry into World War II.

2. SPB Minutes, 13–14 August 1942; "Texas Today," *Waco Times-Herald,* November (n.d.) 1940; Richardson, *Texas,* p. 328. The inventory of active Texas recreation parks in 1942 not built by the

CCC consisted of Frio (Tips), Jim Hogg, San Jose Mission, and Stephen F. Austin state parks. Board of Control state parks in 1936 all received permanent monuments and improvements with Centennial funds; Lipantitlan, accepted in 1937, received only the 1936 standard-issue gray granite monument.

3. Frank D. Quinn, "Maybe Your Nerves Need a Retread," *Texas Parade,* August 1942, pp. 8–12; SPB Minutes, 18–20 May, 13–14 August 1942, 20 March 1943; "Big Bend Park Threatened by Gas Rationing," *Dallas Morning News,* 8 November 1942.

4. Quinn, "Maybe Your Nerves Need a Retread"; Petersen, "Park for the Panhandle," pp. 173–174; "Record of Attendance" and "Statement of Gross Income" in Emery, "History"; Maxwell, *Big Bend Country,* pp. 60–61; SPB Minutes, 7 November 1942; *1942 Yearbook: Park and Recreation Progress* (Washington, D.C.: National Conference on State Parks, 1942); Barry Mackintosh, "Parks and People," in Sontag (ed.), *National Park Service,* p. 39; Wirth, *Parks,* pp. 225–227; "Big Bend Park Threatened by Gas Rationing," *Dallas Morning News,* 8 November 1942.

5. McKay, *Texas Politics,* pp. 376, 389–390, 392.

6. Richardson, *Texas,* p. 362.

7. "The War's Restriction On Travel Is Bringing Increased Appreciation of Texas Playgrounds," SPB press release, 25 April 1943, Neff Papers.

8. 48th Legislature, Regular Session (1943), *General and Special Laws,* pp. 971–978; SPB Minutes, 20 March, 6–8 October, 1943.

9. SPB Minutes, 10 July 1939; 13–14 August 1942; 20 March, 6–8 October 1943; 17–19 June 1944; Maxwell, *Big Bend Country,* p. 39.

10. "Busy State Parks Year," *Dallas News,* 29 December 1943; SPB Minutes, 20 March, 6–8 October 1943; "Record of Attendance," in Emery, "History." While the Palo Duro visitor increases imply an average of eight occupants per automobile, likely the park received many visitors by bus and perhaps military transport.

11. SPB Minutes, 20 March 1943; Maxwell, *Big Bend Country,* p. 61; Kenneth Baxter Ragsdale, *Quicksilver: Terlingua and the Chisos Mining Company* (College Station: Texas A&M University Press, 1976), p. 66; Jameson, *Big Bend National Park,* p. 14; "Governor Signs Deed for Big Bend Park," 27 August and "Texas Wants Legal Rights in Big Park," 3 September 1943, Hillory A. Tolson, quoted in *Dallas Morning News.*

12. Jameson, *Big Bend National Park,* p. 13; Maxwell, *Big Bend Country,* pp. 61, 64; John E. King, "Big Bend Park Deed Given F. R.," *Dallas Morning News,* 7 June; Victor Schoffelmayer, "Big Bend Area Is Biological Island in Expanse of Desert," *Dallas Morning News,* 6 July 1944.

13. SPB Minutes, 6 April, 17–19 June 1944; "Bentsen-Rio Grande Valley State Park," *Ray Miller's Texas Parks,* p. 224; Michael L. Collins, "Lloyd Bentsen [Jr.]," in Hendrickson & Collins, ed. (1993), p. 259.

14. SPB Minutes, 17–19 June 1944

15. Ibid.; SPB Minutes, 22 February 1945; "Address of Frank D. Quinn. National Citizens Planning Conference. June 18, 1959," manuscript in Frank Quinn papers, Barker Texas History Collections.

16. McKay, *Texas Politics,* pp. 396, 445–446, 464.

17. SPB Minutes, 22 February 1945, with additional attachments from Neff Papers; Emery to Tolson, 23 March 1945, Neff Papers.

18. *Ray Miller's Texas Parks,* pp. 508–510; Bernard Asbell, "Death of FDR," in Graham and Wander (eds.), *Franklin D. Roosevelt,* pp. 91–93.

19. David McCullough, *Truman* (New York: Simon & Schuster, 1992), pp. 340–341, 347.

20. Paul D. Casdorph, *Let the Good Times Roll: Life at Home in America During World War II* (New York: Paragon House, 1989), p. 226.

21. 49th Legislature, Regular Session (1945), *General and Special Laws,* pp. 897–904, *Senate Journal,* p. 1297; SPB Minutes, 24–25 June, 5–7 October 1945.

22. Casdorph, *Let the Good Times Roll,* pp. 253, 256; Ise, *National Park Policy,* p. 455.

23. "Investigator Claims Parks Well Operated," *Dallas Morning News,* 28 August 1945; "Address of Frank D. Quinn. National Citizens Planning Conference. June 18, 1959," MS in Frank Quinn papers, Barker Texas History Collections; SPB Minutes, 5–7 October 1945.

24. Quinn to Neff, 2 August 1945; Neff to Quinn, 10 August 1945; SPB Minutes, 5–7 October 1945.

25. SPB Minutes, 3–4 November 1945.

Epilogue

1. *Operation Ten-Seventy: A State Park Improvement Program,* handout of statistics from the Texas State Parks Board, 1960, at Texas State Archives.

2. Petersen, "Park for the Panhandle," pp. 175–177.

3. Ibid.; Frank David Quinn papers, Barker Texas History Collections, especially typed address to National Citizens Planning Conference, 18 June 1959, Memphis, Tennessee.

4. *Operation Ten-Seventy;* "Neglected State Parks To Get More Attention, Bigger Budget," *Dallas Times Herald,* 28 April 1963; Elo J. Urbanovsky, et al., *Texas State Parks: A General Report of Functions, Space Requirements, Financial Considerations and Policies for the Future* (Lubbock: Texas Technological College, August 1963); "Two-Year State Parks Study Ends," *Dallas News,* 20 October 1963; "Texas' Master Plan for Parks Outlined," *Houston Chronicle,* 16 January 1966.

5. Vivian Elizabeth Smyrl, "Texas Parks and Wildlife Department," *New Handbook of Texas* (Austin: Texas State Historical Association, 1996).

6. Jim Cox, "CCC: Fond Memories from a Time of National Hardship" (reprinted from September 1978) and Sue Moss, "CCC 50th Anniversary," *Texas Parks & Wildlife,* September 1983, pp. 2–7. While these articles listed 33 CCC-built state parks in the current system, the authors included Lake Mineral Wells State Park, which instead features 1933–1934 CWA buildings, and they separately listed Old Fort Parker, the 1936 reconstruction aided by CCC enrollees from adjacent Fort Parker State Park.

7. Ezekial Rhodes, Jr., personal interview with Terri Myers of Hardy-Heck-Moore consultants, 19 August 1993; W. R. Bowers, personal letter to author, 1 September 1994; Raymond Rigsby, personal interview with Peter L. Petersen of West Texas State University, 27 October 1977.

BIBLIOGRAPHY

Sources and Comments

Examining the New Deal can be downright exciting when the researcher actually visits the *places* created during this phenomenal era. Equally stimulating can be the discovery in musty National Archives folders of photographs recording the moment of creation by youthful workers laboring at the receiving end of New Deal relief funds. Most rewarding of all, though, is a personal encounter with one of these workers some half a century after that recorded moment, confirming the very personal impact of the New Deal and a lifelong pride in creating a special place that still serves the public as a state park.

Many parks described, if only briefly, in *Parks for Texas*—in addition to numerous associated personalities—definitely are worth separate book-length studies. In many cases information on these parks and individuals abounds in federal, state, and local sources. For others, details and illustrations are more obscure, even if they have survived the half century of time that moves us rapidly away from the New Deal era. For oral histories, New Dealers will be with us for just a few more years, as their time is fleeting, too. Following is a summary of sources employed for this study of the early Texas state park system, with comments for further use in future studies.

Contact with Major Resources

Barker Collections (see University of Texas at Austin)

CCC veterans:

National Association of Civilian Conservation Corps Alumni, P.O. Box 16429, St. Louis, Missouri 63125-0429.

Center for Research Libraries:

6050 South Kenwood Avenue, Chicago, Illinois 60637.

(New) Handbook of Texas:

Texas State Historical Association, 2.306 Sid Richardson Hall, Austin, Texas 78712.

Legislative Reference Library:

Capitol Building, P.O. Box 12488, Austin, Texas 78711-2488.

Library of Congress:

Washington, D.C. 20540.

National Archives:

National Archives and Records Administration, Washington, D.C. 20408.

Archives II, 8601 Adelphi Road, College Park, Maryland 20740-6001.

Lyndon Baines Johnson Presidential Library, 2312 Red River Street, Austin, Texas 78705.

Rocky Mountain Region, P.O. Box 25307, Denver, Colorado 80225.

National Park Service:

Historic Photographic Collections, Harpers Ferry Center, Harpers Ferry, West Virginia 25425.

NPS publications (note: all NPS publications cited are out of print [in 1997]).

State Archives:

Archives and Information Services Division, Texas State Library, P.O. Box 12927, Austin, Texas 78711-2927.

Texas Historical Commission:

P.O. Box 12276, Austin, Texas 78711.

Texas Parks and Wildlife Department:

4200 Smith School Road, Austin, Texas 78744.

University of Texas at Austin:

General Libraries, Austin, Texas 78711.

Barker Texas History Collections, Center for American History, Austin, Texas 78712.

Federal Sources

Because federal agencies funded and supervised development of New Deal state parks, in the 1930s and 1940s voluminous records accumulated at Washington, D.C., and eventually moved to the National Archives for permanent curation. Record Group 79, impounding the raw history of the National Park Service, contains the greatest volume of information on this era's Texas state park development. Entries 30, 39, and 40—field inspectors' reports—and Entry 41—park superintendents' reports—contain snapshots, project summaries, and lists of personnel employed. On other shelves the National Archives holds a small collection of 1930s large-format negatives showcasing completed facilities, as well as drawings used in the NPS's 1935 publication *Park Structures and Facilities* and its 1938 *Park and Recreation Structures* (reprinted in 1990 by Graybooks of Boulder, Colorado), all including parks in Texas.

National Archives Record Group 35, annals of the Civilian Conservation Corps, also includes project summaries and personnel lists in its Entry 115. The CCC's own traveling inspectors concerned themselves directly with the health and welfare of enrollees, and information here cites camp conditions, daily menus, and off-hours educational activities. Of tremendous background interest is the weekly newspaper *Happy Days,* bound in Entry 18, that informed enrollees between 1933 and 1940 of their Corps' achievements.

These NPS and CCC records now reside at Archives II in College Park, Maryland, in somewhat remote but very comfortable quarters for researchers. Here also are Record Group 95 of the USDA Forest Service, and Record Group 114 of the USDA Soil Conservation Service, which both supervised many Texas CCC camps, as well as Record Group 69 of the 1935–1942 Work Projects Administration. War Department (U.S. Army) records remain at the original National Archives building in Washington, D.C., and document CCC operations reporting to the Adjutant General's Office, Record Group 407.

More papers from NPS western regional offices, including those for state parks directed from Oklahoma City and Santa Fe, linger in uninventoried boxes at the National Archives repository in Denver. The Lyndon Baines Johnson Presidential Library in Austin, a National

Archives branch, contains Johnson's New Deal papers incorporating much evidence of the National Youth Administration.

CCC enrollment records, for those interested in tracing individuals, are housed at the military's National Personnel Records Center in St. Louis. A recently assembled collection of CCC camp newsletters—such as Davis Mountains' *Checker Upper* and Mother Neff's *Blue Eagle News*—is available on microfilm from the Center for Research Libraries in Chicago.

Another important NPS source is the agency's own huge Historic Photographic Collections at the Harpers Ferry Center in West Virginia. Many of the photographs reproduced in this work came from a group of ca. 1937 photo albums in the center's collection. Further NPS internal records are summarized conveniently in its 1985 *The Civilian Conservation Corps and the National Park Service, 1933–1942,* and its 1993 *Presenting Nature: The Historic Landscape Design of the National Park Service* (reprinted in 1997 as *Building the National Parks* by Johns Hopkins Press).

The Library of Congress in Washington, D.C., yields not only secondary information on the Texas congressional delegation, but obscure publications of the National Conference on State Parks. The reading rooms of this library, as well as those of the National Archives in Washington and College Park, dramatically convey the importance of records they hold through magnificent architectural spaces, some even New Deal products themselves.

State Sources

The very agency that manages Texas state parks sadly for too many years gave little priority to retaining original records and passed few items to the State Archives. Fortunately, at least three important collections of original state park materials are available at TPWD. First, hundreds of plans and drawings for New Deal facilities have been saved, with growing concern for their proper curation. With special permission these can be studied in original form or viewed on microfiche. Second, the agency holds informative State Parks Board minutes from 1933 through 1963, available on microfilm. Third, land-acquisition records reveal obscure details (and near scandals) on many park properties, but these files are not consistently organized nor readily available for research. Tragically, drawings and land records for decommissioned parks long ago exited in the trash.

TPWD and the Texas Historical Commission in 1983–1985 jointly conducted a survey of surviving CCC facilities in 30 parks still operated by the state. Survey results in maps, inventory pages, and photographs are found at both TPWD and THC offices in Austin. The resulting 1986 booklet *The Civilian Conservation Corps in Texas State Parks* will soon be out of print (in 1998). An inventory of CCC-produced furnishings still used in state parks is currently in process.

In addition, TPWD recently commissioned a number of land-use and administrative histories of certain state parks. To date these include Abilene, Balmorhea, Bastrop, Bonham, Cleburne, Daingerfield, Fort Parker, Garner, Goliad, Inks Lake, Lockhart, Meridian, and Mother Neff, available through TPWD or these parks. More thorough documentation on the development of Goliad State Park, Mother Neff State Park, and Austin's Zilker Park appear in their nominations to the National Register of Historic Places, and similar detail is available on Bastrop State Park through its nomination as a National Historic Landmark; these documents are at the Texas Historical Commission.

The State Archives hold the original minutes of the State Parks Board, 1933–1963. Here also are valuable records of the State Board of Control, umbrella organization of the 1930s Texas Relief Commission, the 1936 Centennial Commission, and from 1919 to 1949 the several "historical" state parks. The relief commission and its successors managed all recruitment of CCC enrollees in Texas, and briefly in 1933 selected all CCC work projects, although few records of this early New Deal activity survive. The relief agency also distributed federal funds of the Reconstruction Finance Corporation, Federal Emergency Relief Administration, Civil Works Administration, and Works Progress Administration, but again, few of these records survive outside limited federal copies in the National Archives. In the State Archives also are history-rich papers of the governors—Sterling, Ferguson, Allred, O'Daniel, and Stevenson—who served through the Great Depression and the Second World War.

The Legislative Reference Library in Austin's State Capitol is an inestimable state government resource, housed in an impressive and hospitable space. Here are biennial summaries and audit reports of the State Parks Board beginning in 1934, plus the Board of Control and other agencies associated with parks, including the reluctant Game, Fish and Oyster Commission that merged in 1963 with the parks board to create TPWD. This library thankfully has maintained a newspaper-clipping service since the 1920s and offers many key articles on state parks and Big Bend National Park on microfilm. Most valuable—though as tricky to use as they are rewarding with insight—are the *House Journals, Senate Journals,* and *General Laws* that chronicle each session of the legislature through distribution of funds to recreation and historical park operations.

The General Libraries of the University of Texas at Austin contain a surprising collection of period books and resources on the New Deal and the CCC in particular. The University's Barker Texas History Collections, housed in the Center for American History, feature above all the papers of David Edward Colp, 1923–1935 chairman of the State Parks Board; also vertical files on virtually every state park and New Deal topic, with obscure clippings and period brochures; the papers of Sam Rayburn and other New Deal congressmen; and the pitiful remnants of John Nance Garner's life record, since he defiantly burned his own files in the 1940s.

Important historic state publications include the priceless 1938 catalog *Monuments Commemorating the Centenary of Texas Independence* documenting incredible New Deal support for the 1936 Centennial. Of lesser detail but rich with spirit of the era, the 1940 *WPA Guide to Texas* (most recently reprinted in 1986 by Texas Monthly Press) placed then-new recreation parks in context for travelers through the state. Ironically, the State Parks Board turned down an offer to co-sponsor this publication with the WPA Writers' Program, whereupon the Texas Highway Department accepted that role with associated credit.

The General Land Office produced in 1991 a fine brace of parkland inventory volumes, *Real Property Evaluation Report of the Texas Parks and Wildlife Department for the 72nd Legislature.* These detailed appraisals are available in the Texas State Library and Legislative Reference Library in Austin. Also valuable is the 1970 *Geologic and Historic Guide to the State Parks of Texas* issued by the University of Texas at Austin's Bureau of Economic Geology.

Local Sources

Local newspapers can be the greatest source of summarized information on construction of nearby parks. Communities viewed any 1930s public works project as welcome relief from the depression, and considerable publicity generally tracked this keen citizen interest. From insightful *Dallas News* and *Fort Worth Star-Telegram* coverage of the state park system, to such local craft as the *Hamilton Herald-Record* and *Lampasas Leader*—which covered the entire New Deal in remarkable detail—these papers reveal the local impact of state park projects through starting dates, dedication celebrations, and occasional special columns by park personnel. If historic editions are not available at the current newspaper office or local library, the Barker Collections may have copies.

Popular county historical volumes usually acknowledge park development and sometimes include accurate details. In recent years, many county historical commissions have documented their local CCC and WPA parks for official historical marker applications; these are available at the Texas Historical Commission and include Bastrop, Fort Parker, Grayson (Loy), Mineral Wells, and Possum Kingdom.

Several local and regional repositories hold valuable papers and artifacts with information of statewide interest. Baylor University's Texas Collection at Waco houses the papers of Pat M. Neff, governor-at-the-creation and later chairman of the State Parks Board, including much official board correspondence, clippings, and photographs. The Panhandle-Plains Historical Museum in Canyon features papers of architect Guy Carlander, Congressman Marvin Jones, and parks board charter-member Phebe K. Warner, all influential in the regional impact of Palo Duro Canyon State Park. The Austin History Center maintains daybooks of Arthur Fehr, architect of Bastrop State Park, which constitute a Rosetta Stone of translation from official policy to day-to-day building of a park.

The Bell County Museum contains the hodge-podge but very useful Miriam Ferguson Collection. The Southwest Collection at Texas Tech holds the detailed congressional files of George Mahon. And vest-pocket Fort Croghan Museum in Burnet offers the unusual library of J. B. Braziel, CCC alumnus who assembled an amazing stack of Corps information, including camp assignments, enrollment statistics, photographs and uniforms, and priceless copies of the 1936 CCC *Official Annuals* peddled to Texas enrollees.

Other Resources

Thoughtful studies on such broad topics as the Great Depression and the New Deal are invaluable for understanding the context from which Texas state parks materialized. Robert S. McElvaine's *The Great Depression* (Times Books, 1985) presents a sweeping but very human chronicle of this bittersweet American episode. Paul K. Conkin's *The New Deal* (Thomas Y. Crowell, 1967) offers a compact summary of President Franklin Roosevelt's programs and policies that addressed the crisis. For the Texas experience during this era, the best works are Seth McKay's 1952 *Texas Politics, 1906–1944,* Lionel Patenaude's 1983 *Texans, Politics and the New Deal,* Rupert Richardson's 1958 textbook *Texas: The Lone Star State,* the Texas Memorial Museum's 1973 *Texas Cities and the Great Depression,* and Donald Whisenhunt's 1980 editing of *The Depression in the Southwest,* and his 1983 *The Depression in Texas: The Hoover Years.*

By far the most detailed and inspiring, from a still unceasing parade of new volumes on the depression and FDR's New Deal, is The Age of Roosevelt series begun by Arthur M. Schlesinger, Jr., in 1957. These include *The Crisis of the Old Order, The Coming of the New Deal,* and *The Politics of Upheaval* from various publishers. A handy "encyclopedic view" of this president and his entourage has been assembled into *Franklin D. Roosevelt: His Life and Times,* edited by Otis L. Graham and Meghan Robinson Wander (Da Capo, 1985).

The CCC entry in Graham and Wander's encyclopedia came from John Salmond, who wrote the single scholarly look at the agency, *The Civilian Conservation Corps, 1933–1942: A New*

Deal Case Study (Duke University Press, 1967). Here this incredibly complex program is explained through the personalities that drove its successes and setbacks. Little acknowledgment is given to the physical products of the CCC, but this administrative background is indispensable. A suitable counterbalance to Salmond's academic approach is Stan Cohen's *The Tree Army: A Pictorial History of the Civilian Conservation Corps, 1933–1942* (Pictorial Histories Publishing Co. 1980).

The CCC served as but one conservation instrument of the New Deal, within a diverse group of agencies that literally changed the face of the United States. Phoebe Cutler's *The Public Landscape of the New Deal* (Yale University Press, 1985) describes, illustrates, and graphs the results of a decade of nationwide physical improvements and social engineering. Even the federal agency that arguably benefited most from CCC handiwork also played a larger role in the New Deal. The windfall of 1930s development for the National Park Service is admirably presented, if personally inclined, by the agency's later director Conrad L. Wirth in *Parks, Politics, and the People* (University of Oklahoma Press, 1980).

Texas politics remain an ever-intriguing topic, particularly concerning the New Deal when the state's very senior congressional delegation exercised unprecedented influence directly within its home districts. Until Herbert Hoover's very late, and Franklin Roosevelt's very early, presidential support brought federal relief for local unemployment, the Washington, D.C., government rarely had appeared any closer to communities than their downtown post offices. In fact, the vast majority of Americans had encountered federal buildings—public works secured by their congressman—only in the form of those well-designed, durably built postal temples. But after 1932 Congressmen and U.S. Senators channeled New Deal monies toward an unparalleled boom in federal construction projects across the American landscape, from highways and dams to schools and state parks.

Few studies have looked at our federal officials—elected and appointed—in quite this way, but Jordan A. Schwarz's *The New Dealers: Power Politics in the Age of Roosevelt* (Knopf, 1993) makes a great effort. His title characters include Texans Lyndon Johnson, Jesse Jones, Wright Patman and Sam Rayburn. Handy biographies on these New Deal figures, plus Vice President John Garner and senators Morris Sheppard and Tom Connally, appear in *Profiles in Power: Twentieth Century Texans in Washington* (Harlan Davidson, 1993), edited by Kenneth E. Hendrickson, Jr., and Michael L. Collins. Unfortunately missing here is an index, as well as profiles on critical Texan New Dealers such as Henry Patrick Drought, Neal Guy, Margie Elizabeth Neal, and Lawrence Westbrook, plus other congressmen who brought home the CCC camps: Thomas Blanton, James Buchanan, Martin Dies, Marvin Jones, George Mahon, J. J. Mansfield, Maury Maverick, Hatton Sumners, Fritz Lanham, Sam Russell, Charles South (Garner's successor), and R. E. Thomason.

Most—but not all—of these pivotal figures can be found as brief biographies in the *New Handbook of Texas,* issued in 1996 by the Texas State Historical Association from its excellent editorial staff headed by Ron Tyler. Perhaps part of the blame for the obscurity of these power brokers can be laid upon Garner, and even Rayburn, who promulgated low-key profiles amongst fellow members of Congress. Note that only one New Deal state park in Texas is named for its benefactor in Washington—ironically for Garner but purportedly over his objections—although corresponding CCC camp assignments hung upon the specific influence of all these gentlemen. Nonetheless, the *New Handbook* features insightful articles on the CCC, WPA,

NYA, and Great Depression, and the governors (though few legislators) who conducted state affairs through the era.

The *New Handbook* also contains entries on all active state parks, yet most of their development information filtered through *Ray Miller's Texas Parks: A History and Guide* (Cordovan Press, 1984). Miller's guide resulted from much original research conveyed in honest language. Laurence Parent's 1997 *Official Guide to Texas State Parks* from the University of Texas Press fulfills the need for an attractive update.

Oral Histories

The University of North Texas in Denton through the 1980s gathered a large number of oral histories from CCC veterans, and transcriptions are available from the university library. A number of TPWD park administration histories (see above) drew upon the memories of CCC veterans who helped build those parks, and live nearby today, or who returned for reunions of their fellow company members. Many park managers keep lists of CCC veterans who return to a park for vacations and reunions, or who settled in the nearby community upon discharge a half century ago.

Surviving CCC enrollees in 1977 formed the National Association of Civilian Conservation Corps Alumni. The organization publishes its monthly *NACCCA Journal,* maintains headquarters and a museum at Jefferson Barracks south of St. Louis, and fosters communication among members and regional chapters in the states. In 1990 NACCCA published a hefty volume of personal stories from CCC members, including many photographs of camp life and work projects, as *Civilian Conservation Corps: The Way We Remember It, 1933–1942.* Inquiries on membership, chapter and national gatherings, and efforts of alumni to reinstitute a national CCC organization may be directed to NACCCA at the address above.

INDEX

Page numbers in **boldface** indicate Appendix A entry, with capsule history of park; page numbers in *italics* indicate illustrations.

Study, 118, 129, 158, 169; postwar retrenchment, 188; project classifications, 40, 150;
reorganizations, 47, 87, 125; San Jose as
first area in Texas, 160, 165, 224; search for
potential national parks, 64, 119, 146, 174;
on SPB operations budget, 50, 68–70, 82,
127, 138, 141

national parks: 1933 state enabling legislation,
27; architecture, 24; origins, 2; and state
parks, 7

National Youth Administration, xx; 1935 creation, 94; at Tips SP, 226; extended to 1943,
175, 182; furniture shops, 152, 157, 160, 167,
172; at Mother Neff SP, 142, 151; moves toward defense, 168, 172; placed under FSA,
152; and roadside parks, 97, 104, 178

Neal, Margie Elizabeth, state senator, 8,
69, 83

Neff, Isabella Shepherd, first mother, xiii,
6, 72

Neff, Pat Morris, *xxiv*, 5, 25, 44, 219; appointed to SPB, 21; becomes chairman
of SPB, 100, 107; as custodian of Mother
Neff SP, 151, 179; death of, 192; departure
from SPB, 146; donates additional acres,
72; elected vice chairman of SPB, 48; final
CCC work at Mother Neff, 132, 134; loans
Quinn 1923 SPB photo, 189; on Palo Duro
Canyon, 49; on preparedness, 141; president of Baylor University, 8, 22, 151; prose,
1, 6, 106; seeks CCC camp for Mother Neff
SP, 55, 68; trip to Washington, D.C., 131

New Deal, 40, 63; 1937 reduction, 127; 1939
reorganization, 152; 50th anniversary, 194;
bows to defense, 156, 172; first initiatives,
17, 36; programs at Bastrop SP, 200; programs at Goliad SP, 208; programs at San
Jacinto SP, 144, 224; programs at San Jose,
224; proposed by FDR, 8; Second New
Deal, 86, 93; summary of state park work,
177; support for Centennial, 103; support
for state parks, 61, 178; Texan administrators, 67, 83, 127; total expenditures
in Texas, 178

Newhall, Guy, architect, 220

Normangee State Park, 21, 58, 119, **220**, 238

Obert, Donald D., NPS inspector, 79

Ochiltree State Park: returned, 148

O'Daniel, Wilbert Lee "Pappy," governor,
135; on Big Bend, 146; names Beauchamp
secretary of state, 142; prose, 180; resigns
to U.S. Senate, 167; at San Jacinto, 144,
164, 224

Odle, Hugh, park activitist, 106, 107, 217

Olmsted, Frederick Law, landscape architect, 67

Ottine. *See* Palmetto State Park

Page & Southerland, architects, 219

Page, Charles Henry, architect, 58, 76, 209

Palisades State Park, 32, 33, 49, 52, 57, 60,
67, 85, 104, 107, **220**; returned, 148;
tables 1, 3–4

Palmetto State Park, 49, 64, 68, 70, 72, 73,
76, 90, 99, 104, 115, 120, 121, 125, 128, *196,*
221, 238; tables 3–5, 8–10

Palo Duro Canyon State Park, 7, 13, 19, 25–
26, 29, 33, *42, 43,* 49, 51, 54, 64–65, 69–
72, 85, 90, 104, 107, 115–116, *176,* 195, **221**,
238, 253; 1934 dedication, 77; CCC camp
closes, 128; Coronado Lodge, 66, 74, 179;
Emery's land deal, 31, 45–46, 49, 84, 180;
first CCC camps assigned, 31; gains fourth
CCC company, 57; "Goodnight Trail,"
26; "Hamblin Drive," 13, 239; initial land
costs, 32, 50, 54; reduced to one CCC camp,
99; repayment of debt, 179–180, 191; RFC
loan for improvement, 8, 26; segregation
results, 96; tables 1–10

Paris State Park, 58, 99, 104, 115, 125, 203,
222; CCC unit at Centennial exhibit, 111;
tables 6–9

Park and Recreation Structures, 132, 196

Park Structures and Facilities, 90. See also
Park and Recreation Structures

Parker, Edith, Senate secretary, 172

Patenaude, Lionel, 16, 127, 158, 164

patronage: in park development, 29, 123

Patton, Nat, congressman, 4, 92, 198, 235

Payne, Harry D., architect, 212

Payne, John Barton, NCSP founder, 73–74

Petersen, Peter L., 33, 50, 54, 84, 96, 179

Pfeiffer, "Uncle Joe," craftsman, 66, 111, 199,
203

Phelps, Henry Truman, architect, 84, 199,
209

Possum Kingdom State Park, 147, 150, 174,

89555

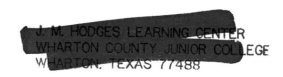